NETHERLANDS

COMPANY LAWS AND REGULATIONS HANDBOOK

VOLUME 1

STRATEGIC INFORMATION AND BASIC LAWS

International Business Publications, USA
Washington DC, USA - Netherlands

NETHERLANDS

COMPANY LAWS AND REGULATIONS HANDBOOK

VOLUME 1 STRATEGIC INFORMATION AND BASIC LAWS

UPDATED ANNUALLY

We express our sincere appreciation to all government agencies and international organizations which provided information and other materials for this handbook

2018 Edition Updated Reprints International Business Publications, USA
ISBN 1-4330-7038-3

For additional analytical, business and investment opportunities information,
please contact Global Investment & Business Center, USA
at (703) 370-8082. Fax: (703) 370-8083. E-mail: ibpusa3@gmail.com
Global Business and Investment Info Databank - www.ibpus.com

Printed in the USA

NETHERLANDS

COMPANY LAWS AND REGULATIONS HANDBOOK

VOLUME 1

STRATEGIC INFORMATION AND BASIC LAWS

TABLE OF CONTENTS

STRATEGIC & DEVELOPMENT PROFILES

STRATEGIC & BUSINESS PROFILE

Capital (and largest city)	Amsterdam[2] 52°19′N 05°33′E52.317°N 5.55°E
Official language(s)	Dutch
Recognised regional languages	Frisian (in Friesland), Papiamento (in Bonaire), English (in Sint Eustatius and Saba)[3]
Ethnic groups	80.7% Dutch, 5% EU varieties, 2.4% Indonesians, 2.2% Turks, 2% Surinamese, 2% Moroccans, 0.8% Caribbean 4.8% others
Demonym	Dutch
Government	Constitutional monarchy, Unitary parliamentary representative democracy
- Monarch	Beatrix
- Prime Minister	Mark Rutte (VVD)
- Deputy Prime Minister	Maxime Verhagen (CDA)
- Current coalition	VVD-CDA Coalition
Legislature	States-General
- Upper House	Senate
- Lower House	House of Representatives
Independence	As result of the Eighty Years' War from the Habsburg Empire
- Declared	26 July 1581
- Recognised	30 January 1648[4]
	Area
- Total	41,543 km² (135th) 16,039 sq mi
- Water (%)	18.41
	Population
- 2012 estimate	16,847,007 (61st)
- Density	403.4/km² (30th) 1,044.8/sq mi
GDP (PPP)	2011 estimate
- Total	$694.574 billion (21st)
- Per capita	$41,691 (9th)
GDP (nominal)	2011 estimate
- Total	$832.160 billion (16th)
- Per capita	$49,950 (9th)
Gini (2006)	30.9 (medium)
HDI	▲0.910 (very high) (3rd)
Currency	Euro (€): Netherlands, United States dollar ($): Caribbean Netherlands
Time zone	CET and AST (UTC+1 and −4)
- Summer (DST)	CEST and AST (UTC+2 and −4)
Drives on the	right
Internet TLD	.nl[7]
Calling code	31, +599[8]

The **Netherlands** is a constituent country of the Kingdom of the Netherlands, located mainly in North-West Europe and with several islands in the Caribbean. Mainland Netherlands borders the North Sea to the north and west, Belgium to the south, and Germany to the east, and shares maritime borders (image) with Belgium, Germany and the United Kingdom. It is a parliamentary democracy organised as a unitary state. The country capital is Amsterdam and the seat of government is The Hague. The *Netherlands* in its entirety is often referred to as Holland, although North and South Holland are actually only two of its twelve provinces (a case of *pars pro toto*; see terminology of "the Netherlands").

The Netherlands is a geographically low-lying country, with about 25% of its area and 21% of its population located below sea level, and 50% of its land lying less than one metre above sea level.[9] This distinct feature contributes to the country's name in many other European languages (e.g. German: *Niederlande*, Croatian: *Nizozemska*, French: *Les Pays-Bas*, Italian: *Paesi Bassi* and Spanish: *Países Bajos*, literally mean "(The) Low Countries"). Significant land area has been gained through land reclamation and preserved through an elaborate system of polders and dikes. Much of the Netherlands is formed by the estuary of three important European rivers, which together with their distributaries form the Rhine-Meuse-Scheldt delta. Most of the country is very flat, with the exception of foothills in the far southeast and several low-hill ranges in the central parts.

The Netherlands was one of the first countries to have an elected parliament. Among other affiliations the country is a founding member of the EU, NATO, OECD and WTO. With Belgium and Luxembourg it forms the Benelux economic union. The country is host to the Organization for the Prohibition of Chemical Weapons and five international courts: the Permanent Court of Arbitration, the International Court of Justice, the International Criminal Tribunal for the Former Yugoslavia, the International Criminal Court and the Special Tribunal for Lebanon. The first four are situated in The Hague as is the EU's criminal intelligence agency Europol and judicial co-operation agency Eurojust. This has led to the city being dubbed "the world's legal capital".[10] The Netherlands has a capitalist market-based economy, ranking 13th of 157 countries according to the Index of Economic Freedom. In May 2011, the Netherlands was ranked as the "happiest" country according to results published by the Organisation for Economic Co-operation and Development

The Kingdom of the Netherlands was formed in 1815. In 1830 Belgium seceded and formed a separate kingdom. The Netherlands remained neutral in World War I but suffered a brutal invasion and occupation by Germany in World War II. A modern, industrialized nation, the Netherlands is also a large exporter of agricultural products. The country was a founding member of NATO and the EC, and participated in the introduction of the euro in 1999.

GEOGRAPHY

Location: Western Europe, bordering the North Sea, between Belgium and Germany
Geographic coordinates: 52 30 N, 5 45 E
Map references: Europe

Area:
total: 41,532 sq km *land:* 33,889 sq km *water:* 7,643 sq km

Area - comparative: slightly less than twice the size of New Jersey
Land boundaries:
total: 1,027 km
border countries: Belgium 450 km, Germany 577 km
Coastline: 451 km
Maritime claims:
exclusive fishing zone: 200 nm
territorial sea: 12 nm
Climate: temperate; marine; cool summers and mild winters
Terrain: mostly coastal lowland and reclaimed land (polders); some hills in southeast
Elevation extremes:
lowest point: Prins Alexanderpolder -7 m
highest point: Vaalserberg 321 m
Natural resources: natural gas, petroleum, arable land

Base 800382 (A01914) 3-87

Land use:
arable land: 25% *permanent crops:* 3% *permanent pastures:* 25% *forests and woodland:* 8%
other: 39%

Irrigated land: 6,000 sq km
Natural hazards: the extensive system of dikes and dams protects nearly one-half of the total area from being flooded
Environment - current issues: water pollution in the form of heavy metals, organic compounds, and nutrients such as nitrates and phosphates; air pollution from vehicles and refining activities; acid rain

Environment - international agreements:
party to: Air Pollution, Air Pollution-Nitrogen Oxides, Air Pollution-Sulphur 85, Air Pollution-Sulphur 94, Air Pollution-Volatile Organic Compounds, Antarctic-Environmental Protocol, Antarctic Treaty, Biodiversity, Climate Change, Desertification, Endangered Species, Environmental Modification, Hazardous Wastes, Law of the Sea, Marine Dumping, Marine Life Conservation, Nuclear Test Ban, Ozone Layer Protection, Ship Pollution, Tropical Timber 83, Tropical Timber 94, Wetlands, Whaling
signed, but not ratified: Air Pollution-Persistent Organic Pollutants, Biodiversity, Climate Change-Kyoto Protocol

Geography - note: located at mouths of three major European rivers (Rhine, Maas or Meuse, and Schelde

PEOPLE

Population: 15,892,237

Age structure:
0-14 years: 18% (male 1,497,290; female 1,431,671)
15-64 years: 68% (male 5,490,518; female 5,305,848)
65 years and over: 14% (male 885,839; female 1,281,071)

Population growth rate: 0.57%
Birth rate: 12.12 births/1,000 population
Death rate: 8.72 deaths/1,000 population
Net migration rate: 2.3 migrant(s)/1,000 population

Sex ratio:
at birth: 1.05 male(s)/female
under 15 years: 1.05 male(s)/female
15-64 years: 1.03 male(s)/female
65 years and over: 0.69 male(s)/female
total population: 0.98 male(s)/female

Infant mortality rate: 4.42 deaths/1,000 live births

Life expectancy at birth:
total population: 78.28 years
male: 75.4 years
female: 81.28 years

Total fertility rate: 1.64 children born/woman

Nationality:
noun: Dutchman(men), Dutchwoman(women)
adjective: Dutch

Ethnic groups: Dutch 91%, Moroccans, Turks, and other 9%

Religions: Roman Catholic 34%, Protestant 25%, Muslim 3%, other 2%, unaffiliated 36% (1991)

Languages: Dutch

Literacy:
definition: age 15 and over can read and write
total population: 99%

GOVERNMENT

conventional long form: Kingdom of the Netherlands
conventional short form: Netherlands
local long form: Koninkrijk der Nederlanden
local short form: Nederland
etymology: the country name literally means "the lowlands" and refers to the geographic features of the land being both flat and down river from higher areas (i.e., at the estuaries of the Scheldt, Meuse, and Rhine Rivers; only about half of the Netherlands is more than 1 meter above sea level)

Government type:
parliamentary constitutional monarchy; part of the Kingdom of the Netherlands

Capital:
name: Amsterdam; note - The Hague is the seat of government
geographic coordinates: 52 21 N, 4 55 E
time difference: UTC+1 (6 hours ahead of Washington, DC, during Standard Time)
daylight saving time: +1hr, begins last Sunday in March; ends last Sunday in October
note: time descriptions apply to the continental Netherlands only, not to the constituent countries in the Caribbean

Administrative divisions:
12 provinces (provincies, singular - provincie); Drenthe, Flevoland, Fryslan (Friesland), Gelderland, Groningen, Limburg, Noord-Brabant (North Brabant), Noord-Holland (North Holland), Overijssel, Utrecht, Zeeland (Zealand), Zuid-Holland (South Holland)
note 1: the Netherlands is one of four constituent countries of the Kingdom of the Netherlands; the other three, Aruba, Curacao, and Sint Maarten, are all islands in the Caribbean; while all four parts are considered equal partners, in practice, most of the Kingdom's affairs are administered by the Netherlands, which makes up about 98% of the Kingdom's total land area and population

note 2: three other Caribbean islands, Bonaire, Saint Eustatius, and Saba, are considered to be special municipalities of the Netherlands proper

Dependent areas:
Aruba, Curacao, Sint Maarten

Independence:
23 January 1579 (the northern provinces of the Low Countries conclude the Union of Utrecht breaking with Spain; on 26 July 1581 they formally declared their independence with an Act of Abjuration; however, it was not until 30 January 1648 and the Peace of Westphalia that Spain recognized this independence)
National holiday:
King's Day (birthday of King WILLEM-ALEXANDER), 27 April (1967); note - King's or Queen's Day are observed on the ruling monarch's birthday; celebrated on 26 April if 27 April is a Sunday

Constitution:
history: previous 1597, 1798; latest adopted 24 August 1815 (substantially revised in 1848)
amendments: proposed as an “Act of Parliament” by or on behalf of the king or by the Second Chamber of the States General; the Second Chamber is dissolved after its first reading of the “Act”; passage requires a second reading by both the First Chamber and newly elected Second Chamber, followed by at least two-thirds majority vote of both chambers, and ratification by the king; amended many times, last in 2010 (2016)

Legal system:
civil law system based on the French system; constitution does not permit judicial review of acts of the States General

International law organization participation:
accepts compulsory ICJ jurisdiction with reservations; accepts ICCt jurisdiction

Citizenship:
citizenship by birth: no
citizenship by descent only: at least one parent must be a citizen of the Netherlands
dual citizenship recognized: no
residency requirement for naturalization: 5 years

Suffrage:
18 years of age; universal

Executive branch:

chief of state: King WILLEM-ALEXANDER (since 30 April 2013); Heir Apparent Princess Catharina-Amalia (since 30 April 2013)
head of government: Prime Minister Mark RUTTE (since 14 October 2010; Deputy Prime Ministers (since 26 October 2017) Hugo DE JONGE, Karin Kajsa OLLONGREN, and Carola SCHOUTEN (since 26 October 2017); note - Mark RUTTE heads his third cabinet since 26 October 2017
cabinet: Council of Ministers appointed by the monarch
elections/appointments: the monarchy is hereditary; following Second Chamber elections, the leader of the majority party or majority coalition usually appointed prime minister by the monarch; deputy prime ministers appointed by the monarch

Legislative branch:
description: bicameral States General or Staten Generaal consists of the First Chamber or Eerste Kamer (75 seats; members indirectly elected by the country's 12 provincial council members by proportional representation vote; members serve 4-year terms) and the Second Chamber or Tweede Kamer (150 seats; members directly elected in multi-seat constituencies by proportional representation vote to serve up to 4-year terms)
elections: First Chamber - last held on 26 May 2015 (next to be held in May 2019); Second Chamber - last held on 15 March 2017 (next to be held 15 March 2021)

election results: First Chamber - percent of vote by party - NA; seats by party - VVD 13, CDA 12, D66 10, PVV 9, SP 9, PvdA 8, GL 4, CU 3, other 7; Second Chamber - percent of vote by party - VVD 21.3%, PVV 13.1%, CDA 12.4%, D66 12.2%, GL 9.1%, SP 9.1%, PvdA 5.7%, CU 3.4%, PvdD 3.2%, 50 Plus 3.1%, other 7.4%; seats by party - VVD 33, PVV 20, CDA 19, D66 19, GL 14, SP 14, PvdA 9, CU 5, PvdD 5, 50 Plus 4, other 8

Judicial branch:
highest court(s): Supreme Court or Hoge Raad (consists of 41 judges: the president, 6 vice presidents, 31 justices or raadsheren, and 3 justices in exceptional service, referred to as buitengewone dienst); the court is divided into criminal, civil, tax, and ombuds chambers

judge selection and term of office: justices appointed by the monarch from a list provided by the Second Chamber of the States General; justices appointed for life or until mandatory retirement at age 70

subordinate courts: courts of appeal; district courts, each with up to 5 subdistrict courts; note in mid-July 2017, legislation was proposed to establish a new commericial court for international trade disputes with the Netherlands

Political parties and leaders:
Christian Democratic Appeal or CDA [Sybrand VAN HAERSMA BUMA]
Christian Union or CU [Gert-Jan SEGERS]
Democrats 66 or D66 [Alexander PECHTOLD]
Denk [Tunahan KUZU]
50 Plus [Henk KROL]
For the Netherlands or VNL [Jan ROOS]
Forum for Democracy or FvD [Thierry BAUDET]
Green Left or GL [Jesse KLAVER]
Labor Party or PvdA [Lodewik ASSCHER]
Party for Freedom or PVV [Geert WILDERS]
Party for the Animals or PvdD [Marianne THIEME]
People's Party for Freedom and Democracy or VVD [Mark RUTTE]
Reformed Political Party or SGP [Kees VAN DER STAAIJ]
Socialist Party or SP [Emile ROEMER]
plus a few minor parties

Political pressure groups and leaders:
Christian Trade Union Federation or CNV [Maurice LIMMEN]
Confederation of Netherlands Industry and Employers or VNO-NCW [Hans DE BOER]
Federation for Small and Medium-sized Businesses or MKB [Michael VAN STRAALEN]
Netherlands Trade Union Federation or FNV [Han BUSKER]
Social Economic Council or SER [Mariette HAMER]
Trade Union Professionals or VDP [Nic VAN HOLSTEIN]

International organization participation:
ADB (nonregional member), AfDB (nonregional member), Arctic Council (observer), Australia Group, Benelux, BIS, CBSS (observer), CD, CE, CERN, EAPC, EBRD, ECB, EIB, EITI (implementing country), EMU, ESA, EU, FAO, FATF, G-10, IADB, IAEA, IBRD, ICAO, ICC (national committees), ICCt, ICRM, IDA, IEA, IFAD, IFC, IFRCS, IGAD (partners), IHO, ILO, IMF, IMO, IMSO, Interpol, IOC, IOM, IPU, ISO, ITSO, ITU, ITUC (NGOs), MIGA, MINUSMA, NATO, NEA, NSG, OAS (observer), OECD, OPCW, OSCE, Pacific Alliance (observer), Paris Club, PCA, Schengen Convention, SELEC (observer), UN, UNCTAD, UNDOF, UNESCO, UNHCR, UNIDO, UNMISS, UNRWA, UNTSO, UNWTO, UPU, WCO, WHO, WIPO, WMO, WTO, ZC

Diplomatic representation in the US:
chief of mission: Ambassador Hendrik SCHUWER (since 17 September 2015)
chancery: 4200 Linnean Avenue NW, Washington, DC 20008
telephone: [1] (202) 244-5300, [1] 877-388-2443
FAX: [1] (202) 362-3430
consulate(s) general: Chicago, Miami, New York, San Francisco

Diplomatic representation from the US:
chief of mission: Ambassador Peter HOEKSTRA (since 10 January 2018)
embassy: Lange Voorhout 102, 2514 EJ, The Hague
mailing address: PSC 71, Box 1000, APO AE 09715
telephone: [31] (70) 310-2209
FAX: [31] (70) 310-2207
consulate(s) general: Amsterdam

Flag description:
three equal horizontal bands of red (bright vermilion; top), white, and blue (cobalt); similar to the flag of Luxembourg, which uses a lighter blue and is longer; the colors were derived from those of WILLIAM I, Prince of Orange, who led the Dutch Revolt against Spanish sovereignty in the latter half of the 16th century; originally the upper band was orange, but because its dye tended to turn red over time, the red shade was eventually made the permanent color; the banner is perhaps the oldest tricolor in continuous use

National symbol(s):

lion, tulip; national color: orange

National anthem:
name: "Het Wilhelmus" (The William)
lyrics/music: Philips VAN MARNIX van Sint Aldegonde (presumed)/unknown
note: adopted 1932, in use since the 17th century, making it the oldest national anthem in the world; also known as "Wilhelmus van Nassouwe" (William of Nassau), it is in the form of an acrostic, where the first letter of each stanza spells the name of the leader of the Dutch Revolt

ECONOMY

The Netherlands, the sixth-largest economy in the European Union, plays an important role as a European transportation hub, with a persistently high trade surplus, stable industrial relations, and low unemployment. Industry focuses on food processing, chemicals, petroleum refining, and electrical machinery. A highly mechanized agricultural sector employs only 2% of the labor force but provides large surpluses for food-processing and underpins the country's status as the world's second largest agricultural exporter.

The Netherlands is part of the euro zone, and as such, its monetary policy is controlled by the European Central Bank. The Dutch financial sector is highly concentrated, with four commercial banks possessing over 80% of banking assets, and is four times the size of Dutch GDP.

In 2008, during the financial crisis, the government budget deficit hit 5.3% of GDP. Following a protracted recession from 2009 to 2013, during which unemployment doubled to 7.4% and household consumption contracted for four consecutive years, economic growth began inching forward in 2014. Since 2010, Prime Minister Mark RUTTE's government has implemented significant austerity measures to improve public finances and has instituted broad structural reforms in key policy areas, including the labor market, the housing sector, the energy market, and the pension system. In 2016, the government budget returned to a surplus of 0.3% of GDP, with economic growth of 2.1%, and GDP per capita finally surpassed pre-crisis levels. The Dutch government projects steady but modest economic growth of 2.1% in 2017 and unemployment decreasing to 4.9%.

GDP (purchasing power parity):

$870.8 billion (2016 est.)
$852.9 billion (2015 est.)
$836.2 billion (2014 est.)
note: data are in 2016 dollars
country comparison to the world: 28

GDP (official exchange rate):
$773.9 billion (2016 est.)

GDP - real growth rate:
2.1% (2016 est.)
2% (2015 est.)
1.4% (2014 est.)
country comparison to the world: 129

GDP - per capita (PPP):
$50,800 (2016 est.)
$50,300 (2015 est.)
$49,500 (2014 est.)
note: data are in 2016 dollars
country comparison to the world: 23

Gross national saving:
28.6% of GDP (2016 est.)

30.1% of GDP (2015 est.)
29.3% of GDP (2014 est.)
country comparison to the world: 30

GDP - composition, by end use:
household consumption: 44.4%
government consumption: 24.9%
investment in fixed capital: 20.3%
investment in inventories: -0.2%
exports of goods and services: 81.6%
imports of goods and services: -71% (2016 est.)

GDP - composition, by sector of origin:
agriculture: 1.6%
industry: 17.8%
services: 70.4% (2016 est.)

Agriculture - products:
vegetables, ornamentals, dairy, poultry and livestock products; propagation materials
Industries:
agroindustries, metal and engineering products, electrical machinery and equipment, chemicals, petroleum, construction, microelectronics, fishing

Industrial production growth rate:
2.6% (2016 est.)
country comparison to the world: 142

Labor force:
8.942 million (2016 est.)
country comparison to the world: 57

Labor force - by occupation:
agriculture: 1.2%
industry: 17.2%
services: 81.6% (2015 est.)

Unemployment rate:
6% (2016 est.)
6.9% (2015 est.)
country comparison to the world: 72

Population below poverty line:
8.8% (2015 est.)

Household income or consumption by percentage share:
lowest 10%: 2.3%
highest 10%: 24.9% (2014 est.)

Distribution of family income - Gini index:
30.3 (2015 est.)
25.1 (2013 est.)
country comparison to the world: 124
Budget:
revenues: $340.8 billion
expenditures: $337.6 billion (2016 est.)

Taxes and other revenues:
44% of GDP (2016 est.)
country comparison to the world: 25

Budget surplus (+) or deficit (-):

0.4% of GDP (2016 est.)
country comparison to the world: 28

Public debt:
61.8% of GDP (2016 est.)
65.1% of GDP (2015 est.)
note: data cover general government debt, and includes debt instruments issued (or owned) by government entities other than the treasury; the data include treasury debt held by foreign entities; the data include debt issued by subnational entities, as well as intra-governmental debt; intra-governmental debt consists of treasury borrowings from surpluses in the social funds, such as for retirement, medical care, and unemployment, debt instruments for the social funds are not sold at public auctions

country comparison to the world: 64

Fiscal year:
calendar year
Inflation rate (consumer prices):
0.3% (2016 est.)
0.6% (2015 est.)
country comparison to the world: 44

Central bank discount rate:
0% (31 December 2016)
0.05% (31 December 2015)
note: this is the European Central Bank's rate on the marginal lending facility, which offers overnight credit to banks in the euro area
country comparison to the world: 149

Commercial bank prime lending rate:
2.59% (31 December 2016 est.)
2.93% (31 December 2015 est.)
country comparison to the world: 171

Stock of narrow money:
$498.3 billion (31 December 2016 est.)
$475.2 billion (31 December 2015 est.)
note: see entry for the European Union for money supply for the entire euro area; the European Central Bank (ECB) controls monetary policy for the 18 members of the Economic and Monetary Union (EMU); individual members of the EMU do not control the quantity of money circulating within their own borders
country comparison to the world: 13

Stock of broad money:
$1.119 trillion (31 December 2014 est.)
$1.158 trillion (31 December 2013 est.)
country comparison to the world: 17

Stock of domestic credit:
$1.455 trillion (31 December 2016 est.)
$1.425 trillion (31 December 2015 est.)
country comparison to the world: 15

Market value of publicly traded shares:
$652.7 billion (31 December 2015 est.)
$735.1 billion (31 December 2014 est.)
$675 billion (31 December 2013 est.)
country comparison to the world: 18

Current account balance:
$74.3 billion (2016 est.)

$65.13 billion (2015 est.)
country comparison to the world: 8

Exports:
$480.1 billion (2016 est.)
$474.3 billion (2015 est.)
country comparison to the world: 8

Exports - commodities:
machinery and transport equipment, chemicals, mineral fuels; food and livestock, manufactured goods

Exports - partners:
Germany 24.5%, Belgium 11.1%, UK 9.3%, France 8.4%, Italy 4.2%

Imports:
$422.3 billion (2016 est.)
$425.4 billion (2015 est.)
country comparison to the world: 8

Imports - commodities:
machinery and transport equipment, chemicals, fuels, foodstuffs, clothing
Imports - partners:
Germany 14.7%, China 14.5%, Belgium 8.2%, US 8.1%, UK 5.1% (2015)

Reserves of foreign exchange and gold:
$39.03 billion (31 December 2016 est.)
$35.39 billion (31 December 2015 est.)
country comparison to the world: 43

Debt - external:
$4.063 trillion (31 December 2016 est.)
$4.054 trillion (31 December 2015 est.)
country comparison to the world: 6

Stock of direct foreign investment - at home:
$844 billion (31 December 2016 est.)
$739.9 billion (31 December 2015 est.)
country comparison to the world: 12

Stock of direct foreign investment - abroad:
$1.207 trillion (31 December 2016 est.)
$1.102 trillion (31 December 2015 est.)
country comparison to the world: 12

Exchange rates:
euros (EUR) per US dollar -
0.9214 (2016 est.)
0.885 (2015 est.)
0.885 (2014 est.)
0.7634 (2013 est.)
0.7752 (2012 est.)

ENERGY

Electricity - production:
98.57 billion kWh
country comparison to the world:
34

Electricity - consumption:
116.8 billion kWh
country comparison to the world:
29

Electricity - exports:

15.02 billion kWh
country comparison to the world:
14

Electricity - imports:

33.25 billion kWh
country comparison to the world:
5

Electricity - installed generating capacity:

29.92 million kW
country comparison to the world:
29

Electricity - from fossil fuels:

85.1% of total installed capacity
country comparison to the world:
88

Electricity - from nuclear fuels:

1.6% of total installed capacity
country comparison to the world:
29

Electricity - from hydroelectric plants:

0.1% of total installed capacity
country comparison to the world:
149

Electricity - from other renewable sources:

13.2% of total installed capacity
country comparison to the world:
17

Crude oil - production:

29,400 bbl/day
country comparison to the world:
67

Crude oil - exports:

35,500 bbl/day
country comparison to the world:
48

Crude oil - imports:

1.202 million bbl/day
country comparison to the world:
9

Crude oil - proved reserves:

352 million bbl
country comparison to the world:
54

Refined petroleum products - production:

1.248 million bbl/day
country comparison to the world:
17

Refined petroleum products - consumption:

1.01 million bbl/day
country comparison to the world:
21

Refined petroleum products - exports:

2.138 million bbl/day
country comparison to the world:
4

Refined petroleum products - imports:

2.079 million bbl/day
country comparison to the world:
3

Natural gas - production:

81.52 billion cu m
country comparison to the world:
11

Natural gas - consumption:

44.11 billion cu m
country comparison to the world:
21

Natural gas - exports:

63.42 billion cu m
country comparison to the world:

6

Natural gas - imports:

24.65 billion cu m
country comparison to the world:
19

Natural gas - proved reserves:

1.09 trillion cu m
country comparison to the world:
26

Carbon dioxide emissions from consumption of energy:

58.1 million Mt

COMMUNICATIONS

Telephones - main lines in use:

7.086 million

country comparison to the world: 25

Telephones - mobile cellular:

19.643 million

country comparison to the world: 50

Telephone system:

general assessment: highly developed and well maintained
domestic: extensive fixed-line fiber-optic network; large cellular telephone system with 5 major operators utilizing the third generation of the Global System for Mobile Communications (GSM) technology; one in five households now use Voice over the Internet Protocol (VoIP) services
international: country code - 31; submarine cables provide links to the US and Europe; satellite earth stations - 5 (3 Intelsat - 1 Indian Ocean and 2 Atlantic Ocean, 1 Eutelsat, and 1 Inmarsat

Broadcast media:

more than 90% of households are connected to cable or satellite TV systems that provide a wide range of domestic and foreign channels; public service broadcast system includes multiple broadcasters, 3 with a national reach and the remainder operating in regional and local markets; 2 major nationwide commercial television companies, each with 3 or more stations, and many commercial TV stations in regional and local markets; nearly 600 radio stations with a mix of public and private stations providing national or regional coverage

Internet country code:

.nl

Internet hosts:

13.699 million

country comparison to the world: 11

Internet users:

14.872 million

country comparison to the world: 27

TRANSPORTATION

Airports

:

29

country comparison to the world:

120

Airports - with paved runways:

total:

23

over 3,047 m:

3

2,438 to 3,047 m:

11

1,524 to 2,437 m:

1

914 to 1,523 m:

6

under 914 m:

2

Airports - with unpaved runways:

total:

6

914 to 1,523 m:

4

under 914 m:

2

Heliports:

1

Pipelines:

condensate 81 km; gas 8,531 km; oil 578 km; refined products 716 km

Railways:

total:

3,013 km

country comparison to the world:

56

standard gauge: 3,013 km 1.435-m gauge (2,195 km electrified)

Roadways:

total:
139,295 km (includes 2,758 km of expressways)
country comparison to the world:
36

Waterways:
6,237 km (navigable for ships of 50 tons)
country comparison to the world:
22

Merchant marine:

total:
744
country comparison to the world:
15

by type: bulk carrier 4, cargo 514, carrier 15, chemical tanker 56, container 67, liquefied gas 21, passenger 17, passenger/cargo 14, petroleum tanker 4, refrigerated cargo 10, roll on/roll off 19, specialized tanker 3
foreign-owned: 196 (Australia 1, Bermuda 1, Denmark 27, Finland 13, France 2, Germany 86, Ireland 8, Italy 6, Japan 1, Norway 19, Sweden 12, UAE 4, US 16)
registered in other countries: 233 (Antigua and Barbuda 17, Bahamas 23, Belize 1, Canada 1, Curacao 43, Cyprus 23, Germany 1, Gibraltar 34, Italy 2, Liberia 31, Luxembourg 3, Malta 3, Marshall Islands 21, Panama 6, Paraguay 1, Philippines 17, Russia 2, Saint Vincent and the Grenadines 1, Singapore 1, UK 1, unknown 1)

Ports and terminals:
major seaport(s):
IJmuiden, Vlissingen
river port(s):
Amsterdam (Nordsee Kanaal); Moerdijk (Hollands Diep River); Rotterdam (Rhine River); Terneuzen (Western Scheldt River)
container port(s) (TEUs):
Rotterdam (11,876,920)

MILITARY

Military branches:

Royal Netherlands Army, Royal Netherlands Navy (includes Naval Air Service and Marine Corps), Royal Netherlands Air Force (Koninklijke Luchtmacht, KLu), Royal Military Police

Military service age and obligation:

17 years of age for an all-volunteer force (2014)

Manpower available for military service:

males age 16-49: 3,734,610
females age 16-49: 3,687,940 (2014 est.)

Manpower fit for military service:

males age 16-49: 3,479,509
females age 16-49: 3,435,564

Manpower reaching militarily significant age annually:

male: 100,446
female: 94,750 (2014 est.)

Military expenditures:

1.27% of GDP

country comparison to the world: 82
1.35% of GDP
1.27% of GDP

TRANSNATIONAL ISSUES

Disputes - international:

none

Refugees and internally displaced persons:

refugees (country of origin): 18,799 (Somalia); 15,533 (Iraq); 6,269 (Afghanistan)
stateless persons: 2,005

Illicit drugs:

major European producer of synthetic drugs, including ecstasy, and cannabis cultivator; important gateway for cocaine, heroin, and hashish entering Europe; major source of US-bound ecstasy; large financial sector vulnerable to money laundering; significant consumer of ecstasy

IMPORTANT INFORMATION FOR UNDERSTANDING THE COUNTRY[1]

PROFILE

OFFICIAL NAME: Kingdom of the Netherlands

Geography
Area: 41,526 sq. km. (16,485 sq. mi.); about half the size of South Carolina.
Cities: *Capital*--Amsterdam (pop. 767,457). *Other cities*--The Hague, seat of government (488,553); Rotterdam (593,049); Utrecht (307,081).
Terrain: Coastal lowland.
Climate: Northern maritime, with cool summers and mild winters.

People
Population: 16.6 million.
Nationality: *Noun*--Dutchmen and Dutchwomen. *Adjective*--Dutch.
Ethnic groups: Predominantly Dutch; large minority communities are Moroccans, Turks, Surinamese, and Dutch Caribbean.
Religions: Largest groups are Roman Catholic, Protestant, and Muslim.
Language: Dutch.
Education: *Years compulsory*--13. *Attendance*--nearly 100%. *Literacy*--98%.
Health: *Infant mortality rate*--4.4/1000. *Life expectancy*-- 78.3 years for men and 82.3 years for women.
Civilian employment (7.887 million): *industry*--16.6%; *services*--81.8%; *agriculture*--1.6%.

Government
Type: Parliamentary democracy under a constitutional monarch.
Constitution: 1814 and 1848.
Branches: *Executive*--monarch (chief of state), prime minister (head of government), cabinet. *Legislative*--bicameral parliament (First and Second Chambers). *Judicial*--Supreme Court.
Subdivisions: 12 provinces.
Political parties: Christian Democratic Appeal (CDA), Freedom Party (PVV), Labor Party (PvdA), Liberal Party (VVD), Socialist Party (SP), other minor parties.
Suffrage: Universal at 18.

Economy*
Natural resources: Natural gas, petroleum, fertile soil.
Agriculture (2% of GDP): *Products*--dairy, poultry, meat, livestock, flower bulbs, cut flowers, vegetables and fruits, sugar beets, potatoes, wheat, barley.
Industry (24% of GDP): *Types*--agro-industries, steel and aluminum, metal and engineering products, electric machinery and equipment, bulk chemicals, natural gas, petroleum products, construction, transport equipment, microelectronics, fishing.
Services (74% of GDP): *Types*--trade, hotels, restaurants, transport, storage and communication, financial (banking and insurance) and business services, care, and other.
Trade : *Exports*--$523.3 billion f.o.b.: machinery and transport equipment, chemicals, mineral fuels, processed food and tobacco, agricultural products. *Imports*--$468.4 billion f.o.b.: mineral fuels and crude petroleum, machinery, transportation equipment, chemicals, mineral fuels and crude petroleum, consumer goods, foodstuffs. *Major trading partners (exports/imports*--EU (74.0%/53.3%), Germany (24.2%/17.7%), Belgium (11.1%/9.6%), China (1.5%/9.3%), United Kingdom (8.04%/6.7%), and U.S. (4.6%/7.6%), and France (8.7%/4.5%)..
*Figures are based on a June 2011 exchange rate of 0.70 euro to the dollar.

HISTORY

[1] US State Department Profile

The Dutch are primarily of Germanic stock with some Gallo-Celtic mixture. Their small homeland frequently has been threatened with destruction by the North Sea and has often been invaded by the great European powers.

Julius Caesar found the region which is now the Netherlands inhabited by Germanic tribes in the first century B.C. The western portion was inhabited by the Batavians and became part of a Roman province; the eastern portion was inhabited by the Frisians. Between the fourth and eighth centuries A.D., most of both portions were conquered by the Franks. The area later passed into the hands of the House of Burgundy and the Austrian Habsburgs. Falling under harsh Spanish rule in the 16th century, the Dutch revolted in 1558 under the leadership of Willem of Orange. By virtue of the Union of Utrecht in 1579, the seven northern Dutch provinces became the Republic of the United Netherlands.

During the 17th century, considered its "golden era," the Netherlands became a great sea and colonial power. Among other achievements, this period saw the emergence of some of painting's "Old Masters," including Rembrandt, Vermeer, and Hals, whose works--along with those of later artists such as Mondriaan and Van Gogh--are today on display in museums throughout the Netherlands and the world.

The country's importance declined, however, with the gradual loss of Dutch technological superiority and after wars with Spain, France, and England in the 17th and 18th century. The Dutch United Provinces supported the Americans in the Revolutionary War. In 1795, French troops ousted Willem V of Orange, the Stadhouder under the Dutch Republic and head of the House of Orange. The Netherlands experienced a brief period of being a client state of France, under the Batavian Republic , then as the Kingdom of Holland, ruled by Louis Bonaparte, and finally as part of France.

Following Napoleon's defeat in 1815, the Netherlands and Belgium became the "Kingdom of the United Netherlands" under King Willem I, son of Willem V of Orange. The Belgians withdrew from the union in 1830 to form their own kingdom. King Willem II was largely responsible for the liberalizing revision of the constitution in 1848.

The Netherlands prospered during the long reign of Willem III (1849-90). At the time of his death, his daughter Wilhelmina was 10 years old. Her mother, Queen Emma, reigned as regent until 1898, when Wilhelmina reached the age of 18 and became the monarch.

The Netherlands proclaimed neutrality at the start of both world wars. Although it escaped occupation in World War I, German troops overran the country in May 1940. Queen Wilhelmina fled to London and established a government-in-exile. During the war, the Nazis rounded up the Jewish population before deporting them to camps in the East. Over 75% of the Netherlands' 140,000 Jews died at the hands of the Nazis. Shortly after the Netherlands was liberated in May 1945, the Queen returned. Crown Princess Juliana acceded to the throne in 1948 upon her mother's abdication. In April 1980, Queen Juliana abdicated in favor of her daughter, now Queen Beatrix. Crown Prince Willem-Alexander was born in 1967.

Elements of the Netherlands' once far-flung empire were granted either full independence or nearly complete autonomy after World War II. Indonesia formally gained its independence in 1949, and Suriname became independent in 1975. In the Caribbean, what was known as the Netherlands Antilles dissolved on October 10, 2010. The islands of Aruba and Curacao, and Sint Maarten (the Dutch two-fifths of the island of Saint Martin) enjoy a large degree of autonomy as constituent members of the Kingdom of the Netherlands. Meanwhile, the islands of Bonaire, Saba, and Sint Eustatius are considered to be special public bodies within the Netherlands.

GOVERNMENT AND POLITICAL CONDITIONS

The present constitution--which dates from 1848 and has been amended several times, most recently in 1983--protects individual and political freedoms, including freedom of religion. Although church and state are separate, a few historical ties remain; the royal family belongs to the Dutch Reformed Church (Protestant). Freedom of speech also is protected.

Government Structure

The country's government is based on the principles of ministerial responsibility and parliamentary government. The national government comprises three main institutions: the Monarch, the Council of Ministers, and the States General (parliament). There also are local governments.

The Monarch. The monarch is the titular head of state. The Queen's function is largely ceremonial, but she does have some influence deriving from the traditional veneration of the House of Orange, from which Dutch monarchs for more than 3 centuries have descended. Her influence also derives from her personal qualities and her power to appoint the "formateur," who forms the Council of Ministers following elections.

Council of Ministers. The Council of Ministers plans and implements government policy. The Monarch and the Council of Ministers together are called the Crown. Most ministers also head government ministries, although ministers-without-portfolio exist. The ministers, collectively and individually, are responsible to the States General. Unlike the British system, Dutch ministers cannot simultaneously be members of parliament.

The Council of State is a constitutionally established advisory body to the government that consists of members of the royal family and Crown-appointed members generally having political, academic, diplomatic, or military experience. The Council of State must be consulted by the cabinet on proposed legislation before a law is submitted to the parliament. The Council of State also serves as the country's highest administrative court .

States General. The Dutch parliament consists of two houses, the First Chamber ("Senate") and the Second Chamber ("House of Representatives"). Historically, Dutch governments have been based on the support of a majority in both houses of parliament. The Second Chamber is by far the more important of the two houses. It alone has the right to initiate legislation and amend bills submitted by the Council of Ministers. It shares with the First Chamber the right to question ministers and state secretaries.

The Second Chamber consists of 150 members, elected directly for a 4-year term--unless the government falls prematurely--on the basis of a nationwide system of proportional representation. This system means that members represent the whole country--rather than individual districts as in the United States--and are normally elected on a party slate, not on a personal basis. There is no threshold for small-party representation. Campaigns are relatively short, lasting usually about a month, and the election budgets of each party tend to be less than $2 million. The electoral system makes a coalition government almost inevitable. The last election of the Second Chamber was in June 2010.

The First Chamber is composed of 75 members elected for 4-year terms by the 12 provincial legislatures. It cannot initiate or amend legislation, but its approval of bills passed by the Second Chamber is required before bills become law. The First Chamber generally meets only once a week, and its members usually have other full-time jobs. The current First Chamber was elected following provincial elections in May 2011.

Courts. The judiciary comprises 62 cantonal courts, 19 district courts, five courts of appeal, and a Supreme Court that has 24 justices. All judicial appointments are made by the Crown. Judges nominally are appointed for life but actually are retired at age 70.

Local Government. The first-level administrative divisions are the 12 provinces, each governed by a locally elected provincial council and a provincial executive appointed by members of the provincial council. The province is formally headed by a queen's commissioner appointed by the Crown.

Current Government. General elections (of the Second Chamber) were held in June 2010. On October 14, 2010, a new minority government of the Liberal Party (VVD) and Christian Democratic Appeal (CDA) was sworn in, headed by Prime Minister Mark Rutte (VVD). This government relies on parliamentary support from the Freedom Party (PVV). Given the consensus-based nature of Dutch politics, a change of government does not usually result in drastic changes in foreign or domestic policy. Descriptions of the four main parties follow.

The Liberal Party (VVD), which is considered "liberal" in the European rather than American sense, emerged from the June elections as the largest party with 31 seats, although with a slim margin. Considered the most conservative of the major parties, the Liberals attach great importance to private enterprise and the freedom of the individual in political, social, and economic affairs.

The second-place finisher in the June elections was the Labor Party (PvdA), with 30 seats. PvdA is a classic European social democratic party, which is left of center. Labor's emphasis is economic equality for citizens, though the party has debated the role of the central government in that process. PvdA has no formal links to the country's trade unions.

The right wing, populist Freedom Party (PVV) achieved more gains than any other party in June, becoming the third-largest with 24 seats. PVV, lead by Geert Wilders, primarily runs on an anti-Islam and anti-immigrant ticket, along with a nationalist agenda that voices little support for European integration, Dutch participation in crisis management operations, or development assistance. On socio-economic issues, however, PVV tends to be "conservatively" left-of-center.

The once-dominant Christian Democratic Appeal Party (CDA) slipped into fourth position, losing 20 of its previous 41 seats. CDA supports free enterprise and holds to the principle that government activity should supplement but not supplant communal action by citizens. On the political spectrum, the CDA sees its philosophy as standing between the "individualism" of the Liberals and the "statism" of the Labor Party.

Domestic Drug Policy

Despite the government's long-term efforts to combat production of and trafficking in narcotic drugs, the Netherlands continues to be a significant transit point for drugs entering Europe (especially cocaine), and an important producer and exporter of synthetic drugs, particularly Ecstasy (MDMA), although MDMA production appears to have declined significantly in recent years. Dutch authorities received no reports of ecstasy tablet seizures in the United States linked to the Netherlands in 2009 . Cultivation of Dutch-grown cannabis ("Nederwiet") is extensive. In July 2008, the Justice and Interior Ministers established a task force to combat the criminal organizations behind cannabis plantations. In June 2011, the Cabinet approved measures to reduce drug-related nuisance and drug tourism. The Cabinet proposed that coffeeshops become private clubs for the local market only accessible to Dutch citizens upon display of their ID's. A maximum ceiling will be set on membership per individual coffeeshop. The "100% controls" at Schiphol airport in Amsterdam on inbound flights from the Caribbean and some South American and West African countries have resulted in a sharp decline in the number of drug couriers from those countries.

The Dutch Opium Act punishes possession, commercial distribution, production, import, and export of all illicit drugs. Drug use, however, is not an offense. The act distinguishes between "hard" drugs that have "unacceptable" risks (e.g., heroin, cocaine, Ecstasy) and "soft" drugs (cannabis products). One of the main aims of this policy is to separate the markets for soft and hard drugs so that soft drug users are less likely to come into contact with hard drugs. Sales of small quantities (under five grams) of cannabis products are tolerated in "coffeeshops" operating under strict conditions and controls. The United States continues to disagree with this aspect of Dutch drug policy. Trafficking in "hard" drugs is prosecuted vigorously. Overall, the Health Ministry coordinates drug policy, while the Ministry of Justice is responsible for law enforcement. At the municipal level, policy is coordinated in tripartite consultations among the mayor, the chief public prosecutor, and the police.

The Netherlands has a wide variety of demand-reduction and harm-reduction programs reaching about 70% of the country's 24,000-46,000 opiate addicts. The number of opiate addicts has stabilized over the past few years, with the average age rising to 44, and the number of overdose deaths related to opiates stabilizing at between 30 and 50 per year.

Counterterrorism/Homeland Security

The Netherlands supports counterterrorism efforts with leadership, personnel, and material. The Netherlands is a party to all 12 UN counterterrorism conventions.

In August 2004, the Act on Terrorist Crimes, implementing the 2002 European Union (EU) framework decision on combating terrorism, became effective. The act makes recruitment for the Jihad and conspiracy with the aim of committing a serious terrorist crime separate criminal offenses. A first government assessment of Dutch counterterrorist measures over the past 10 years, published in January 2011, concluded that Dutch counterterrorism policy is solid and reliable, and the package of measures is well-balanced and in line with the members of the European Convention on Human Rights. In December 2010, the appeals court in Amsterdam found the seven members of the "Hofstad" terror group guilty of participating in a criminal and terrorist organization and imposed prison sentences of between 15 months and 13 years against the seven. The appeals court verdict was the latest in a long legal process against the group. In June 2011, the National Counterterrorism Coordinator's Office (NCTb) maintained the terror threat level at "limited." (The Netherlands has four threat levels: minimum, limited, substantial, and critical.) According to the NCTb, this means that the chance of an attack in the Netherlands or against Dutch interests is relatively small but cannot be ruled out. The NCTb believes that the threat of an attack against Dutch interests abroad is greater in countries and regions where groups affiliated with al Qa'ida are more active than in the Netherlands itself.

The Dutch have taken a leading role in the European Union, the Financial Action Task Force (FATF), and other bodies to establish financial protocols to combat terrorism. They have assisted countries that lack the capacity to implement measures to combat terrorist financing. The Dutch Government takes steps to freeze the assets of individuals and entities included on the UN Security Council Resolution (UNSCR) 1267 Sanctions Committee's consolidated list. In August 2008, the Prevention of Money Laundering and Financing of Terrorism Act (WWFT) became effective. The act incorporated the EU's third Money Laundering Directive into Dutch national law.

The Netherlands is an active participant in the Container Security Initiative at Rotterdam, one of Europe's busiest ports. The Dutch Government also permits U.S. CBP Immigration Liaison Officers at Schiphol airport to assist with U.S.-bound passenger screening (the program is now known as the Immigration Advisory Program - IAP). In April 2009 , Dutch and U.S. authorities performed the opening of the new FLUX (Fast Low Risk Universal Crossing) system at some 20 U.S. airports enabling registered travelers that have submitted to a security assessment to go straight through U.S. immigration controls using iris scanners. The Netherlands deploys full body scanners on flights from Schiphol airport to the U.S. In November 2010, the Netherlands and the U.S. signed an agreement on Preventing and Combating Serious Crime (PCSC) that allows for the exchange of fingerprints and other data of known terrorists and criminals while protecting individual privacy.

Principal Government Officials

	Portfolio / Name		Party
Prime Minister	General Affairs	Mark Rutte	VVD
Deputy Prime Minister / Minister	Social Affairs and Employment	Lodewijk Asscher	PvdA
Minister	Interior and Kingdom Relations	Ronald Plasterk	PvdA
Minister	Foreign Affairs	Frans Timmermans	PvdA
Minister	Finance	Jeroen Dijsselbloem	PvdA
Minister	Security and Justice	Ivo Opstelten	VVD
Minister	Economic Affairs	Henk Kamp	VVD
Minister	Defence	Jeanine Hennis-Plasschaert	VVD
Minister	Health, Welfare and Sport	Edith Schippers	VVD
Minister	Education, Culture and Science	Jet Bussemaker	PvdA
Minister	Infrastructure and the Environment	Melanie Schultz van Haegen	VVD
Minister without portfolio	Housing and Civil Service (within Interior and Kingdom Relations)	Stef Blok	VVD
Minister without portfolio	Foreign Trade and Development Cooperation (within Foreign Affairs)	Lilianne Ploumen	PvdA
State Secretary	Finance (Fiscal affairs, Finances of lower governments)	Frans Weekers (2012-2014) Eric Wiebes (2014-)	VVD
State Secretary *	Security and Justice (Prevention, Family law, Youth justice, Copyright law)	Fred Teeven	VVD
State Secretary *	Economic Affairs (Agriculture, Nature, Food quality, Tourism, Postal affairs)	Co Verdaas (2012) Sharon Dijksma (2012-)	PvdA
State Secretary	Health, Welfare and Sport (Nursing and care, Elderly policy, Youth policy, Biotechnology)	Martin van Rijn	PvdA
State Secretary	Education, Culture and Science	Sander Dekker	VVD

	(Higher education, Science and Knowledge, Teachers, Culture)		
State Secretary *	Infrastructure and the Environment (Water policy, Environment, Aviation)	Wilma Mansveld	PvdA
State Secretary	Social Affairs and Employment (Unemployment insurances (partial), Equality, Long-term unemployment, Poverty, Health and Safety)	Jetta Klijnsma	PvdA

The Netherlands' **embassy** in the U.S. is at 4200 Linnean Avenue, NW, Washington, DC 20008; tel: 877-388-2443; fax: 202-362-3430.

ECONOMY

Currency	Euro (EUR) = € 1
Fiscal year	calendar year
Trade organisations	EU, WTO and OECD
	Statistics
GDP	$752 billion (nominal, 2015) $908 billion (PPP, 2017)
GDP rank	17th (nominal) / 27th (PPP)
GDP growth	+2.2% (2016 est.)
GDP per capita	$48,860 (nominal, 2015 est.) $50,338 (PPP, 2016 est.)[5]
GDP by sector	agriculture: 1.6%; industry: 18.8%; services: 79.6% (2015 est.)
Inflation (CPI)	0.2% (2016 est.)
Population below poverty line	9.1% (2013 est.)
Gini coefficient	25.1 (2013 est.)
Labour force	8.4 million (2016 est.)
Labour force by occupation	agriculture: 2%; industry: 18%; services: 80%
Unemployment	4.8% (July 2017)
Average gross salary	3,073 € / month (2016)
Average net salary	2,263 € / month (2016)
Main industries	agriculture-related industries, oil and natural gas, metal and engineering products, electronic machinery and equipment, chemicals, petroleum, construction, microelectronics, fishing
Ease-of-doing-business rank	28th (2017)
	External
Exports	$488.3 billion (2015 est.)
Export goods	natural gas, machinery and equipment, chemicals, fuels; foodstuffs
Main export partners	Germany 24.5%% Belgium 11.1%% France 8.4% United Kingdom 9.3% Italy 4.2% (2015 est.)[12]
Imports	$404.6 billion (2015 est.)
Import goods	machinery and transport equipment, chemicals, fuels, foodstuffs, clothing
Main import partners	Germany 14.7% China 14.5% Belgium 8.2% United Kingdom 5.1% Russia 5.7%

	Norway 4.1% (2015 est.)
FDI stock	$608.9 billion (31 December 2012 est.)
Gross external debt	$4.154 trillion (31 December 2014 est.)
	Public finances
Public debt	65.1% of GDP (2015 est.)
Revenues	$327.7 billion (2016)
Expenses	$324.6 billion (2016)
Economic aid	€ 4 bn
Credit rating	Standard & Poor's: AAA (Domestic) AAA (Foreign) AAA (T&C Assessment) Outlook: Stable Moody's: Aaa Outlook: Stable Fitch: AAA Outlook: Stable
Foreign reserves	US$42.92 billion (31 December 2014 est.)

According to the World Bank and the International Monetary Fund, the Netherlands was the 18th largest economy of the world in 2012, while the country has only about 17 million inhabitants. (see: List of countries by GDP (nominal)). GDP per capita is roughly $48,860 which makes it one of richest nations in the world (see: List of countries by GDP (PPP) per capita). Between 1996 and 2000 annual economic growth (GDP) averaged over 4%, well above the European average. Growth slowed considerably in 2001-05 as part of the global economic slowdown. 2006 and 2007 however showed economic growth of 3.4% and 3.9%. The Dutch economy was hit considerably by the ongoing global financial crisis and the ensuing European debt crisis.

The Netherlands has discovered huge natural gas resources since 1959. The sale of natural gas generated enormous revenues for the Netherlands for decades, adding hundreds of billions of euros to the government's budget.[17] However, the unforeseen consequences of the country's huge energy wealth impacted the competitiveness of other sectors of the economy, leading to the theory of Dutch disease.[17]

The Netherlands have a prosperous and open economy, which depends heavily on foreign trade. The economy is noted for stable industrial relations, fairly low unemployment and inflation, a very big sizable current account surplus (compared to the size of the country even more than Germany) and an important role as a European transportation hub, with Rotterdam as by far the biggest port in Europe and Amsterdam with one of the biggest airports in Europe. Industrial activity is predominantly in food processing, chemicals, petroleum refining, hightech, financial services, creative sector and electrical machinery. A highly mechanised agricultural sector employs no more than 2% of the labour force but provides large surpluses for the food-processing industry and for exports. The Netherlands, along with 11 of its EU partners, began circulating the euro currency on 1 January 2002.

The stern financial policy has been abandoned in 2009 because of the current credit crises. The relatively large banking sector was partly nationalised and bailed out through government interventions. The unemployment rate dropped to 5.0% in the summer of 2011, but increased with a sharp rate since then to 7.3% in May 2013, 6.8% in 2015 and 4.8% in july 2017.[18][19][20] The state budget deficit is about 2.2% in 2015 well below the norm of 3.0% in the EU.[21] Historically, the Dutch introduced and invented the stock market[22] by the merchandise trading through Dutch East India Company. The Netherlands is a founding member of the European Union, the OECD and the World Trade Organization.

The global financial crisis hit the Netherlands hard in the fall 2008; the Dutch economy entered recession in the fourth quarter of 2008, but annual GDP growth that year was still 1.9%. In 2009 , however, the economy shrank by 3.9%. The economy recovered slowly in 2010 with an annual growth rate of 1.8%. The recovery is forecasted to continue with an expected growth of 2% in 2011.This is mainly due to the increase in international trade, the largest engine of the Dutch economy; however, growth is expected to slow to 1.75% in 2012. In 2010, the exports increased by 12.8% and imports by 11.7%, in 2011 the forecasted figures are 6.75% and 5.25%. The expected national budget deficit (3.7% of GDP) and government debt (64.1%) still are cause for concern as they exceed the limits set by the European Growth and Stability Pact.

In order to fight against the consequences of the crisis, the government launched three economic stimulus packages since November 2008. The first package was worth about $8.3 billion, the second consisted mainly of government guarantees to stimulate lending and exports, and the third was worth $9 billion, bringing the total value of the stimulus measures to $17.3 billion, or approximately 2% of GDP. The state finances deteriorated further due to government interventions in the financial sector, including the nationalization of the Dutch activities of ABN Amro/Fortis Bank (costing a total of $37.6 billion), and capital injections to ING ($12.5 billion total) and other financial institutions whose balance sheets were compromised by U.S. mortgage-backed securities and other toxic assets. The financial institutions are repaying their government loans.

Private consumption dropped by 2.5% in 2009 and recovered by 0.3% in 2010. The slow recovery is expected to continue by 0.5%. in 2011 and 2012. The unemployment rate remained relatively low during the recession with 3.7% in 2009 , peaking at 4.5% in 2010. It is forecasted to decrease to 4.25% in 2011 and 4% in 2012. After a drop in the early 2000s, business investment (excluding the housing sector) staged a recovery from 2005 onwards. In 2008, business investment was up 7.4%, but it decreased sharply by 18.2% in 2009 . Despite predictions, the business investment's downfall did not continue as sharply as the drop was 'only' 1.5% in 2010; in 2011 the investments are predicted to grow by 5.75% and 4.25% in 2012.

Before the onset of the financial crisis, many firms in the Netherlands cited a loss of competitiveness as a major impediment to growth as unit labor costs outpaced those of their major competitors, including within the euro area. Smaller wage increases codified in collective bargaining agreements before growth accelerated in 2006 helped Dutch firms stay competitive during this period. However, an increasing labor shortage resulted in higher wage demands in the second half of 2007 and into 2008, with the average wage increasing by 3.3%. The pace of job growth steadily increased up to 2008, but then declined sharply in 2009 as fallout from the financial crisis constricted demand. The labor productivity is increasing from the pit of -3.1% in 2009 to 3.5% in 2010 and to an expected 2.25% in 2011 and 1.75% in 2012. Inflation ranged from 1.1% to 2.5% between 2004 and 2008. In 2009 , it fell to 1.2% and remained low at 1.3% in 2010. Due to international developments including the rapid demand growth in the emerging markets, the inflation is expected to grow by 2.25% in 2011 and 2012.

The Netherlands was one of the first EU member states to qualify for the Economic and Monetary Union (EMU). Traditionally, Dutch fiscal policy sought to strike a balance between further reductions in public spending and lower tax and social security contributions. During the first half of the current decade, the government struggled to keep the budget deficit within the limit of 3% of GDP set by the EU's Growth and Stability Pact. The government achieved a budget surplus of 0.5% in 2006, 0.2% in 2007, and 0.7% in 2008. This shifted to a deficit of 5.4% in 2009 as a result of the crisis, more specifically increased government spending on stimulus packages, unemployment benefits, and financial sector bailouts.. The deficit remained the same in 2010, but is expected to improve to 3.7% in 2011 and 2.2% in 2012, when the Netherlands will thus again comply with the EU's standards. The government debt has also increased rapidly from 45.5% in 2007 to 62.8% in 2010. The debt is expected to grow slowly to 64.1% in 2011 and 64.5% in 2012.

In order to fight against the increasing government debt and deficit levels, the government announced it was going to cut spending by $26 billion by 2015. The largest austerity measures include the downsizing of government ($8.5 billion) and cutting back on 'income transfers,' i.e., subsidies including child daycare and rent subsidies ($6.1 billion). There are other significant cutbacks, for example, on defense, culture and innovation subsidies, and development cooperation.

Government Role

Although the private sector is the cornerstone of the economy, the Netherlands has traditionally had an important and vibrant public sector. Despite the fact that the government still plays a significant role through permit requirements and regulations pertaining to almost every aspect of economic activity, the goal of the new government is to reduce significantly the administrative burden on business and shrink the public sector. The government had steadily reduced its role in the economy since the 1980s, but it was forced to become somewhat more active again as the economic downturn necessitated its intervention in the financial sector. The financial institutions that received government aid in the midst of the crisis have almost paid back all the loans. The exception is nationalized ABN Amro Bank that will not be re-privatized before 2013. The new government also aims to privatize the public transport companies in the largest cities. In general, the government's ownership of private businesses continues to be limited.

Trade and Investment
The Netherlands, where the total of goods, imports and exports is greater than the GDP, had a record trade surplus of approximately $47 billion in 2007. In 2008, this surplus decreased to approximately $43.2 billion, and in 2009 to $42.2 billion. With the escalation of the international trade in 2010, the Dutch trade surplus grew to $57 billion. With no significant trade or investment barriers, the Netherlands remains a receptive market for U.S. exports and an important investment partner. The Netherlands is the ninth-largest destination for U.S. exports ($35 billion in 2010), as well as the third-largest direct investor in the United States. Dutch accumulated direct investment in the United States in 2009 was $238 billion. The same year, the Netherlands was the largest destination for U.S. direct investment abroad with approximately $471 billion, representing approximately 13% of the total foreign direct investments. There are more than 1,600 U.S. companies with subsidiaries or offices in the Netherlands. The Dutch are strong proponents of free trade and staunch allies of the U.S. in international forums such as the World Trade Organization (WTO) and the Organization for Economic Cooperation and Development (OECD).

Sectors of the Economy
Services account for about three-quarters of the national income and are primarily in transportation, distribution, logistics, and financial areas such as banking and insurance. Industrial activity generates about a fourth of the national product and is dominated by the metalworking, oil refining, chemical, and food processing industries. The agriculture and fisheries sector account for some 2% of GDP.

Although Dutch crude oil production is small, in 2009 the Netherlands was the second-largest producer and the second-largest net exporter of natural gas in Europe (both after Norway). At the beginning of 2010, the country had 1.4 trillion cubic feet of natural gas reserves; the government earns approximately $14 billion annually from gas exploration and extraction through taxes and other levies. The port city of Rotterdam is one of the world's major centers for crude oil imports, trading, refining, and petrochemical production. Key sources of imported petroleum products include Russia, Saudi Arabia and Norway. Domestic gas resources are forecast to run out by 2030. To remain an energy player after its own resources are depleted, the Netherlands is cultivating energy relationships with potential long-term supplier countries such as Algeria, Kazakhstan, Libya, Qatar, and--most importantly--Russia. For example, Dutch gas pipeline company Gasunie, wholly owned by the Dutch Government, holds a 9% stake in Gazprom's Nord Stream pipeline, which will transport gas from Russia to Germany under the Baltic Sea. The Netherlands's goal is to become a gas "roundabout" for the Western Europe, meaning a hub that gathers natural gas from various sources (including the North Sea, Algerian and Qatari liquefied natural gas (LNG), and Russia), and then distributes it via pipeline to continental Europe.

Environmental Policy
The Netherlands is a small and densely populated country. Its economy depends on industry (particularly chemicals and metal processing), intensive agriculture and horticulture, and infrastructure, which takes advantage of the country's geographical position at the heart of Europe's transportation network. These factors have led to major pressure on the environment. The government works closely with industry and nongovernmental organizations to reach environmental targets. The Dutch welcomed the EU's 2008 directive to cut greenhouse gas (GHG) emissions 20% from 1990 levels and increase power derived from renewable sources to 20% by 2020. The Netherlands has a binding national target to reduce emissions in sectors not covered by the EU emissions trading system by 16% in 2020. It also has a binding national target of 14% in 2020 for renewable energy. Many independent energy experts, however, consider the government's aggressive climate change targets to be overly optimistic.

FOREIGN RELATIONS

The Netherlands abandoned a longstanding policy of neutrality after World War II. The Dutch are engaged participants in international affairs. Dutch foreign policy is geared to promoting a wide variety of goals: the rule of law, human rights, and democracy. Priority is given to enhancing European integration, ensuring

European security and stability (mainly through the mechanism of NATO and the EU, and by emphasizing the important role the United States plays in the security of Europe), and participating in conflict management and peacekeeping missions. In August 2010, the Netherlands withdrew its ground forces after more than 8 years in Afghanistan. It returned to Afghanistan in July 2011 with a police training mission in an EU and NATO context.

The Netherlands generally pursues its foreign policy interests within the framework of multilateral organizations. The Netherlands is an active and responsible participant in the United Nations as well as other multilateral organizations such as NATO, the EU, the Organization for Security and Cooperation in Europe (OSCE), the Council of Europe (CoE), the Organization for Economic Cooperation and Development (OECD), the World Trade Organization (WTO), and the International Monetary Fund (IMF). A centuries-old tradition of legal scholarship has made the Netherlands the home of the International Court of Justice; the Permanent Court of Arbitration; the Yugoslavia War Crimes Tribunal; the Special Tribunal for Lebanon; the European judicial and police organizations Eurojust and Europol; and the International Criminal Court. Dutch security policy is based primarily on membership in NATO, which the Netherlands joined as a charter member in 1949.

The Netherlands' post-war customs union with Belgium and Luxembourg (the Benelux group) paved the way for the formation of the European Community (precursor to the EU). Likewise, the Benelux abolition of internal border controls was a model for the wider Schengen accord, which today has 25 European signatories, including the Netherlands, pledged to common visa policies and free movement of people and goods across common borders. The Dutch have traditionally been strong advocates of European integration, and most aspects of their foreign, economic, and trade policies are coordinated through the European Union. However, Dutch voters rejected the EU constitutional treaty in June 2005. Parliament later approved the Lisbon Treaty in September 2008.

The Dutch were key proponents of the 1992 Maastricht Treaty and were the architects of the 1998 Treaty of Amsterdam. They have embraced the introduction of new member states and the common currency (euro). In recent years, however, the Dutch have become increasingly skeptical of the way the EU is run, its perceived inclination of taking on more tasks, and further enlargements.

Foreign Aid

The Netherlands has traditionally been one of the world's most generous aid donors. Although the government reduced spending on Official Development Assistance (ODA) from 0.8% (approximately USD 6.3 billion in 2010) to a fixed 0.7% of GDP by 2012, the Netherlands still is the fifth largest aid donor in relative terms and the eight largest in absolute terms. For budgetary and ideological reasons, the aid policy was significantly restructured in 2011. The number of countries to which the Netherlands provides direct bilateral assistance was reduced from 33 to 15 countries. The remaining beneficiary countries include a number of fragile states and low-income countries that have insufficient resources to make investments needed to achieve the Millennium Development Goals. Dutch aid was also restructured to focus on four spearheads: security and the rule of law; food security; water; and HIV/AIDS and Sexual Reproductive Health and Rights (SRHR). Those areas were selected in the belief that the Netherlands with its specific expertise can make a difference in the areas.

The Netherlands used to spend about 26 percent of its aid budget (on average USD 1.8 billion a year in the period 2006-2009) through multilateral channels, such as the World Bank, UNICEF, UNDP, FAO, ILO, WHO. However, it now believes these donations are too fragmented and it seeks to restructure them on the basis of the organizations' effectiveness and the added value of the Dutch priorities.

International Drug-Trafficking Control

The Dutch work closely with the United States and other countries on international programs against drug trafficking and organized crime. There is close Dutch-U.S. cooperation on joint counternarcotics operations in the Caribbean. The Netherlands actively participates in the Drug Enforcement Administration's (DEA) El Paso Intelligence Center (EPIC) and is a full member of DEA's International Drug Enforcement Conference (IDEC). The U.S. Coast Guard and the Royal Netherlands Navy actively work together in the drug transit zone in the Caribbean Sea through a bilateral Law Enforcement Detachment (LEDET) Arrangement. The Netherlands is a signatory to international counternarcotics agreements, a member of the UN Office on Drugs and Crime (UNODC), the UN Commission on Narcotic Drugs, and the 1990 Strasbourg Convention on Money Laundering and Confiscation, and is a major contributor to international counternarcotics projects.

U.S. RELATIONS

The U.S. partnership with the Netherlands is one of its oldest continuous relationships and dates back to the American Revolution. The excellent bilateral relations are based on close historical and cultural ties as well as a common dedication to individual freedom and human rights. The Netherlands shares with the United States a liberal economic outlook and firm commitment to free trade. The United States attaches great value to its strong economic and commercial ties with the Dutch. In 2009 , the Netherlands was the largest destination for United States direct foreign investment, with 13.4% of the total. This made the United States the largest direct foreign investor in the Netherlands. Vice versa, the Netherlands was the third-largest direct foreign investor in the United States in 2009 , and the Netherlands kept the same position in 2010.

The United States and the Netherlands often have similar positions on issues and work together both bilaterally and multilaterally in such institutions as the United Nations and NATO. The Dutch have worked with the United States at the WTO and in the OECD, as well as within the EU to advance the shared goal of a more open, market-led global economy.

The United States and the Netherlands joined NATO as charter members in 1949. The Dutch fought alongside the United States in the Korean War and the first Gulf War and have been active in global peacekeeping efforts in the former Yugoslavia, Afghanistan, and Iraq. The Netherlands played a leading role in the 1999 Kosovo air campaign. They currently are contributing to EU peacekeeping forces in Bosnia. The Dutch also support and participate in NATO training efforts in Iraq, the EU and NATO police training efforts in Afghanistan, the NATO mission in Libya and in both EU as well as NATO counter-piracy operations.

Principal U.S. Embassy Officials

chief of mission: Ambassador Peter HOEKSTRA (since 10 January 2018)

Deputy Chief of Mission--Edwin R. Nolan
Political-Economic Counselor-- Andrew Mann
Legal Counselor--John J. Kim
Public Affairs Counselor--Julie Moyes
Management Counselor--Graham L. Webster
Regional Security Officer--John L. Bush
Defense Attaché--Captain Daniel Braswell
Office of Defense Cooperation--Colonel Kevin Leek
Commercial Counselor--Maria J. Andrews
Agriculture Counselor-- Mary Allan Smith
Consul General, Amsterdam--Julie A. Ruterbories

The **U.S. Embassy** is located at Lange Voorhout 102, 2514 EJ The Hague; tel: 31-70-310-2209; fax: 31-70-310-2307. The Consulate General is at Museumplein 19, 1071 DJ Amsterdam; tel: 31-20-575-5309; fax: 31-20-679-0321.

TRAVEL AND BUSINESS INFORMATION

Travel Alerts, Travel Warnings, Trip Registration
The U.S. Department of State's Consular Information Program advises Americans traveling and residing abroad through Country Specific Information, Travel Alerts, and Travel Warnings. **Country Specific Information** exists for all countries and includes information on entry and exit requirements, currency regulations, health conditions, safety and security, crime, political disturbances, and the addresses of the U.S. embassies and consulates abroad. **Travel Alerts** are issued to disseminate information quickly about terrorist threats and other relatively short-term conditions overseas that pose significant risks to the security of American travelers. **Travel Warnings** are issued when the State Department recommends that Americans avoid travel to a certain country because the situation is dangerous or unstable.

For the latest security information, Americans living and traveling abroad should regularly monitor the Department's Bureau of Consular Affairs Internet web site at http://travel.state.gov, where current Worldwide Caution, Travel Alerts, and Travel Warnings can be found. The travel.state.gov website also includes information about passports, tips for planning a safe trip abroad and more. More travel-related information also is available at http://www.usa.gov/Citizen/Topics/Travel/International.shtml.

The Department's Smart Traveler app for U.S. travelers going abroad provides easy access to the frequently updated official country information, travel alerts, travel warnings, maps, U.S. embassy locations, and more that appear on the travel.state.gov site. Travelers can also set up e-tineraries to keep track of arrival and departure dates and make notes about upcoming trips. The app is compatible with iPhone, iPod touch, and iPad (requires iOS 4.0 or later).

The Department of State encourages all U.S. citizens traveling or residing abroad to enroll in the State Department's Smart Traveler Enrollment Program (STEP). A link to the registration page is also available through the Department's Smart Traveler app. U.S. citizens without internet access can enroll directly at the nearest U.S. embassy or consulate. By enrolling, you make your presence and whereabouts known in case it is necessary to contact you in an emergency and so you can receive up-to-date information on security conditions.

Emergency information concerning Americans traveling abroad may be obtained by calling 1-888-407-4747 toll free in the U.S. and Canada or the regular toll line 1-202-501-4444 for callers outside the U.S. and Canada

FAQS ABOUT THE NETHERLANDS

THE TEN MOST FREQUENTLY ASKED QUESTIONS ABOUT THE NETHERLANDS

1. **How many parts does the Kingdom of the Netherlands have?** The Kingdom of the Netherlands has three parts: the Netherlands and two countries in the Caribbean - the Netherlands Antilles and Aruba. With an area of 41,528 km and a population of over 16 million, the Netherlands (the European part of the Kingdom) is one of the world's smaller countries.
2. **Is there a difference between the Netherlands and Holland?** The Netherlands is often called Holland. But North Holland and South Holland are in fact the two coastal provinces in the west that played an important part in the country's history. The official name is the Kingdom of the Netherlands or the Netherlands for short.
3. **What is the system of government? Which city is the capital?** The Netherlands is a constitutional monarchy with a parliamentary system, in which the government consists of the queen and the ministers. For historical reasons, The Hague is the seat of government, but Amsterdam is the capital. The current government is a coalition between the Christian democrats (CDA) and two liberal parties (VVD & D66). Jan Peter Balkenende (CDA) is the Prime Minister. Queen Beatrix is the head of state.
4. **How flat is the Netherlands?** Very flat. A quarter of its surface area is below sea level. The lowest point in the Netherlands, near Rotterdam, is 6.7 metres below sea level. Its highest point, the Vaalserberg, is 323 metres above sea level. The Vaalserberg is in the province of Limburg, where the borders of the Netherlands, Belgium and Germany meet.

5. **What is the weather like?** The Netherlands has a temperate climate, thanks to its long coastline. The average temperatures are 18°C in summer and 3°C in winter. Average annual rainfall is 800 mm.
6. **What language is spoken?** The official language is Dutch, but a second official language, Frisian, is spoken by approximately 400,000 people in the province of Friesland. Frisian bears some similarities to English and the Scandinavian languages. Dutch is the language of instruction in schools throughout the Netherlands.
7. **Which currency can you use?** The euro is now the official currency in the Netherlands. As part of the drive towards European integration, many European countries replaced their national currencies with the euro (€) on 1 January 2002. There are coins of 1, 2, 5, 10, 20 and 50 eurocents and 1 and 2 euros, and notes of 5, 10, 20, 50, 100 and 500 euros. The notes are the same in all 12 euro countries. Only the coins have a European and a national side. You can pay with the euro in many European countries - the Netherlands, Germany, France, Italy, Luxembourg, Belgium, Spain, Portugal, Finland, Ireland, Austria and Greece.
   Exchange rate:
   € 1 = US$ 1.32 (rate in March 2005)
8. **What is the best way to travel in the Netherlands?** The Netherlands has an excellent infrastructure, with good roads and first-rate public transport services, thanks to its close-knit network of trains and buses. The Dutch themselves like to get around by bike.
9. **When is the day of national celebration?** The Queen's Birthday on 30 April. Queen Beatrix's actual birthday is on 31 January, but she celebrates it on 30 April, her late mother's birthday. Events like parades, street markets and sports days are organised throughout the country.
10. **What are the Netherlands' economic strengths?** The Dutch economy has a strong international focus, the Netherlands being one of the European Union's most dynamic centres of trade and industry. Due to its favourable location by the North Sea, the Netherlands plays an important role as a main port and distribution centre for companies operating worldwide. The port of Rotterdam handles some 327 million tonnes of goods every year, and is the biggest port in the world. Amsterdam Schiphol international airport is the fourth biggest cargo-handling airport in Europe. That is why the Netherlands is often called the Gateway to Europe. In 2003, the Netherlands was ranked the eighth largest exporter in the world.

CORPORATE LAW BASICS

Corporate law (also "company" or "corporations" law) is the law of the most dominant kind of business enterprise in the modern world. Corporate law is the study of how shareholders, directors, employees, creditors, and other stakeholders such as consumers, the community and the environment interact with one another under the internal rules of the firm.

Corporate law is a part of a broader companies law (or law of business associations). Other types of business associations can include partnerships (like most law firms), or trusts (like a pension fund) or companies limited by guarantee (like some universities or charities). Corporate law is about big business, which has separate legal personality, with limited liability for its shareholders, who buy and sell their stocks depending on the performance of the board of directors. It deals with the firms that finish their titles with "plc" (UK), "Inc" (US) or "AG and GmbH" (Germany). According to the American Professors Hansmann (of Yale University) and Kraakman (of Harvard University), the five defining characteristics of the modern corporation are:[1]

separate legal personality of the corporation (the right to sue and be sued in its own name)

limited liability of the shareholders (so that when the company is insolvent, they only owe the money that they subscribed for in shares)

transferrable shares (usually on a listed exchange, such as the London Stock Exchange, New York Stock Exchange or Euronext in Paris) delegated management, in other words, control of the company placed in the hands of a board of directors

investor ownership, which Hansmann and Kraakman take to mean, ownership by shareholders.

The last of these defining features is contested. For a start, it is pointed out that shareholders do not own corporations, they own their shares.[2] Ownership of a corporation is complicated by increasing social and economic interdependence, as different stakeholders compete to have a say in corporate affairs. In most developed countries excluding the English speaking world, company boards have representatives of both shareholders and employees to "codetermine" company strategy. Corporate law is often divided into corporate governance (which concerns the various power relations within a corporation) and corporate finance (which concerns the rules on how capital is used).

LEGAL ENTITIES TYPES

UNITED STATES

S corporation ·
C corporation
LLC ·
LLLP ·
Series LLC
Delaware corporation
Nevada corporation
Massachusetts business trust

UK / IRELAND / COMMONWEALTH

Limited company
(by shares ·
by guarantee
Public ·
Proprietary)
Community interest company

EUROPEAN UNION

EEA
SE ·
SCE ·
SPE ·
EEIG

ELSEWHERE

AB · AG · ANS · A/S · AS · GmbH
K.K. · N.V. · OY · S.A. ·

The word "corporation" is generally synonymous with large publicly owned companies. In the United States, a company may or may not be a separate legal entity, and is often used synonymously with "firm" or "business." A corporation may accurately be called a company; however, a company should not necessarily be called a corporation, which has distinct characteristics. According to Black's Law Dictionary, in the U.S. a company means "a corporation — or, less commonly, an association, partnership or union — that carries on industrial enterprise."

The defining feature of a corporation is its legal independence from the people who create it. If a corporation fails, shareholders will lose their money, and employees will lose their jobs, but neither will be liable for debts that remain owing to the corporation's creditors. This rule is called limited liability, and it is why corporations end with "Ltd." (or some variant like "Inc." and "plc"). In the words of British judge, Walton J, a company is...

> "...only a juristic figment of the imagination, lacking both a body to be kicked and a soul to be damned."[4]

But despite this, corporations are recognised by the law to have rights and responsibilities like actual people. Corporations can exercise human rights against real individuals and the state,[5] and they may be responsible for human rights violations.[6] Just as they are "born" into existence through its members obtaining a certificate of incorporation, they can "die" when they lose money into insolvency. Corporations can even be convicted of criminal offences, such as fraud and manslaughter.[7]

HISTORY

Although some forms of companies are thought to have existed during Ancient Rome and Ancient Greece, the closest recognizable ancestors of the modern company did not appear until the second millennium. The first recognizable commercial associations were medieval guilds, where guild members agreed to abide by guild rules, but did not participate in ventures for common profit. The earliest forms of joint commercial enterprise under the *lex mercatoria* were in fact partnerships.

But with the expansion of international trade, Royal charters were increasingly granted in Europe (notably in England and Holland) to merchant adventurers.

The Royal charters usually conferred special privileges on the trading company (including, usually, some form of monopoly). Originally, traders in these entities traded stock on their own account, but later the members came to operate on joint account and with joint stock, and the new Joint stock company was born.

Early companies were purely economic ventures; it was only belatedly realized that an incidental benefit of holding joint stock was that the company's stock could not be seized for the debts of any individual member.[9] The development of company law in Europe was hampered by two notorious "bubbles" (the South Sea Bubble in England and the Tulip Bulb Bubble in Holland) in the 17th century, which set the development of companies in the two leading jurisdictions back by over a century in popular estimation.

But companies, almost inevitably, returned to the forefront of commerce, although in England to circumvent the Bubble Act 1720 investors had reverted to trading the stock of unincorporated associations, until it was repealed in 1825. However, the cumbersome process of obtaining Royal charters was simply insufficient to keep up with demand. In England there was a lively trade in the charters of defunct companies. However, prevarication amongst the legislation meant that in England it was not until the Joint Stock Companies Act 1844 that the first equivalent of modern companies, formed by registration, appeared.

Soon after came the Limited Liability Act 1855, which in the event of a company's bankruptcy limited the liability of all shareholders to the amount of capital they had invested. The beginning of modern company law came when the two pieces of legislation were codified under the Joint Stock Companies Act 1856 at the behest of the then Vice President of the Board of Trade, Mr Robert Lowe. That legislation shortly gave way to the railway boom, and from there the numbers of companies formed soared. In the later nineteenth century depression took hold, and just as company numbers had boomed, many began to implode and fall into insolvency. Much strong academic, legislative and judicial opinion was opposed to the notion that businessmen could escape accountability for their role in the failing businesses.

The last significant development in the history of companies was the decision of the House of Lords in *Salomon v. Salomon & Co.* where the House of Lords confirmed the separate legal personality of the company, and that the liabilities of the company were separate and distinct from those of its owners.

In a December 2006 article, *The Economist* identified the development of the joint stock company as one of the key reasons why Western commerce moved ahead of its rivals in the Middle East in post-renaissance era.[10] Of course one should not underestimate the effects of early industrialisation either.[*citation needed*]

CORPORATE GOVERNANCE

Corporate governance is primarily the study of the power relations between the board of directors and those who elect them (shareholders in the "general meeting" and employees). It also concerns other stakeholders, such as creditors, consumers, the environment and the community at large. One of the main differences between different countries in the internal form of companies is between a two-tier and a one tier board. The United Kingdom, the United States, and most Commonwealth countries have single unified boards of directors. In Germany, companies have two tiers, so that shareholders (and employees) elect a "supervisory board", and then the supervisory board chooses the "management board". There is the option to use two tiers in France, and in the new European Companies (Societas Europea).

Recent literature, especially from the United States, has begun to discuss corporate governance in the terms of management science. While post-war discourse centred on how to achieve effective "corporate democracy" for shareholders or other stakeholders, many scholars have shifted to discussing the law in terms of principal-agent problems. On this view, the basic issue of corporate law is that when a "principal" party delegates his property (usually the shareholder's capital, but also the employee's labour) into the control of an "agent" (i.e. the director of the company) there is the possibility that the agent will act in his own interests, be "opportunistic", rather than fulfill the wishes of the principle. Reducing the risks of this opportunism, or the "agency cost", is said to be central to the goal of corporate law.

CORPORATE CONSTITUTION

The rules for corporations derive from two sources. These are the country's statutes (in the US, usually the Delaware General Corporation Law (DGCL); in the UK, the Companies Act 2006 (CA 2006); in Germany, the Aktiengesetz (AktG) and the Gesetz betreffend die Gesellschaften mit beschränkter Haftung (GmbH-Gesetz, GmbHG). The law will set out which rules are mandatory, and which rules can be derogated from.

Examples of important rules which cannot be derogated from would usually include how to fire the board of directors, what duties directors owe to the company or when a company must be dissolved as it approaches bankruptcy.

Examples of rules that members of a company would be allowed to change and choose could include, what kind of procedure general meetings should follow, when dividends get paid out, or how many members (beyond a minimum set out in the law) can amend the constitution. Usually, the statute will set out model articles, which the corporation's constitution will be assumed to have if it is silent on a bit of particular procedure.

The United States, and a few other common law countries, split the corporate constitution into two separate documents (the UK got rid of this in 2006). The memorandum of Association (or articles of incorporation) is the primary document, and will generally regulate the company's activities with the outside world. It states which objects the company is meant to follow (e.g. "this company makes automobiles") and specifies the authorised share capital of the company. The articles of association (or by-laws) is the secondary document, and will generally regulate the company's internal affairs and management, such as procedures for board meetings, dividend entitlements etc. In the event of any inconsistency, the memorandum prevails[11] and in the United States only the memorandum is publicised. In civil law jurisdictions, the company's constitution is normally consolidated into a single document, often called the charter.

It is quite common for members of a company to supplement the corporate constitution with additional arrangements, such as *shareholders' agreements*, whereby they agree to exercise their membership rights in a certain way. Conceptually a shareholders' agreement fulfills many of the same functions as the corporate constitution, but because it is a contract, it will not normally bind new members of the company unless they accede to it somehow.

One benefit of shareholders' agreement is that they will usually be confidential, as most jurisdictions do not require shareholders' agreements to be publicly filed. Another common method of supplementing the corporate constitution is by means of *voting trusts*, although these are relatively uncommon outside of the United States and certain offshore jurisdictions. Some jurisdictions consider the company seal to be a party of the "constitution" (in the loose sense of the word) of the company, but the requirement for a seal has been abrogated by legislation in most countries.

BALANCE OF POWER

The most important rules for corporate governance are those concerning the balance of power between the board of directors and the members of the company. Authority is given or "delegated" to the board to manage the company for the success of the investors. Certain specific decision rights are often reserved for shareholders, where their interests could be fundamentally affected. There are necessarily rules on when directors can be removed from office and replaced. To do that, meetings need to be called in order to vote on the issues. How easily the constitution can be amended and by who necessarily affects the relations of power.

It is a principle of corporate law that the directors of a company have the right to manage. This is expressed in statute in the DGCL, where §141(a) states,

> (a) The business and affairs of every corporation organized under this chapter shall be managed by or under the direction of a board of directors, except as may be otherwise provided in this chapter or in its certificate of incorporation.

In Germany, §76 AktG says the same for the management board, while under §111 AktG the supervisory board's role is stated to be to "supervise" (*überwachen*). In the UK, the right to manage is not laid down in law, but is found in Art.2 of the Model Articles. This means it is a default rule, which companies can opt out of (s.20 CA 2006) by reserving powers to members, although companies rarely do. UK law specifically reserves shareholders right and duty to approve "substantial non cash asset transactions" (s.190 CA 2006), which means those over 10% of company value, with a minimum of £5,000 and a maximum of £100,000.[14] Similar rules, though much less stringent, exist in §271 DGCL[15] and through case law in Germany under the so called *Holzmüller* doctrine.

Probably the must fundamental guarantee that directors will act in the members' interests is that they can easily be sacked. During the Great Depression, two Harvard scholars, Adolf Berle and Gardiner Means wrote *The Modern Corporation and Private Property*, an attack on American law which failed to hold directors to account, and linked the growing power and autonomy of directors to the economic crisis. In the UK, the right of members to remove directors by a simple majority is assured under s.168 CA 2006[17] Moreover, Art.20 of the Model Articles requires a third of the board to put themselves up for re-election every year (in effect creating maximum three year terms). 10% of shareholders can demand a meeting any time, and 5% can if it has been a year since the last one (s.303 CA 2006).

In Germany, where employee participation creates the need for greater boardroom stability, §84(3) AktG states that management board directors can only be removed by the supervisory board for an important reason (*ein wichtiger Grund*) though this can include a vote of no-confidence by the shareholders. Terms last for five years, unless 75% of shareholders vote otherwise. §122 AktG lets 10% of shareholders demand a meeting. In the US, Delaware lets directors enjoy considerable autonomy. §141(k) DGCL states that directors can be removed without any cause, unless the board is "classified", meaning that directors only come up for re-appointment on different years. If the board is classifed, which every board in Delaware is, then directors cannot be removed unless there is gross misconduct.

Director's autonomy from shareholders is seen further in §216 DGCL, which allows for plurality voting and §211(d) which states shareholder meetings can only be called if the constitution allows for it.[18] The problem is that in America, directors usually choose where a company is incorporated and §242(b)(1) DGCL says any constitutional amendment requires a resolution by the directors. By contrast, constitutional amendments can be made at any time by 75% of shareholders in Germany (§179 AktG) and the UK (s.21 CA 2006[19]).

CORPORATE PERSONALITY

One of the key legal features of corporations are their separate legal personality, also known as "personhood" or being "artificial persons". However, the separate legal personality was not confirmed under English law until 1895 by the House of Lords in *Salomon v. Salomon & Co.*[20] Separate legal personality often has unintended consequences, particularly in relation to smaller, family companies. In *B v. B* [1978] Fam 181 it was held that a discovery order obtained by a wife against her husband was not effective against the husband's company as it was not named in the order and was separate and distinct from him.[21] And in *Macaura v. Northern Assurance Co Ltd*[22] a claim under an insurance policy failed where the insured had transferred timber from his name into the name of a company wholly owned by him, and it was subsequently destroyed in a fire; as the property now belonged to the company and not to him, he no longer had an "insurable interest" in it and his claim failed.

However, separate legal personality does allow corporate groups a great deal of flexibility in relation to tax planning, and also enables multinational companies to manage the liability of their overseas operations. For instance in *Adams v. Cape Industries plc*[23] it was held that victims of asbestos poisoning at the hands of an American subsidiary could not sue the English parent in tort.

There are certain specific situations where courts are generally prepared to "pierce the corporate veil", to look directly at, and impose liability directly on the individuals behind the company. The most commonly cited examples are:

- where the company is a mere façade
- where the company is effectively just the agent of its members or controllers
- where a representative of the company has taken some personal responsibility for a statement or action[24]
- where the company is engaged in fraud or other criminal wrongdoing
- where the natural interpretation of a contract or statute is as a reference to the corporate group and not the individual company
- where permitted by statute (for example, many jurisdictions provide for shareholder liability where a company breaches environmental protection laws)
- in many jurisdictions, where a company continues to trade despite inevitable bankruptcy, the directors can be forced to account for trading losses personally

CAPACITY AND POWERS

Historically, because companies are artificial persons created by operation of law, the law prescribed what the company could and could not do. Usually this was an expression of the commercial purpose which the company was formed for, and came to referred to as the company's *objects*, and the extent of the objects are referred to as the company's capacity. If an activity fell outside of the company's capacity it was said to be *ultra vires* and void.

By way of distinction, the organs of the company were expressed to have various *corporate powers*. If the objects were the things that the company was able to do, then the powers were the means by which it could do them.

Usually expressions of powers were limited to methods of raising capital, although from earlier times distinctions between objects and powers have caused lawyers difficulty.[25] Most jurisdictions have now modified the position by statute, and companies generally have capacity to do all the things that a natural person could do, and power to do it in any way that a natural person could do it.

However, references to corporate capacity and powers have not quite been consigned to the dustbin of legal history. In many jurisdictions, directors can still be liable to their shareholders if they cause the company to engage in businesses outside of its objects, even if the transactions are still valid as between the company and the third party. And many jurisdictions also still permit transactions to be challenged for lack of "corporate benefit", where the relevant transaction has no prospect of being for the commercial benefit of the company or its shareholders.

As artificial persons, companies can only act through human agents. The main agent who deals with the company's management and business is the board of directors, but in many jurisdictions other officers can be appointed too.

The board of directors is normally elected by the members, and the other officers are normally appointed by the board. These agents enter into contracts on behalf of the company with third parties.

Although the company's agents owe duties to the company (and, indirectly, to the shareholders) to exercise those powers for a proper purpose, generally speaking third parties' rights are not impugned if it transpires that the officers were acting improperly. Third parties are entitled to rely on the ostensible authority of agents held out by the company to act on its behalf. A line of common law cases reaching back to *Royal British Bank v Turquand* established in common law that third parties were entitled to assume that the internal management of the company was being conducted properly, and the rule has now been codified into statute in most countries.

Accordingly, companies will normally be liable for all the act and omissions of their officers and agents. This will include almost all torts, but the law relating to crimes committed by companies is complex, and varies significantly between countries.

DIRECTOR'S DUTIES

In most jurisdictions, directors owe strict duties of good faith, as well as duties of care and skill, to safeguard the interests of the company and the members.

The standard of skill and care that a director owes is usually described as acquiring and maintaining sufficient knowledge and understanding of the company's business to enable him to properly discharge his duties.

Directors are also strictly charged to exercise their powers only for a proper purpose. For instance, were a director to issue a large number of new shares, not for the purposes of raising capital but in order to defeat a potential takeover bid, that would be an improper purpose.[26]

Directors also owe strict duties not to permit any conflict of interest or conflict with their duty to act in the best interests of the company. This rule is so strictly enforced that, even where the conflict of interest or conflict of duty is purely hypothetical, the directors can be forced to disgorge all personal gains arising from it. In *Aberdeen Ry v. Blaikie* (1854) 1 Macq HL 461 Lord Cranworth stated in his judgment that,

> "A corporate body can only act by agents, and it is, of course, the duty of those agents so to act as best to promote the interests of the corporation whose affairs they are conducting. Such agents have duties to discharge of a fiduciary nature towards their principal. And it is a rule of universal application that no one, having such duties to discharge, shall be allowed to enter into engagements in which he has, *or can have*, a personal interest conflicting *or which possibly may conflict*, with the interests of those whom he is bound to protect... So strictly is this principle adhered to that no question is allowed to be raised as to the fairness or unfairness of the contract entered into..."

However, in many jurisdictions the members of the company are permitted to ratify transactions which would otherwise fall foul of this principle. It is also largely accepted in most jurisdictions that this principle should be capable of being abrogated in the company's constitution.

CORPORATE LITIGATION

Members of a company generally have rights against each other and against the company, as framed under the company's constitution. In relation to the exercise of their rights, minority shareholders usually have to accept that, because of the limits of their voting rights, they cannot direct the overall control of the company and must accept the will of the majority (often expressed as *majority rule*). However, majority rule can be iniquitous, particularly where there is one controlling shareholder.

Accordingly, a number of exceptions have developed in law in relation to the general principle of majority rule.

Where the majority shareholder(s) are exercising their votes to perpetrate a fraud on the minority, the courts may permit the minority to sue[27]

members always retain the right to sue if the majority acts to invade their personal rights, e.g. where the company's affairs are not conducted in accordance with the company's constitution (this position has been debated because the extent of a personal right is not set in law). *Macdougall v Gardiner* and *Pender v Lushington* present irreconcilable differences in this area.

in many jurisdictions it is possible for minority shareholders to take a *representative* or *derivative action* in the name of the company, where the company is controlled by the alleged wrongdoers

CORPORATE FINANCE

SHARES AND SHARE CAPITAL

Companies generally raise capital for their business ventures either by debt or equity. Capital raised by way of equity is usually raised by issued shares (sometimes called "stock" (not to be confused with stock-in-trade)) or warrants.

A share is an item of property, and can be sold or transferred. Holding a share makes the holder a member of the company, and entitles them to enforce the provisions of the company's constitution against the company and against other members. Shares also normally have a nominal or par value, which is the limit of the shareholder's liability to contribute to the debts of the company on an insolvent liquidation.

Shares usually confer a number of rights on the holder. These will normally include:

voting rights

rights to dividends declared by the company

rights to any return of capital either upon redemption of the share, or upon the liquidation of the company

in some countries, shareholders have preemption rights, whereby they have a preferential right to participate in future share issues by the company

Many companies have different classes of shares, offering different rights to the shareholders. For example, a company might issue both ordinary shares and preference shares, with the two types having different voting and/or economic rights. For example, a company might provide that preference shareholders shall each receive a cumulative preferred dividend of a certain amount per annum, but the ordinary shareholders shall receive everything else.

The total number of issued shares in a company is said to represent its *capital*. Many jurisdictions regulate the minimum amount of capital which a company may have, although some countries only prescribe minimum amounts of capital for companies engaging in certain types of business (e.g. banking, insurance etc.).

Similarly, most jurisdictions regulate the maintenance of capital, and prevent companies returning funds to shareholders by way of distribution when this might leave the company financially exposed. In some jurisdictions this extends to prohibiting a company from providing financial assistance for the purchase of its own shares.

LIQUIDATIONS

Liquidation is the normal means by which a company's existence is brought to an end. It is also referred to (either alternatively or concurrently) in some jurisdictions as *winding up* and/or *dissolution*.

Liquidations generally come in two forms, either *compulsory liquidations* (sometimes called *creditors' liquidations*) and *voluntary liquidations* (sometimes called *members' liquidations*, although a voluntary liquidation where the company is insolvent will also be controlled by the creditors, and is properly referred to as a *creditors' voluntary liquidation*).

As its names imply, applications for compulsory liquidation are normally made by creditors of the company when the company is unable to pay its debts. However, in some jurisdictions, regulators have the power to apply for the liquidation of the company on the grounds of public good, i.e. where the company is believed to have engaged in unlawful conduct, or conduct which is otherwise harmful to the public at large.

Voluntary liquidations occur when the company's members decide voluntarily to wind up the affairs of the company. This may be because they believe that the company will soon become insolvent, or it may be on economic grounds if they believe that the purpose for which the company was formed is now at an end, or that the company is not providing an adequate return on assets and should be broken up and sold off.

Some jurisdictions also permit companies to be wound up on "just and equitable" grounds.[26] Generally, applications for just and equitable winding-up are brought by a member of the company who alleges that the affairs of the company are being conducted in a prejudicial manner, and asking the court to bring an end to the company's existence. For obvious reasons, in most countries, the courts have been reluctant to wind up a company solely on the basis of the disappointment of one member, regardless of how well-founded that member's complaints are. Accordingly, most jurisdictions which permit just and equitable winding up also permit the court to impose other remedies, such as requiring the majority shareholder(s) to buy out the disappointed minority shareholder at a fair value.

Where a company goes into liquidation, normally a liquidator is appointed to gather in all the company's assets and settle all claims against the company. If there is any surplus after paying off all the creditors of the company, this surplus is then distributed to the members.

CORPORATIONS IN VATIOUS COUNTRIES

Abbreviation	Country	Full term in nation	Full term in English	Notes
AE	Greece	Anonimi Etairia	Anonymous society (Anonymous corporation)	Similar to S.A.
AB	Sweden	Aktiebolag	Stock company	When used within the company's name, it is turned into the definite form (i.e aktiebolaget).
AD	Bulgaria	Aktsionerno drujestvo	Joint Stock Company (JSCO)	
AD	Republic of Macedonia	Akcionersko društvo	Stock corporation	
A.D	Serbia and Montenegro	Akcionarsko društvo	Stock corporation	
AG	Austria	Aktiengesellschaft	Stock corporation	Equivalent to Public Limited Company (PLC) or incorporated company, min. capital 70.000 EUR
AG	Germany	Aktiengesellschaft	Stock corporation	Equivalent to PLC or incorporated company, min. capital 50.000 EUR
AG	Switzerland	Aktiengesellschaft	Stock corporation	Equivalent to PLC or incorporated company, min. capital 100.000 CHF
d.d.	Croatia	Dionicko društvo	Stock corporation	Equivalent to PLC or incorporated company
A/S	Denmark and Norway	Aktieselskab, aksjeselskap	Stock corporation	
a. s.	Czech Republic	Akciová spolecnost	Stock company	Can be both private or public. The minimum share capital is 2 million CZK (20 million CZK for IPOs). Organs: General Assembly, Board of Directors

				and Supervisory Board.
a. s.	Slovakia	Akciová spolocnost	Stock company	Assimilable to Public Limited Company, plc. The minimum share capital is 1 million SKK (approx. 25 000 EUR). Organs: General Assembly, Board and Control Council.
BAT	Ukraine	Vidkryte Aktsionerne Tovarystvo	ie i obr /> Open Joint-Stock Company	Similar to Public Limited Company (PLC) or (Public) Corporation)
Ltd or	Hong Kong, China	Limited, " (in Traditional Chinese)	Can denote either a Private or Public Limited Company (liability limited by share capital)	Similar to a UK LTD/PLC. Under the Hong Kong Companies Ordinance (Chapter 32) the name of a Hong Kong incorporated company may be registered in either the English or Chinese language, or both.
Ltd or 'Cyf' (Welsh)	England & Wales	Limited, or 'Cyfyngedig' Welsh language equivalent	Private Limited Company (liability limited by share capital)	
Plc or 'Ccc' (Welsh)	England & Wales	Public Limited Company, or 'Cwmni Cyfyngedig Cyhoeddus' Welsh language equivalent	Public Limited Company (liability limited by share capital)	Requires authorised minimum share capital of GBP £50,000; of which it must have allotted shares to the value of at least GBP £50,000 and a minimum of 25% must be fully paid up prior to starting business.
Unltd or Ultd	England & Wales	Unlimited, or 'Anghyfyngedig' Welsh language equivalent	Private Unlimited Company (with share capital)	Unlimited Company; as word implies, members or shareholders of the company have no limit placed on their liability for the company's financial obligations in the event of it becoming insolvent, however, it is not a requirement under the Companies Act of GB for an Unlimited Company to state either Unltd, Ultd or Unlimited after its company name. It is nevertheless, a company (a legal entity like its peers Ltd and Plc) registered and formed (incorporated) under the Companies Act of Great Britain and subject to the Companies Act. The advantage of an unlimited company is that they are exempted from filing accounts with the Registrar of Companies for public disclosure (unless, during the accounting period covered, the company is a qualified subsidiary or a parent of a

				limited company undertaking) subject to a few exceptions to this rule.
SE	European Union	Societas Europaea (Latin for 'European Company')	European (Public) Limited Company (liability limited by share capital)	The legal form of the European (Public) Company. Similar to a UK PLC or German AG company etc. An SE (Societas Europaea) may be created on registration in any one of the Member States of the European Union, and is subject to the European Company Statute - Council Regulation (EC) No 2157/2001 on the Statute for a European company (the 'Regulation'). An SE is able to relocate its registered office to any other Member State of the EUand without it being wound up.
Sdn Bhd	Malaysia	Sendirian Berhad	Private limited Company	Equivalent to Public Limited Company in the UK
Bhd	Malaysia	Berhad	Stock Corporation	Denotes publicly listed companies in Malaysia
Co.	USA.	Company	Stock Corporation or Non-stock corporation	In some USA States, it is permissible to use Company or Co. in place of Inc. or Corp. for a corporation. See the table under USA in the article Types of corporations. Allowed by many states but not all; however, individuals and partnerships may register a ficticious name with the word "Company" in it either with the county where they reside or with the state in such areas where the state registers ficticious names.
Corp.	USA	Corporation	Stock corporation or non-stock corporation	"Corporation", "Incorporated" and the abbreviations "Corp." and "Inc." are the only terms universally accepted by all 51 corporation chartering agencies in the USA.
Inc.	U.S.A.	Incorporated	Stock corporation">Stock corporation or non-stock corporation	"Corporation", "Incorporated" and the abbreviations "Corp." and "Inc." are the only terms universally accepted by all 51 corporation chartering agencies in the United States.
K.K.	Japan	Kabushiki kaisha	Business corporation	The predominant form of company in Japan, and the only type that can be publicly traded.
LTD	Australia	Limited	Public Limited Company	Equivalent to PLC Public Limited Company in the UK

LTD	New Zealand	Limited	Public or private Limited Company	All NZ limited liability companies must use LTD
Ltd	India	Limited	Public Limited Company (liability limited in share capital)	Equivalent to a UK PLC.
Pvt Ltd	India	Private Limited	Private Limited Company (liability limited in share capital)	Equivalent to a UK LTD.
Ltd.	Some USA. States.	Limited	Corporation	In some USA States, it is permissible to use Ltd. instead of Inc. or Corp. for a corporation.
N.V.	Belgium and Netherlands	Naamloze Vennootschap	A limited liability company, liability limited by shares. In its articles or corporation it may forbid public trading of its shares. However, it is the only type of company in the Netherlands that may allow public trading of its shares.	
OAO	Russia	Otkrytoye aktsionernoye obshchestvo	Open Joint-Stock Company	Similar to Public Limited Company (PLC). There is also ZAO (zakrytoye aktsionernoye obshchestvo- Close Joint-Stock Company, or closely-held corporation, no more than fifty shareholders)
Oy(j)	Finland	(Julkinen) osakeyhtiö	(Public) Limited Company	
Rt.	Hungary	Részvénytársaság	Stock company	
S.A.	Spain	Sociedad Anónima	Stock Corporation	Minimum capital is 60.101,21€
S.A.	Brazil	Sociedade Anônima	Public Limited Company	
S.A.	Portugal	Sociedade Anónima	Public Limited Company	
S.A.	France	Société Anonyme	Public Limited Company	public corporation.
S.A.	Switzerlan	Société Anonyme Società Anonima	Public Limited Company	
S.p.A.	Italy	Società per Azioni	Stock corporation	Italian plc. As with Ltd., some USA states also permit this designation (in which case, it is synonymous with corporation). Currently, only the state of Connecticut permits this use.
S.A.	Romania	Societate pe Actiuni	Stock corporation	Romanian plc.
S.A.	Poland	"Spólka Akcyjna"	Stock corporation	
Co., ltd.	Thailand	Company Limited	Private limited company or limited company	
PLC.	Thailand	Public Company Limited	Stock corporation	
P.T. / PT	Indonesia	Perseroan Terbatas	Limited Company	
P.T. Tbk. / PT Tbk	Indonesia	Perseroan Terbatas, Terbuka	Stock corporation	

Limited Liability Companies and Partnerships

Name	Country	Type
Denmark	Anpartsselskab. Similar to Limited Liability Company. Taxwise, it is a separate entity. The company capital must be at least DKK 125.000	
BM or B.M.	Israel	Be'eravon Mugbal- The hebrew term for Ltd.. Not used much in English, usually translated as Ltd..
BV	Netherlands	Besloten Vennootschap"", a private limited liability company, liability limited by shares. The most common form of enterprise. Similar to GmbH, LLC, Ltd., BVBA, SPRL.
BVBA	Belgium	Besloten Vennootschap met Beperkte Aansprakelijkheid, a private limited liability company, liability limited by shares. The most common form of enterprise. Similar to GmbH, LLC, Ltd., BV, SPRL.
CC	South Africa	Closed corporation
C.V.	Netherlands	"commanditaire vennootschap"; a partnership with one or more silent partners.
d.o.o.	Slovenia	Družba z omejeno odgovornostjo, "company with limited liability"
d.o.o.	Croatia	ogranicenom odgovornošcu" Društvo s ogranicenom odgovornošcu, "company with limited liability"
d.o.o.	Serbia and Montenegro	Društvo s ogranicenom odgovornošcu , "company with limited liability"
E.P.E.	Greece	Etairia Periorismenis Euthinis (taa esµ)
G.D.K.		, a variant of the American LLC introduced in 2006
	Germany, Austria and Switzerland	limited liability". Similar to Limited Liability Company (LLC). In Germany, min. capital €25,000, in Austria €35,000, in Switzerland CHF 20,000
Inc.	Australia	An
Kft.	Hungary	Korlátolt felelosségu társaság (Limited liability company)
LLC LC Ltd. Co.	U.S.A.	Limited liability company, similar to a corporation and a limited liability partnership. May be legally abbreviated in multiple ways. The most common abbreviation is LLC. Allowable abbreviations may vary by USA State. Note: Ltd. by itself is not a valid abbreviation for an LLC, because in some states, like Texas Ltd. may mean a Corporation instead of an LLC.
LLP	U.S.A.	Limited liability partnership where each partner is fully liable for the debts of the partnership, not including acts of professional negligence or malpractice.
Ltd.	U.K. and others	Private company with liability limited by shares (not traded publicly) or by guarantee. Established under English law and used by countries with similar company laws. In Australia, a company with the suffix Ltd may be a company limited by guarantee (e.g. for charities, universities etc). Such companies may obtain dispensation from the Registrar of Companies to operate without the suffix to distinguish their activities from those of a commercial company.
NL	Australia	Mining company not entitled to call on the unpaid issue price of shares; no liability for shareholders as distinct from limited liability
PLC	U.K. and Ireland	A public limited company, liability limited by shares which are

		traded publicly.
OOD /	Bulgaria	Limited liability company (drujestvo s ogranichena otgovornost,).
OOO	Russia	Obshchestvo s ogranichennoy otvetstvennostyu - (Limited Liability Company)
Pty. / Pte.	Various	a prefix used to distinguish a Proprietary Limited company (Pty. Ltd.), essentially the same as a UK private limited company (Ltd.) Used in Australia, South Africa and others. A Proprietary company generally (depending on jurisdiction) is one with less then 50 members (shareholders), and not exceeding a certain annual revenue. In Australia, proprietary companies are classified as either small or large depending on the number of employees and the quantum of gross assets and operating capital.
Pvt. Ltd.	India	Private Limited Company, can have up to 50 shareholders and min 2 shareholders . Shares are not traded on a stock exchange.
Sàrl or SARL or SàRL	France Switzerland	Société à responsabilité limitée
SDN BHD	Malaysia	Sendirian Berhad (Private Limited)
S.L.	Spain	Sociedad Limitada. Minimum capital is 3.012€
S.L.N.E.		Sociedad Limitada Nueva Empresa Similar to SL, it was introduced in 2003 to speed up the registration of a new company (it takes one day to register). Minimum capital is 3.012€
SPRL	Belgium	Société privée à responsabilité limitée, a private limited liability company, liability limited by shares.
Sp.z o.o.	Poland	Spólka z ograniczona odpowiedzialnoscia, limited liability
S.R.L.	Romania	Societate cu Raspundere Limitata
Srl or S.r.l or S.R.L.	Italy Switzerland	Società a responsibilità limitata
S.R.L.	Spain	Sociedad de Responsabilidad Limitada (equivalent to S.L.)
s.r.o.	Czech Republic	Spolecnost s ruceni

EUROPEAN COMPANY LAW

THE EUROPEAN COMPANY – FREQUENTLY ASKED QUESTIONS

(see also IP/04/1195)

1. What is the European Company Statute?

It is a legal instrument based on European Community law that gives companies the **option** of forming a European Company – known formally by its Latin name of 'Societas Europeae' (SE). An SE can operate on a European-wide basis and be governed by Community law directly applicable in all Member States. The European Company Statute is established by two pieces of legislation, namely a Regulation (directly applicable in Member States) establishing the company law rules and a Directive (which will have to be implement in national law in all Member States) on worker involvement.

2. How can a European Company be set up?

In one of four ways:

By the merger of two or more existing public limited companies from at least two different EU Member States;
By the formation of a holding company promoted by public or private limited companies from at least two different Member States;
By the formation of a subsidiary of companies from at least two different Member States;
By the transformation of a public limited company which has, for at least two years, had a subsidiary in another Member State.

3. What are the advantages of setting up a European Company?

The creation of the European Company Statute will mean in practice, that companies established in more than one Member State will be able to merge and operate throughout the EU on the basis of a single set of rules and a unified management and reporting system. They will therefore avoid the need to set up a financially costly and administratively time-consuming complex network of subsidiaries governed by different national laws. In particular, there will be advantages in terms of significant reductions in administrative and legal costs, a single legal structure and unified management and reporting systems. The potential savings in terms of administrative costs were estimated to be up to €30 billion per year by the Competitiveness Advisory Group of industrialists convened in 1995 by the Heads of State and Government and chaired by Carlo Ciampi.

By setting up as a European Company a business can restructure fast and easily to take the best possible advantage of the trading opportunities offered by the Internal Market. European Companies with commercial interests in more than one Member State will be able to move across borders easily as the need arises in response to the changing needs of their business.

This is because the Statute will allow an SE registered in Member State A to move its registered office to Member State B without, as is the case now, having to wind up the company in Member State A and re-register it in Member State B. For pan-European projects, for example Trans-European Network projects in the transport or energy sectors (the upgrading of railway lines/road networks) a single European Company could attract private venture capital more easily than a series of national companies all operating under national rules.

4. Are companies obliged to become European Companies?

No. But if they wish to operate in a series of different Member States without establishing themselves as an SE they will have to respect a series of national laws governing company start-ups, often at considerable legal and administrative cost.

5. Will there be a central register of European Companies?

No. Each SE will be registered in a Member State on the same register as companies established under national law. However, the registration of each SE will be published in the EC's Official Journal

6. Can a European Company be registered in any Member State in which it operates (e.g. where it has a mailbox) or must it be registered where it has its operational headquarters?

The European Company must be registered in the Member State where it has its administrative head office. This is the only system that allows effective supervision of the whole SE, so as to avoid the SE being used for doubtful practices such as tax fraud or money laundering.

7. Where will a European Company be taxed?

Despite Commission proposals to this effect, the SE statute does not contain any tax arrangements. An SE will therefore, for tax purposes, be treated as any other multinational company according to the national fiscal legislation applicable at company level or branch level.

All EU Directives in the tax field either do or will, shortly, apply to the EU company. The Council has already adopted a Directive (for details of proposal see IP/03/1214) which extends to European Companies the benefit of the Parent-Subsidiary Company which eliminates tax obstacles for groups of companies in the EU by abolishing withholding taxes on payments of dividends between associated companies of different Member States and preventing double taxation of parent companies on the profits of their subsidiaries.

Once the Council has adopted the Commission's proposals for modifications of the Mergers Directive (see IP/03/1418) and the Interest and Royalties Directive (2003/49/EC), it will be the case that the creation and the running of an European Company will be subject to the same tax rules as that of any other Plc, SA, AG, SpA etc. under national law. The same principle applies with respect to VAT.

In one aspect the European Company will even be better off: Currently from a company law perspective only the European Company can transfer its seat from one Member State to another without winding up and re-creating itself. The proposal to amend the Mergers Directive to apply it to European Companies will ensure that this transaction will - subject to some conditions - not trigger any tax charges.

Finally, the Commission has launched the idea of testing the common consolidated EU company tax base with a European Company pilot scheme. There are pros and cons for this idea and we will need to deepen the discussion when we make progress with the work on the tax base. In any event, any possible discrimination would need to be avoided. Concluding, the Commission has done its utmost to see that the European Company at the very least has the same company tax treatment as any other company.

8. What are the provisions for worker involvement in European Companies?

Under the Directive on worker involvement, the creation of a European Company requires negotiations on the involvement of employees with a body representing all employees of the companies concerned. If it proved impossible to negotiate a mutually-satisfactory arrangement then a set of standard principles, laid down in an annexe to the Directive would apply. Essentially these principles oblige SE managers to provide regular reports on the basis of which there must be regular consultation of and information to a body representing the companies' employees. These reports must detail the companies' current and future business plans, production and sales levels, implications of these for the workforce, management changes, mergers, divestments, potential closures and layoffs.

In certain circumstances, where managers and employee representatives were unable to negotiate a mutually-satisfactory agreement and where the companies involved in the creation of an SE were previously covered by participation rules, a European Company would be obliged to apply standard principles on participation of its workers. This would be the case of a European Company created as a holding company or joint-venture when a majority of the employees had the right, prior to the creation of the SE, to participate in company decisions.

In the case of a European Company created by a merger, the standard principles on participation of its workers would have to be applied when at least 25 % of employees had the right to participate before the merger. It is on this element that agreement on the Directive had, until the Nice Summit in December 2000, not proved possible. The compromise struck by Heads of State and Government was to authorise a Member State not to implement the Directive on participation in the case of SEs created by merger, but in that case the SE could be registered in that Member State only if an agreement was concluded or when no employees were covered by participation rules before the SE was created.

In the case of a transformation of a national company into an SE, the arrangements for worker participation applied by this national company prior to its transformation as a European Company would have to continue to apply.

9. Must European Companies be publicly quoted?

No – private companies and medium sized companies may also opt to become European Companies. If an SE's shares are quoted, it must be treated in the same way as public companies established under national law.

The minimum capital requirement has been set at 120,000 euros so as to enable medium-sized companies from different Member States to create an SE.

10. Why has it taken more than 30 years to put in place this measure?

Partly because the European Company, in order to be based on Community law valid in each Member State, has to be established by a Regulation (directly applicable in all Member States) as opposed to a Directive (implemented through national law). Agreement therefore required consensus amongst all Member States on aspects of company law where there are still widely varying rules in national law. Moreover, it has required finding common ground between those Member States with a tradition of worker involvement (anxious that European Companies should not be used as a means to avoid national worker involvement requirements) and those Member States where worker involvement is not imposed (anxious that European Companies should not be used to introduce worker involvement obligations). In the end, it required a compromise at the EU's highest political level, the European Council (at Nice).

11. Does the European Company Statute include provisions on employment contracts and pensions?

No. Employment contracts and pensions are not covered by the Regulation. They would be subject to national law in the Member States where the headquarters and branches operated.

As regards company pension schemes, European Companies would stand to benefit from the provisions of the proposal for a Directive on occupational retirement provision presented by the Commission in October 2000 (see IP/00/1141), notably as regards the possibility for a company to set up a single pension fund for all employees throughout the EU.

STATUTE FOR A EUROPEAN COMPANY (SE)

Whereas:

(1) The completion of the internal market and the improvement it brings about in the economic and social situation throughout the Community mean not only that barriers to trade must be removed, but also that the structures of production must be adapted to the Community dimension. For that purpose it is essential that companies the business of which is not limited to satisfying purely local needs should be able to plan and carry out the reorganisation of their business on a Community scale.

(2) Such reorganisation presupposes that existing companies from different Member States are given the option of combining their potential by means of mergers. Such operations can be carried out only with due regard to the rules of competition laid down in the Treaty.

(3) Restructuring and cooperation operations involving companies from different Member States give rise to legal and psychological difficulties and tax problems. The approximation of Member States' company law by means of Directives based on Article 44 of the Treaty can overcome some of those difficulties. Such approximation does not, however, release companies governed by different legal systems from the obligation to choose a form of company governed by a particular national law.

(4) The legal framework within which business must be carried on in the Community is still based largely on national laws and therefore no longer corresponds to the economic framework within which it must develop if the objectives set out in Article 18 of the Treaty are to be achieved. That situation forms a considerable obstacle to the creation of groups of companies from different Member States.

(5) Member States are obliged to ensure that the provisions applicable to European companies under this Regulation do not result either in discrimination arising out of unjustified different treatment of European companies compared with public limited-liability companies or in disproportionate restrictions on the formation of a European company or on the transfer of its registered office.

(6) It is essential to ensure as far as possible that the economic unit and the legal unit of business in the Community coincide. For that purpose, provision should be made for the creation, side by side with companies governed by a particular national law, of companies formed and carrying on business under the law created by a Community Regulation directly applicable in all Member States.

(7) The provisions of such a Regulation will permit the creation and management of companies with a European dimension, free from the obstacles arising from the disparity and the limited territorial application of national company law.

(8) The Statute for a European public limited-liability company (hereafter referred to as "SE") is among the measures to be adopted by the Council before 1992 listed in the Commission's White Paper on completing the internal market, approved by the European Council that met in Milan in June 1985. The European Council that met in Brussels in 1987 expressed the wish to see such a Statute created swiftly.

(9) Since the Commission's submission in 1970 of a proposal for a Regulation on the Statute for a European public limited-liability company, amended in 1975, work on the approximation of national company law has made substantial progress, so that on those points where the functioning of an SE does not need uniform Community rules reference may be made to the law governing public limited-liability companies in the Member State where it has its registered office.

(10) Without prejudice to any economic needs that may arise in the future, if the essential objective of legal rules governing SEs is to be attained, it must be possible at least to create such a company as a means both of enabling companies from different Member States to merge or to create a holding company and of enabling companies and other legal persons carrying on economic activities and governed by the laws of different Member States to form joint subsidiaries.

(11) In the same context it should be possible for a public limited-liability company with a registered office and head office within the Community to transform itself into an SE without going into liquidation, provided it has a subsidiary in a Member State other than that of its registered office.

(12) National provisions applying to public limited-liability companies that offer their securities to the public and to securities transactions should also apply where an SE is formed by means of an offer of securities to the public and to SEs wishing to utilise such financial instruments.

(13) The SE itself must take the form of a company with share capital, that being the form most suited, in terms of both financing and management, to the needs of a company carrying on business on a European scale. In order to ensure that such companies are of reasonable size, a minimum amount of capital should be set so that they have sufficient assets without making it difficult for small and medium-sized undertakings to form SEs.

(14) An SE must be efficiently managed and properly supervised. It must be borne in mind that there are at present in the Community two different systems for the administration of public limited-liability companies. Although an SE should be allowed to choose between the two systems, the respective responsibilities of those responsible for management and those responsible for supervision should be clearly defined.

(15) Under the rules and general principles of private international law, where one undertaking controls another governed by a different legal system, its ensuing rights and obligations as regards the protection of minority shareholders and third parties are governed by the law governing the controlled undertaking, without prejudice to the obligations imposed on the controlling undertaking by its own law, for example the requirement to prepare consolidated accounts.

(16) Without prejudice to the consequences of any subsequent coordination of the laws of the Member States, specific rules for SEs are not at present required in this field. The rules and general principles of private international law should therefore be applied both where an SE exercises control and where it is the controlled company.

(17) The rule thus applicable where an SE is controlled by another undertaking should be specified, and for this purpose reference should be made to the law governing public limited-liability companies in the Member State in which the SE has its registered office.

(18) Each Member State must be required to apply the sanctions applicable to public limited-liability companies governed by its law in respect of infringements of this Regulation.

(19) The rules on the involvement of employees in the European company are laid down in Directive 2001/86/EC(4), and those provisions thus form an indissociable complement to this Regulation and must be applied concomitantly.

(20) This Regulation does not cover other areas of law such as taxation, competition, intellectual property or insolvency. The provisions of the Member States' law and of Community law are therefore applicable in the above areas and in other areas not covered by this Regulation.

(21) Directive 2001/86/EC is designed to ensure that employees have a right of involvement in issues and decisions affecting the life of their SE. Other social and labour legislation questions, in particular the right of employees to information and consultation as regulated in the Member States, are governed by the national provisions applicable, under the same conditions, to public limited-liability companies.

(22) The entry into force of this Regulation must be deferred so that each Member State may incorporate into its national law the provisions of Directive 2001/86/EC and set up in advance the necessary machinery for the formation and operation of SEs with registered offices within its territory, so that the Regulation and the Directive may be applied concomitantly.

(23) A company the head office of which is not in the Community should be allowed to participate in the formation of an SE provided that company is formed under the law of a Member State, has its registered office in that Member State and has a real and continuous link with a Member State's economy according to the principles established in the 1962 General Programme for the abolition of restrictions on freedom of establishment. Such a link exists in particular if a company has an establishment in that Member State and conducts operations therefrom.

(24) The SE should be enabled to transfer its registered office to another Member State. Adequate protection of the interests of minority shareholders who oppose the transfer, of creditors and of holders of other rights should be proportionate. Such transfer should not affect the rights originating before the transfer.

(25) This Regulation is without prejudice to any provision which may be inserted in the 1968 Brussels Convention or in any text adopted by Member States or by the Council to replace such Convention, relating to the rules of jurisdiction applicable in the case of transfer of the registered offices of a public limited-liability company from one Member State to another.

(26) Activities by financial institutions are regulated by specific directives and the national law implementing those directives and additional national rules regulating those activities apply in full to an SE.

(27) In view of the specific Community character of an SE, the "real seat" arrangement adopted by this Regulation in respect of SEs is without prejudice to Member States' laws and does not pre-empt any choices to be made for other Community texts on company law.

(28) The Treaty does not provide, for the adoption of this Regulation, powers of action other than those of Article 308 thereof.

(29) Since the objectives of the intended action, as outlined above, cannot be adequately attained by the Member States in as much as a European public limited-liability company is being established at European level and can therefore, because of the scale and impact of such company, be better attained at Community level, the Community may take measures in accordance with the principle of subsidiarity enshrined in Article 5 of the Treaty. In accordance with the principle of proportionality as set out in the said Article, this Regulation does not go beyond what is necessary to attain these objectives,

HAS ADOPTED THIS REGULATION:

TITLE I GENERAL PROVISIONS

Article 1

1. A company may be set up within the territory of the Community in the form of a European public limited-liability company (Societas Europaea or SE) on the conditions and in the manner laid down in this Regulation.

2. The capital of an SE shall be divided into shares. No shareholder shall be liable for more than the amount he has subscribed.

3. An SE shall have legal personality.

4. Employee involvement in an SE shall be governed by the provisions of Directive 2001/86/EC.

Article 2

1. Public limited-liability companies such as referred to in Annex I, formed under the law of a Member State, with registered offices and head offices within the Community may form an SE by means of a merger provided that at least two of them are governed by the law of different Member States.

2. Public and private limited-liability companies such as referred to in Annex II, formed under the law of a Member State, with registered offices and head offices within the Community may promote the formation of a holding SE provided that each of at least two of them:

(a) is governed by the law of a different Member State, or

(b) has for at least two years had a subsidiary company governed by the law of another Member State or a branch situated in another Member State.

3. Companies and firms within the meaning of the second paragraph of Article 48 of the Treaty and other legal bodies governed by public or private law, formed under the law of a Member State, with registered offices and head offices within the Community may form a subsidiary SE by subscribing for its shares, provided that each of at least two of them:

(a) is governed by the law of a different Member State, or

(b) has for at least two years had a subsidiary company governed by the law of another Member State or a branch situated in another Member State.

4. A public limited-liability company, formed under the law of a Member State, which has its registered office and head office within the Community may be transformed into an SE if for at least two years it has had a subsidiary company governed by the law of another Member State.

5. A Member State may provide that a company the head office of which is not in the Community may participate in the formation of an SE provided that company is formed under the law of a Member State, has its registered office in that Member State and has a real and continuous link with a Member State's economy.

Article 3

1. For the purposes of Article 2(1), (2) and (3), an SE shall be regarded as a public limited-liability company governed by the law of the Member State in which it has its registered office.

2. An SE may itself set up one or more subsidiaries in the form of SEs. The provisions of the law of the Member State in which a subsidiary SE has its registered office that require a public limited-liability company to have more than one shareholder shall not apply in the case of the subsidiary SE. The provisions of national law implementing the twelfth Council Company Law Directive (89/667/EEC) of 21 December 1989 on single-member private limited-liability companies(5) shall apply to SEs mutatis mutandis.

Article 4

1. The capital of an SE shall be expressed in euro.

2. The subscribed capital shall not be less than EUR 120000.

3. The laws of a Member State requiring a greater subscribed capital for companies carrying on certain types of activity shall apply to SEs with registered offices in that Member State.

Article 5

Subject to Article 4(1) and (2), the capital of an SE, its maintenance and changes thereto, together with its shares, bonds and other similar securities shall be governed by the provisions which would apply to a public limited-liability company with a registered office in the Member State in which the SE is registered.

Article 6

For the purposes of this Regulation, "the statutes of the SE" shall mean both the instrument of incorporation and, where they are the subject of a separate document, the statutes of the SE.

Article 7

The registered office of an SE shall be located within the Community, in the same Member State as its head office. A Member State may in addition impose on SEs registered in its territory the obligation of locating their head office and their registered office in the same place.

Article 8

1. The registered office of an SE may be transferred to another Member State in accordance with paragraphs 2 to 13. Such a transfer shall not result in the winding up of the SE or in the creation of a new legal person.

2. The management or administrative organ shall draw up a transfer proposal and publicise it in accordance with Article 13, without prejudice to any additional forms of publication provided for by the Member State of the registered office. That proposal shall state the current name, registered office and number of the SE and shall cover:

(a) the proposed registered office of the SE;

(b) the proposed statutes of the SE including, where appropriate, its new name;

(c) any implication the transfer may have on employees' involvement;

(d) the proposed transfer timetable;

(e) any rights provided for the protection of shareholders and/or creditors.

3. The management or administrative organ shall draw up a report explaining and justifying the legal and economic aspects of the transfer and explaining the implications of the transfer for shareholders, creditors and employees.

4. An SE's shareholders and creditors shall be entitled, at least one month before the general meeting called upon to decide on the transfer, to examine at the SE's registered office the transfer proposal and the report drawn up pursuant to paragraph 3 and, on request, to obtain copies of those documents free of charge.

5. A Member State may, in the case of SEs registered within its territory, adopt provisions designed to ensure appropriate protection for minority shareholders who oppose a transfer.

6. No decision to transfer may be taken for two months after publication of the proposal. Such a decision shall be taken as laid down in Article 59.

7. Before the competent authority issues the certificate mentioned in paragraph 8, the SE shall satisfy it that, in respect of any liabilities arising prior to the publication of the transfer proposal, the interests of creditors and holders of other rights in respect of the SE (including those of public bodies) have been adequately protected in accordance with requirements laid down by the Member State where the SE has its registered office prior to the transfer.

A Member State may extend the application of the first subparagraph to liabilities that arise (or may arise) prior to the transfer.

The first and second subparagraphs shall be without prejudice to the application to SEs of the national legislation of Member States concerning the satisfaction or securing of payments to public bodies.

8. In the Member State in which an SE has its registered office the court, notary or other competent authority shall issue a certificate attesting to the completion of the acts and formalities to be accomplished before the transfer.

9. The new registration may not be effected until the certificate referred to in paragraph 8 has been submitted, and evidence produced that the formalities required for registration in the country of the new registered office have been completed.

10. The transfer of an SE's registered office and the consequent amendment of its statutes shall take effect on the date on which the SE is registered, in accordance with Article 12, in the register for its new registered office.

11. When the SE's new registration has been effected, the registry for its new registration shall notify the registry for its old registration. Deletion of the old registration shall be effected on receipt of that notification, but not before.

12. The new registration and the deletion of the old registration shall be publicised in the Member States concerned in accordance with Article 13.

13. On publication of an SE's new registration, the new registered office may be relied on as against third parties. However, as long as the deletion of the SE's registration from the register for its previous registered office has not been publicised, third parties may continue to rely on the previous registered office unless the SE proves that such third parties were aware of the new registered office.

14. The laws of a Member State may provide that, as regards SEs registered in that Member State, the transfer of a registered office which would result in a change of the law applicable shall not take effect if any of that Member State's competent authorities opposes it within the two-month period referred to in paragraph 6. Such opposition may be based only on grounds of public interest.

Where an SE is supervised by a national financial supervisory authority according to Community directives the right to oppose the change of registered office applies to this authority as well.

Review by a judicial authority shall be possible.

15. An SE may not transfer its registered office if proceedings for winding up, liquidation, insolvency or suspension of payments or other similar proceedings have been brought against it.

16. An SE which has transferred its registered office to another Member State shall be considered, in respect of any cause of action arising prior to the transfer as determined in paragraph 10, as having its registered office in the Member States where the SE was registered prior to the transfer, even if the SE is sued after the transfer.

Article 9

1. An SE shall be governed:

(a) by this Regulation,

(b) where expressly authorised by this Regulation, by the provisions of its statutes

or

(c) in the case of matters not regulated by this Regulation or, where matters are partly regulated by it, of those aspects not covered by it, by:

(i) the provisions of laws adopted by Member States in implementation of Community measures relating specifically to SEs;

(ii) the provisions of Member States' laws which would apply to a public limited-liability company formed in accordance with the law of the Member State in which the SE has its registered office;

(iii) the provisions of its statutes, in the same way as for a public limited-liability company formed in accordance with the law of the Member State in which the SE has its registered office.

2. The provisions of laws adopted by Member States specifically for the SE must be in accordance with Directives applicable to public limited-liability companies referred to in Annex I.

3. If the nature of the business carried out by an SE is regulated by specific provisions of national laws, those laws shall apply in full to the SE.

Article 10

Subject to this Regulation, an SE shall be treated in every Member State as if it were a public limited-liability company formed in accordance with the law of the Member State in which it has its registered office.

Article 11

1. The name of an SE shall be preceded or followed by the abbreviation SE.

2. Only SEs may include the abbreviation SE in their name.

3. Nevertheless, companies, firms and other legal entities registered in a Member State before the date of entry into force of this Regulation in the names of which the abbreviation SE appears shall not be required to alter their names.

Article 12

1. Every SE shall be registered in the Member State in which it has its registered office in a register designated by the law of that Member State in accordance with Article 3 of the first Council Directive (68/151/EEC) of 9 March 1968 on coordination of safeguards which, for the protection of the interests of members and others, are required by Member States of companies within the meaning of the second paragraph of Article 58 of the Treaty, with a view to making such safeguards equivalent throughout the Community(6).

2. An SE may not be registered unless an agreement on arrangements for employee involvement pursuant to Article 4 of Directive 2001/86/EC has been concluded, or a decision pursuant to Article 3(6) of the Directive has been taken, or the period for negotiations pursuant to Article 5 of the Directive has expired without an agreement having been concluded.

3. In order for an SE to be registered in a Member State which has made use of the option referred to in Article 7(3) of Directive 2001/86/EC, either an agreement pursuant to Article 4 of the Directive must have been concluded on the arrangements for employee involvement, including participation, or none of the participating companies must have been governed by participation rules prior to the registration of the SE.

4. The statutes of the SE must not conflict at any time with the arrangements for employee involvement which have been so determined. Where new such arrangements determined pursuant to the Directive conflict with the existing statutes, the statutes shall to the extent necessary be amended.

In this case, a Member State may provide that the management organ or the administrative organ of the SE shall be entitled to proceed to amend the statutes without any further decision from the general shareholders meeting.

Article 13

Publication of the documents and particulars concerning an SE which must be publicised under this Regulation shall be effected in the manner laid down in the laws of the Member State in which the SE has its registered office in accordance with Directive 68/151/EEC.

Article 14

1. Notice of an SE's registration and of the deletion of such a registration shall be published for information purposes in the Official Journal of the European Communities after publication in accordance with Article 13. That notice shall state the name, number, date and place of registration of the SE, the date and place of publication and the title of publication, the registered office of the SE and its sector of activity.

2. Where the registered office of an SE is transferred in accordance with Article 8, notice shall be published giving the information provided for in paragraph 1, together with that relating to the new registration.

3. The particulars referred to in paragraph 1 shall be forwarded to the Office for Official Publications of the European Communities within one month of the publication referred to in Article 13.

TITLE II FORMATION

Section 1

General

Article 15

1. Subject to this Regulation, the formation of an SE shall be governed by the law applicable to public limited-liability companies in the Member State in which the SE establishes its registered office.

2. The registration of an SE shall be publicised in accordance with Article 13.

Article 16

1. An SE shall acquire legal personality on the date on which it is registered in the register referred to in Article 12.

2. If acts have been performed in an SE's name before its registration in accordance with Article 12 and the SE does not assume the obligations arising out of such acts after its registration, the natural persons, companies, firms or other legal entities which performed those acts shall be jointly and severally liable therefor, without limit, in the absence of agreement to the contrary.

Section 2

Formation by merger

Article 17

1. An SE may be formed by means of a merger in accordance with Article 2(1).

2. Such a merger may be carried out in accordance with:

(a) the procedure for merger by acquisition laid down in Article 3(1) of the third Council Directive (78/855/EEC) of 9 October 1978 based on Article 54(3)(g) of the Treaty concerning mergers of public limited-liability companies(7) or

(b) the procedure for merger by the formation of a new company laid down in Article 4(1) of the said Directive.

In the case of a merger by acquisition, the acquiring company shall take the form of an SE when the merger takes place. In the case of a merger by the formation of a new company, the SE shall be the newly formed company.

Article 18

For matters not covered by this section or, where a matter is partly covered by it, for aspects not covered by it, each company involved in the formation of an SE by merger shall be governed by the provisions of the law of the Member State to which it is subject that apply to mergers of public limited-liability companies in accordance with Directive 78/855/EEC.

Article 19

The laws of a Member State may provide that a company governed by the law of that Member State may not take part in the formation of an SE by merger if any of that Member State's competent authorities opposes it before the issue of the certificate referred to in Article 25(2).

Such opposition may be based only on grounds of public interest. Review by a judicial authority shall be possible.

Article 20

1. The management or administrative organs of merging companies shall draw up draft terms of merger. The draft terms of merger shall include the following particulars:

(a) the name and registered office of each of the merging companies together with those proposed for the SE;

(b) the share-exchange ratio and the amount of any compensation;

(c) the terms for the allotment of shares in the SE;

(d) the date from which the holding of shares in the SE will entitle the holders to share in profits and any special conditions affecting that entitlement;

(e) the date from which the transactions of the merging companies will be treated for accounting purposes as being those of the SE;

(f) the rights conferred by the SE on the holders of shares to which special rights are attached and on the holders of securities other than shares, or the measures proposed concerning them;

(g) any special advantage granted to the experts who examine the draft terms of merger or to members of the administrative, management, supervisory or controlling organs of the merging companies;

(h) the statutes of the SE;

(i) information on the procedures by which arrangements for employee involvement are determined pursuant to Directive 2001/86/EC.

2. The merging companies may include further items in the draft terms of merger.

Article 21

For each of the merging companies and subject to the additional requirements imposed by the Member State to which the company concerned is subject, the following particulars shall be published in the national gazette of that Member State:

(a) the type, name and registered office of every merging company;

(b) the register in which the documents referred to in Article 3(2) of Directive 68/151/EEC are filed in respect of each merging company, and the number of the entry in that register;

(c) an indication of the arrangements made in accordance with Article 24 for the exercise of the rights of the creditors of the company in question and the address at which complete information on those arrangements may be obtained free of charge;

(d) an indication of the arrangements made in accordance with Article 24 for the exercise of the rights of minority shareholders of the company in question and the address at which complete information on those arrangements may be obtained free of charge;

(e) the name and registered office proposed for the SE.

Article 22

As an alternative to experts operating on behalf of each of the merging companies one or more independent experts as defined in Article 10 of Directive 78/855/EEC, appointed for those purposes at the joint request of the companies by a judicial or administrative authority in the Member State of one of the merging companies or of the proposed SE, may examine the draft terms of merger and draw up a single report to all the shareholders.

The experts shall have the right to request from each of the merging companies any information they consider necessary to enable them to complete their function.

Article 23

1. The general meeting of each of the merging companies shall approve the draft terms of merger.

2. Employee involvement in the SE shall be decided pursuant to Directive 2001/86/EC. The general meetings of each of the merging companies may reserve the right to make registration of the SE conditional upon its express ratification of the arrangements so decided.

Article 24

1. The law of the Member State governing each merging company shall apply as in the case of a merger of public limited-liability companies, taking into account the cross-border nature of the merger, with regard to the protection of the interests of:

(a) creditors of the merging companies;

(b) holders of bonds of the merging companies;

(c) holders of securities, other than shares, which carry special rights in the merging companies.

2. A Member State may, in the case of the merging companies governed by its law, adopt provisions designed to ensure appropriate protection for minority shareholders who have opposed the merger.

Article 25

1. The legality of a merger shall be scrutinised, as regards the part of the procedure concerning each merging company, in accordance with the law on mergers of public limited-liability companies of the Member State to which the merging company is subject.

2. In each Member State concerned the court, notary or other competent authority shall issue a certificate conclusively attesting to the completion of the pre-merger acts and formalities.

3. If the law of a Member State to which a merging company is subject provides for a procedure to scrutinise and amend the share-exchange ratio, or a procedure to compensate minority shareholders, without preventing the registration of the merger, such procedures shall only apply if the other merging companies situated in Member States which do not provide for such procedure explicitly accept, when approving the draft terms of the merger in accordance with Article 23(1), the possibility for the shareholders of that merging company to have recourse to such procedure. In such cases, the court, notary or other competent authorities may issue the certificate referred to in paragraph 2 even if such a procedure has been commenced. The certificate must, however, indicate that the procedure is pending. The decision in the procedure shall be binding on the acquiring company and all its shareholders.

Article 26

1. The legality of a merger shall be scrutinised, as regards the part of the procedure concerning the completion of the merger and the formation of the SE, by the court, notary or other authority competent in the Member State of the proposed registered office of the SE to scrutinise that aspect of the legality of mergers of public limited-liability companies.

2. To that end each merging company shall submit to the competent authority the certificate referred to in Article 25(2) within six months of its issue together with a copy of the draft terms of merger approved by that company.

3. The authority referred to in paragraph 1 shall in particular ensure that the merging companies have approved draft terms of merger in the same terms and that arrangements for employee involvement have been determined pursuant to Directive 2001/86/EC.

4. That authority shall also satisfy itself that the SE has been formed in accordance with the requirements of the law of the Member State in which it has its registered office in accordance with Article 15.

Article 27

1. A merger and the simultaneous formation of an SE shall take effect on the date on which the SE is registered in accordance with Article 12.

2. The SE may not be registered until the formalities provided for in Articles 25 and 26 have been completed.

Article 28

For each of the merging companies the completion of the merger shall be publicised as laid down by the law of each Member State in accordance with Article 3 of Directive 68/151/EEC.

Article 29

1. A merger carried out as laid down in Article 17(2)(a) shall have the following consequences ipso jure and simultaneously:

(a) all the assets and liabilities of each company being acquired are transferred to the acquiring company;

(b) the shareholders of the company being acquired become shareholders of the acquiring company;

(c) the company being acquired ceases to exist;

(d) the acquiring company adopts the form of an SE.

2. A merger carried out as laid down in Article 17(2)(b) shall have the following consequences ipso jure and simultaneously:

(a) all the assets and liabilities of the merging companies are transferred to the SE

(b) the shareholders of the merging companies become shareholders of the SE;

(c) the merging companies cease to exist.

3. Where, in the case of a merger of public limited-liability companies, the law of a Member State requires the completion of any special formalities before the transfer of certain assets, rights and obligations by the merging companies becomes effective against third parties, those formalities shall apply and shall be carried out either by the merging companies or by the SE following its registration.

4. The rights and obligations of the participating companies on terms and conditions of employment arising from national law, practice and individual employment contracts or employment relationships and existing at the date of the registration shall, by reason of such registration be transferred to the SE upon its registration.

Article 30

A merger as provided for in Article 2(1) may not be declared null and void once the SE has been registered.

The absence of scrutiny of the legality of the merger pursuant to Articles 25 and 26 may be included among the grounds for the winding-up of the SE.

Article 31

1. Where a merger within the meaning of Article 17(2)(a) is carried out by a company which holds all the shares and other securities conferring the right to vote at general meetings of another company, neither Article 20(1)(b), (c) and (d), Article 29(1)(b) nor Article 22 shall apply. National law governing each merging company and mergers of public limited-liability companies in accordance with Article 24 of Directive 78/855/EEC shall nevertheless apply.

2. Where a merger by acquisition is carried out by a company which holds 90 % or more but not all of the shares and other securities conferring the right to vote at general meetings of another company, reports by the management or administrative body, reports by an independent expert or experts and the documents necessary for scrutiny shall be required only to the extent that the national law governing either the acquiring company or the company being acquired so requires.

Member States may, however, provide that this paragraph may apply where a company holds shares conferring 90 % or more but not all of the voting rights.

Section 3

Formation of a holding SE

Article 32

1. A holding SE may be formed in accordance with Article 2(2).

A company promoting the formation of a holding SE in accordance with Article 2(2) shall continue to exist.

2. The management or administrative organs of the companies which promote such an operation shall draw up, in the same terms, draft terms for the formation of the holding SE. The draft terms shall include a report explaining and justifying the legal and economic aspects of the formation and indicating the implications for the shareholders and for the employees of the adoption of the form of a holding SE. The draft terms shall also set out the particulars provided for in Article 20(1)(a), (b), (c), (f), (g), (h) and (i) and shall fix the minimum proportion of the shares in each of the companies promoting the operation which the shareholders must contribute to the formation of the holding SE. That proportion shall be shares conferring more than 50 % of the permanent voting rights.

3. For each of the companies promoting the operation, the draft terms for the formation of the holding SE shall be publicised in the manner laid down in each Member State's national law in accordance with Article 3 of Directive 68/151/EEC at least one month before the date of the general meeting called to decide thereon.

4. One or more experts independent of the companies promoting the operation, appointed or approved by a judicial or administrative authority in the Member State to which each company is subject in accordance with national provisions adopted in implementation of Directive 78/855/EEC, shall examine the draft terms of formation drawn up in accordance with paragraph 2 and draw up a written report for the shareholders of each company. By agreement between the companies promoting the operation, a single written report may be drawn up for the shareholders of all the companies by one or more independent experts, appointed or approved by a judicial or administrative authority in the Member State to which one of the companies promoting the operation or the proposed SE is subject in accordance with national provisions adopted in implementation of Directive 78/855/EEC.

5. The report shall indicate any particular difficulties of valuation and state whether the proposed share-exchange ratio is fair and reasonable, indicating the methods used to arrive at it and whether such methods are adequate in the case in question.

6. The general meeting of each company promoting the operation shall approve the draft terms of formation of the holding SE.

Employee involvement in the holding SE shall be decided pursuant to Directive 2001/86/EC. The general meetings of each company promoting the operation may reserve the right to make registration of the holding SE conditional upon its express ratification of the arrangements so decided.

7. These provisions shall apply mutatis mutandis to private limited-liability companies.

Article 33

1. The shareholders of the companies promoting such an operation shall have a period of three months in which to inform the promoting companies whether they intend to contribute their shares to the formation of the holding SE. That period shall begin on the date upon which the terms for the formation of the holding SE have been finally determined in accordance with Article 32.

2. The holding SE shall be formed only if, within the period referred to in paragraph 1, the shareholders of the companies promoting the operation have assigned the minimum proportion of shares in each company in accordance with the draft terms of formation and if all the other conditions are fulfilled.

3. If the conditions for the formation of the holding SE are all fulfilled in accordance with paragraph 2, that fact shall, in respect of each of the promoting companies, be publicised in the manner laid down in the national law governing each of those companies adopted in implementation of Article 3 of Directive 68/151/EEC.

Shareholders of the companies promoting the operation who have not indicated whether they intend to make their shares available to the promoting companies for the purpose of forming the holding SE within the period referred to in paragraph 1 shall have a further month in which to do so.

4. Shareholders who have contributed their securities to the formation of the SE shall receive shares in the holding SE.

5. The holding SE may not be registered until it is shown that the formalities referred to in Article 32 have been completed and that the conditions referred to in paragraph 2 have been fulfilled.

Article 34

A Member State may, in the case of companies promoting such an operation, adopt provisions designed to ensure protection for minority shareholders who oppose the operation, creditors and employees.

Section 4

Formation of a subsidiary SE

Article 35

An SE may be formed in accordance with Article 2(3).

Article 36

Companies, firms and other legal entities participating in such an operation shall be subject to the provisions governing their participation in the formation of a subsidiary in the form of a public limited-liability company under national law.

Section 5

Conversion of an existing public limited-liability company into an SE

Article 37

1. An SE may be formed in accordance with Article 2(4).

2. Without prejudice to Article 12 the conversion of a public limited-liability company into an SE shall not result in the winding up of the company or in the creation of a new legal person.

3. The registered office may not be transferred from one Member State to another pursuant to Article 8 at the same time as the conversion is effected.

4. The management or administrative organ of the company in question shall draw up draft terms of conversion and a report explaining and justifying the legal and economic aspects of the conversion and indicating the implications for the shareholders and for the employees of the adoption of the form of an SE.

5. The draft terms of conversion shall be publicised in the manner laid down in each Member State's law in accordance with Article 3 of Directive 68/151/EEC at least one month before the general meeting called upon to decide thereon.

6. Before the general meeting referred to in paragraph 7 one or more independent experts appointed or approved, in accordance with the national provisions adopted in implementation of Article 10 of Directive 78/855/EEC, by a judicial or administrative authority in the Member State to which the company being converted into an SE is subject shall certify in compliance with Directive 77/91/EEC(8) mutatis mutandis that the company has net assets at least equivalent to its capital plus those reserves which must not be distributed under the law or the Statutes.

7. The general meeting of the company in question shall approve the draft terms of conversion together with the statutes of the SE. The decision of the general meeting shall be passed as laid down in the provisions of national law adopted in implementation of Article 7 of Directive 78/855/EEC.

8. Member States may condition a conversion to a favourable vote of a qualified majority or unanimity in the organ of the company to be converted within which employee participation is organised.

9. The rights and obligations of the company to be converted on terms and conditions of employment arising from national law, practice and individual employment contracts or employment relationships and existing at the date of the registration shall, by reason of such registration be transferred to the SE.

TITLE III STRUCTURE OF THE SE

Article 38

Under the conditions laid down by this Regulation an SE shall comprise:

(a) a general meeting of shareholders and

(b) either a supervisory organ and a management organ (two-tier system) or an administrative organ (one-tier system) depending on the form adopted in the statutes.

Section 1

Two-tier system

Article 39

1. The management organ shall be responsible for managing the SE. A Member State may provide that a managing director or managing directors shall be responsible for the current management under the same conditions as for public limited-liability companies that have registered offices within that Member State's territory.

2. The member or members of the management organ shall be appointed and removed by the supervisory organ.

A Member State may, however, require or permit the statutes to provide that the member or members of the management organ shall be appointed and removed by the general meeting under the same conditions as for public limited-liability companies that have registered offices within its territory.

3. No person may at the same time be a member of both the management organ and the supervisory organ of the same SE. The supervisory organ may, however, nominate one of its members to act as a member of the management organ in the event of a vacancy. During such a period the functions of the person concerned as a member of the supervisory organ shall be suspended. A Member State may impose a time limit on such a period.

4. The number of members of the management organ or the rules for determining it shall be laid down in the SE's statutes. A Member State may, however, fix a minimum and/or a maximum number.

5. Where no provision is made for a two-tier system in relation to public limited-liability companies with registered offices within its territory, a Member State may adopt the appropriate measures in relation to SEs.

Article 40

1. The supervisory organ shall supervise the work of the management organ. It may not itself exercise the power to manage the SE.

2. The members of the supervisory organ shall be appointed by the general meeting. The members of the first supervisory organ may, however, be appointed by the statutes. This shall apply without prejudice to Article 47(4) or to any employee participation arrangements determined pursuant to Directive 2001/86/EC.

3. The number of members of the supervisory organ or the rules for determining it shall be laid down in the statutes. A Member State may, however, stipulate the number of members of the supervisory organ for SEs registered within its territory or a minimum and/or a maximum number.

Article 41

1. The management organ shall report to the supervisory organ at least once every three months on the progress and foreseeable development of the SE's business.

2. In addition to the regular information referred to in paragraph 1, the management organ shall promptly pass the supervisory organ any information on events likely to have an appreciable effect on the SE.

3. The supervisory organ may require the management organ to provide information of any kind which it needs to exercise supervision in accordance with Article 40(1). A Member State may provide that each member of the supervisory organ also be entitled to this facility.

4. The supervisory organ may undertake or arrange for any investigations necessary for the performance of its duties.

5. Each member of the supervisory organ shall be entitled to examine all information submitted to it.

Article 42

The supervisory organ shall elect a chairman from among its members. If half of the members are appointed by employees, only a member appointed by the general meeting of shareholders may be elected chairman.

Section 2

The one-tier system

Article 43

1. The administrative organ shall manage the SE. A Member State may provide that a managing director or managing directors shall be responsible for the day-to-day management under the same conditions as for public limited-liability companies that have registered offices within that Member State's territory.

2. The number of members of the administrative organ or the rules for determining it shall be laid down in the SE's statutes. A Member State may, however, set a minimum and, where necessary, a maximum number of members.

The administrative organ shall, however, consist of at least three members where employee participation is regulated in accordance with Directive 2001/86/EC.

3. The member or members of the administrative organ shall be appointed by the general meeting. The members of the first administrative organ may, however, be appointed by the statutes. This shall apply without prejudice to Article 47(4) or to any employee participation arrangements determined pursuant to Directive 2001/86/EC.

4. Where no provision is made for a one-tier system in relation to public limited-liability companies with registered offices within its territory, a Member State may adopt the appropriate measures in relation to SEs.

Article 44

1. The administrative organ shall meet at least once every three months at intervals laid down by the statutes to discuss the progress and foreseeable development of the SE's business.

2. Each member of the administrative organ shall be entitled to examine all information submitted to it.

Article 45

The administrative organ shall elect a chairman from among its members. If half of the members are appointed by employees, only a member appointed by the general meeting of shareholders may be elected chairman.

Section 3

Rules common to the one-tier and two-tier systems

Article 46

1. Members of company organs shall be appointed for a period laid down in the statutes not exceeding six years.

2. Subject to any restrictions laid down in the statutes, members may be reappointed once or more than once for the period determined in accordance with paragraph 1.

Article 47

1. An SE's statutes may permit a company or other legal entity to be a member of one of its organs, provided that the law applicable to public limited-liability companies in the Member State in which the SE's registered office is situated does not provide otherwise.

That company or other legal entity shall designate a natural person to exercise its functions on the organ in question.

2. No person may be a member of any SE organ or a representative of a member within the meaning of paragraph 1 who:

(a) is disqualified, under the law of the Member State in which the SE's registered office is situated, from serving on the corresponding organ of a public limited-liability company governed by the law of that Member State, or

(b) is disqualified from serving on the corresponding organ of a public limited-liability company governed by the law of a Member State owing to a judicial or administrative decision delivered in a Member State.

3. An SE's statutes may, in accordance with the law applicable to public limited-liability companies in the Member State in which the SE's registered office is situated, lay down special conditions of eligibility for members representing the shareholders.

4. This Regulation shall not affect national law permitting a minority of shareholders or other persons or authorities to appoint some of the members of a company organ.

Article 48

1. An SE's statutes shall list the categories of transactions which require authorisation of the management organ by the supervisory organ in the two-tier system or an express decision by the administrative organ in the one-tier system.

A Member State may, however, provide that in the two-tier system the supervisory organ may itself make certain categories of transactions subject to authorisation.

2. A Member State may determine the categories of transactions which must at least be indicated in the statutes of SEs registered within its territory.

Article 49

The members of an SE's organs shall be under a duty, even after they have ceased to hold office, not to divulge any information which they have concerning the SE the disclosure of which might be prejudicial to the company's interests, except where such disclosure is required or permitted under national law provisions applicable to public limited-liability companies or is in the public interest.

Article 50

1. Unless otherwise provided by this Regulation or the statutes, the internal rules relating to quorums and decision-taking in SE organs shall be as follows:

(a) quorum: at least half of the members must be present or represented;

(b) decision-taking: a majority of the members present or represented.

2. Where there is no relevant provision in the statutes, the chairman of each organ shall have a casting vote in the event of a tie. There shall be no provision to the contrary in the statutes, however, where half of the supervisory organ consists of employees' representatives.

3. Where employee participation is provided for in accordance with Directive 2001/86/EC, a Member State may provide that the supervisory organ's quorum and decision-making shall, by way of derogation from the provisions referred to in paragraphs 1 and 2, be subject to the rules applicable, under the same conditions, to public limited-liability companies governed by the law of the Member State concerned.

Article 51

Members of an SE's management, supervisory and administrative organs shall be liable, in accordance with the provisions applicable to public limited-liability companies in the Member State in which the SE's registered office is situated, for loss or damage sustained by the SE following any breach on their part of the legal, statutory or other obligations inherent in their duties.

Section 4

General meeting

Article 52

The general meeting shall decide on matters for which it is given sole responsibility by:

(a) this Regulation or

(b) the legislation of the Member State in which the SE's registered office is situated adopted in implementation of Directive 2001/86/EC.

Furthermore, the general meeting shall decide on matters for which responsibility is given to the general meeting of a public limited-liability company governed by the law of the Member State in which the SE's registered office is situated, either by the law of that Member State or by the SE's statutes in accordance with that law.

Article 53

Without prejudice to the rules laid down in this section, the organisation and conduct of general meetings together with voting procedures shall be governed by the law applicable to public limited-liability companies in the Member State in which the SE's registered office is situated.

Article 54

1. An SE shall hold a general meeting at least once each calendar year, within six months of the end of its financial year, unless the law of the Member State in which the SE's registered office is situated applicable to public limited-liability companies carrying on the same type of activity as the SE provides for more frequent meetings. A Member State may, however, provide that the first general meeting may be held at any time in the 18 months following an SE's incorporation.

2. General meetings may be convened at any time by the management organ, the administrative organ, the supervisory organ or any other organ or competent authority in accordance with the national law applicable to public limited-liability companies in the Member State in which the SE's registered office is situated.

Article 55

1. One or more shareholders who together hold at least 10 % of an SE's subscribed capital may request the SE to convene a general meeting and draw up the agenda therefor; the SE's statutes or national legislation may provide for a smaller proportion under the same conditions as those applicable to public limited-liability companies.

2. The request that a general meeting be convened shall state the items to be put on the agenda.

3. If, following a request made under paragraph 1, a general meeting is not held in due time and, in any event, within two months, the competent judicial or administrative authority within the jurisdiction of which the SE's registered office is situated may order that a general meeting be convened within a given period or authorise either the shareholders who have requested it or their representatives to convene a general

meeting. This shall be without prejudice to any national provisions which allow the shareholders themselves to convene general meetings.

Article 56

One or more shareholders who together hold at least 10 % of an SE's subscribed capital may request that one or more additional items be put on the agenda of any general meeting. The procedures and time limits applicable to such requests shall be laid down by the national law of the Member State in which the SE's registered office is situated or, failing that, by the SE's statutes. The above proportion may be reduced by the statutes or by the law of the Member State in which the SE's registered office is situated under the same conditions as are applicable to public limited-liability companies.

Article 57

Save where this Regulation or, failing that, the law applicable to public limited-liability companies in the Member State in which an SE's registered office is situated requires a larger majority, the general meeting's decisions shall be taken by a majority of the votes validly cast.

Article 58

The votes cast shall not include votes attaching to shares in respect of which the shareholder has not taken part in the vote or has abstained or has returned a blank or spoilt ballot paper.

Article 59

1. Amendment of an SE's statutes shall require a decision by the general meeting taken by a majority which may not be less than two thirds of the votes cast, unless the law applicable to public limited-liability companies in the Member State in which an SE's registered office is situated requires or permits a larger majority.

2. A Member State may, however, provide that where at least half of an SE's subscribed capital is represented, a simple majority of the votes referred to in paragraph 1 shall suffice

3. Amendments to an SE's statutes shall be publicised in accordance with Article 13.

Article 60

1. Where an SE has two or more classes of shares, every decision by the general meeting shall be subject to a separate vote by each class of shareholders whose class rights are affected thereby.

2. Where a decision by the general meeting requires the majority of votes specified in Article 59(1) or (2), that majority shall also be required for the separate vote by each class of shareholders whose class rights are affected by the decision.

TITLE IV ANNUAL ACCOUNTS AND CONSOLIDATED ACCOUNTS

Article 61

Subject to Article 62 an SE shall be governed by the rules applicable to public limited-liability companies under the law of the Member State in which its registered office is situated as regards the preparation of its annual and, where appropriate, consolidated accounts including the accompanying annual report and the auditing and publication of those accounts.

Article 62

1. An SE which is a credit or financial institution shall be governed by the rules laid down in the national law of the Member State in which its registered office is situated in implementation of Directive 2000/12/EC of the European Parliament and of the Council of 20 March 2000 relating to the taking up and pursuit of the business of credit institutions(9) as regards the preparation of its annual and, where appropriate, consolidated accounts, including the accompanying annual report and the auditing and publication of those accounts.

2. An SE which is an insurance undertaking shall be governed by the rules laid down in the national law of the Member State in which its registered office is situated in implementation of Council Directive 91/674/EEC of 19 December 1991 on the annual accounts and consolidated accounts of insurance undertakings(10) as regards the preparation of its annual and, where appropriate, consolidated accounts including the accompanying annual report and the auditing and publication of those accounts.

TITLE V WINDING UP, LIQUIDATION, INSOLVENCY AND CESSATION OF PAYMENTS

Article 63

As regards winding up, liquidation, insolvency, cessation of payments and similar procedures, an SE shall be governed by the legal provisions which would apply to a public limited-liability company formed in accordance with the law of the Member State in which its registered office is situated, including provisions relating to decision-making by the general meeting.

Article 64

1. When an SE no longer complies with the requirement laid down in Article 7, the Member State in which the SE's registered office is situated shall take appropriate measures to oblige the SE to regularise its position within a specified period either:

(a) by re-establishing its head office in the Member State in which its registered office is situated or

(b) by transferring the registered office by means of the procedure laid down in Article 8.

2. The Member State in which the SE's registered office is situated shall put in place the measures necessary to ensure that an SE which fails to regularise its position in accordance with paragraph 1 is liquidated.

3. The Member State in which the SE's registered office is situated shall set up a judicial remedy with regard to any established infringement of Article 7. That remedy shall have a suspensory effect on the procedures laid down in paragraphs 1 and 2.

4. Where it is established on the initiative of either the authorities or any interested party that an SE has its head office within the territory of a Member State in breach of Article 7, the authorities of that Member State shall immediately inform the Member State in which the SE's registered office is situated.

Article 65

Without prejudice to provisions of national law requiring additional publication, the initiation and termination of winding up, liquidation, insolvency or cessation of payment procedures and any decision to continue operating shall be publicised in accordance with Article 13.

Article 66

1. An SE may be converted into a public limited-liability company governed by the law of the Member State in which its registered office is situated. No decision on conversion may be taken before two years have elapsed since its registration or before the first two sets of annual accounts have been approved.

2. The conversion of an SE into a public limited-liability company shall not result in the winding up of the company or in the creation of a new legal person.

3. The management or administrative organ of the SE shall draw up draft terms of conversion and a report explaining and justifying the legal and economic aspects of the conversion and indicating the implications of the adoption of the public limited-liability company for the shareholders and for the employees.

4. The draft terms of conversion shall be publicised in the manner laid down in each Member State's law in accordance with Article 3 of Directive 68/151/EEC at least one month before the general meeting called to decide thereon.

5. Before the general meeting referred to in paragraph 6, one or more independent experts appointed or approved, in accordance with the national provisions adopted in implementation of Article 10 of Directive 78/855/EEC, by a judicial or administrative authority in the Member State to which the SE being converted into a public limited-liability company is subject shall certify that the company has assets at least equivalent to its capital.

6. The general meeting of the SE shall approve the draft terms of conversion together with the statutes of the public limited-liability company. The decision of the general meeting shall be passed as laid down in the provisions of national law adopted in implementation of Article 7 of Directive 78/855/EEC.

TITLE VI ADDITIONAL AND TRANSITIONAL PROVISIONS

Article 67

1. If and so long as the third phase of economic and monetary union (EMU) does not apply to it each Member State may make SEs with registered offices within its territory subject to the same provisions as apply to public limited-liability companies covered by its legislation as regards the expression of their capital. An SE may, in any case, express its capital in euro as well. In that event the national currency/euro conversion rate shall be that for the last day of the month preceding that of the formation of the SE.

2. If and so long as the third phase of EMU does not apply to the Member State in which an SE has its registered office, the SE may, however, prepare and publish its annual and, where appropriate, consolidated accounts in euro. The Member State may require that the SE's annual and, where appropriate, consolidated accounts be prepared and published in the national currency under the same conditions as those laid down for public limited-liability companies governed by the law of that Member State. This shall not prejudge the additional possibility for an SE of publishing its annual and, where appropriate, consolidated accounts in euro in accordance with Council Directive 90/604/EEC of 8 November 1990 amending Directive 78/60/EEC on annual accounts and Directive 83/349/EEC on consolidated accounts as concerns the exemptions for small and medium-sized companies and the publication of accounts in ecu(11).

TITLE VII FINAL PROVISIONS

Article 68

1. The Member States shall make such provision as is appropriate to ensure the effective application of this Regulation.

2. Each Member State shall designate the competent authorities within the meaning of Articles 8, 25, 26, 54, 55 and 64. It shall inform the Commission and the other Member States accordingly.

Article 69

Five years at the latest after the entry into force of this Regulation, the Commission shall forward to the Council and the European Parliament a report on the application of the Regulation and proposals for amendments, where appropriate. The report shall, in particular, analyse the appropriateness of:

(a) allowing the location of an SE's head office and registered office in different Member States;

(b) broadening the concept of merger in Article 17(2) in order to admit also other types of merger than those defined in Articles 3(1) and 4(1) of Directive 78/855/EEC;

(c) revising the jurisdiction clause in Article 8(16) in the light of any provision which may have been inserted in the 1968 Brussels Convention or in any text adopted by Member States or by the Council to replace such Convention;

(d) allowing provisions in the statutes of an SE adopted by a Member State in execution of authorisations given to the Member States by this Regulation or laws adopted to ensure the effective application of this Regulation in respect to the SE which deviate from or are complementary to these laws, even when such provisions would not be authorised in the statutes of a public limited-liability company having its registered office in the Member State.

Article 70

This Regulation shall enter into force on 8 October 2004.

This Regulation shall be binding in its entirety and directly applicable in all Member States.

MAJOR MINISTRIES

Ministerio de Asuntos Generales

Binnenhof 20, Postbus 20001, 2500 EA La Haya
teléfono: +31 70 3564100, fax: +31 70 3564683
Ministerio de Asuntos Generales

Ministerio del Interior y de Relaciones dentro del Reino

Schedeldoekshaven 200, Postbus 20011, 2500 EA La Haya
teléfono: +31 70 4266426, fax: +31 70 3639153
Ministerio del Interior y de Relaciones dentro del Reino

Ministerio de Asuntos Exteriores

Bezuidenhoutseweg 67, Postbus 20061, 2500 EB La Haya
teléfono: +31 70 3486486, fax: +31 70 3484848
Ministerio de Asuntos Exteriores

Ministerio de Defensa

Plein 4, Postbus 20701, 2500 ES La Haya
teléfono: +31 70 3188188, fax: +31 70 3187888
Ministerio de Defensa

MINISTERIO DE ECONOMÍA

Bezuidenhoutseweg 30, Postbus 20101, 2500 EC La Haya
teléfono: +31 70 3798911, fax: +31 70 3474081
Ministerio de Economía

MINISTERIO DE FINANZAS

Korte Voorhout 7, Postbus 20201, 2500 EE La Haya
teléfono: +31 70 3428000, fax: +31 70 3427905
Ministerio de Finanzas

MINISTERIO DE JUSTICIA

Schedeldoekshaven 100, Postbus 20301, 2500 EH La Haya
teléfono: +31 70 3707911, fax: +31 70 3707900
Ministerio de Justicia

MINISTERIO DE AGRICULTURA, NATURALEZA Y CALIDAD ALIMENTARIA

Bezuidenhoutseweg 73 Postbus 20401, 2500 EK La Haya
teléfono: +31 70 3786868, fax: +31 70 3786100
Ministerio de Agricultura, Naturaleza y Calidad Alimentaria

MINISTERIO DE EDUCACIÓN, CULTURA Y CIENCIAS

Europaweg 4, Postbus 25000, 2700 LZ Zoetermeer
teléfono: +31 79 3232323, fax: +31 79 3232320
Ministerio de Educación, Cultura y Ciencias

MINISTERIO DE ASUNTOS SOCIALES Y EMPLEO

Anna van Hannoverstraat 4, Postbus 90801, 2509 LV La Haya
teléfono: +31 70 3334444, fax: +31 70 3334040
Ministerio de Asuntos Sociales y Empleo

MINISTERIO DE TRANSPORTES Y OBRAS PÚBLICAS

Plesmanweg 1, Postbus 20901,2500 EX La Haya
teléfono: +31 70 3516171, fax: +31 70 3517895
Ministerio de Transportes y Obras Públicas

MINISTERIO DE SANIDAD, BIENESTAR Y DEPORTES

Parnassuslaan 5, Postbus 20350, 2500 EJ Den Haag
teléfono: +31 70 3407911, fax: +31 70 3407834
Ministerio de Sanidad, Bienestar y Deportes

MINISTERIO DE LA VIVIENDA, URBANISMO Y MEDIO AMBIENTE

Rijnstraat 8, Postbus 20951, 2500 EZ La Haya
teléfono: +31 70 3393939, fax: +31 70 3391352
Ministerio de la Vivienda, Urbanismo y Medio Ambiente

IMPORTANT LAWS AND REGUILATIONS ON COMPANY FORMATION AND GOVERNANCE

IMPORTANT CORPORATE REGULATIONS IN THE DUTCH CIVIL CODE

TITLE 1. GENERAL PROVISIONS

1The State, provinces, municipalities, water boards, and any bodies under the Constitution which granted regulatory powers, have legal personality.

2 Other bodies, which part of the government was made responsible, possess only a legal personality, if this is in or pursuant to provisions of the law follows.

3 The following articles of this title, except Article 5 shall not apply to legal persons referred to in the preceding paragraphs.

Article 2

1Denominations and their independent parts and bodies in which they are united, have legal personality.

2They are ruled by their own statute, to the extent not in conflict with the law. With the exception of Article 5, the following articles of this title is not for them; corresponding application is permitted, provided it is compatible with their status and the nature of relationships.

Article 3

Associations, cooperatives, mutual associations, limited liability companies, private limited companies and foundations have legal personality.

Article 4

1A corporation does not arise in the absence of a document signed by a notary or a statement of no objection, provided by law for the establishment required. The lack of power of authenticity signed by a notary deed prevents the formation of the corporation only if that entity in a testamentary disposition made by that Act in life would have been created.

2Destruction of the act which created a legal entity, its existence not affected. The expiry of the participation of one or more founders of a legal entity in itself not affect the validity of the participation of the remaining founders.

3Is the name of a nonexistent corporation has a capital formed, then appoints the court at the request of any interested person or the prosecution of one or more liquidators. Article 22 shall apply mutatis mutandis.

4The power is settled like that of a decomposed body in the purported legal. Those who have acted as directors are jointly and severally liable for the debts pertaining to this power that matured during the period in which they did. They are also connected to the obligations arising from that time for this ability legal acts carried out, to the extent that no one under the preceding sentence is connected. Missing persons under the previous two sentences are connected, then those who acted jointly and severally liable.

5 If still a legal entity is formed to follow in the ability, upon request, the court may allow that this is not settled, but that in that legal entity is inserted.

Article 5

A corporation is what the property is concerned with an individual right, unless the law to the contrary arises.

Article 6

1Changes in statutes and regulations and to dissolve the entity, to whom the book should be made public, may before such disclosures and, in case of amendment, the required disclosure of the amended articles were done, not be invoked against a party and others who were unaware thereof.

2A permitted by law upon statutory jurisdiction of the Board or of a director to represent the legal person in a legal action against an opposing party that it was unaware, can not be done if the limitation or exclusion of the jurisdiction is not at the time of provision of that act recuired by law on the point was made public. The same applies to an appeal to limit the authority of others than directors, to whom that power is conferred by the statutes.

3The person may appeal against a party who was unaware of them, not the inaccuracy or incompleteness of the data contained in the register immediately. Correct and complete registration elsewhere or disclosure of the statutes is not in itself sufficient proof that the party of the inaccuracy or incompleteness was not unaware.

4 Unless the law provides otherwise, the party of a legal person can not rely on ignorance of a fact in a manner specified by law is made public, unless that disclosure has not been done in any manner which the law requires it or not the prescribed notice is given.

5 The two preceding paragraphs shall not apply to judicial decisions in the bankruptcy or receivership register register.

Article 7

Performed by a legal act is voidable if the target was exceeded and therefore the other party knew or should have known without its own research, only the person can appeal on this ground for annulment do.

Article 8

1A legal person and those under the law and the statutes involved in its organization, as such should behave towards one another to requirements of reasonableness and fairness.

2 A between them by law, custom, statutes, regulations or applicable decision rule does not apply where this is in the circumstances to standards of reasonableness and fairness.

Article 9

Each driver is facing the person liable to a proper fulfillment of the task entrusted to him. If the issue relates to the job of two or more board members, each of them shall be liable in respect of a failure, unless this is due not to him and he was not negligent in taking measures to consequences to avert.

Article 10

1The Executive Committee of the assets of the corporation and all of the activities of the entity, the requirements arising from these activities, in such a manner and to keep the books, records and other data carriers in such a way preserve that at all times the rights and obligations of the corporation may be known.

2 Subject to the following titles, the board shall annually within six months of the year the balance sheet and statement of income and expenses of the legal person and on paper to set.

3 The Board is required in paragraphs 1 and 2 books, records and other data carriers for seven years to save.

4 On a data carrier provided data, except on paper balance sheet and statement of income and expenses, are on a different carrier are transferred and stored, provided the transfer is done with full and accurate representation of the data and this data during the entire storage time available and within a reasonable time can be made readable.

Article 10a

The fiscal year is the calendar of a legal, if in no other year has been designated statutes.

Article 11

The liability of a person as a director of another legal peace also jointly and severally on all who at the time of the creation of the legal liability of the driver thereof.

Article 12

The voting rights on decisions where the legal entity to certain persons, other than in their capacity as a member, shareholder or member of a body, conferring rights or obligations remission, may by the statutes on which individuals and their spouse, registered partner, and relatives in the straight line can be denied.

Article 13

1A vote is void in cases where a unilateral act is void, a voice can not be destroyed.

2 An incompetent who is a member of an association, may directly exercise voting rights therein, insofar as the statutes themselves do not object, in other cases, the exercise of voting rights to his legal representative.

3Unless the articles otherwise provide, it is in a meeting of a body of a legal opinion expressed by the President on the outcome of a vote shall prevail. The same applies to the contents of a decision, if a vote was not recorded in writing.

4Immediately after the pronouncement of the judgment of the President correctness is contested, then a new vote if the majority of the meeting or, if the original vote was not or in writing, a voting member requires. This new vote the legal consequences of the original vote.

Article 14

1A decision by a body corporate, which is contrary to law or the statutes are void, unless the law otherwise result.

2A decision is invalid because it was taken despite the absence of a law or the statutes prescribed prior act of or notice to anyone other than the institution that made the decision, it can be ratified by the other. Is the missing step is a requirement stipulated, then this also applies to the ratification.

3 Ratification is no longer possible after a reasonable period, on the other is made by the institution that made the decision or by the party to whom it was addressed.

Article 15

1A decision by a body corporate is, subject to elsewhere in the law regarding the possibility of certain destruction, voidable:

adue to conflict with legal or statutory provisions governing the establishment of resolutions;

bbecause contrary to reasonableness and fairness which are required by Article 8;

cdue to conflict with a regulation.

2 Until the provisions referred to in the previous paragraph a, are not those which contain the provisions in Article 14 paragraph 2 refers.

3 Destruction shall be by ruling of the court of the domicile of the corporation:

aa claim against the person of someone who has a legitimate interest in complying with the obligation is not fulfilled, or

bat the request of the corporation itself, set against the person under board resolution by the judge of the court to rely on such a request of the corporation, in which case the costs of the proceedings by the legal act.

4 If a director in his own name institutes the claim asks the person to the judge of the court to appoint someone who respect of the proceedings in place of the board occurs.

5 The power to set aside the decision to claim expires one year after the end of the day on which either the decision sufficient publicity is given or the decision of the party is aware or was notified.

6A decision that is voidable under paragraph 1 under a may by a resolution to that effect be attached to this decision, the same requirements as for the decision to confirm. The confirmation does not work as long as a predetermined action for annulment is pending. If the claim is successful again as the annulled decision taken by the subsequent decision, unless the scope of this decision to the contrary arises.

Article 16

1The final decision that the nullity of a decision of a person who establishes or destroys such a decision, is for anyone, unless revoked or third party proceedings, binding, if the legal party to the proceedings has been. Revocation will allow each member or shareholder.

2Is the decision an act of the corporation, that a party is directed, or is it a requirement for the validity of such an act, then the nullity or annulment of the decision not to which party will be prejudiced if the defect clung to the decision, nor had any need to know. Nevertheless, the nullity or annulment of a decision to appoint a director or a commissioner appointed to be invoked; reimburse the legal however his injury if he knew the defect in the decision nor need to know.

Article 17

A corporation is established for an indefinite period.

Article 18

1A legal person may, subject to the following members into another legal form.

2 For conversion are required:

aimplementing a decision taken in accordance with the requirements for a resolution to amend and, unless a foundation revenue, taken with the votes of at least nine tenths of the votes cast;

ba decision to amend the statutes;

ca notarial deed of conversion that includes the new statutes.

3 In the previous paragraph mentioned under a majority is not required for a conversion of a limited liability company into a private company or vice versa.

4 For the conversion of or into a foundation and a public or private limited company in an association is also required judicial authorization.

5Only the person may request permission for conversion to the court by submitting a notarized draft of the deed. It is in any case be refused if a required act is invalid or if an action for annulment thereof is pending. They will be denied if the interests of stemgerechtdigden who have not consented or others of whom at least someone accustomed to the court, are insufficient spare. If the conversion authorization of the court is required, explains the notary in the instrument of conversion that the authorization to draft the deed was granted.

6After conversion of a foundation under the Statute must prove that the assets they have in the conversion and its benefits only with permission of the court otherwise be spent than was required for the conversion. The same applies to the articles of a legal entity to the extent these capabilities and benefits thereto by virtue of merger or division have been transferred.

7 The legal entity shall indicate the conversion to registers in which he must be and must be enrolled or registered as an association is voluntary.

8 Conversion terminate the existence of the corporation not.

Article 19

1A corporation is dissolved:

aby a decision of the general meeting or, if the person is a foundation, by a decision of the Board unless otherwise provided in the statutes;

bupon the occurrence of an event that according to the statutes the dissolution results, and not a decision or a dissolution action is addressed;

cafter bankruptcy by either lifting the bankruptcy due to the condition of the estate, either by insolvency;

dby the total lack of members, if the legal person, association, cooperative or mutual insurance is;

eby a decision of the Chamber of Commerce and Industry referred to in Article 19a;

fby the court in the cases determined by law.

2The court stated at the request of the board, any interested person or the prosecutor, or at what time the entity is dissolved in a case referred to in paragraph 1 under b or d. The decision is binding for everyone. Is the legal entity is registered, then the entry of final judgment, which includes the statement, by the care of the Registrar registered there.

3 On the registers where the legal entity is registered for the dissolution statement made: in the cases referred to in paragraph 1, sub a, b and d by the liquidator, if any, otherwise by the board, in the case referred to in paragraph 1, c by the bankruptcy trustee in the case referred to in paragraph 1, under e by the Chamber of Commerce and Industry and in the case referred to in paragraph 1 under f by the clerk of the court.

4If the legal entity at the time of its dissolution no longer has benefits, he then cease to exist. In that case, the directors or, in application of Article 19a, the Chamber of Commerce and Industry, giving them to the registers where the legal entity is registered.

5The legal entity remains after dissolution continued as long as the liquidation of its assets is required. In documents and announcements from him, his name should be added: in liquidation.

6The legal means in case of liquidation to exist at the time the liquidation ends. The liquidator or trustee in bankruptcy does to the registers where the legal entity is registered, its statement.

7 The information about the corporation in the registers at the time when he ceases to exist, there for ten years following that date preserved.

Article 19a

1A registered traders public limited company, private limited company, cooperative or mutual insurance by a decision of the Chamber of Commerce and Industry, where that person is registered, dissolved, if the House has shown that at least two of the following conditions:

athe legal person for its commercial registration or registration of a company belonging to him amount not paid for at least one year after the date on which that amount he had to comply;

bthere are at least a year no directors of the corporation in the register, while not giving up registration is done, or there occurs, if there are drivers are registered with respect to all registered drivers one of the following circumstances for:

1driver is deceased,

2the driver is at least one year proved unavailable at the address listed in the register, or to the municipal personal records in the registered address, or in which administration is at least one year no address of the driver named;

cthe person is at least one year in default with the fulfillment of the obligation to disclose the accounts or the balance sheet and the notes in accordance with Articles 394, 396 or 397;

dthe person has at least one year failed to comply with a notice referred to in Article 9, paragraph 3 of the General State Taxes Act to make the declaration for the corporation.

2 A registered traders association or foundation, which is not an enterprise which is registered in the Trade, by a decision of the Chamber of Commerce and Industry, where the legal entity is registered, dissolved, if the House has shown that the circumstance mentioned in paragraph 1 b, and it occurs at least one year in default for the commercial registration due amount.

3If the Chamber on the basis of known data, that a legal person referred to in paragraphs 1 and 2 for dissolution is eligible, it notifies the entity and the registered directors by registered letter to their last known addresses, that it intends to dissolve the legal proceeding, stating the conditions on which the intention is founded. The Chamber supports this notice in the registry. If the circumstance referred to in paragraph 1 b occurs, does the Chamber's intention to dissolve also include a statement in the Dutch Gazette. As far as the cost of this publication is not the assets of the entity can be met, those borne by the Minister of Justice.

4 After eight weeks after the date of the registered letter dissolves the Chamber in the legal decision, unless previously showed that the conditions under paragraph therein, may not or no longer occur.

5 The decision is made known to the legal and registered drivers.

6The dissolution of the Chamber shall include a statement in the Dutch Gazette. Paragraph 3, fourth sentence, shall apply mutatis mutandis.

7If under Article 23, paragraph 1 no liquidators may be appointed, enters the Chamber as liquidator of the assets of the dissolved entity, except as provided in Article 19, paragraph 4. At the request of the Chamber in its place the court appoints one or more other liquidators.

8If against a decision referred to in paragraph 4, an appeal is lodged with the Board of Trade and Industry Appeals Chamber writes that in the registry. The decision on the appeal shall also be registered. If the decision seeks annulment of the decision, the Court shall include a statement in the Dutch Gazette. During the period in which the entity after the decision to terminate had ceased to exist, there is an extension basis as provided in Article 320 of Book 3 in respect of the limitation of claims by or against the corporation.

Article 20

1A legal person whose activity is contrary to public policy, by the court at the request of the prosecutor declared forbidden and disbanded.

2A corporation whose purpose is contrary to public policy, by the court at the request of the prosecutor dissolved. Before winding up the court may order the person the opportunity within a period to be determined so as to its purpose that it is not contrary to pub ic policy.

3An entity named in the list referred to in Article 2, third paragraph, of Regulation (EC) No 2580/2001 of 27 December 2001 (OJ L 344), in Annex I to Regulation (EC) No 881 / 2002 of 27 May 2002 (OJ L 139) or is listed and identified with a star in the Annex to Common Position 2001/931 of 27 December 2001 (OJ L 344) is prohibited by law and not authorized to perform legal acts.

Article 21

1The court dissolve a corporation, if:

ahis creation of imperfections;

bStatutes are not complying with the requirements of the law;

che is not under the legal definition of its legal status is.

2 The court dissolves the legal entity shall not, if she had a deadline and he authorized after such a legal person who meets the requirements of the law.

3 The court may dissolve a legal, if in this book for its legal prohibitions set violates or commits a serious act contrary to its statutes.

4 The dissolution is pronounced at the request of any interested person or the prosecutor.

Article 22

1The court before which an application is pending dissolution of the corporation, the assets of the entity if required under administration; the decision mention the time it enters into force.

2 The judge shall appoint at his disposal one or more administrators, and determine their powers and their compensation.

3 To the extent the court determines otherwise, the bodies of the legal entity without the prior approval of the administrator and can not make decisions without the legal representatives of his co no legal transactions.

4 The decision may at any time by the court, be amended or repealed;'s reign ends in any case, once the decision on the request for dissolution becomes final.

5 The administrator shall send to the registers where the legal entity is registered, stating the decision and the information about themselves on a driver may be required.

6 An act the person despite his incompetence resulting from the administration before registration has done, is nevertheless valid if the other party knew or should have known rule.

Article 22a

1Before or when making a request by the prosecution to dissolve a limited liability company or a private company with limited liability, the Public Prosecutor may ask the court to petition to recommend that the decision on said application becomes final to the shareholders the power to alienate, pledge or usufruct tax receipts will be denied.

2The judge decides after summary examination. The command is given on condition that the set of the request for dissolution by the court shall within a period to be determined. Against this decision no appeal is allowed.

3The order shall be notified, if possible on the same day, notified to the shareholders and the company. The Registrar is responsible for the registration of the decree in the register in which the entity is registered.

4Within eight days of service mentioned in the preceding paragraph, the shareholder revolt against the decision. The objection does not suspend the order, subject to the jurisdiction of the shareholders to them in summary proceedings by the judge of the court to decide. Opposition to the decision may be based on the allegation that the shareholder wishes to transfer his shares.

5The request for dissolution within eight days after it is set to the shareholder to be served.

Article 23

1To the extent that no other court appointed liquidators and the Statute does not appoint other liquidators, the liquidators directors of the assets of a dissolved corporation. On liquidators who are appointed not by the court, the provisions regarding the appointment, suspension, dismissal and supervision of drivers applicable, insofar as the statutes provide otherwise. The ability of an entity is dissolved by the court by one or more paid by him to appoint liquidators.

2Relieve the court a liquidator, he may appoint one or more other. Lack liquidators, then the court appoints one or more liquidators at the request of any interested person or the prosecutor. The liquidator appointed by the court is entitled to the remuneration which it grants him.

3 A liquidator appointed by the court starts the day after the clerk appointing the liquidator has notified the Registrar shall provide the notification immediately, if the decision for the appointment, is enforceable and otherwise, once it becomes final gone.

4 Every liquidator shall send to the registers where the legal entity is registered, stating his actions as such and the information about themselves that a driver may be required.

5 The court may order a liquidator from a certain day, dismiss her, be it at his request or because of serious reasons at the request of a fellow trustee, the public prosecutor or ex officio.

6The layoffs liquidator shall submit the account and responsible to those who continue the settlement. Is the successor appointed by the court, he shall do the accounts in front of the judge.

Article 23a

1A liquidator shall, unless the articles otherwise provide, the same powers, duties and liabilities as a director, provided they are compatible with his duties as liquidator.

2If two or more liquidators, then each of them perform any work, unless otherwise specified. In case of disagreement between the liquidators decided to request one of them to judge who is involved in the settlement, otherwise the court. The judge referred to in the preceding sentence may also be a distribution of wage setting.

3Both the court as a settlement in its appointed magistrate may give necessary orders for the settlement, whether in the form of a writ of execution form. The liquidator is obliged to follow their instructions. Against the orders and instructions are no appeals.

4 Should the liquidator that the debt will likely exceed the benefits, he does declare for bankruptcy unless all known creditors agree to request continuation of the settlement outside bankruptcy.

5 The foregoing provisions of this Article and Articles 23b, 23c are not applicable to liquidation in bankruptcy.

Article 23b

1The liquidator shall, after which the payment of creditors of the assets of the dissolved legal person is left in proportion to their rights over to them under the statutes are so entitled, or otherwise to the members or shareholders. Has no other right to the surplus, it jumps out of the State, which as far as possible according to the purpose of the corporation pays.

2The liquidator shall prepare a presentation of accounts on the settlement, showing the extent and composition of the surplus expressions. If two or more claimants to the surplus, then the liquidator proposes a plan of distribution that the basis of the distribution contains.

3 To the extent that the surplus is something other than money and the statutes or court order no further instructions comprise, as modes of distribution are considered:

aallocation of a portion of the excess of each of the recipients;

boverendowment to one or more shareholders against payment of the surplus value;

cdistribution of the net proceeds after sale.

4The liquidator shall submit the accounts and the plan of distribution at the office of the registers in which the entity is registered, and in any event at the offices of the corporation, if any, or any other place in the district where the legal domiciled. The pieces are there for two months for each perusal. The liquidator is in a newspaper where and when to consult them. The court may order notice in the Gazette.

5Within two months after the accounts and the plan are deposited and the deposit under paragraph 4 has been published and announced, any creditor or creditor against a petition to the court in revolt. The liquidator does notice of objection made in the same way as the deposit of the accounts and the plan of distribution are communicated.

6Whenever the position of the Company so requires, the liquidator a payment in advance to the beneficiaries do. After the start of the objection period does so without authorization from the court.

7Once the withdrawal of or opposition to any decision is final, the liquidator shall so inform the way the application has been notified. Does the decision to change the plan of distribution, it is also the amended plan of division in this way communicated.

8 The liquidator consigneert sums not collected within six months after the last payment is available.

9 The settlement ends at the time not known to the liquidator benefits remain.

10 Over a month after the liquidation is finished, does the liquidator accounts of his administration to the court, if the settlement is involved.

Article 23c

1If after the time the person has ceased to exist a creditor or owner of the balance rises or the existence of a clear benefit, the court may at the request of an interested party to reopen the settlement and if necessary appoint a liquidator. In that case revives the legal, but only for settlement of the reopened wound. The liquidator has the power of each of the claimants to recover what is this too much from the surplus received.

2 During the period in which the person had ceased to exist, there is an extension basis as provided in Article 320 of Book 3 in respect of the limitation of claims by or against the corporation.

Article 24

1The books, records and other data carriers of a dissolved entity must be kept for seven years after the person has ceased to exist. Custodian is the person in or under the statutes or by the general meeting or, if the corporation has a foundation, the board is designated as such.

2Missing a custodian and is the final liquidator unwilling to save, then a custodian, if possible from among those who were involved in the legal entity at the request of an interested party appointed by the magistrate of the court of the district where the legal residence had. Remedies are not open.

3 Within eight days after the commencement of its retention, the custodian's name and address to the records of the dissolved legal person was registered.

4 In paragraph 2 subdistrict can so requested permission to consult the books, records and other data carriers give any party, if the corporation has a foundation, and also to anyone who proves to inspect a reasonable interest in his capacity as former member or shareholder of the entity or holder of certificates of his shares, or as assignee of such person.

Article 24a

1Subsidiary of a legal person:

awhere a legal entity or one or more of its subsidiaries, whether or not under contract with other voters, alone or together, more than half of the voting rights at the general meeting can exercise;

ba legal entity whose legal entity or one or more of its subsidiaries is a member or shareholder and, whether or not under contract with other voters, alone or together, more than half of the directors or the board may appoint or dismiss, even if all voters vote.

2 Is equated with a subsidiary under its own name acting company in which the legal entity or one or more subsidiaries as partner is fully liable to creditors for the debts.

3For the purposes of paragraph 1, rights attached to shares not allocated to the person who holds shares on behalf of others. Rights attached to shares attributable to the person on whose behalf the shares are held, if it has jurisdiction to determine how the rights are exercised and the shares are to provide.

4For the purposes of paragraph 1, voting rights attached to shares pledged, assigned to the lienholder, if he can determine how the rights are exercised. However, the shares pledged for a loan that the pledgee has provided in the ordinary course of business, then the voting rights attributable to him only if he has exercised it in their own interest.

Article 24b

A group is an economic unit in which legal and companies are connected. Group companies are legal entities and companies together in a group are connected.

Article 24c

1A legal person or company has a shareholding in a corporation if he or any of its subsidiaries for its own account alone or together to provide that legal capital or do in order to provice that legal permanently linked to the service of their own efficacy. If a fifth or more of the issued share capital is provided, the existence of a holding suspected.

2 A person has a shareholding in a company if he or a subsidiary:

atherein as a partner is fully liable to creditors for debts; or

botherwise it is a partner in order with this company are permanently linked to the service of their own efficacy.

Article 24d

In determining whether the voting members or shareholders present or represented, or the extent of the share capital is represented, no account is taken of memberships or shares which the law provides that no vote may be cast.

Article 25

The provisions of this book can only be waived, provided that from the law.

TITLE 2. ASSOCIATIONS

Article 26

1The association is a legal entity with members who focuses on a particular purpose, other than that specified in Article 53 paragraph 1 or 2.

2 An association is established by multilateral legal act.

3 An association may not distribute profits among its members.

Article 27

1Is an association established by a deed, then the following provisions must be observed.

2The deed is executed in the Dutch language. A power of attorney to cooperate with the act must be in writing granted. If the association has its seat in the province of Friesland, the Frisian language in the deed be executed.

3 The document sets out the rules of the association.

4 The statutes include:

athe name of the association and the municipality in the Netherlands where it has its seat;

bthe purpose of the association;

cobligations to the association members, or the manner in which such obligations may be imposed;

dthe manner of convening the general meeting;

ethe manner of appointment and dismissal of directors;

fthe destination of the surplus of the association in case of dissolution, or the manner in which the destination will be determined.

5The notary, in front of whom the deed shall assume that the instrument complies with the provisions in paragraphs 2-4. If he fails, he is personally against those who damaged thereby, liable.

Article 28

1Is not an association under the first paragraph of the preceding article constituted, the general meeting may decide to do the statutes included in a notarial deed.

2 Paragraphs 2-5 of the preceding Article shall apply mutatis mutandis.

Article 29

1The directors of an association whose statutes are contained in a deed are required her to do in the commercial register, and an authentic copy of the deed, or an authentic extract of the deed containing the articles at the office of the register set to explain.

2 While the task at initial registration and deposit have not been done, each director for a legal act by which he connects the association, besides the union liable.

Article 30

1An association whose statutes are not included in a deed, can not acquire real property and can not be heir.

2The directors are jointly and severally for debts connected in addition to the association of an act during their administration fall due. After their retirement, they are also jointly and severally liable for debts arising from legal acts carried out during their administration, to the extent that no one under the next preceding sentence, the association is affiliated. Liability under any of the preceding sentence does not rest on those who do not advance the act is consulted and who has refused her, when she became known, as director for his take responsibility. Missing persons following the first or second sentence in addition to the association are connected, are the ones who acted jointly and severally liable.

3The directors of such an association can do it in the commercial register. Where the statutes be in writing, then they lay a copy thereof at the office of the register set.

4 Has the registration referred to in the preceding paragraph, place, person who is under paragraph 2 is connected only liable, if the party demonstrates that the association will not meet the commitment.

Article 31 [repealed on 01/01/1992]

Article 32 [repealed on 01/09/1994]

Article 33

Unless the statutes provide otherwise, the board decides on the admission of a member and may not yet meeting the general admission to admission decisions.

Article 34

1The membership of the association is personal, unless the articles provide otherwise.

2Unless the articles of association provide otherwise, the membership of a corporation by merger or division ceases to exist on the acquiring legal entity respectively according to the deed of division attached to a description of the acquiring entities.

Article 34a

Commitments can only by or under the statutes of membership are attached.

Article 35

1The membership ends:

aby the death of the member, unless the articles authorize transfer by inheritance;

btermination by the member;

ctermination by the association;

dby expulsion.

2The Association may unsubscribe in the cases in the articles mentioned, also if a member has ceased to meet the requirements under the statutes for membership made to comply, and if reasonable the association can not be required to let the membership continue. Unless the statutes delegate this to another body, it shall be terminated by the Board.

3 Disqualification can be imposed only when a member in violation of the statutes, regulations or decisions of the Association, or the association in an unreasonable manner.

4Unless the statutes delegate this to another body, made the disqualification by the Board. The member is at the earliest writing of the decision, stating reasons, informed. It stands, unless the constitution the decision by the general meeting is taken within one month of receiving notification of the decision, appeal to the general meeting or a specially designated body in the statutes or third open. The bylaws may contain other regulation of the profession, but the term can not be shorter than one month are made. During the appeal and pending the appeal the member is suspended.

5 When membership in the course of a financial year, remains, unless the articles otherwise provide, nevertheless the annual contribution payable in full.

Article 36

1Unless the articles provide otherwise, termination of membership only at the end of a year and serving a notice of four weeks, at this period, the General Extension does not apply. In any case, the membership may be terminated by termination at the end of the year following that in which notice is given, or immediately, if not reasonably be a member to continue.

2 A termination in violation in the preceding paragraph, shall terminate membership at the earliest possible time following the date of termination.

3A member can cancel his membership with immediate effect within one month after a decision by which his rights are limited or his obligations, he has become known or communicated, the resolution shall not apply to him. This right of denunciation, the members of the association be denied in case of modification of the rights and obligations as defined in general and also in case of change of financial rights and obligations.

4 A member may terminate its membership with immediate effect within one month after being informed of a decision to change the association is another legal merger or demerger.

Article 37

1The Board is appointed from the members, the statutes may provide that directors outside members can be appointed.

2The appointment is made by the general meeting. The statutes may also the method of appointment otherwise regulate, provided that each member directly or indirectly to the vote on the nomination of directors may participate.

3 Regulations may provide that one or more of the directors, provided that less than half, by persons other than members are appointed.

4Does the statute provides that a director in a meeting from a binding nomination must be appointed, then that the nomination be withdrawn by binding with at least two thirds of the votes cast by decision of that meeting. The statutes can be determined at this meeting at least a certain number of votes must be cast, this number may be set no higher than two thirds of the votes by the voters together can be cast.

5Where under the constitution of board members or departments outside a meeting being appointed, the members should be allowed to candidates. The bylaws may provide that this right only some members jointly, provided that their number is not higher states than a fifth of the number of members that can participate in the election. The statutes may also provide that only candidates nominated so fixed, if it has at least a certain number of votes have united, that this number is not greater than two thirds of the votes cast.

6A board member may, even if he is appointed for a certain time, at any time by the body that appointed him, be dismissed or suspended. A conviction for the recovery of the employment contract between the association and director can not be pronounced by the court.

7 Unless the statutes provide otherwise, the Board points out of a chairman, a secretary and a treasurer.

Article 38

1Subject to the following article, all members who are not suspended, access to the general meeting and have one each voice, a suspended member has access to the meeting where the decision to suspend is treated, and is authorized thereon the word to be carried. The statutes may to some members more than one vote.

2 Unless the statutes provide otherwise, join the President and the Secretary of the Board or their alternates, as such also by the general meeting.

3The bylaws may provide that persons belonging to other organs of the association and who are not members, in the general meeting voting exercise. The number of votes cast by them, together, however, will not be greater than half of the number of votes cast by the members.

4 Unless the articles provide otherwise, a person under paragraph 1 or 3 are entitled to vote, voting in another written proxy to cast his vote.

5The requirement of a written power of attorney is met if the proxy is recorded electronically.

6The bylaws may provide that a person under paragraph 1 or 3 voting, voting rights may exercise by means of electronic communication.

7For the purposes of paragraph 6 requires that the voting through electronic means of communication can be identified, directly take note of the proceedings of the meeting and exercise his voting rights. The bylaws may provide that additional requirement that the voting through electronic means of communication can participate in the deliberations.

8Regulations may provide that votes cast at the general meeting by electronic communication may be released not earlier than the thirtieth day of the meeting, be equated with the votes cast at the meeting.

9By or under the statutes may impose conditions on the use of electronic communication. If these conditions are made under the Statute, those disclosed in the notice.

Article 39

1The bylaws may provide that the General Assembly will consist of delegates by and from members are chosen. The manner of election and the number of delegates by the statutes, each member must directly or indirectly participate in the election. Paragraphs 4 and 5 of Article 37 shall apply mutatis mutandis to the election. Article 38, paragraph 3 shall apply to persons who belong to other organs of the association and who are not delegates.

2The bylaws may provide that certain decisions of the General Assembly will be subject to a referendum. The statutes cover cases where the time within which, and how the referendum will be held. Pending the outcome of the referendum, the implementation of the decision is suspended.

Article 40

1At the general meeting are in the association all powers not authorized by the law or the articles entrusted to other bodies.

2 A unanimous vote of all members or delegates, even if they are not in a meeting, has provided with knowledge of the board adopted the same force as a decision of the General Assembly.

Article 41

1The board calls the general meeting, as often as it deems desirable, or when to do so by law or the statutes is required. The bylaws may delegate this power to others than the government grant.

2 At the written request of at least one such number of members or delegates as is entitled to cast one tenth of the votes at the general meeting or such lesser number as in the statute, the board is obliged to convene a general meeting within a period no longer than four weeks after submission of the request.

3If the request within fourteen days of no action is taken, may, unless the statutes the way of convening of the general assembly for this event has been arranged, the applicants themselves to convene the meeting go the way the board the general meeting convenes or by advertisement in at least one spot where the association is established, widely read newspaper. The applicants may then others than members with chairing the meeting and the minutes.

4Unless the articles otherwise provide, to the requirement of written form of the application referred to in paragraph 2 are met if the request is recorded electronically.

5Unless the statutes provide otherwise, if a member or representative agrees, the convening done by an electronically readable and reproducible message sent to the address provided by him for this purpose is disclosed.

Article 41a

Articles 37-41 shall apply mutatis mutandis to the sections of an association with no legal person and that a general meeting and have a board, which in those Articles concerning the statute, may be deposited in a department regulations.

Article 42

1In the articles of association can not be changed except by a decision of a general meeting which is convened by stating that an amendment of the statutes will be proposed. The deadline for convening such a meeting shall be at least seven days.

2Those convening the general meeting to discuss a proposal to amend the articles have done, at least five days before the meeting a copy of that proposal, which the proposed amendment verbatim, in a suitable place for members to inspect until after the end of the day the meeting is held. To the departments from which the association exists and delegates, the proposal should at least fourteen days before the meeting to have been notified to the preceding sentence will not then apply.

3 The provisions in the first two paragraphs shall not apply if the general meeting all members or delegates present or represented and the decision to amend the Articles is passed unanimously.

4 In this article and the first two members of the following article shall apply mutatis mutandis to a decision to dissolve.

Article 43

1Unless the statutes provide otherwise, requires a resolution to amend at least two thirds of the votes cast.

2 As far as the power to amend the statutes might be excluded, is nevertheless possible amendment unanimously in a meeting where all members or delegates present or represented.

3 A provision in the statutes which the power to change one or more other provisions are restricted, may only be amended in accordance with the same restriction.

4 A provision in the statutes which the power to change one or more other rules, may only be amended unanimously in a meeting where all members or delegates present or represented.

5The association has full jurisdiction, then the modification shall not take effect after a notarial deed. The Directors are required to deposit an authentic copy of the amendment and the amended statute to deposit at the office of the Trade.

6 The directors of an association with limited jurisdiction with a statute pursuant to Article 30 paragraph 3 of this book copy in the office of the trade have been deposited, are required there is also a copy of the amendment and the amended statute to deposit.

Article 44

1Subject to restrictions under the statutes, the board is charged with the management of the association.

2Only if the statute arises, the board is authorized to decide to enter into agreements to acquire, alienate or encumber registered property, and to enter into agreements whereby the Association commits itself as surety or debtor, is for a third or provides security for a debt of another party. The bylaws may delegate this power to restrictions and conditions bind. The exclusion, limitations and conditions also apply for the authority to represent the Association in respect of such acts, unless the articles provide otherwise.

Article 45

1The board represents the association, except where the law provides otherwise.

2The articles may also be authorized to represent to one or more directors. They may provide a driver's association only with the cooperation of one or more others may represent.

3Power of representation to the board or to a director belongs to, indefinitely and unconditionally, to the extent the law provides otherwise. A legally permitted or prescribed restriction or requirement for the power of representation can only be invoked by the association.

4 The statutes can to persons other than directors power to grant representation.

Article 46

The association may, except where the statutes are not the opposite result, for the benefit of the members rights and obligations to the extent expressly provided in the statutes, their dependents commitments. They can fulfill stipulated rights against and recover damages to a member, unless opposed.

Article 47

In all cases where the association has a conflict of interest with one or more directors or supervisory directors the general meeting may appoint one or more persons to represent the Association.

Article 48

1The Board At a general meeting within six months of the year, unless this period is extended by the General Assembly, an annual report on the affairs of the association and its policies. It explains the balance sheet and statement of income and expenditure with notes submitted to the meeting. These documents are signed by the directors, if the signature of one or more of them is giving the reasons therefor. After expiration of the period, any member of the joint board for the enforcement of these obligations.

2Missing a supervisory board and is on the fairness of the documents to the general meeting not submitted a statement from an accountant as defined in Article 393, paragraph 1, appoint the General Assembly annually a committee of at least two members who are not part of the board may decide. The committee shall examine the documents referred to in the second sentence of paragraph 1, and report to the General Assembly report of its findings. The Board is required the commission to conduct its investigation, all information requested by her to provide her the cashbook and the values to show and the books, records and other data carriers of the association available for consultation.

3An association with one or more undertakings which maintains under the Act must be entered in the commercial mentions in the statement of income and expenses, net sales of these companies.

Article 49

1Annually, within six months after the year of an association referred to in Article 360 paragraph 3, subject to extension of this deadline by up to five months by the general meeting under special circumstances, the Board shall prepare annual accounts and submit them for members at the offices of the association. Within this period, the board also the annual report for inspection by the members unless the Articles 396 paragraph 7 or 403 for the association funds.

2The financial statements are signed by the directors and the auditors; if the signature of one or more of them shall be stated and reasons given.

3The financial statements are adopted by the General Meeting that the Board not later than one month after the expiry of the period is to keep. Adoption of the annual discharge shall not serve as a director respectively commissioner.

4Article 48 paragraph 1 shall not apply to the association referred to in Article 360 paragraph 3. Article 48 paragraph 2 is applicable thereto except that bottoms means the documents under paragraph 1 shall be presented.

5An association referred to in Article 360 paragraph 3 may be covered by the statutory reserves amortize a deficit only to the extent permitted by law.

6Our Minister of Economic Affairs may upon request, compelling reasons to waive the obligation to draw up, furnishing and setting the financial statements.

Article 50

The association referred to in Article 360 paragraph 3, provides that the annual accounts, annual report and pursuant to Article 392 paragraph 1 to add data from the call for the General Assembly intended to handle the financial statements, its premises are present. Members may inspect the documents at that place and obtain a free copy of.

Article 50a

Articles 131, 138, 139, 149 and 150 shall apply mutatis mutandis in case of bankruptcy of an association whose statutes are contained in a deed and that the corporate tax is subject.

Article 51

In the event of bankruptcy or receivership of an association which is registered in the trade, the notice shall be granted under the Bankruptcy Act in the Dutch Gazette be taken up by him with that disclosure is in charge, also for inclusion in the register specified.

Article 52

Where the provisions of this title in the statutes may be waived, this deviation can only be in with written statutes.

TITLE 3. COOPERATIVES AND MUTUALS

Section 1. General Provisions

Article 53

1The cooperative is a cooperative established by notarial deed and association. They should aim to clear from the statutes in certain material needs of its members to provide under contracts other than insurance, concluded with them in the company that to this end to them for exercising or doing exercise.

2The mutual insurance is a notarial deed as a mutual insurance association founded. They should aim to clear the association and its members insurance agreements, all this in the insurance industry that to this end for the benefit of its members exercises.

3 The statutes of a cooperative may her afford agreements as those of its members, with others to enter, the same applies to the articles of a mutual association with any obligation of members or former members to the deficits contribute is excluded.

4 If a cooperative or mutual insurance in the preceding paragraph, exercise jurisdiction, it may not do to an extent that the agreements with the members of only minor significance.

Article 53a

The provisions of the previous title, with the exception of Articles 26 paragraph 3 and 44 paragraph 2, to the cooperative and mutual insurance applies, unless otherwise provided in this title is not deviated.

Article 54

1A cooperative and mutual insurance are established by a multilateral legal act by notarial deed.

2The name of a cooperative, the word "cooperative" as that of a mutual association the word "mutual" or "reciprocal". The name of the entity must, at the end the letters WA, BA or UA in accordance with Article 56 bear.

Article 54a [repealed on 11/25/1988]

Article 55

1Those who at the dissolution were members, or less than a year before have ceased to be members, are against the legal entity in the statutes specified criterion for a deficit liable; a cooperative or mutual insurance association dissolved by its insolvency after they bankruptcy is declared, then the term of one year from the date of dissolution, but the day of bankruptcy counted. The bylaws may prescribe a longer period than one year fix.

2 The statutes do not contain a measure of everyone's liability, are all liable in equal shares.

3Can one or more members or former members, the amount of his share in the deficit not be recovered, then for the other missing members and former members, each in proportion to its share liability. This liability exists even if the story liquidators waive one or more members or former members on the ground that the exercise of the right to redress a benefit to the estate would not be obtained. If the settlement is carried out under the supervision of persons by law charged with that oversight, the liquidators of that story just dispense with the authorization of those persons.

4 The guaranteeing members and former members are obliged to immediately pay their share of a projected deficit increased by 50 percent, or much less as the liquidators deem sufficient, to cover a further interim cover for the costs of collection and the proportion of those who were allowed to remain in default on their obligation.

5 A member or former member is not entitled to set off its debt under this article.

Article 56

1A cooperative or mutual insurance company may deviate from it in the previous article in its constitution any obligation of its members or former members to a deficit to help exclude or to a maximum limit. Members can call this only if the entity at the end of his name in the first case the letters UA (disclaimer), and in the second case the letters BA (limited liability) has posted. A legal entity which the first sentence has not been applied, place the letters WA (liability) at the end of his name.

2 The legal entities mentioned, except telegrams and advertisements, obliged to carry her name completely.

Article 57

1The statutes may provide that a board of commissioners will be. The board consists of one or more natural persons.

2The supervisory board is responsible for supervising the policy of the government and the general affairs of the entity and the related enterprise. He is the Board with advice. In the performance of their duties, the commissioners of the importance of the legal and related business.

3Unless the statutes provide otherwise, the Supervisory Board authorized the General Assembly appointed by each driver at all times be suspended. This suspension may at any time by the general meeting be removed.

4Except as provided in Article 47 represents the supervisory body in the other cases of conflict of interest with one or more directors than the closing or changing agreements like this with all members in equal conditions are concluded. The statutes may derogate from this provision.

5 The articles may contain additional provisions regarding the duties and powers of the board and its members include.

6 Unless the articles provide otherwise, the general meeting to the board as such a salary grant.

7 Unless the statutes granting the commissioners voting, they have as such in the General Assembly only an advisory vote.

8 The Board provides the Supervisory Board in time for the performance of its duties.

Article 57a

1On the appointment of commissioners who are not already in the memorandum have been appointed, Article 37 shall apply, unless made pursuant to Article 63f.

2A recommendation or nomination of a Commissioner from the candidate's age, his profession and the positions he holds or has held in the extent of interest in connection with the performance of the duties of a commissioner. It also sets out the legal, he is already a; if these include legal persons, belonging to the same group, may with the designation of the group will be sufficient. The recommendation and nomination shall be reasoned.

Article 58

1Annually within six months of the year, subject to extension of this deadline by up to five months by the general meeting under special circumstances, the Board shall prepare annual accounts and submit them to the members at the offices of the legal . Within this period, the board also the annual report for inspection by the members unless the Articles 396 paragraph 7, or 403 for the legal funds. The financial statements are adopted by the General Meeting that the Board not later than one month after the expiry of the period is to keep. Article 48 paragraph 2 shall apply mutatis mutandis. Adoption of the annual discharge shall not serve as a director respectively commissioner.

2 The financial statements shall be signed by the directors and the auditors; if the signature of one or more of them shall be stated and reasons given.

3The entity provides that the annual accounts, annual report and pursuant to Article 392 paragraph 1 to add data from the call for the General Assembly intended to handle the accounts, his premises are present. Members may inspect the documents at that place and obtain a free copy of.

4 Charged by the statutory reserves A deficit may only be extinguished to the extent permitted by law.

5 Our Minister of Economic Affairs may upon request, compelling reasons to waive the obligation to draw up, furnishing and setting the financial statements.

Article 59

1Cooperatives and mutuals are not authorized by a resolution with the changes in its members in the exercise of its company entered agreements to bring this power unless they are clearly in the agreement are reserved. A reference to statutes, regulations, terms and conditions or the like, is not sufficient.

2 In a change as in the previous paragraph, the legal professions themselves against a member only if the change was communicated in writing to the member.

Article 60

For further holds that the cooperative, with preservation of the freedom of retirement from the cooperative, it conditions the statutes, in accordance with its object and purpose, can be connected. A condition which goes beyond what is permitted, is to that extent not written.

Article 61

For a cooperative, which in its constitution, not every obligation of its members or former members to contribute to a deficit had been eliminated by the following provisions also apply:

aThe membership will be requested in writing. The applicant shall also be notified in writing, that as a member is admitted or denied. When he was admitted, he is also reported the number under which he was a member in the administration of the cooperative is registered. Nevertheless order to prove the acquisition of membership, a written application and written notice as referred to above, not to prove.

bThe writings, in which membership is applied for at least ten years by the Board retained. However require the writings referred to here is not to be kept as it concerns those whose membership can be substantiated by them signed, dated statement in the records of the cooperative.

cThe termination of membership may only be made from either a separate document, either by the member signed, dated statement in the records of the cooperative. The member that termination occurs, will receive a written acknowledgment of the board. The written approval is not given within fourteen days, then the member is entitled to termination costs of the cooperative by writ to repeat.

dBy the board certified copy of the list of members is at the Commercial filed with the registration of the cooperative. Within a month after the end of each financial year by the board a written statement of the changes the list of members during the year has undergone, the office of the trade laid down list added or, if the Chamber of Commerce Industry considers this necessary, a new set list.

Article 62

For a mutual insurance company shall also apply the following provisions:

aThose who as a policyholder in a mutual agreement of current insurance, are automatically members of the insurance company. The mutual insurance company under its articles also policyholders who are not members should ensure that provision may be waived.

bUnless the statutes provide otherwise, the membership takes out an insurance contract arises, shall continue until all the member with the insurance association insurance contracts have ended. For transfer of the rights and obligations under such agreement, the membership, provided under that contract, the transferee or transferees on the new, all this barring provisions in the statutes.

cIf the guarantee capital of a mutual insurance is divided into shares, Articles 79-89, 90-92, 95, 96 paragraph 1, 98, paragraphs 1 and 6, and 98c paragraphs 1 and 2 of this Book shall apply.

Article 63

1It is a person who is not cooperative or mutual insurance company is prohibited from doing business with use of the term "cooperative", "concerted" or "reciprocal".

2 In case of violation of this prohibition, any cooperative or mutual insurance claim, that the offender, on pain of a penalty by the court to determine the offending word remember when doing business use.

Section 2. The Board of Commissioners in the large cooperative and among the mutual insurance

Article 63a

In this section, a dependent company means:

aa legal entity to which the cooperative or mutual insurance company or one or more dependent companies, alone or together for their own account at least half of the issued capital.

ba partnership, a company is incorporated and for which the cooperative or mutual insurance company as a partner towards third parties fully liable for all debts.

Article 63b

1A cooperative or mutual insurance, if paragraph 2 applies to it, within two months after the adoption of its financial statements by the general meeting, to specify the trade that it meets the conditions laid down in paragraph 2. Until Article 63c paragraph 3 have been applied, the board shall in each subsequent annual report when the task is done, the statement is deleted, it will be recorded in the first annual report after the cancellation is made.

2 The obligation to challenge applies if:

aequity according to the balance sheet and notes at least a threshold amount established by Royal Decree [Editor: At Stb. 2000/290, this amount including September 1, 2000 set at 13 million euros.] Amounts,

bthe legal person or a dependent company under a legal obligation Works has set, and

cthe legal entity and its dependent companies together in the rule at least one hundred employees working in the Netherlands.

3In subparagraph a of paragraph 2 above limit shall be no more than once in two years increased or decreased in proportion to the development of a by general government to designate price index since a bee that measure date to be determined, it is then rounded to the nearest multiple of one million. The amount will not be re-established as long as the unrounded amount less than one million differs from the previously fixed amount.

4 Under the equity is in part a of paragraph 2, including the joint made and yet to be input from members by way of guarantee or in dependent companies which are limited partnerships, where this does not lead to double counting.

Article 63c

1Articles 63f to 63j shall apply to a legal entity on which a statement referred to in Article 63b for three years continuously enrolled. This period shall be deemed not to be interrupted if a cancellation of the statement, which during that period was made in error, undone.

2 The cancellation of the registration on the grounds that the entity no longer meets the requirements of Article 63b paragraph 2, the applicability of Articles 63f to 63j terminate only if the cancellation after three years have elapsed in which the person was not re- The statement has been obliged.

3 The cooperative or mutual insurance brings its constitution in accordance with Articles 63f to 63j for which its funds, the latest from the date of such items pursuant to paragraph 1 of its operation.

Article 63d

1Articles 63f to 63j shall not apply to a legal person whose activity is exclusively or almost exclusively limited to the management and financing and its dependent companies and their holdings in other entities, provided that the employees of the Dutch dependent companies represented in a works council has the powers referred to in Articles 158 and 268.

2Our Minister of Justice, having heard the Economic and Social Council, a cooperative or mutual insurance upon request to waive one or more of Articles 63f to 63j. The exemption may be granted under restrictions and conditions may be attached thereto. They may be modified or withdrawn.

Article 63rd

A cooperative or mutual insurance does not apply where Article 63c may, at its statutes the manner of appointment and dismissal of auditors and the duties and powers of the supervisory control under Articles 63f to 63j, if they or a dependent society is a Works set to which the provisions of the Works Councils Act apply. This arrangement in the statutes loses its validity when the council ceases to exist or that counsel is no longer the provisions of the Works Councils Act apply.

Article 63f

1The large cooperative and have a large mutual insurance supervisory board.

2 The Board shall, subject to paragraph 8, on the recommendation of the Supervisory Board appointed by the General Assembly, where the appointment has not already been done with the memorandum or before this article on the person became applicable.

3The supervisory board consists of at least three members. Is the number of commissioners less than three, the Board promotes immediate measures to supplement its membership.

4The general meeting, the council and the board may participate in the Supervisory Board recommend persons to nominate Commissioner. The Supervisory Board shall inform them in a timely manner when due and in which a vacancy must be filled.

5 The supervisory board gives to the general meeting and the works of the name of the person he recites, in compliance with Article 57a paragraph 2.

6 The general meeting appoints the person nominated, unless the council within two months of notification or the general meeting by themselves in the first meeting after those two months against the nomination object:

a on the ground that the requirements of paragraph 4, second sentence, or paragraph 5 does not properly complied with;

b based on the expectation that the nominee will be unsuitable for the performance of the duties of the Commissioner, or

c based on the expectation that the supervisory board appointed in accordance with the plan will not properly constituted.

7 The objection is to the Board of Commissioners stating the reasons stated.

8 Notwithstanding the opposition of the council nominated candidate may be appointed if the Enterprise Chamber of the Amsterdam Court unfounded objections on the request of a designated by the Board of Commissioners designated representative. At his request the Enterprise Chamber appoints the nominated candidate, if the general meeting has objected or did not do so in its meeting convened appointed, unless the company has room an objection by the general meeting to be justified.

9 Defense may be conducted by a representative designated by the assembly or the council established in paragraph 6 above objects.

10The decision of the Enterprise can not be appealed. The Enterprise can not express condemnation of the proceedings.

11For the purposes of this section, the council means the council of the business of the corporation or of a dependent society. If two or more works, these are equally competent. Does the company or companies concerned a central works council, then the powers of the council under this section to the Central Works Council. The council takes no decision referred to in this article only after at least once about having consulted with the legal entity.

Article 63 g

1If all members, then the council and the board recommend persons for appointment to the meeting. The person who convenes the general meeting, shall notify the council and the administration time that the appointment of commissioners subject of treatment will be.

2The appointment is effective unless the council within two months under Article 63f paragraph 5 has been informed of the name of the person appointed pursuant to Article 63f paragraph 6 to the legal objection. Notwithstanding this objection, the appointment of force if the Enterprise Chamber of the Amsterdam Court at the request of a duly designated representative of the general meeting the objection unfounded.

3 The members of 10 and 11 of Article 63f shall apply mutatis mutandis

Article 63h

1Commissioner can not be:

apersons employed by the entity;

bpersons employed by a dependent company;

cdirectors and persons in the service of an employee organization that is usually involved in the determination of the conditions of the persons referred to under a and b.

2 Those rules may not exceed two thirds of the commissioners determine that they are appointed from a circle to which at least the members of the legal belong.

Article 63i

1Commissioner shall not later than if after his appointment last four years has been Commissioner. The deadline may be extended by the statutes to the day of the next general meeting after the four years or after the date of this article for the legal person will apply.

2The Enterprise Chamber of the Amsterdam Court may dismiss a commissioner request for neglecting his duties, for other important reasons or for radical change in the circumstances in which enforcement of the Commissioner of the corporation can not reasonably be required. The request may be submitted by a representative designated by the Board, by the general meeting or by the council. Article 63f paragraph 11 shall apply mutatis mutandis.

3A member may only be suspended by the Supervisory Board. The suspension shall automatically expire if not used within one month after the commencement of the suspension with a request referred to in paragraph 2 has been submitted to the Enterprise

Article 63j

1The approval of the Supervisory Board are subject to the decisions of the Board concerning:

aissuance of debentures of the corporation;

bissuance of debentures by a limited partnership or general partnership of which the entity is fully liable partner;

capplication for admission of a and b referred debentures to trading on a regulated market or multilateral trading facility, as defined in Article 1:1 of the Act on financial supervision or with a regulated market or multilateral trading facility from a State not a Member State or requesting a withdrawal of such authorization;

dthe commencement or termination of a continuing collaboration of the legal person or a dependent company and another entity or company or as fully liable partner in a limited partnership or partnership, if such cooperation or termination of major significance to the entity;

etaking a stake worth at least a fourth of the amount of equity in the balance sheet and notes of the corporation, or a dependent by this company in the capital of a company, or any material increase or decrease of such a participation;

finvestments requiring an amount equal to one fourth of the equity according to the balance sheet and notes of the corporation;

ga proposal to amend the statutes;

ha proposal to dissolve the legal entity;

ifiling for bankruptcy and petition for suspension of payment;

jtermination of employment of a substantial number of employees of the entity or a dependent company simultaneously or within a short period of time;

kradical change in the employment of a substantial number of employees of the corporation or of a dependent society.

2 The lack of approval of the Supervisory Board on a decision as referred to in paragraph 1 affect the authority of the board of directors not to.

3 For decisions of the entity referred to in subparagraphs d, e, f, j and k of paragraph 1, requires any decision of the Board.

TITLE 4. LIMITED LIABILITY COMPANIES

Section 1. General Provisions

Article 64

1The limited company is a legal entity with a share capital divided into transferable shares. A shareholder is not personally liable for what in the name of the company is carried out and is not held above the amount that ought to be paid his share in the losses of the company to contribute. At least one share is held by someone other than and other than on behalf of the company or any of its subsidiaries.

2The company is one or more persons established by notarial deed. For establishment shall require a statement of the Minister of Justice that it has proved of no objection. The deed is signed by each and every founder who, according to this Act shall take one or more shares.

3The memorandum must be made within three months after the date of the declaration of no objection his past, on pain of forfeiture of the statement. The Minister may at the request of interested parties on the basis of compelling reasons this term not exceeding three months.

Article 65

The Constitution of a corporation is executed in the Dutch language. A power of attorney to cooperate in such deed must be in writing granted.

Article 66

1The memorandum must contain articles of the corporation. The bylaws contain the name, seat and purpose of the company.

2 The name starts or ends with the words Limited Liability Company, written either in full or abbreviated "NV".

3 The seat must be located in the Netherlands.

Article 67

1The statutes specify the amount of the share capital and the number and amount of shares in euro up to two decimal places. Are there different types of shares, the articles mention the number and amount of each species. The memorandum shall state the amount of subscribed capital and paid part of it. Are there different types of shares than the amounts of the issued and paid-up capital broken down by type. The document also mentions the creation of all those who take shares in Article 86 paragraph 2 sub b and c data with the number and type of shares held by him and paid-in amount.

2The authorized and subscribed capital must be at least the minimum capital. The minimum capital is forty-five thousand euro. By Order in Council, this amount increased if the law of the European Communities required to increase the subscribed capital. For public corporations which exist on the day before this increase in force, they first eighteen months after that day of power.

3 The paid portion of the subscribed capital must be at least forty-five thousand euros.

4 Of capital must be at least one-fifth are placed.

5A corporation that has arisen before 1 January 2002, the amount of capital and the amount of the shares in golden state up to two decimal places.

Article 67a

1If a public company in the statutes, the amount of the share capital and the amount of the shares in guilders into euros, the amount of shares subscribed and paid-up share in euro calculated under Article 109l fourth member of the Treaty on European Union finally fixed conversion rate, rounded up to two decimal places. The rounded amount of each share in euros may not exceed 15% higher or lower than the original amount of the share in guilders. The total amount of the shares referred to in Article 67 in euros, the share capital into euro. The sum of the amounts of the shares subscribed and paid-up part thereof in euro is the amount of the issued and paid-up share capital in euro. The deed shall state the amount of the issued and paid-up share capital in euro.

2After conversion in accordance with paragraph 1, the sum of the amounts of the issued shares higher than in accordance with Article 109l fourth paragraph of the Treaty on European Union finally fixed conversion rate converted amount of the subscribed capital, the difference is charged of distributable reserves or the reserves referred to in Article 389 or 390. If these reserves are not sufficient, then the company is a negative crediting reserve the size of the difference that is not borne out of distributable or non-distributable reserves is charged. Until the difference in retained earnings or reserves are met, the company may no benefits referred to in Article 105 do. By complying with the provisions of this paragraph shall be deemed to have the shares are fully paid.

3After conversion in accordance with paragraph 1, the sum of the amounts of the issued shares lower than according to the Article 109l fourth paragraph of the Treaty on European Union finally fixed conversion rate converted amount of the subscribed capital, the company keeps a non-distributable reserve the size of the difference. Article 99 is not applicable.

Article 67b

If the company is in derogation of Article 67a the amount of the shares changes, this change requires the approval of any group of shareholders whose rights the amendment would affect. Arises under the right to change money or debt, then the total amount of one tenth of the modified nominal amount of shares not exceeding.

Article 67c

1A limited liability company whose articles of the share capital and the amount of the shares in golden state, may in society use the equivalent in euro up to two decimal places, provided it is made to this article. This use of the equivalent in euro has no legal effect.

2If a corporation whose articles of the amount of the share capital and the amount of the shares in golden state, after 1 January 2002 a change in one or more provisions which amounts are expressed in guilders, in the Statutes, all amounts converted to euro. The items 67a and 67b are applicable.

Article 68

1To obtain a statement from the Minister of Justice that it has proved of no objection must be to him all the information necessary to assess the application. Our Minister should also benefit from the State Funds amounting to? 90.76 are met. We may by order increase the amount of administration associated with the increase in wages and prices.

2 The declaration may only be refused on the grounds that, in view of the intentions or antecedents of the people the policy of the Company shall determine or help determine a risk that the company will be used for illicit purposes or that its activity will lead discriminate against its creditors.

3For the purpose of exercising the supervision referred to in paragraph 2 providing the Institute for employee insurance and the national tax office at his request to the Minister the information it needs. The institute and the national tax office give the Minister on request free of charge access to data held by or providing free extracts thereof.

Article 69

1The directors are required the company to do in the commercial register and a certified copy of the memorandum and of the associated under Articles 93a, 94 and 94a attached documents, and copies of documents prepared in accordance with Article 94a paragraph 4 last sentence, to resign the office of the trade. At the same time they must make a declaration of the total of fixed and estimated costs associated with the establishment and against the company as a result.

2 The directors have been with the company liable for any act done during their administration so that the company is linked in the period before:

a the task at first enrollment in the trade, accompanied by the deposited copies was done, b the paid up capital at least the prescribed minimum capital formation, and

c the issued capital in establishing at least one fourth of the nominal amount is paid.

3 The liability referred to in paragraph 2, parts b and c, does not apply if application is made to Article 94a paragraph 4, last sentence, and immediately upon completion of the audit on behalf of the Company's deposits are obtained which are necessary to meet Article 67 paragraph 3 and Article 80 paragraph 1.

Article 70 [repealed on 01/01/1992]

Article 71

1 When the corporation itself under Article 18 into an association, cooperative or mutual insurance company, any shareholder member, unless he has asked the compensation referred to in paragraph 2.

2 The decision to transpose Article 100 applies, unless the company itself into a private company. After such a decision, any shareholder who is not with the decision agreed, asking the company compensation for the loss of his shares. The request for compensation must be made in writing to the company within one month after the shareholder has indicated that he may seek such compensation. The notification shall be in the same manner as the notice convening a general meeting.

3Failing agreement, the compensation determined by one or more independent experts, at the request of either party to be appointed by the court to authorize conversion or by the judge of the court. The items 351 and 352 are applicable.

Article 72

1 When a private company pursuant to Article 18 into a limited company to be the instrument of conversion attached:

a a statement by the Minister of Justice, to which Article 235 applies, that he objected to the conversion and amendment has not been proved;

b a statement by an accountant as defined in Article 393 paragraph 1, which shows that the equity of the company on a day within five months for the conversion of at least equivalent to the paid-up capital.

2 When another person is under Article 18 into a limited company to be the instrument of conversion attached:

a a statement by the Minister of Justice, to which Article 68 applies, that he objected to the conversion and amendment has not been proved;

b a statement by an accountant as defined in Article 393 paragraph 1, which shows that the equity of the corporation on a day within five months for the conversion amounts to at least the amount of the paid portion of the subscribed capital in accordance with the instrument of conversion; in equity, the value of which will be counted after that day no later than immediately after the conversion to shares will be deposited;

c if the legal members, the written consent of each member whose shares are not paid by conversion of the reserves of the corporation;

dif a foundation is converted, judicial authorization.

3When an association, cooperative or mutual insurance commitments under Article 18 into a limited liability company, each member shareholder. The conversion can not be, as long as one member can still terminate under Article 36 paragraph 4.

Article 73 [repealed on 01/09/1994]

Article 74

1At the request of the prosecutor, the court dissolves the corporation when its purpose, by a lack of income, can not reach, and the court may dissolve the company, when its activity to achieve its purpose has ceased. The public prosecutor shall notify the Chamber of Commerce and Industry, the trade in whose company is registered, that it intends to set action for rescission.

2 The court dissolve the company at the request of the prosecutor when the paid-up capital or part thereof is less than the minimum capital.

3 Before winding up the court the company the opportunity within a period specified by him to correct the omission or transforming themselves into a private company with limited liability.

Article 75

1From all writings, printed documents and notices in which the corporation is a party or which it produces, except telegrams and advertisements, the full name of the company and its address clearly.

2 Where reference is made to the capital of the company, must in any case must state the amount is placed, and how much of the issued amount is paid.

Article 76 [repealed on 11/25/1988]

Article 76a

1Under the investment company means a limited liability company,

awho simply seek to invest its assets so that risk? s are spread, in order to its shareholders in the profits share

bwhose directors are statutorily authorized shares of its capital to spend, acquire and dispose

cfor which an administrator is authorized under the Act on financial supervision for placement of its shares, and

dwhose statutes provide that the company investment company with variable capital.

2The company makes to the business and the Financial Markets Authority stating that they are an investment company with variable capital. These words should in all writings, printed documents and notices in which the investment company is a party or which it produces, except telegrams and advertisements, to clear her name used.

Article 77

When in this title the office of the commercial is listed under the trade means the register kept by the Chamber of Commerce and Industry in accordance with Article 18, sixth and seventh paragraph of the Trade Register Act 2007 is authorized to tender.

Article 78

When the statute refers to the holders of any shares together as a certain portion of the share capital of the company members, shall, unless the contrary appears from the statutes, including capital means the portion of the issued share capital.

Article 78a

For the purposes of Articles 87, 96, 96a, 101 and 129, paragraph 6 under the body of the company means the general meeting, the meeting of holders of shares of a particular species, the board, the supervisory board and the joint meeting of the Board and the Supervisory Board.

Section 2. The shares

Article 79

1Shares are the parts where the capital is divided by the statutes.

2 Fractions are parts in which the shares under the statutes are or may be split.

3 The provisions of this title on shares and shareholders shall apply to holders of fractional shares and fractional shares provided that those provisions do not indicate otherwise.

Article 80

1When taking a share, the nominal amount paid up and, if the share for a higher amount, the difference between those amounts. It may be provided that a part, not exceeding three quarters of the nominal amount need only be paid after the Company has requested.

2 It is lawful to them that their professional charge for their own account place shares by agreement to allow the shares taken by them to pay less than the nominal amount, provided that at least ninety-four percent of this amount look at taking the money is paid in shares

3 A shareholder may not be fully or partially relieved of the obligation to pay, except as provided in Article 99.

4 The shareholder and, in the case of Article 90, the former shareholders are not entitled to set off their debt under this article.

Article 80a

1Payment for a share in cash to the extent that no other contribution has been agreed.

2Prior to or at the establishment may deposit in foreign currency only if the memorandum states that payment in a foreign currency is permitted, after the establishment this can occur only with the consent of the corporation. Payment in a currency that is a unit of the euro under Article 109l fourth paragraph of the Treaty on European Union is not considered payment in foreign currency.

3With payment in a foreign money is the payment obligation for the amount paid against the amount deposited freely in Dutch money can be exchanged. Determines the exchange rate on the day of the deposit or, if earlier than one month before the establishment is paid on the day of the establishment or, after applying the following sentence, on the day mentioned therein. The company may require payment at the exchange rate on a specified date within two months before the last day shall be paid, provided that the shares or certificates immediately after the issue will be admitted to trading on a regulated market or multilateral trading facility, as provided Article 1:1 of the Act on Financial Supervision which is authorized in another member state or a regulated market or multilateral trading facility from a State not a Member State.

Article 80b

1If consideration other than cash has been agreed, which is inserted in economic terms can be appreciated. A right to perform work or services may not be contributed.

2 Consideration other than cash must be carried out immediately after taking a share, or after the day on which an additional payment is issued or on which they agreed.

Article 81

A shareholder can not, even by amending the statute, against his will any obligation above the deposit to the nominal amount of the share may be imposed.

Article 82

1The statutes or registered shares or bearer.

2 If shares both name as bearer could read, the limited company at the request of a shareholder's name denominated paid bearer share or vice versa shall, insofar as the statutes provide otherwise, and have a maximum at cost.

3 Proofs of bearer share shall not be issued to shareholders than to deposit at least the full amount of such shares, subject to the provision of the second paragraph of Article 80 of this Book.

4If bearer shares through an amendment in the name can be made to the shareholder a share rights not exercise until after surrender of the share certificate to the company. These regulations shall apply if holders of bearer shares by merger or division holders of shares, except that the presentation of the share certificate is sufficient.

Article 83

Opposite the subsequent purchaser in good faith is on the corporation failed to prove open, that a bearer share is not paid, or to a registered share is not paid what one due to the Company on the share certificate statement made as a deposit on the nominal amount mentions.

Article 84

The liquidator of a corporation and, in case of bankruptcy, the trustee is authorized to deregistration and recovery of all payments not yet made on the shares no matter what the statutes thereto is determined.

Article 85

1The Board of the Company shall maintain a register containing the names and addresses of all holders of registered shares are recorded, indicating the date the shares were acquired, the date of acknowledgment or service, as well as on each share amount paid. It shall also contain the names and addresses of those who have a right of usufruct or pledge on those shares, stating the date they acquired the right, the date of acknowledgment or service, and specifying the rights attached to shares their accordance with paragraphs 2 and 4 of Articles 88 and 89 of this book forward.

2 The register is updated regularly, it shall also record any discharge of liability for payments not yet made.

3The board provided on request to a shareholder, a usufructuary or a pledgee an extract from the register in respect of his right to a share. If the share is a right of usufruct or a pledge, the extract to whom in paragraphs 2 and 4 of Articles 88 and 89 of this Book rights referred.

4The board shall make the register office of the company for inspection by the shareholders and users of the fruit and pledgees who in paragraph 4 of Articles 88 and 89 of this Book rights referred. The preceding sentence shall not apply to the portion of the registry outside the Netherlands to comply with the applicable legislation or under stock exchange rules will be held. The data from the register regarding non-paid shares are available for inspection by any person; copy or extract of this data at no more than cost price.

Article 86

1For the issuance and delivery of registered shares, other than a share referred to in Article 86c, or the transfer of a right thereto, requires a dedicated in front of a Netherlands-rank civil law notary registered with the concerned parties . No separate document is required for the issuance of shares to be placed in the establishment.

2 Acts of issuance or delivery must state:

athe title of the act and how the share or the limited right to it is acquired;

bname, first name, birth date, birthplace, residence and address of the natural persons who are parties to the transaction;

c, name, residence and address of the persons who are parties to the transaction;

dthe number and type of shares to which the act relates to, or

ename, residence and address of the company in whose shares the act relates.

Article 86a

1The delivery of a share or the transfer of a right thereto in accordance with Article 86 paragraph 1, part of law against the company.

Except in the event that the company itself is party to the transaction, they may attached to the share rights can only be exercised after the act has acknowledged that the deed has been served in accordance with the provisions of Article 86b, or it has been recognized by registration in the shareholders register as referred to in paragraph 2.

2The company who has knowledge of the act referred to in the first paragraph, as long as its not their recognition is requested or notification of the deed has been done, that act on its own motion recognizing the registration of the transferee of the share or the limited right thereon in the shareholders register. They do it immediately by registered letter notifying the parties to the transaction with the request still a copy or extract referred to in Article 86b paragraph 1 to submit to her. Following receipt of such places it in proof of recognition, a note on the piece in the manner described in Article 86b of the recognition is prescribed, the date of acceptance is the date of registration stated.

3 If an act referred to in the first paragraph has taken place without this has led to a corresponding change in the register of shareholders, this neither the company nor to others who in good faith in the shareholders register person as a shareholder or owner a limited right to a share considered, be pleaded.

Article 86b

1Subject to Article 86a paragraph 2 shall take the acknowledgment in the deed or on the basis of submission of a notarized copy or extract of the deed.

2 In recognition under submission of a notarized copy or extract is a dated statement posted on the document produced.

3 The service is made by a notarial copy or extract of the deed.

Article 86c

1For the delivery of a share or the provision of a limited right to a company, whose shares or depositary receipts for shares admitted to trading on a regulated market or multilateral trading facility, as defined in Article 1:1 of the Act The Financial Supervision or a regulated market or multilateral trading facility from a non-Member State, or whose shares or depositary shares at the time of the act may legitimately be expected to do so will soon be allowed, The following provisions apply.

2For the delivery of a share or the transfer of a right thereto shall require a deed and, except in the event that the company itself is a party to the legal act, written acknowledgment by the company of the transfer. The acknowledgment shall be in the deed, or by a dated statement of acknowledgment on the deed or a notary or by the transferor certified copy or extract thereof, or in the manner referred to in paragraph 3. Acknowledgement is equal to the service of that document, copy or extract on the company. If the transfer of partly paid shares, the acknowledgment may be made only if the instrument bears a fixed date.

3If a share is a share certificate is issued, the statutes provide that the provision also issue share certificate to the company that is required. This requirement does not apply if the share certificate is lost, stolen or destroyed and not according to the statutes can be replaced. If the share certificate is issued to the company, the company may acknowledge the delivery by that share an annotation of the places from which approval has been issued by the evidence or to substitute a new share certificate denominated in the name of the transferee.

4A lien may also be established without acknowledgment or service to the company. In such case, Article 239 of Book 3, mutatis mutandis, with acknowledgment or service to the company takes the place of paragraph 3 of that Article.

Article 86d

1The holder of a bearer share certificate of the company may ask him to provide a duplicate of the lost share certificate.

2The holder must demonstrate that the share certificate is lost, indicating the identity of the share certificate.

3The company publishes the application for a duplicate in the listing of a regulated market or multilateral trading facility, as defined in Article 1:1 of the Act on financial supervision or with a regulated market or multilateral trading facility from a state not Member State referred to in Article 86c paragraph 1 or, if the shares are not included therein, in a national newspaper.

4Any interested party may within six weeks from the day after the publication of the application by petition to the court in revolt against the issue of the duplicate.

5If no timely objection is set or if an objection to final judgment was dismissed, the duplicate fee of expense. The duplicate replaces the lost share certificate. After issuing a duplicate certificate to replace the share is not legally binding.

6This Article shall not apply where the articles of association provide for a system to replace lost share certificates.

Article 87

1In the statute, the transfer ability of registered shares are restricted. This restriction can not be Such That They transfer makes it impossible or excessively difficult. The Same Applies To the allocation of shares or any community. A transfer in violation of a restriction is invalid.

2Where the statutes the transfer of shares subject to the approval or an organ of the company or third party, the approval is Deemed Granted if not in the statutes within-a Prescribed period not Exceeding three months, the decision has Reached leg or if the shareholder together with the refusal of approval task Receives one or more candidates who are willing to share When The application for approval relates to buy. This arrangement Should Be Such That the shareholder who so requests will receive a price equal to the value of his share or to transfer shares, Determined by one or more independent experts.

3Where the statutes providence That a shareholder who wants to alienate one or more shares must first offer it to fellow shareholders or by a body or company to designate the third, the scheme must be Such That the shareholder who so requests a price equal to the Receives value or to transfer his share or shares, Determined by one or more independent experts. The shareholder will be Entitled to with draw the offer if this is done within-one month after he Announced to the candidates he has the All which the offer relates to shares to sell and at what price. If it is Determined That not all of the All which the offer relates to shares are purchased, the supplier shares within-a period specified in the statutes or at least three months after adoption That may Freely transfer.

4The company itself may only with the consent of the shareholder referred to in the second or third paragraph, a prospective purchaser.

5Bepalingen in the statutes regarding the transferability of shares shall not apply if the holder under the law to transfer his share to a previous holder is required.

Article 87a

1The Regulations may provide that in cases specified in the Statute, the shareholder has held his shares to offer and transfer. The statutes may determine thereby that while shareholder obligations to offer or transfer fails, his voting rights, its right to participate in the meeting and its right to benefits is suspended.

2nd Regulations may provide that if a shareholder is not in the statutes within a reasonable time to determine its statutory obligations to offer and transfer of its shares outstanding, the Company is irrevocably authorized to offer shares and transfer. If no candidates to whom the shareholder will be able to transfer all his shares in accordance with rules in the statutes, lacks the authority and consent of the shareholder as provided in paragraph 1 relieved.

3rd arrangement should be such that the shareholder who so requests will receive a price equal to the value of his share or shares, determined by one or more independent experts.

Article 87b

1The Regulations may provide that the shareholder who is not or no longer meets the requirements set out in the statutes the vote, the right to participate in the general assembly and the right to benefits is suspended.

2Indien the shareholder one or more of the rights mentioned in paragraph 1 can not exercise and the shareholder is not obliged to offer its shares and transfer, was irrevocably in the statutes of the requirements relieved when the company within three months at the request of the shareholder has nominated candidates to whom he will be able to transfer all his shares in accordance with rules in the statutes.

3rd arrangement should be such that the shareholder who so requests will receive a price equal to the value of his share or shares, determined by one or more independent experts.

Article 88

1The right to establish a share of usufruct of the statutes can not be excluded or limited.

2 The shareholder has the right to vote the shares subject to a usufruct.

3 Notwithstanding the preceding paragraph, the voting rights to the usufructuary, if that is the establishment of the usufruct and the usufructuary is a person to whom the shares may be freely transferred. If the fruit is a person to whom the shares are not freely transferable, is it the right to vote solely, if at the establishment of the usufruct and both that provision and - upon transfer of the usufruct - the transfer of voting rights approved by the corporate body designated by the statutes to grant approval to a proposed transfer of shares, or - in the absence of such designation - by the general meeting. The provisions of the preceding sentence may be waived in the statutes. A usufruct referred to in Articles 19 and 21 of Book 4, the voting rights also to the usufructuary, unless the establishment of the usufruct by the parties or by the magistrate on the basis of article 23 paragraph 4 of Book 4, otherwise .

4 The shareholder who has no voting rights, and the usufructuary right to vote shall have the rights which by law are granted to the holders of depositary receipts for shares issued energy company. The usufructuary has no voting rights, these rights, unless it by the constitution or the transfer of the usufruct or the statutes of the company will be remembered.

5 If the statutes of the company provide otherwise, are also the shareholder from the share arises rights, seeking to acquire shares, except that he was the value of those rights shall reimburse to the beneficiary, provided that under his right of usufruct thereto entitled.

Article 89

1The power to pledge a bearer share in the statutes can not be excluded or limited. Lien on shares may be located, insofar as the statutes provide otherwise.

2 The shareholder has voting rights on the pledged shares.

3 Notwithstanding the preceding paragraph, the voting rights to the lienholder, if that is the establishment of the pledge and the pledgee is a person to whom the shares may be freely transferred. If the pledgee is a person to whom the shares are not freely transferable, is it the right to vote solely, if at the creation of the pledge, and the provision is approved by the corporate body by the articles designated for approval to grant a proposed transfer of shares, or - in the absence of such designation - by the general meeting. Another occurs in the rights of the pledgee, then only allow him to vote, if the institution referred to in the preceding sentence or, failing that, the general meeting approves transfer of the franchise. The provisions of the preceding three sentences can be made in the statutes.

4 The shareholder who has no voting rights, and lienholders who vote shall have the rights conferred by law upon the holders of depositary receipts for shares issued energy company. The pledgee who has no voting rights, these rights, unless it by the constitution or the transfer of the lien or the statutes of the company will be remembered.

5 The provisions of the statutes regarding the sale and transfer of shares shall apply to the sale and transfer of shares by the pledgee or verblijving of the shares to the pledgee, provided that the pledgee all regarding the alienation and transfer to the shareholder rights accruing to exercise and fulfill its obligations in this respect.

6 Is the lien established in accordance with Article 86c paragraph 4, then the rights under this article first increases after the pledgee's lien by the company admitted or has been served.

Article 89a

1The limited liability company may own shares or depositary receipts in pledge, if:

ade to be pledged shares are fully paid,

BThe nominal amount to be pledged and already held in pledge or held as treasury shares and depositary receipts combined does not exceed one tenth of the issued capital, and

cde general meeting has approved the pledge agreement.

2This article does not apply to shares and depositary receipts for which a financial undertaking that the business of banking in the Netherlands may exercise under the Act on Financial Supervision in the ordinary course of its business in pledge. These shares and certificates are excluded from the application of Articles 98 paragraph 2 sub b and 98a paragraph 3.

Article 90

1NA transfer or allocation of a share will not be paid any of the previous shareholders for the amount due thereon are jointly and severally liable towards the corporation. The Board may, together with the Supervisory Board the previous shareholder in authentic or registered deed of further liability release, in which event the liability nonetheless existed for deposits, issued within one year after the date of the authentic instrument or private is registered.

2 If a previous shareholder pays, he enters into the rights that the company has against subsequent holders.

Article 91 [repealed on 01/01/1992]

Article 91a

1The holder of bearer shares, all shares in the capital of the company has acquired, gives written notice thereof to the company within eight days after the last acquisition.

2 The holder of bearer shares who ceases holders of all shares in the capital of the company by a third one or more of its shares, this gives written notice to the company within eight days thereafter. If the holder of all shares dies or by merger or division ceases to exist, give the purchasers thereof in writing to the company within one month after the death respectively the merger or the division.

3 If all shares in the capital of the company belong to a marriage community or a community of a registered partnership, the company is considered a single shareholder within the meaning of this article and rest on each of the participants the obligation to notify under this article.

4 For the purposes of this article shares held by the company or its subsidiaries are not counted.

Article 92

1For where the statutes do not otherwise specified, all shares in proportion to their amount equal rights and obligations.

2 The limited liability company, the shareholders or certificate holders who are in similar circumstances, the same treatment.

3rd statutes may provide that shares of a certain kind of special rights as specified in the Statute on the control of the company are connected.

Article 92a

1Hij as a shareholder for its own account at least 95% of the issued capital of the corporation provides, be made against the other joint shareholders a claim to transfer their shares to the plaintiff. The same applies if two or more group companies this part of the capital together, and together provide the claim set to transfer to one of them.

2 About the application judge at first instance the Enterprise Chamber of the Amsterdam Court. From the statement is only cassation.

3 If one or more defendants against default is granted, the court of its own motion whether the plaintiff or plaintiffs fulfill the requirements of paragraph 1.

4 The court rejects the claim against all defendants off, if a defendant despite the fee would suffer serious physical injury by the transfer, a defendant is the holder of a share to which the statutes, a special law on the control of the company or undertake a plaintiff against a defendant has waived his claim in the jurisdiction.

5 If the court finds that paragraphs 1 and 4 the assignment of the claim does not prevent, he may recommend that one or three experts, messages about the value of the shares to be transferred. The first three sentences of Article 350 paragraph 3 and Articles 351 and 352 apply. The judge sets the price at which the shares to be transferred on a day set by him. As long and as far as the price is not paid, he is plus

interest at the statutory rate, from that day to the transfer, distributions on the shares during this period will be payable, stretching on the day of payment to partial payment of the price.

6 The judge who assigns the claim, condemns the transferee to those to whom the shares belong or will belong to the set price, with interest payable against delivery of the unencumbered right to the shares. The court indicates that the costs of the proceedings if he believes that such a statement belongs. A defendant who has made no defense, does not pay the costs.

7 State the order to transfer to judicial res fixed, it shall notify the transferee of the day and place of payment and the price in writing to the holders of the offered shares of whom know the address. He also announced in a national newspaper, unless he knows all the address.

8 The buyer can always its obligations under paragraphs 6 and 7 by ridding the fixed price with interest for all outstanding shares not taken to consign, including notice of his known rights of pledge and usufruct and herds known to him. This communication is batter of the shares on the entitlement. By consign it goes right to the shares transferred to him and go unencumbered rights of pledge or usufruct on the entitlement. To share and dividend coupons which after the transition payments are made payable may thereafter no claim against the company more binding. The buyer makes consign and the price per share at that time known in the manner of paragraph 7.

Section 3. The ability of the corporation

Article 93

1Uit acts performed on behalf of a limited company to be established, rights and obligations arise only for the company when such acts after its inception, express or implied endorsement or pursuant to paragraph 4 is connected.

2 Those who perform a legal act on behalf of a limited company to be established, unless with respect to that act otherwise expressly stipulated, therefore jointly and severally liable, until the company after its creation the act ratified.

3 If the company has its obligations under the ratified act fails, those who on behalf of the company to be formed acted jointly and severally liable for the damages that the third consequently suffers, when they knew or could reasonably know that the company's commitments was unable to perform Without prejudice to the liability in respect of the directors because of the ratification. The knowledge that the company was unable to perform its obligations, it is presumed to exist if the company within one year after the establishment in a state of bankruptcy.

4 The founders, the company in the memorandum only connect by issuing shares accepting deposits thereon, to appoint directors, the appointment of commissioners and perform legal acts referred to in Article 94 paragraph 1. If a founder has not been adequately diligence, Articles 9 and 138, mutatis mutandis.

Article 93a

1Indien before or at the creation of shares shall be paid in cash, must comply with the memorandum attached to one or more statements, alleging that the amounts on the establishment to place shares must be paid:

ahetzij immediately after the establishment will be available from the limited liability company,

bhetzij all at the same time not earlier than five months before the creation, in a separate account which were available only after the establishment of the company will stand, if the company accepts deposits in the deed.

2 If foreign money is deposited must prove the statement against how much money could be freely traded in a day when under Article 80a paragraph 3 the price determines the payment requirement.

3Een statement referred to in paragraph 1 may only be made by a financial undertaking under Article 1:1 of the Act on Financial Supervision in the European Union or a State Party to the Agreement on the European Economic Area business of a bank may exercise. The certificate may be issued only to a notary.

4 Are the creation of the account referred to in subparagraph b of paragraph 1, shall be removed, then the founders jointly and severally against the company related to reimbursement of such amounts, until the company has explicitly endorsed the withdrawals.

5th notary, the bank whose statement he received immediate notification of the establishment. If the establishment does not continue, he must return the bank statement.

6 If after the establishment in a foreign currency is deposited, explains the company within two weeks after the deposit a declaration referred to in paragraph 2, of a bench in the third paragraph at the office of the trade.

Article 94

1Rechtshandelingen:

ain relation to the acquisition of shares with special obligations to the corporation be placed,

vomiting acquire shares other than those on which participation in the public company is open to the public,

cstrekkende for any advantage to ensure a founder of the limited liability company or a third in the establishment,

dbetreffende for shares other than cash,

in its entirety should be included in the memorandum or in a document given to it in original or certified copy is attached and to which the memorandum refers. If the preceding sentence not been complied with, can the company from such acts no rights or obligations.

2 After the founding, in the preceding paragraph, legal transactions without prior approval of the general meeting may be made only if and insofar as the government the necessary powers expressly granted by the statutes.

3 From the provisions of this article except as provided in paragraph 2 of Article 80 agreements.

Article 94a

1Indien in establishing payment for shares other than in cash is agreed, the founders make a description of the contribution, stating the value assigned and the valuation methods applied. These methods must conform to standards in society be considered acceptable. The description refers to the condition of the contribution on a day not earlier than six months before the establishment is located. The description shall be signed by all founders and the attached memorandum.

2 About the description of the contribution to an accountant as defined in Article 393, paragraph a statement that the memorandum should be attached. It declares that the value of the contribution, applying in society accepted accounting methods, at least the amount of the payment obligation, expressed in money, to which the contribution must be met. If it is known that the value after the description has been significantly reduced, a second explanation is required.

3rd description and the auditors are not required, when required in the memorandum provided regarding:

ainbreng of securities or money market instruments referred to in Article 1:1 of the Act on Financial Supervision, provided that such securities or money market instruments are valued at the weighted average price at which they are three months preceding the date of the contribution on a regulated market as referred Article 1:1 of the Act on Financial Supervision are traded;

binbreng other than cash, other than securities or instruments referred to in subparagraph a, that is valued by an independent person who according to his training and efficacy is experienced in performing valuations, provided expert valuation made by applying in society as accepted accounting principles and the value of the contribution is determined on a day not earlier than six months before the date of the contribution is;

cinbreng other than cash, other than securities or money market instruments referred to in subparagraph a, whose value is derived from financial statements that is determined over the last year that the asset's contribution and in accordance with Directive 2006/43/EC of the European Parliament and Council of 17 May 2006 on statutory audits of annual accounts and consolidated accounts, amending Council Directives 78/660/EEC and 83/349/EEC and repealing Directive 84/253/EEC (OJ L 157) is subject to an audit.

4Indien the establishment is known that the rate is affected by exceptional circumstances which cause the value of securities or instruments referred to in paragraph 3, subparagraph a, on the day of the contribution will be significantly modified or if the creation is known that the value of contributions referred to in paragraph 3, b or c, on the day of the transfer as a result of new qualifying circumstances have changed significantly, the founders still required to make a description which is signed by all founders and on which an auditor referred to in paragraph 2 shall be taken. The description and the audit are attached to the memorandum. Made the contribution after the establishment and in the period between the creation and insertion known that circumstances referred to in the first sentence have occurred, then the board is obliged to still obtain a description to which an auditor referred to in paragraph 2 shall be taken.

5Indien in establishing payment for shares other than in cash is agreed upon under the provisions of paragraph 3, explains the company within one month after the day of the input to the Commercial a statement from the founders down where the input is described, indicating of its assigned value and valuation methods applied. The statement shall also indicate whether the value assigned at least the amount of the payment obligation, expressed in money, to which input is to be met and further provides that in the period between the valuation and contribution no new qualifying circumstances have occurred. The founders sign the declaration, if the signature of one or more of them shall be stated and reasons given.

6 The description and auditors are not required if the following conditions:

aAll founders have decided to waive the preparation of expert testimony;

leg or more persons in whose accounts Title 9 applies, or under applicable law to meet the requirements of the Fourth Council Directive of the European Communities on the company, all shares to be issued for a consideration other than cash ;

celke transferring entity has at the time of the contribution of non-distributable reserves, as necessary by the board to do so apart from distributable reserves, the size of the par value of shares held by the entity;

delke transferring entity certify that an amount of at least the nominal value of the products he acquired shares will make available for the payment of debts of the company to third parties, arising in the period between the placement of the shares and one year after the adopted annual accounts of the Company for the year of the contribution was deposited at the office of the trade, where the company is unable to satisfy the creditors and their claims within two years after such deposit in writing to one of the transferring persons have given up;

Eelke transferring entity has its last adopted balance sheet and notes, with auditors thereto, deposited at the office of the trade and since the balance sheet date are not yet eighteen months have passed;

Felke transferring entity excludes a reserve on the size of the par value of shares held by him and can do so from the nature reserves, this does not prevent;

gde company does at the office of the register referred to in a statement of the decision or transferring entity does the same office stating his declaration mentioned under d.

7 If the preceding paragraph is applied, an transferring legal entity against the contribution of shares taken not to alienate the period mentioned in that paragraph d, and he must reserve referred to in that paragraph f persist until two years after that period . Afterwards, the reserve will be held until the specified amount of outstanding claims as referred to in paragraph d. The original reserve is reduced by payments on the specified claims.

8 The transferring entity and all of paragraph 6 d referred to creditors, the subdistrict of residence of the company requests a government on the progress to set up, seeking their satisfaction thereof pursuant to paragraph 6 d amounts made available. Where necessary, the provisions of the Bankruptcy Act concerning the verification of claims and settlement of analogy. A creditor can not claim with a debt to a transferring legal reckoning. About the progress made only under the burden of government are available and they can only be realized under this burden, except for debts arising out of acts which the trustee in his capacity have been made. The subdistrict regulates the powers and remuneration of the trustee, he may be available at any time.

Article 94b

1Indien after the establishment for shares other than in cash is agreed, the company pursuant to Article 94a paragraph 1 a description of the contribution. The description refers to the state on a day not earlier than six months before the date on which the shares are taken or at which an increase it is issued or on which they agreed. The directors sign the description, if the signature of one or more of them shall be stated and reasons given.

2 Article 94a paragraph 2 shall apply mutatis mutandis.

3in in Article 94a paragraph 3, section a, b and c cases referred to the board may decide to refrain from drawing up the description and the audit report. Is known for the contribution that circumstances referred to in Article 94a paragraph 4, first sentence, has occurred, then the board is obliged to still obtain a description to which an auditor referred to in Article 94a paragraph 2 shall be taken.

4Indien after the establishment for shares other than in cash is agreed upon under the provisions of paragraph 3, explains the company no later than the eighth day before the input to the Commercial an announcement which is inserted down which is described indicating the value assigned, the valuation methods applied, the names of the contributors, the amount of said unpaid part of subscribed capital and the date of the Article 96 paragraph 1 decision to issue. The notice shall also indicate whether the value assigned at least the amount of the payment obligation, expressed in money, to which input is to be met and further provides that with respect to the valuation of the contribution no new qualifying circumstances have occurred . The directors shall sign the notice, if the signature of one or more of them shall be stated and reasons given. Within a month after the date of the contribution puts the company at the Commercial submitting a declaration stating that in the period between the notice referred to in the first sentence and the input no new qualifying circumstances with regard to the valuation have occurred . The directors sign the declaration, if the signature of one or more of them shall be stated and reasons given.

5Blijven a description and audit referred to in paragraph 3, second sentence, omitted and is the insertion site in accordance with Article 94a paragraph 3, b or c, then one or more holders of shares on the day of the Article 96 paragraph 1 decision referred to issue solely or jointly at least five percent of the issued capital of the board that still require a description format for which an audit referred to in Article 94a paragraph 2 shall be taken. The board will address this implementation, provided that the shareholders' desire later than the day preceding the date of the contribution to the board have made themselves known and they at the time of submission of the application is still at least five percent of the issued capital, such that the decision was issued, represent.

6 If all shareholders have decided to waive the preparation of the description and audit in accordance with Article 94a paragraph 6, in bg, is pursued, no description or audit is required, and Article 94a paragraphs 7 and 8 shall apply mutatis mutandis.

7 The Company shall, within eight days after the day the shares are acquired or on which the additional payment became due, the auditor's contribution or a copy thereof at the office of the register stating the names of the contributors and the amount thus paid part of the capital.

8 This Article shall not apply where the contribution consists of shares or certificates of shares, therein convertible rights or profit shares of another legal entity, which the company, a public bid, provided such securities or any part thereof are admitted to trading on a regulated market or multilateral trading facility, as defined in Article 1:1 of the Act on financial supervision or with a regulated market or multilateral trading facility from a State not a Member State.

Article 94c

1one act the corporation has done without the approval of the General Assembly or without the declaration referred to in paragraph 3, for the benefit of the company be destroyed, if the transaction:

astrekt to obtain goods, including claims that are settled, that a year before the incorporation or subsequently owned by a founder, and

ba done before two years have elapsed since the registration of the company in the commercial.

2 If the approval is requested, the company should include a description of the available goods and the consideration. The description refers to the condition of the described on a day which are not affect the setting lies. In describing the values that have to return the goods and be granted, the valuation methods applied. These methods must conform to standards in society be considered acceptable. The directors sign the description, if the signature of one or more of them shall be stated and reasons given.

3 Article 94a paragraph 2 shall apply, except that the statement must include the value of the goods to obtain, by applying in society accepted accounting methods, corresponding to at least the value of the consideration.

4Article 94b paragraph 3 shall apply mutatis mutandis. Does an act carried out applying the preceding sentence, it can not be destroyed under paragraph 1 in the absence of the declaration referred to in paragraph 3. Article 94b paragraph 4 shall apply, except that the date of the transaction referred to in paragraph 1 is mentioned in the description.

5 On the availability for inspection and copy at the disposal of the documents referred to in the preceding paragraphs, Article 102 shall apply mutatis mutandis.

6 The company shall, within eight days after the act or after the approval, if granted afterwards, in the third paragraph statement or a copy thereof at the office of the trade.

7 For the purposes of this article are excluded:

averkrijgingen at public auction or exchange,

bverkrijgingen under the stipulated conditions for the ordinary operations of the company belong

cverkrijgingen which a declaration referred to in Article 94a paragraph 2 has been made,

dverkrijgingen due to merger or division.

Article 94d [repealed on 20/01/1986]

Article 95

1The limited liability company may not own shares.

2 Shares held by the company in violation of the preceding paragraph has taken go at the time of taking over the joint administrators. Each director is severally liable for the paying of these shares with the legal interest from that date. Are the shares placed in the establishment, then this paragraph shall apply to the joint founders.

Take another 3 a share in his own name but on behalf of the company, he shall be considered for his own account.

Article 96

1The following the setting up limited liability company may only issue shares pursuant to a resolution of the general meeting or other corporate body for that purpose by resolution of the general meeting or by the statutes for a specified period not exceeding five years is appropriate. In the designation must state the number of shares may be issued. The designation may be renewed for no longer than five years renewable. Unless the appointment provides otherwise, it may not be withdrawn.

2 Are there different types of shares, then the validity of the decision of the general meeting to issue or to designate a prior or concurrent resolution of approval by each group of holders of shares of the same class whose rights are affected by the issue.

3 The company shall, within eight days after a decision by the general meeting to issue or to designate a full text thereof at the office of the trade.

4The company shall within eight days after each calendar quarter at the Commercial description of any issue of shares in the last calendar quarter, stating the number and type.

5 This article shall apply mutatis mutandis to the granting of rights to subscribe for shares, but shall not apply to the issuance of shares to a person who exercises a previously acquired right to subscribe for shares.

Article 96a

1Behoudens the two following paragraphs, every shareholder has a preferential issue of shares in proportion to the aggregate amount of his shares. Unless the statutes provide otherwise, it nevertheless made in respect of shares issued for consideration other than cash. He has no respect of shares issued to employees of the corporation or of a group company.

2 Where the statutes provide otherwise, shareholders who have

aniet above a certain percentage of the nominal amount or only slightly above the share in profits, or

bniet above the nominal amount or only slightly above share in a liquidation surplus,

no pre-emptive shares to be issued.

3 To the extent the statutes provide otherwise, the shareholders have no pre-emptive shares to be issued in one of the preceding paragraph a and b defined types.

4 The company announces the issuance of pre-emption rights and the time that can be exercised in the Government Gazette and in a national newspaper, unless all the shares are denominated and the announcement to all shareholders in writing to the address stated by them.

5 The preferential right may be exercised for at least two weeks after the date of announcement in the Gazette or after dispatch of the notice to shareholders.

6 The preferential right may be limited or excluded by the general meeting. In this proposal, the reasons for the proposal and the selection of the proposed issue price will be explained in writing. The preferential right may be limited or excluded by virtue of Article 96 paragraph 1 designated corporate body, if decided by the general meeting or by the statutes for a fixed period not exceeding five years has been designated to limit or exclude the emption. The designation may be renewed for no longer than five years renewable. Unless the appointment provides otherwise, it may not be withdrawn.

7 For a decision of the General Assembly to restrict or exclude pre-emptive or to designate a majority of at least two thirds of the votes cast if less than half of the issued capital is represented at the meeting. The company shall within eight days after the decision full text thereof at the office of the trade.

8 By the granting of rights to subscribe for shares, the shareholders a preferential right; the preceding paragraphs shall apply mutatis mutandis. Shareholders do not have shares that are issued to a person who exercises a previously acquired right to subscribe for shares.

Article 96b

Articles 96 and 96a do not apply to an investment company with variable capital

Article 97

If, in the case of issue of shares after its founding, announced what amount will be issued and only a smaller amount can be placed, that amount is placed only if the conditions of issue so provide.

Article 98

1Verkrijging by the corporation of partly paid shares in its capital is void.

2Volgestorte own shares The Company may not obtain or if equity less the acquisition price is not less than the paid-up capital plus the reserves required by law or the statutes must be observed. Notwithstanding the preceding sentence, amounts, if shares of the company are admitted to trading on a regulated market or multilateral trading facility, as defined in Article 1:1 of the Act on Financial Supervision in a regulated market or an or multilateral trading facility from a non-Member State is the nominal amount of shares in its capital which the company acquires, holds or pledge, or which are held by a subsidiary, not more than half of the issued capital.

3 The requirement in paragraph 2, the amount of equity according to the last balance sheet, less the purchase price for shares in the capital of the company, the amount of loans referred to in Article 98c paragraph 2 and distributions of profits or reserves to others that it and its subsidiaries after the balance sheet date. Is a more than six months without the financial statements were adopted, then an acquisition under paragraph 2 is not allowed.

4Verkrijging other than to be permitted only if and insofar as the general meeting is authorized by the board. This authorization is valid for five years. Notwithstanding the previous sentence applies in case the shares of a company are admitted to trading on a regulated market or multilateral trading facility, as defined in Article 1:1 of the Act on Financial Supervision in a regulated market or an or multilateral trading facility from a state outside this authorization for a maximum of eighteen months.

The general meeting determines the number of authorized shares may be acquired, how they may be obtained and the limits within which the price should be. The articles may acquire the company's own shares exclude or limit.

5 The authorization is not required, insofar as the statutes allow the company to acquire own shares under a scheme applicable, transfer to employees of the company or its group companies. These shares must be included in the listing of a scholarship.

6 Paragraphs 1-4 do not apply to shares held by the Company under the overall title.

7th paragraphs 2-4 shall not apply to shares held by a financial undertaking under the Act on Financial Supervision in the Netherlands the business of banking may exercise, on behalf and on behalf of another obtains.

8 The paragraphs 2-4 shall not apply to an investment company with variable capital. The issued capital of such an investment, minus the amount of shares that it holds itself, at least one tenth of the share capital.

9 Under the concept of equity in this article includes depositary receipts.

Article 98a

1Verkrijging of shares in contravention of paragraphs 2-4 of the previous article shall be void. The directors are jointly and severally liable to the vendor in good faith by the nullity damage.

2 Shares and share certificates in bearer form that the corporation in contravention of paragraphs 2-4 of the preceding Article has obtained, go at the time of the acquisition of the joint administrators. Each director is liable for compensation to the company of the purchase price with legal interest thereon from that date.

3 The company may no longer than three years after conversion to a corporation or after its own shares for no consideration or under general title has been obtained, together with its subsidiaries hold shares in its capital more than one tenth of the subscribed capital, own shares they pledge themselves has to be counted. The shares which the company holds too much, go to the end of the last day of those years on the joint board. These are jointly and severally liable for payment to the company of the value of the shares at that time with the legal interest from that date. The term shares in this paragraph includes depositary receipts.

4 The preceding paragraph shall not apply to any fully paid their own share of the Company under the general title has been obtained and within three years since then, disposed of or withdrawn.

5 The third paragraph shall apply to any certificate or own share of the company pursuant to paragraph five of the preceding Article has been obtained without the authorization of the general meeting and that they hold for one year.

Article 98b

If another person in his own name on behalf of the public company shares in its capital or depositary receipts obtained, it shall forthwith upon payment to the company transfer. If these shares are denominated is the second paragraph of the preceding Article shall apply mutatis mutandis.

Article 98c

1The company may not, with a view to taking or acquisition by others of shares in its capital or depositary receipts, provide security, a price guarantee, is any other way or be severally or otherwise next to or for others. This prohibition also applies to its subsidiaries.

2nd Company and its subsidiaries may not, with a view to taking or acquisition by others of shares in the capital of the company or depositary receipts, loans, unless the board so decides, and there met the following conditions:

aThe granting the loan, including interest received by the company and the securities which the company provided, shall be at fair market conditions;

BThe equity, less the amount of the loan is not smaller than the paid-up capital plus the reserves required by law or the statutes must be held;

cde creditworthiness of the third or, when the multiparty transactions, of each counterparty thereto is carefully examined;

dindien the loan is provided in order to subscribe for shares in the context of an increase in the subscribed capital of the company or with a view to the acquisition of shares by the company in its own capital, the price at which the shares are or acquired equitable.

3Voor the requirement in paragraph 2, subsection b, the amount of equity according to the last balance sheet, less the purchase price for shares in the capital of the company and distributions of profits or reserves to others that it and its subsidiaries after the balance sheet date. Is a more than six months without the financial statements were adopted, then a transaction referred to in paragraph 2 is not allowed.

4th Company maintains a non-distributable reserve equal to the amount of the loans referred to in paragraph 2.

5Een decision of the Board to provide a loan referred to in paragraph 2 is subject to the prior approval of the General Assembly. The decision to adopt is taken by a majority of two thirds of the votes cast if less than half of the issued share capital represented at the meeting. Notwithstanding the previous sentence in the case of shares or certificates of shares of the company are admitted to trading on a regulated market as referred to in Article 1:1 of the Act on Financial Supervision or on a multilateral trading facility as referred to in Article 1:1 of the Act on Financial Supervision clearance decision taken by at least 95 percent of the votes cast.

6Wanneer to the general meeting referred to in paragraph 5 approval is sought shall be prescribed by the notice convening the general meeting. Simultaneously with the notice is at the offices of the company a report for inspection by the shareholders and holders of depositary receipts issued by the Company of its shares placed stating the reasons for granting the loan, the company related interest, the conditions of the loan will be provided, the rate at which the shares by the third will be taken or obtained and attached to the loan involve risks for the liquidity and solvency of the company.

7th Within eight days after the approval referred to in paragraph 5, in paragraph 6 shall report or a copy thereof at the office of the trade.

8th paragraphs 1 to 7 do not apply if shares or share certificates or acquired by or on behalf of employees of the company or its group companies.

9th paragraphs 1 to 7 do not apply to a financial undertaking under the Act on Financial Supervision in the Netherlands may exercise the business of banking, where it acts in the ordinary course of its business.

Article 98d

1one subsidiary may own account or ensure that no shares in the capital of the corporation. Such shares may only acquire subsidiaries for its own account or do obtain, if the corporation itself under paragraphs 1-6 of Article 98 may acquire own shares.

2 If any breach of the previous paragraph, the directors of the corporation are jointly and severally liable to pay compensation to the subsidiary of the purchase price with legal interest thereon from the time when the shares have been taken or obtained. Payment of compensation made against transfer of such shares. A director need not reimburse the purchase price, if he proves that the subscription or acquisition does not meet the limited liability company is to blame.

3 A subsidiary may,

anadat she subsidiary has become

bnadat the subsidiary company of which it is converted into a limited liability company, or

cnadat it as a subsidiary of the capital of the corporation for no consideration or under general title has been obtained,

no longer than three years with the corporation and its other subsidiaries of these shares for its own account or make love than a tenth of the issued capital. The directors of the corporation are jointly and severally liable for compensation to the subsidiary of the value of the shares that they too hold or does hold at the end of the last day of those years, with legal interest from that date. Payment of compensation made against transfer of the shares. A director need not pay compensation if he proves that it is not the corporation is attributable to the shares still held.

4 Under the concept of equity in this article includes depositary receipts.

Article 99

1The general meeting may resolve to reduce the issued capital by canceling shares or by the amount of shares by reducing. In this decision the shares to which the decision relates shall be designated and must implement the decision governs.

2 A decision to withdraw may only relate to shares that the company itself or for which they hold certificates or all shares of a class for which the issuance of the Constitution states that they can be withdrawn with repayment, either the shares uitgelote of a species for which the issuance of the Constitution states that they can be chosen at random with repayment.

3 Reducing the amount of shares without repayment and without waiver of the obligation to pay must be in proportion to all shares of the same class. The requirement of proportionality may be waived by agreement of all shareholders involved.

4 Partial repayment on shares or exemption from the obligation to pay is only possible to implement a decision to reduce the amount of the shares. Such repayment or release must be in proportion to all shares, except for the issuance of a particular class of shares in the statutes provide that reimbursement or exemption may be made only to those shares for which shares are subject to the requirement of proportionality. The requirement of proportionality may be waived by agreement of all shareholders involved.

5 Are there different types of shares, then a decision to reduce capital a prior or concurrent resolution of approval is required from each group of holders of shares of the same class whose rights are prejudiced.

6 For a decision to reduce capital, a majority of at least two thirds of the votes cast if less than half of the issued capital is represented at the meeting. This provision shall apply mutatis mutandis to a decision referred to in the fifth paragraph.

7 The convocation of a meeting where a decision mentioned in this article is taken, state the purpose of capital reduction and the manner of implementation. The second, third and fourth paragraph of Article 123 shall apply mutatis mutandis.

Article 100

1The limited company explains in Article 99 paragraph 1 shall decide at the office of the Company Registry and announced the filing in a national newspaper.

2 The company must, on pain of a statement founded objection referred to in the following paragraph, for each creditor who requires collateral or make him give any other guarantee for the satisfaction of his claim. This does not apply if the creditor has adequate safeguards or the assets of the company provide sufficient assurance that the claim will be met.

3 Within two months after the notice mentioned in the first paragraph, any creditor by a petition to the court against the decision to reduce capital in revolt, indicating the guarantee that is sought. The court shall reject the application if the applicant has failed to show that as a result of the capital reduction doubt about the satisfaction of his claim is legitimate and that the company has given enough guarantees for the satisfaction of his claim.

4 Before the court decides, he can the company the opportunity to complete it within a certain period specified by him deposit it. On a legal remedy he may, if the capital has already been reduced, the lodging of a deposit plus a penalty recommended link.

5 A resolution to reduce the subscribed capital shall not take effect until resistance can be done. If timely objection is made, the decision will take effect once the application has been withdrawn or the elimination of the resistance is feasible. A reduction of the capital requirement deed of amendment can not be earlier past.

6 If the company reduces its capital because of losses to an amount not lower than that of its own funds, it shall not guarantee to give the decision immediately.

7 This Article shall not apply if an investment company with variable capital shares acquired lawfully withdraw.

Article 101

1Jaarlijks within five months of the year the company, subject to extension of this deadline by up to six months by the general meeting under special circumstances, the Board shall prepare annual accounts and submit them to shareholders for inspection at the offices of the company. Within this period, the board also the annual report for inspection by the shareholders unless the Articles 396 paragraph 7, or 403 for the company funds. The board of the company to which Articles 158 to 161 and 164 apply, send annual accounts to in Article 158, paragraph 11 shall Works.

2 The accounts shall be signed by the directors and the auditors; if the signature of one or more of them shall be stated and reasons given.

3rd annual accounts are adopted by the General Assembly. Adoption of the annual discharge shall not serve as a director respectively commissioner.

4Besluiten which the accounts are established by the statutes are not subject to the approval of an organ of the company or third parties.

5th statutes contain no provisions that allow binding rules or proposals for the accounts or any item shall be given.

6th statutes may provide that a body other than the company's general meeting has the power to determine what part of the profit for the year is set aside or how the loss will be processed.

7 Our Minister of Economic Affairs may upon request, compelling reasons to waive the obligation to draw up, discuss it and adopt the financial statements.

Article 102

1The limited company ensures that its annual accounts, annual report and pursuant to Article 392 paragraph 1 to add data from the call for the general meeting, for their treatment, its premises are present. The holders of its shares or depositary receipts issued with its cooperation, the documents there and there is no charge obtain a copy.

2 read these shares or bearer certificates or the Company has outstanding debentures to bearer, it may also examine any documents, for if they should be made public after adoption, and realize the maximum cost thereof to obtain a copy. This authority lapses if the documents are deposited at the office of the trade.

Article 103 [Repealed at 31-12-2006]

Article 104

Charged by the statutory reserves A deficit may only be extinguished to the extent permitted by law.

Article 105

1For where the statutes do not provide otherwise, the profit the shareholders benefit.

2 The limited liability company may pay shareholders and others entitled to the distributable profits benefits only insofar as its equity exceeds the amount of the paid-up capital plus the reserves required by law or the statutes must be observed.

3 Payment of profits made after adoption of the annual accounts showing that this is permissible.

4 The Company may make interim distributions, if the rules permit and the requirement of paragraph is evidenced by an interim accounts. This relates to the position of the Company not earlier than the first day of the third month before the month in which the decision to pay is made public. It is prepared in accordance with the society deemed acceptable valuation methods. The net assets are under the law or the reserve amounts. It shall be signed by the directors; if the signature of one or more of them shall be stated and reasons given. The Company shall file the statement of assets in the Commercial Register within eight days after the date of the decision to pay is announced.

5 In calculating the distribution of profits the shares that the company in its own capital, in part, unless the statute otherwise.

6 In calculating the amount of profit that each share will be paid, is only the amount of the payments due to the nominal amount of the shares eligible, unless the statute otherwise.

7 The statutes may provide that the claim of a shareholder is not barred by lapse of five years, but only after a longer term expires. Such determination shall then apply mutatis mutandis to the claim of a holder of a certificate of a share of the shareholder.

8 A benefit in violation of the second or fourth paragraph should be repaid by the shareholder or other profit owner who knew or should have known that the distribution was not permissible.

9Geen of shareholders may be entirely excluded from sharing in the profits.

10The Regulations may provide that the profits to which holders of shares of a certain kind of entitled wholly or partly for their benefit will be reserved.

Article 106 [repealed on 09/01/1981]

Section 4. The general meeting

Article 107

1Aan the General Assembly should, within the law and the Articles of powers within the limits, not to the Board or assigned to others.

2 The board and the supervisory board shall provide it with all requested information, unless an overriding interest of the company opposes.

Article 107a

1Aan the approval of the general meeting are subject to the decisions of the board on a major change in the identity or character of the company or its business, in any case:

aoverdracht of the business or virtually the entire enterprise to a third party;

BThe into or termination of sustained cooperation of the company or a subsidiary with another legal entity or partnership or as fully liable partner in a limited partnership or partnership, if such cooperation or termination of major significance to the company;

chet acquiring or disposing of a participation in the capital of a company worth at least a third of the amount of assets per balance sheet with explanatory notes, if the company consolidated balance sheet, the consolidated balance sheet and notes according to the last adopted annual accounts of the Company, by or a subsidiary.

2The lack of approval of the General Assembly in a resolution referred to in paragraph 1 affect the authority of directors or not directors.

Article 108

1Jaarlijks at least one general meeting.

2 When the statutes are not a shorter period is prescribed, the annual meeting held within six months of the year the company.

Article 108a

Within three months after its administration is likely that the equity of the corporation has decreased to an amount equal to or less than half the paid-up capital, a general meeting held to discuss if necessary to be taken.

Article 109

The Board and the Supervisory Board are authorized to convene a general meeting in the statutes may be granted authority to others.

Article 110

1one or more shareholders who together hold at least one tenth of the issued capital, or such lesser amount as the statute, can the judge of the court at their request, be authorized to convene a general meeting . The court rejects the application if it does not appear that the applicants before the Board and the Supervisory Board in writing stating specifically the items to be discussed this request, addressed a general meeting be convened, and that neither the board nor the supervisory board - so in this case equally competent - the necessary measures taken to ensure that the general meeting within six weeks of the request could be held.

2 For the purposes of this article with holders of shares equivalent to the holders of depositary receipts issued with the cooperation of the company are issued.

3Tenzij the articles otherwise provide, to the requirement of written form of the request referred to in paragraph 1 are met if the request is recorded electronically.

Article 111

1The judge of the court shall, after hearing or notice of the limited liability company, the requested authorization, if the applicant summarily have do show that in the previous article have been fulfilled, and that they have a legitimate interest in keeping the meeting. The judge of the court shall determine the form and the deadlines for convening the general meeting. He may also appoint someone who with the guidance of the general meeting shall be responsible.

2 When the notice under paragraph stated that, under court authorization shall. The notice made in this way is valid, even if it appears that the authorization was wrongly granted.

3 Against the decision of the judge is no provision allowed, subject to cassation in the interest of the law.

Article 112

If they are, under Article 109 of this book or the articles to convene competent, have failed by Article 108 or Article 108a of the Book or the articles prescribed general meeting to hold, each shareholder by the judge the court be empowered to do so themselves. Article 110 paragraph 2 and Article 111 of this Book shall apply mutatis mutandis.

Article 113

1 Until the general meeting called for the shareholders and holders of depositary receipts issued with the cooperation of the company are issued.

2 The notice shall be published in a national newspaper.

3rd Regulations may provide that the holders of shares are called by means of written notices sent to the addresses of those shareholders as stated in the register of shareholders.

4Tenzij the statutes provide otherwise, if the holder of shares and the holder of the share certificates issued with the cooperation of the company are issued, consent, the notice made by an electronically readable and reproducible message sent to the address provided by him for this purpose the company has announced.

5th Regulations may provide that the holders of bearer shares and the holders of depositary receipts issued with the cooperation of the company are issued, be recalled by electronic notice made to the general meeting which directly and permanently accessible is.

Article 114

1When the notice shall state the business to be transacted or shall state that the shareholders and holders of depositary receipts issued by the Company of its shares at the offices of the company unable to examine.

2 With respect to subjects whose treatment was not stated in the notice or in the same fashion, with due observance of the notice period, can not lawfully be taken, unless the decision is taken unanimously at a meeting at which the entire issued capital is represented.

3 Notice that under the law or the statutes to the General Assembly should be directed, may be included either in the notice or in the document for inspection at the office of the company is filed, provided thereof in the notice mentioned.

Article 114a

1one item, which requested in writing by one or more shareholders who are authorized under the following paragraph entitled, is included in the notice or in the same way if the company has announced the request no later than the sixtieth day prior to the meeting and provided no major interest of the company opposes.

2To treatment may be requested by one or more shareholders who individually or collectively at least one hundredth of the issued capital or, if the shares are admitted to trading on a regulated market or multilateral trading facility, as defined in Article 1 1 of the Act on financial supervision or with a regulated market or multilateral trading facility from a non-Member State is at least a value of? 50 million. By Order in Council, this amount can be increased or decreased in relation to the development of wages and prices.

3in the statutes, the required portion of the capital or the value of the shares be reduced by and the deadline for submission of the request be shortened.

4For the purposes of this article with the holders of shares equivalent to the holders of certificates representing shares with the cooperation of the company are issued.

5Tenzij the articles otherwise provide, to the requirement of written form of the request referred to in paragraph 1 are met if the request is recorded electronically.

Article 115

Subject to the second sentence of the first paragraph of Article 111 of this Book, the notice shall be given not later than the fifteenth day before the meeting. That period was shorter or if the notice did not take place, then no valid resolutions may be adopted unless unanimously at a meeting at which the entire issued capital is represented.

Article 116

The general meetings are held in the Netherlands spot in the bylaws, or otherwise in the municipality where the corporation is domiciled. In a general meeting, held elsewhere than one may legitimately decide only be adopted if the entire issued capital is represented.

Article 117

1Iedere shareholder is entitled, in person or by written proxy, general meetings to attend, to speak and to vote. Holders of fractional shares, together constituting the value of a share shall exercise these rights jointly or by one of them, or by written proxy. The statutes, the power of shareholders to be represented should be limited. The power of shareholders to be represented by a lawyer, notary, notary, accountant or accounting consultant can not be excluded.

2 Each holder of a cooperation of the company issued a share certificate shall, in person or by written proxy, the general meeting to attend and to speak. The penultimate and the last sentence of paragraph 1 shall apply mutatis mutandis.

3rd statutes may provide that a shareholder is not entitled to participate in the meeting as long as he fails to comply with a legal or statutory obligation. Where the statute provides that the holders of shares of the evidence of their right before the general meeting must give in custody, be in the notice for that meeting listed the place and date at the latest to be made. That day can not be earlier than the seventh day of the meeting. If the association rules in accordance with the preceding provisions of this paragraph shall contain, these apply also to the holders of certificates representing shares with the cooperation of the company are issued.

4 The directors and auditors as such in the general meetings in an advisory capacity.

5th accountant to whom the assignment to audit the financial statements has been granted under Article 393 paragraph 1, shall be entitled to the general meeting which decides on the adoption of the accounts to attend and speak.

6Aan the requirement of a written power of attorney is met if the proxy is recorded electronically.

Article 117a

1The Regulations may provide that each shareholder is entitled to, in person or by written proxy, by means of electronic communication to the General Assembly to participate in it to speak and to vote.

2for the purposes of paragraph 1 requires that the shareholder via the electronic communication can be identified, directly take note of the proceedings of the meeting and exercise his voting rights. The bylaws may provide that additional requirement that the shareholder by electronic communication may participate in the deliberations.

° 3 or pursuant to the statutes may impose conditions on the use of electronic communication. If these conditions are made under the Statute, those disclosed in the notice.

4Lid 1 to 3 shall apply mutatis mutandis to the rights of any holder of a cooperation of the company issued a share certificate.

5Aan the requirement of a written power of attorney is met if the proxy is recorded electronically.

Article 117b

1The Regulations may provide that votes cast at the general meeting by electronic communication to be released on the same footing with the votes cast at the meeting. These votes will not be released earlier than in the third paragraph, last registration day.

2for the purposes of paragraph 1 as voting or meeting rights are those on the convening of a general meeting to determine when those rights and are registered as such in one appointed by the Board registry, regardless of who at the time of general meeting the persons entitled to the shares.

3rd final day of registration must not be earlier than the thirtieth day prior to the meeting.

4Bij the notice, the day of registration, together with the way the voting or meeting rights can register and how they can exercise their rights.

Article 118

1Slechts shareholders have voting rights. Each shareholder has at least one vote. The bylaws may provide that a shareholder is not entitled to exercise voting rights as long as he fails to comply with a legal or statutory obligation.

2 If the share capital into shares of the same figure was divided, each shareholder brings many voices as he shares.

3 If the share capital into shares of different amount is divided, the number of votes each shareholder equal to the number of times that the amount of the smallest share is included in the aggregate amount of his shares, fractional votes shall be disregarded.

4 However, the same by a shareholder to bring vote on the statute be limited, provided that shareholders whose shares amount to equal the same number of votes and the restriction for the holders of a larger amount of shares is not more favorable than is provided for Holders of a smaller amount of shares.

5 From the provisions of the second and third paragraph, the statutes in other ways be waived, subject to the same shareholder not more than six votes are awarded if the share capital is divided into one hundred shares or more, and no more than three vote if the capital in less than one hundred shares is divided.

6 Under Shares which together constitute a share of the amount to be equated with such share.

7 For a share belonging to the company or a subsidiary in general meeting may not exercise voting rights, nor for a share for which one of them holds. Usufructuaries and pledgees of shares to the company and its accessories, are not excluded from voting if the usufruct or pledge was established before the shares to the Company or a subsidiary. The company or a subsidiary can not vote for a share which it has a right of usufruct or pledge.

Article 118a

1Indien with the cooperation of the company shares have been issued certificates admitted to trading on a regulated market or multilateral trading facility, as defined in Article 1:1 of the Act on financial supervision or with a regulated market or multilateral trading facility system from a non-Member State is the holder of the certificates are authorized to request the principal to the exclusion of the voting rights attached to the relevant shares or the shares to exercise a power of attorney given in the general meeting. A certificate holder may thus authorized to vote at their discretion. Articles 88 paragraph 4 and 89 paragraph 4 shall not apply.

2nd voting the proxy may only restrict or exclude a given power of attorney revoked if:

aa bid is announced or issued share capital of the company or certificates or the legitimate expectation that purpose shall be made without the bid has been agreed with the company;

leg holder of certificates or more holders of certificates and shares according to a mutual agreement to cooperate or not with subsidiaries at least 25% of the issued capital of the company provide or do provide, or

cnaar the judgment of the voting exercise of voting rights by a holder of certificates in substantial conflict with the interests of the company and its business.

The voting takes its decision to limit, withdraw or revoke motivated communicated to the depositary and the other shareholders.

3rd power of limitation, exclusion or revocation does not exist if the voting right personality and the majority of the directors of the corporation may be cast by

abestuurders or former directors and auditors or former auditors of the company or its group companies;

bnatuurlijke persons employed by the company or its group companies;

cvaste advisers of the company or its group companies.

4Bij the decision to limit, exclude or revoke the proxy and the decision on how the voting right is exercised, the persons referred to in paragraph 3 not voting.

Article 119

1The general meeting, the board for a period not exceeding five years authorize the convening of a general meeting to determine that the application of Article 117 paragraphs 1 and 2 and Article 117a paragraph 1 and 4 as voting or meeting rights are to apply someone on a date to be determined taking those rights and are registered as such in a register designated by the board, regardless of who at the time of the general meeting the persons entitled to the shares or certificates. The authorization may also be granted for an indefinite time in the statutes.

2The final day of registration must not be earlier than the thirtieth day before the meeting.

° 3 The notice convening the meeting, the date of registration and whether the way the voting or meeting rights can register and how they can exercise their rights.

Article 120

1All decisions whereof the law or the statutes do not prescribe a larger majority, are taken by absolute majority of votes cast. If the votes in an election of persons, decided by lot, crossed the votes in a vote other than the proposal is rejected, one another and to the extent of the law or the statutes are another solution is indicated. This solution can be to entrust the decision to a third party.

2 Unless the law or the bylaws provide otherwise, is not dependent on the validity of decisions of the meeting represented part of the capital.

3 If the statute provides that the validity of an act depends on the represented at the meeting portion of the capital and this part at the meeting was not represented, may, unless the articles provide otherwise, a new meeting be convened at which the decision can be taken independently of the represented at the meeting portion of the capital. The notice to the new meeting must state that and why a decision can be taken independently of the meeting represented part of the capital.

4 The management of the company likes the resolutions passed. The records office of the company for inspection by the shareholders and the holders with the cooperation of the company issued certificates for its shares. Each of them will request a copy or extract of such record at the maximum cost.

Article 121

1The general meeting is authorized to amend the statutes, insofar as the statutes the power to amend should have been excluded, is nevertheless possible amendment unanimously in a meeting where the entire issued capital is represented.

2 A provision in the statutes, which the authority to amend any other provisions of the statutes is limited, may only be amended in accordance with the same restriction.

3 A provision in the statutes, that the power to change one or more other rules, may only be amended unanimously in a meeting where the entire issued capital is represented.

Article 121a

1The decision to increase the amount of the shares of the capital, according to Article 67a is taken by an absolute majority. The decision to reduce the amount of the shares and the cap tal is taken by a majority of at least two-thirds of the votes cast if less than half of the issued capital is represented. Are there different types of shares, then in addition to the decision to increase or decrease a prior or simultaneous approval decision is required from each group of shareholders which affects the conversion.

2for the application of this provision, shares of a particular species also include stocks with a distinct denomination.

Article 122

Amendment of a provision of the statute, where a party other than shareholders of the company as such any right is awarded, if the recipient in the change not consent, his right not prejudicial, unless at the time of the granting of the right ability to change to that provision was expressly reserved.

Article 123

1When to the General Assembly a proposal to amend the statutes will be made, this must always be in the notice convening the general meeting shall be stated.

2 Those who have done such a notice must be simultaneously a copy of the proposal which the proposed amendment verbatim, at the offices of the company deposit for inspection by any shareholder until the end of the meeting. Article 114 paragraph 2 shall apply mutatis mutandis.

3 The shareholders must be given the opportunity of the day of deposit to that of the general meeting a copy of the proposal, as in the previous paragraph, to obtain. These copies shall be provided free of charge.

4 The provisions in this article relating to shareholders is determined, shall apply to holders of depositary receipts issued for shares of the company.

Article 124

1of a change in the statutes, under penalty of nullity, a notarial deed. The deed is executed in the Dutch language.

2 The deed may consist of a notarial record of the general meeting at which the amendment is adopted, or at a later notarial deed. The board is authorized the deed, without purpose by the general meeting to be authorized. The general meeting, the board or one or more other persons authorized to make the changes, necessary to prove the statement referred to in the following article available.

3 If the share capital changed, please state what part of the instrument is placed.

Article 125

1The change in the statutes shall not take effect, until by the Minister of Justice stated that his objections are not shown.

2nd statement referred to in paragraph one shall be refused on the grounds that by amending the company would acquire a prohibited character or that there is a danger that by amending the company will be used for illicit purposes.

3b obtaining this statement must meet the Minister of Justice with all the information are necessary to assess the application. Our Minister should also benefit from the State Funds amounting to? 90.76 are met. We may by order increase the amount of administration associated with the increase in wages and prices.

4th statement is not required for conversion of the amounts of the shares or the share or the issued capital in euros, according to Article 67a.

Article 126

The Directors are required to deposit an authentic copy of the amendment and the amended statute to deposit at the office of the Trade.

Article 127

During the bankruptcy of the limited liability company may in its constitution not be altered without the consent of the trustee.

Article 128

1The Regulations may provide that decisions of shareholders other than in a meeting can take place unless bearer shares or, with the cooperation of the company, share certificates have been issued. If the statutes contain such a scheme, such a decision is possible only with the unanimous vote of the voting shareholders. The votes will be made in writing.

2Tenzij the statutes provide otherwise, the vote also electronically delivered.

Section 5. The board of the corporation and supervision of the Board

Article 129

1Behoudens restrictions under the statutes, the board is charged with the management of the company.

2nd Regulations may provide that a particular function or designated driver more than one vote is granted. A director may not cast more votes than the other drivers combined.

3Besluiten of the Board may by or under the statutes are subject to the approval of an organ of the company.

4th Regulations may provide that the board should behave to the instructions of an organ of the company that the general lines of the policy in more detail in the articles relate to the areas identified.

Article 130

1The board represents the company, insofar as the law provides otherwise.

2 The power of representation is partly to allow each driver. The bylaws may provide to the board except that it only belongs to one or more directors. They may also provide that a director the company only with the cooperation of one or more others may represent.

3 Entitlement to representation at the board or to an operator belongs to, indefinitely and unconditionally, to the extent the law provides otherwise. A legally permitted or prescribed restriction or requirement for the power of representation can only be invoked by the company.

4 The statutes can to persons other than directors power to grant representation.

Article 131

The court, within whose jurisdiction the company is domiciled, take note of all legal actions relating to the agreement between the corporation and the director, including the claim referred to in Article 138 of this Book, the amount of which is undetermined or? 5000 to beyond. The same court took

note of requests under Article 685 of Book 7 on the first sentence in the said agreement.

Article 132

1The appointment of directors shall be for the first time in the memorandum and later by the general meeting, unless extended in accordance with Article 162 of this Book by the supervisory board is made.

2The Association, the group of eligible individuals by limiting requirements which the directors must meet. The requirements may be refused by a decision of the General Assembly require two-thirds of the votes cast representing more than half of the issued capital.

Article 133

1When the statutes may provide that the appointment by the general meeting will take place from a list of at least two persons for each vacancy to be filled contains.

2 The general meeting may, to such nomination of its binding nature of a resolution passed by two thirds of the votes cast, representing more than half of the issued capital.

3 The preceding paragraphs shall not apply if the appointment is made by the supervisory board.

Article 134

1Iedere director may at any time be suspended or dismissed by a person authorized to appoint.

2 Where the statute provides that the decision to suspend or dismiss may only be taken with a strengthened majority in a general meeting at which a certain portion of the capital is represented, should this enhanced two-thirds majority of votes cast, representing more than half of the capital, not to exceed.

3 A conviction for the recovery of the employment contract between a public company director can not be pronounced by the court.

4 The statutes must contain provisions concerning the manner in which the directors of the company is provisionally foreseen in case of absence or inability of directors.

Article 135

1The company has a policy on the remuneration of the Board. This policy is determined by the general meeting. The remuneration policy at least in Article 383c to e defined topics, insofar as they relate to the board.

2Indien the company pursuant to statutory provisions, a works council has set the remuneration policy and written simultaneously with the offer to the general meeting be forwarded to the works offered. For the purposes of the preceding sentence, the provisions of Article 158, paragraph 11 apply mutatis mutandis to the subsidiary referred to in paragraphs 1 and 2 of Article 24a.

3rd remuneration of directors is in compliance with the policy referred to in paragraph 1, adopted by the general meeting, unless the statutes another body has been designated.

4Indien in the Constitution states that a body other than the General Assembly determines the remuneration, explains that body with regard to benefits in the form of shares or rights to acquire shares of a proposal for approval to the General Assembly. The proposal must state the number of shares or rights to acquire shares may be granted to the board and the criteria for granting or amendment. The lack of approval of the General Assembly affect the authority of the agency does not comply.

Article 136

Unless the statutes provide otherwise, the board is without command of the general meeting has no power to declare the bankruptcy of the corporation.

Article 137

1Rechtshandelingen of the company against the holder of all shares in the capital of the company or against a partner in a marriage community or a community of a registered partnership which all shares in the capital of the company include, where the company is represented by such shareholder or by one of the partners, be recorded in writing. For the purposes of the preceding sentence, shares held by the company or its subsidiaries are not counted. If the first sentence not been complied with, the legal act on behalf of the company be destroyed.

2 Paragraph 1 shall not apply to operations under the stipulated conditions for the ordinary operations of the company properly.

Article 138

1In the case of bankruptcy of the corporation, each director against the estate liable for the amount of the debt to the extent not by liquidation of the remaining benefits will be satisfied if the board task manifestly improper has fulfilled and it is plausible that this a major cause of bankruptcy.

2 If the board has not fulfilled its obligations under Articles 10 or 394, it has fulfilled its task improperly and suspected improper performance of duties is an important cause of bankruptcy. The same applies if the company fully liable partner of a partnership or limited partnership and not fulfilled the obligations under Article 15i of Book 3. An important omission is not taken into account.

3 Do not liable, the director who proves that the improper performance of duties by the board not attributable to him and that he was not negligent in taking measures to avert the consequences.

4 The court may the amount for which the directors are liable if it this reduce excessive songs, given the nature and seriousness of the improper performance of duties by the board, the other causes of bankruptcy, and how this is settled. The judge may also, the amount of the liability of an individual driver reducing this excessive if it occurs, given the time during which the driver has been in office as such in the period in which the improper performance of duties took place.

5 Is the size of the deficit is not yet known, the court may, with or without application of the fourth paragraph, provide that the deficit for the payment of which they are directors condemning a state is prepared in accordance with the provisions of the sixth title of the second book of the Code of Civil Procedure.

6 The claim may be brought only on the basis of improper performance of duties during the period of three years preceding the bankruptcy. A discharge is granted to the driver to adjust the claim is not in the way.

7 With a driver, for the purposes of this article, the one who equated the policy of the Company has determined whether co has determined, as if he was a director. The claim can not be brought against the trustee appointed by the court.

8 This article shall affect the jurisdiction of the bankruptcy trustee to bring a claim under the agreement with the director or pursuant to Article 9.

9 If a director under this section is liable and is unable to pay his debt matter, the trustee by that driver voluntarily performed acts which means that the story on him is reduced to the benefit of the estate by an extrajudicial statement destroy, if it is likely that entirely or almost entirely for the purpose of reduction of that story have been made. Article 45 paragraphs 4 and 5 of Book 3 shall apply mutatis mutandis.

10 If the estate is insufficient to bring an action under this Article or Article 9 or to set up a preliminary investigation into the possibility to do so, the liquidator may request the Minister of Justice by way of advance him the funds necessary provision. Our Minister may adopt rules for the assessment of the merits of the request and the limits within which the request can be assigned. The request must contain the grounds on which it rests, and a reasoned estimate of the cost and scope of the investigation. The application, insofar as it concerns the establishment of a preliminary inquiry, require the approval of the judge.

Article 139

If the financial statements, interim figures by which the company has published the annual report or a misleading representation is given the status of the company, the directors against third parties liable for the damages suffered by them as a result. The director who proves that this is not due to him, is not liable.

Article 140

1When the statutes may provide that a board of commissioners will be. The board consists of one or more natural persons.

2 The supervisory board is responsible for supervising the policy of the government and the general affairs of the company and its business. He is the Board with advice. In the performance of their duties, the commissioners themselves to the interests of the company and its business.

3 The articles may contain additional provisions regarding the duties and powers of the board and its members include.

4th statutes may provide for a particular function or designated commissioner more than one vote is granted. A member may not cast more votes than the other commissioners together.

Article 141

1The Board provides the Supervisory Board in time for the performance of its duties.

2The Board shall at least once a year the Supervisory Board in writing of the outline of the strategic policy, the general and financial risks and the management and control of the company.

Article 142

1The commissioners who are not already in the memorandum have been designated, appointed by the General Assembly. The statutes may the circle of eligible persons limited by requirements which the Board must comply. The requirements may be refused by a decision of the General Assembly require two-thirds of the votes cast representing more than half of the issued capital.

2 The first two paragraphs of Article 133 of this Book shall apply mutatis mutandis, if the appointment by the general meeting takes place.

3 In a recommendation or nomination of a Commissioner from the candidate's age, occupation, the amount of shares held by him in the capital of the company and the positions he holds or has held to the extent of interest in connection with the performance of the duties of a commissioner. It also sets out the legal, he is already a; if these include legal persons, belonging to the same group, may with the designation of the group will be sufficient. The recommendation and the recommendation for appointment or reappointment shall be justified. For reappointment, with the way the candidate has fulfilled his duties as commissioner.

Article 143

The statutes may provide that one or more commissioners, but not more than a third of the whole number, will be appointed other than by the general meeting. Is the appointment of commissioners settled in accordance with Articles 158 and 159 of this Book, you will find the preceding sentence shall not apply.

Article 144

1one Board may be suspended or dismissed by the person who is authorized to appoint, unless Article 161 paragraphs 2 and 3 of Article 161a of this book is applicable.

2The second and third paragraph of Article 134 of this Book shall apply mutatis mutandis.

Article 145

The general meeting may grant a remuneration to the auditors.

Article 146

Unless the statutes provide otherwise, the limited liability company in all cases where a conflict of interest with one or more directors, represented by Commissioners. The general meeting is authorized one or more other persons to be appointed.

Article 147

1Tenzij the statutes provide otherwise, the Board of Commissioners authorized any driver at all times be suspended.

2 The suspension may at any time by the general meeting may be canceled, unless the power to appoint directors to the Board of Commissioners based.

Article 148 [repealed on 01/01/1984]

Article 149

The provisions of Articles 9, 131 and 138 shall apply mutatis mutandis with respect to the performance of duties by the Board of Commissioners.

Article 150

If the financial statements give a misleading representation is given the status of the company, the board next to the drivers against third parties liable for the damages suffered by them as a result. The Commissioner proves that this is not a shortcoming on his part in the supervision is due, is not liable.

Article 151

1Allen, auditors or others who, without being part of the governance of public company, under any provision of the constitution or by resolution of the general assembly, for a certain time or under certa n conditions, acts of governing conduct in this respect are, what their rights and obligations towards the company and third parties, as designated drivers.

2 The approval of certain administrative acts or mandate to do this does not count as performing acts of directors.

Section 6. The supervisory board at the large public company

Article 152

In this section, a dependent company means:

aa legal entity to which the corporation or one or more dependent companies, alone or together for their own account at least half of the issued capital;

leg partnership, a company is incorporated and for which the limited liability company or a dependent company as a partner towards third parties fully liable for all debts.

Article 153

1one limited liability company, if the following paragraph shall apply to her, within two months after the adoption of its financial statements by the general meeting at the offices of the trade 'declarations that they meet the conditions laid down in that paragraph. Until Article 154 paragraph 3 of this book has been applied, the board shall in each subsequent annual report if the statement is made, the statement is deleted, it will be recorded in the first annual report after the date of such cancellation is made.

2 The obligation to make a declaration applies if:

aThe issued capital of the company together with the reserves of the balance sheet and notes at least one established by Royal Decree threshold amount,

bde company or a dependent company under a legal obligation Works has set, and

cbij the company and its dependent companies, together usually at least one hundred employees working in the Netherlands.

3 The obligation to make a statement does not apply to:

aa company dependent company is a legal entity which Articles 63f to 63j, Articles 158 to 161 and 164 or Articles 268 to 271 and 274 apply, a company dependent company is a European limited company within the meaning of Regulation (EC) Nr. 2157/2001 (OJ L 294) in which the Constitution states that Articles 158 Paragraphs 1 to 12, 159, 161, 161a and 164 shall apply, or a company which is dependent company of a European Cooperative Society the meaning of Regulation (EC) Nr. 1435/2003 (OJEU L 207) which in the Constitution states that Articles 158 Paragraphs 1 to 12, 159, 161a and 164 shall apply and that the dismissal of members of the supervisory board by the General Assembly, Article 52 of the Regulation, by absolute majority of the votes cast representing at least one third of the total voting rights under the statute,

leg company whose activity is exclusively or almost exclusively limited to the management and financing of group companies and its and their shareholdings in other entities, provided that the employees of the company and group companies outside the Netherlands are in majority,

ceen company owned exclusively or almost exclusively to a company referred to in Article 263 b of paragraph 3 b, and the provisions mentioned in that group companies and legal services for the management and funding grants, and

deen company in which at least half the subscribed capital in accordance with a mutual cooperation arrangement brings together two or more persons covered by Articles 63f to 63j, Articles 158 to 161 and 164 or Articles 268 to 271 and 274 applies or who are dependent company of such corporation.

4 The in subparagraph a of paragraph 2 above limit shall be no more than once in two years increased or decreased in proportion to the development of a by general government to designate price index since a bee that measure date to be determined, it is then completed to the nearest multiple of one million. The amount will not be re-established as long as the unrounded amount less than one million differs from the previously fixed amount.

5 Under the issued capital and reserves are included in paragraph 2 under a joint made and yet to be input from members by way of guarantee or in dependent companies which are limited partnerships, where this does not lead to double counting.

Article 154

1The Articles 158-164 of this book are applicable to a company on which a statement referred to in the previous article for three years continuously enrolled, this period shall be deemed not to be interrupted if a cancellation of the statement, which during that period wrongly held, is canceled.

2 The cancellation of the registration by virtue of the fact that the company no longer meets the conditions specified in the second paragraph of the preceding Article, the applicability of Sections 158-164 of the Book terminate only if three years after the cancellation has expired and the company during that period was not re-doing the giving has been required.

3 The company markets its statutes in accordance with Articles 158-164 for which its funds, the latest from the date of such items pursuant to paragraph 1 of its operation.

4In the next meeting after the company which Articles 158 to 164 or 158 to 161 and 164 apply will meet the conditions referred to in Articles 153 paragraph 3, 154 paragraph 2, 155 or 155a, does the board to the General Assembly the proposal in the statutes the manner of appointment and dismissal of auditors and the duties and powers of the board of commissioners to settle without the application of Articles 158 to 164, respectively, Articles 158 to 161 and 164 or the proposal in whole or in these articles except Article 162 continue to apply. The decision is taken by an absolute majority. The competence of the General Assembly to take a decision pursuant to this Article may not be limited.

5Uiterlijk twelve months after the decision referred to in paragraph 4 is taken, the board shall submit to the General Assembly a proposal to amend the statutes. If the Assembly decides not to amend shall notify the Enterprise Chamber of the Amsterdam Court at the request of the person appointed under the following paragraph has jurisdiction, the statutes. The last two sentences of paragraph 4 shall apply mutatis mutandis.

6One request for adoption of the statutes can be submitted by a designated representative of the board or the supervisory board and the person who is authorized for inclusion under Article 114a.

7th Enterprise controls as necessary consequences of its decision. The clerk of the Enterprise is doing at the office of the commercial where the company is registered a copy of the decision of the Enterprise deposit.

Article 155

1In Notwithstanding Article 154 Article 162 shall not apply to a company in which a participation of at least half of the issued share capital is held:

Adoor a legal entity whose majority of employees work outside the Netherlands or by dependent companies thereof

bvolgens a mutual cooperation arrangement by a number of such entities or companies, or

cvolgens a mutual cooperation arrangement by one or more of such entities, and one or more legal entities for which Article 153 paragraph 3, under a or Article 263 paragraph 3 under a force or which Articles 63f to 63j, Articles 158 to 161 and 164 or Articles 268 to 271 and 274 apply.

2 The exception under the preceding paragraph shall not apply if the employees of the company, together with those employed by the entity or entities, the majority working in the Netherlands.

3 For the purposes of this Article, employees, employed by a corporation, include the employees of group companies.

Article 155a

1In Notwithstanding Article 154 Article 162 shall not apply to a company in which:

aa natural person or the entire issued capital does provide, or two or more natural persons according to a mutual agreement to cooperate the entire issued capital or do provide;

bone foundation, association or legal entity referred to in Article 1, the entire issued capital for their own account provided or does provide, or two or more of such entities, according to a mutual agreement to cooperate the entire issued capital to provide for its own account or do provide.

2 Using the natural person referred to in paragraph 1 shall be treated as the spouse and registered partner. Also be equated to relatives in a straight line, provided that they are within six months after the death of the individual is a mutual cooperation arrangement entered into.

Article 156

Our Minister of Justice, having heard the Economic and Social Council, to a company at its request to waive one or more of Articles 158-164 of the Book, the exemption may be granted under restrictions and conditions may be attached thereto, which may also be amended or withdrawn.

Article 157

1one company to which Article 154 of this book does not apply, may by its statutes the manner of appointment and dismissal of auditors and the duties and powers of the supervisory control in accordance with Articles 158-164 of this book if they or a dependent society is a Works set to which the provisions of the Works Councils Act apply. She may refrain from applying Article 162. The rules in this paragraph in the statutes loses its validity when the council ceases to exist or no longer works on the provisions of the Works Councils Act apply.

2A company to which Article 155 or 155a applies, the authority to regulate the appointment and dismissal of directors under Article 162.

Article 158

1The company has a supervisory board.

2nd supervisory board consists of at least three members. Is the number of commissioners less than three, the Board takes immediate measures to supplement its membership.

3rd Board of Commissioners adopt a profile of its size and composition, taking into account the nature of the business, its activities and the desired expertise and background of the board. The board discusses the profile for the first down and then for any change in the general meeting and with the works.

4The Board shall, subject to paragraph 9, on the recommendation of the Supervisory Board appointed by the general meeting, provided the appointment has not already been done with the memorandum or before this article on the company became applicable. The Supervisory Board makes recommendations simultaneously to the General Assembly and the Works. The nomination is reasoned. Without prejudice to Article 160 the statutes the circle of eligible persons is not limited.

5th general meeting and the council may participate in the Supervisory Board recommend persons to be nominated Commissioner. The Board shall inform them in due time when, as a result and according to which profile a vacancy to be filled. If the place referred to in paragraph 6 enhanced right of recommendation applies, the Board of Commissioners also notice thereof.

6for a third of the members of the supervisory board is that the supervisory board by the council person recommended the nomination, unless the Supervisory Board objects to the recommendation under the expectation that the recommended person would be unfit for the performance of the duties of Commissioner or the supervisory board appointed pursuant to the recommendation will not properly constituted. If the number of members of the Supervisory Board can not be divided by three, the next lower number that can be divided by three is taken into account for determining the number of members to which this enhanced right of recommendation applies.

7Indien the supervisory objection, it shall inform the works council objection and the reasons for it. The Board shall immediately consult with the works with a view to reaching agreement on the nomination. If the Supervisory Board finds that no agreement can be reached, a designated representative of the board of the Enterprise Chamber of the Amsterdam Court of the objection well founded. The request shall not be filed until four weeks have elapsed after the start of the consultation with the council. The board shall place the person recommended the nomination if the Enterprise's objection unfounded. The Enterprise Division upholds the objection, the works council can make a new recommendation in accordance with paragraph 6.

8The Enterprise, the council calls. The decision of the Enterprise can not be appealed. The Enterprise can not express condemnation of the proceedings.

9th general meeting may by an absolute majority of votes cast, representing at least one third of the issued capital, reject the nomination. If the shareholders by an absolute majority of votes their support to the candidate remember, but this majority is not at least one third of the issued capital, a new meeting may be convened at which the nomination may be rejected by an absolute majority. Then, the board shall make a new nomination. The members 5 to 8 are applied. If the Assembly does not appoint the nominated person and does not decide to reject the nomination, appoints the Supervisory Board of the nominated person.

10th General Assembly, the power conferred by paragraph 5 is due for a to be determined by duration of not more than two consecutive years, transfer to a committee of shareholders, it enables members to designate in which case, the supervisory board to the committee the notice referred to in paragraph 5. The general meeting may at any time undo the transfer.

11Voor the purposes of this section, the council means the council of the business of the company or the company of a dependent society. If more than one works, the powers of this article by these councils separately exercised, if there is a nomination referred to in paragraph 6, the powers of this paragraph by these councils jointly. Does the company or companies concerned a central works council, then the powers of the council under this section to the Central Works Council.

12In the statutes may be made to paragraphs 2, 4 to 7 and 9, except that no derogation from the first two sentences of paragraph 9. The decision to amend the statutes require the prior approval of the Supervisory Board and the consent of the works required.

Article 159

1Ontbreken all Commissioners, other than pursuant to Article 161a, the appointment shall be by the general meeting.

2nd council may recommend persons for appointment as Commissioner. Whoever the General Assembly convenes, shall notify the council in a timely manner that the appointment of commissioners subject of treatment in the general meeting will be, whether the appointment is taking place under the right of recommendation of the council under Article 158, paragraph 6.

3rd paragraphs 6, 7, 8, 10 and 11 of the preceding article shall apply mutatis mutandis.

Article 160

Commissioner can not be:

apersonen employed by the company;

bpersonen employed by a dependent society;

cbestuurders and persons in the service of an employee organization that is usually involved in the determination of the conditions of the persons referred to under a and b.

Article 161

1one Commissioner shall not later than if after his appointment last four years has been Commissioner. The deadline may be extended by the statutes to the day of the next general meeting after the four years or after the date of this article for the legal person will apply.

2 The Enterprise Chamber of the Amsterdam Court may on a request to dismiss a commissioner for neglecting his duties, for other important reasons or for substantial change of circumstances justifying enforcement as Commissioner of the Company can not reasonably be required. The request may be submitted by the company, represented by the Board, or by a duly designated representative of the general meeting or of the works referred to in paragraph 11 of Article 158. The members 10 and 11 of Article 158 shall apply mutatis mutandis.

3 A member may be suspended by the supervisory board, the suspension shall expire by law, if the company within one month after the commencement of the suspension with a request referred to in the preceding paragraph at the Enterprise Chamber has submitted.

Article 161a

1The general meeting may by an absolute majority of votes cast, representing at least one third of the issued capital, confidence in the supervisory board terminate. The decision is reasoned. The decision can not be taken with regard to commissioners appointed by the Enterprise in accordance with paragraph 3.

2A resolution referred to in paragraph 1 shall be taken before the administration of the council's proposal for decision and the reasons therefore has informed. Such notice shall be at least 30 days before the general meeting at which the proposal is discussed. If the works a position on the proposal, the Board proposes the

Supervisory Board and the General Assembly informed of this position. The works can have its position in the General Assembly do explain.

3The decision referred to in paragraph 1, the immediate dismissal of the members of the supervisory board as a result. Then asks the board immediately to the Enterprise Chamber of the Amsterdam Court temporarily one or more commissioners to be appointed. The Enterprise Chamber regulates the consequences of the appointment.

4th Board of Commissioners encourages that, within a deadline set by the Enterprise a new board be composed in accordance with Article 158.

Article 162

The supervisory board appoints the directors of the company, this authority may not be limited by any binding nomination. He gives the general meeting of an intended appointment of a director of the company, he does not absolve a director until after the general meeting on the proposed dismissal. The eleventh paragraph of Article 158 of this Book shall apply mutatis mutandis.

Article 163 [repealed on 01/10/2004]

Article 164

1Aan the approval of the Supervisory Board are subject to the decisions of the Board concerning:

auitgifte and acquisition of shares and debentures of the company or of debentures of a limited partnership or general partnership of which the company fully liable partner;

bmedewerking to the issuance of certificates of shares;

chet application for admission of the documents referred to under a and b to trading on a regulated market or multilateral trading facility, as defined in Article 1:1 of the Act on financial supervision or with a regulated market or multilateral trading facility from a State not a Member State or requesting a withdrawal of such authorization;

Dhet into or termination of sustained cooperation of the Company or a related company with another entity or company or as fully liable partner in a limited partnership or partnership, if such cooperation or termination of major significance to the company;

ehet taking a stake worth at least a fourth of the amount of the issued capital and reserves according to the balance sheet and notes of the company, by it or a related company in the capital of another company, or any material increase or reducing such participation;

finvesteringen requiring an amount equal to at least one fourth of the issued capital and reserves of the company in its balance sheet with explanatory notes;

No proposal to amend the statutes;

over proposal to dissolve the company;

iaangifte of bankruptcy and application for suspension of payments;

jbeëindiging of the employment of a substantial number of employees of the company or of a dependent company simultaneously or within a short period of time;

tion ripening changes in the employment of a substantial number of employees of the company or of a dependent company;

loan proposal to reduce the issued capital.

2 The lack of approval of the Supervisory Board on a decision as referred to in paragraph 1 affect the authority of directors or not directors.

Articles 165-174 [repealed on 01/04/1987]

Section 7. The dissolution of the corporation

Article 174a

The applicant may appeal to the Appeals Board against the business:

ade refusal of an application referred to in Article 64, paragraph 3, second sentence;

bde refusal of a declaration under Article 68, paragraph 2;

cde refusal of a declaration under Article 125, paragraph 2 and

deen decision to refuse, vary or revoke the exemption and a decision to grant an exemption to appropriate and necessary conditions, or limitations thereby imposed under Article 156.

TITLE 5. PRIVATE LIMITED LIABILITY

Article 175

1The private company with limited liability is a legal person with share capital divided into shares. Share certificates are not issued, the shares are not freely transferable. A shareholder is not personally liable for what in the name of the company is carried out and is not held above the amount that its shares should be deposited in the losses of the company to contribute.

2nd company by one or more persons established by notarial deed. For establishment shal require a statement of the Minister of Justice that it has proved of no objection. The deed is signed by each and every founder who, according to this Act shall take one or more shares.

3 The memorandum within three months after the date of the declaration of no objection his past, on pain of forfeiture of the statement. The Minister may at the request of interested parties on the basis of compelling reasons this term not exceeding three months.

Article 176

The memorandum of the company is executed in the Dutch language. A power of attorney to cooperate in such deed must be in writing granted.

Article 177

1 The memorandum must contain the articles of association. The bylaws contain the name, seat and purpose of the company.

2 The name starts or ends with the words private company with limited liability, either written in full or abbreviated to "Ltd".

3 The seat must be located in the Netherlands.

Article 178

1The statutes mention the amount of the share capital and the number and amount of shares in euro up to two decimal places. Are there different types of shares, the articles mention the number and amount of each species. The memorandum shall state the amount of subscribed capital and paid part of it. Are there different types of shares than the amounts of the issued and paid-up capital broken down by type. The document also mentions the creation of all those who take the shares in Article 196 paragraph 2 under b and c data with the number and type of shares held by him and paid-in amount.

2 The social and the subscribed capital and paid-up part of the establishment must at least the minimum capital [Editor: At Stb. 2000/322, this amount including September 1, 2000 on 18 000.] That has been established by royal decree. The minimum capital is not more than once in two years increased or decreased in proportion to the trend since January 1, 1985 with an Order in Council to designate price index, it is then rounded to the nearest multiple of two thousand five hundred euros. The minimum capital is not re-established as long as less than two thousand euro differs from the unrounded amount.

3 Is the sum of the paid-up capital and reserves under any other provision of law or the statutes must be maintained less than the last minimum capital, the company must maintain a reserve equal to the difference.

4 The share capital must be at least one-fifth are placed.

5Een private company that was created before 1 January 2002, the amount of the share capital and the amount of golden shares in state up to two decimal places.

Article 178A

1Indien a private company in the statutes, the amount of the share capital and shares in the amount of guilders into euros, the amount of shares subscribed and paid-up share in euro calculated under Article 109l fourth member of the Treaty on European Union finally fixed conversion rate, rounded up to two decimal places. The rounded amount of each share in euros may not exceed 15% higher or lower than the original amount of the share in guilders. The total amount of the shares in euro referred to in Article 178, the share capital into euro. The sum of the amounts of the shares subscribed and paid-up part thereof in euro is the amount of the issued and paid-up share capital in euro. The deed shall state the amount of the issued and paid-up share capital in euro.

2Is after conversion in accordance with paragraph 1, the sum of the amounts of the issued shares higher than in accordance with Article 109l fourth paragraph of the Treaty on European Union finally fixed conversion rate converted amount of the subscribed capital, the difference is charged of distributable reserves or the reserves referred to in Article 389 or 390. If these reserves are not sufficient, then the company is a negative crediting reserve the size of the difference that is not borne out of distributable or non-distributable reserves is charged. Until the difference in retained earnings or reserves are met, the company may no benefits referred to in Article 216 do. By complying with the provisions of this paragraph shall be deemed to have the shares are fully paid.

3Is after conversion in accordance with paragraph 1, the sum of the amounts of the issued shares lower that according to Article 109l fourth paragraph of the Treaty on European Union finally fixed conversion rate converted amount of the subscribed capital, the company keeps a non- distributable reserve the size of the difference. Article 208 is not applicable.

Article 178B

If the company is in derogation of Article 178A, the amount of the shares changes, this change requires the approval of any group of shareholders whose rights the amendment would affect. Arises under the right to change money or debt, then the aggregate amount of one tenth of the modified nominal amount of shares not exceeding.

Article 178c

1one private company whose articles of the share capital and the amount of shares in the golden state, may in society use the equivalent in euro up to two decimal places, provided it is made to this article. This use of the equivalent in euro has no legal effect.

2Indien a private company whose articles of the amount of the share capital and the amount of shares in the golden state, after 1 January 2002 a change in one or more provisions which amounts are expressed in guilders, in the Statutes, all amounts converted to euro. Articles 178A and 178B apply.

Article 179

1b obtaining a statement from the Minister of Justice that it has proved of no objection must be to him all the information necessary to assess the application. Our Minister should also benef t from the State Funds amounting to? 90.76 are met. We may by order increase the amount of administration associated with the increase in wages and prices.

2 The declaration may only be refused on the grounds that, in view of the intentions or antecedents of the persons that the policy of the Company shall determine or help determine a risk that the company will be used for illicit purposes or that its activity will penalize its creditors.

3Ten purpose of exercising the supervision referred to in paragraph 2 providing the Institute for employee insurance and the national tax office at his request to the Minister the information it needs. The institute and the national tax office give the Minister on request free of charge access to data held by or providing free extracts thereof.

Article 180

1The directors require the company to do in the commercial register and a certified copy of the memorandum and of the associated under Articles 203a, 204 and 204A of documents attached to resign the office of the trade. At the same time they must make a declaration of the total of fixed and estimated costs associated with the establishment and against the company as a result.

2 The directors with the company liable for any act done during their administration so that the company is linked in the period before:

ade task for initial registration in the Commercial Register, together with the deposited copies was done,

BThe paid-up capital at least the prescribed minimum capital formation, and

the cop in the founding capital issued at least one fourth of the nominal amount is paid.

Article 181

1When the private company itself under Article 18 into an association, cooperative or mutual insurance company, any shareholder, member, unless he has asked the compensation referred to in paragraph 2.

2 On the decision to transpose Article 209 is applicable, unless the company itself into a limited company. After such a decision, any shareholder who is not with the decision agreed, asking the company compensation for the loss of his shares. The request for compensation must be made in writ ng to the company within one month after the shareholder has indicated that he may seek compensation. The notification shall be in the same manner as the notice convening a general meeting.

° 3 Failing agreement, the compensation determined by one or more independent experts, at the request of either party to be appointed by the court to authorize conversion or by the judge of the court. The items 351 and 352 are applicable.

Article 182 [repealed on 01/01/1992]

Article 183

1When a corporation pursuant to Article 18 into a private company, be attached to the instrument of conversion:

aa declaration of the Minister of Justice, to which Article 125 applies, that he objected to the conversion and amendment has not been proved;

leg declaration of an expert referred to in Article 393, which shows that the equity of the company on a day within five months for the conversion of at least equivalent to the paid-up capital according to the instrument of conversion.

2 When another person is under Article 18 into a private company, be attached to the instrument of conversion:

aa declaration of the Minister of Justice to which Article 179 applies, that he objected to the conversion and amendment has not been proved;

leg declaration of an expert referred to in Article 393, which shows that the equity of the corporation on a day within five months for the conversion amounts to at least the amount of the paid portion of the subscribed capital in accordance with the instrument of conversion, when equity, the value of which will be counted after that day no later than immediately after the conversion to shares will be deposited;

cindien the legal members, the written consent of each member whose shares are not paid by conversion of the reserves of the corporation;

dindien a foundation is converted, judicial authorization.

3 When an association, cooperative or mutual insurance pursuant to Article 18 into a private company, any member shareholder. The conversion can not be, as long as one member can still terminate under Article 36 paragraph 4.

4 After the conversion to a shareholder, a usufructuary or a pledgee to a share rights not exercise until they are referred to in Article 194 in the register. As far as share certificates have been issued, no registration rather than by issuing the share certificates to the company.

Article 184 [repealed on 09/01/1994]

Article 185

1Based request of the prosecutor, the court dissolves the company, when its purpose, by a lack of income, can not reach, and the court may dissolve the company, when its business to achieve its purpose has ceased. The public prosecutor shall notify the Chamber of Commerce and Industry, the trade in whose company is registered, that it intends to terminate a request to set.

2on request of the prosecutor, a company whose equity is less than the minimum capital last dissolved by the court if:

azij in illegal profits or reserves has paid

bzij in violation of the law has reduced its capital,

czij or a subsidiary in its share capital or depository receipts in violation of the law has acquired or

Dhet equity never at least in setting minimum capital requirement has equaled.

3 Before the winding up the court the company the opportunity within a period specified by him to correct the omission.

Article 186

1Uit all writings, printed documents and notices, which the company is a party or which it produces, except telegrams and advertisements, the full name of the company and its address clearly.

2 Where reference is made to the capital of the company, must in each case must state the amount is placed, and how much of the issued amount is paid.

Article 187 [repealed on 11/25/1988]

Article 188

When in this title the office of the commercial is listed under the trade means the register kept by the Chamber of Commerce and Industry in accordance with Article 18, sixth and seventh paragraph of the Trade Register Act 2007 is authorized to tender.

Article 189

When the statute refers to the holders of any shares together as a certain portion of the share capital of the company members, shall, unless the contrary appears from the statutes, including capital means the portion of the issued share capital.

Article 189a

For the purposes of Articles 195, 206, 210 and 239 paragraph 6 below is part of the company means the general meeting of shareholders, the meeting of holders of shares of a particular species, the board, the supervisory board and the joint meeting of the Board and the Supervisory Board.

Section 2. The shares

Article 190

Shares are the parts where the capital is divided by the statutes.

Article 191

1When taking a share, the nominal amount. It may be provided that a part, not exceeding three quarters of the nominal amount need only be paid after the Company has requested.

2 A shareholder may not be fully or partially relieved of the obligation to pay, except as provided in Article 208.

3 The shareholder and, in the case of Article 199, the former shareholders are not entitled to set off their debt under this article.

Article 191A

1Storting a share in cash to the extent that no other contribution has been agreed.

2 For in the creation or deposit in foreign currency can only be made if the memorandum states that payment in a foreign currency is permitted, after setting this can occur only with the consent of the company. Payment in a currency that is a unit of the euro under Article 109l fourth paragraph of the Treaty on European Union is not considered payment in foreign currency.

3 With payment in a foreign money is the payment obligation for the amount paid against the amount deposited freely in Dutch money can be exchanged. Determines the exchange rate on the day of the deposit or, if earlier than one month before the establishment is paid on the day of its founding.

Article 191b

1Indien consideration other than cash has been agreed, which is inserted in economic terms can be appreciated. A right to perform work or services may not be contributed.

2 Contributions other than cash must be carried out immediately after taking the share or the day after which an additional payment is issued or on which they agreed.

Article 192

A shareholder can not, even by amending the statute, against his will any obligation above the deposit to the nominal amount of the share may be imposed.

Article 193

The liquidator of a company and, in case of bankruptcy, the trustee, are entitled to enrollment and receipt of all payments not yet made on the shares, no matter what the statutes thereto is determined.

Article 194

1The Board of the Company shall maintain a register containing the names and addresses of all shareholders, stating the date on which the shares were acquired, the date of acknowledgment or service, as well as the amount paid on each share. It shall also contain the names and addresses of those who have a right of usufruct or pledge of shares, stating the date they acquired the right, the date of acknowledgment or service, and specifying the rights attached to shares their accordance with paragraphs 2 and 4 of the Articles 197 and 198 of this book forward.

2 The register is updated regularly, it shall also record any discharge of liability for payments not yet made.

3 The directors shall provide upon request by a shareholder, a usufructuary or a pledgee an extract from the register in respect of his right to a share. If the share is a right of usufruct or a pledge, the extract to whom in paragraphs 2 and 4 of the Articles 197 and 198 of this book rights referred.

4 The Board shall make the register at the office of the company for inspection by the shareholders and users of the fruit and pledgees who in paragraph 4 of Articles 197 and 198 of this book rights referred. The data from the register regarding non-paid shares are available for inspection by any person; copy or extract of this data at no more than cost price.

Article 195

1one shareholder, if the statute this power does not limit or exclude one or more of its shares freely transfer his or her spouse or registered partner, to his blood relatives, in a straight line without restriction and in the sidelines in the second degree , a co-shareholder and the company. The circle of persons to whom one or more of the shareholder may freely transfer his shares, the statutes are extended to his blood relatives in the sidelines, or some of them, in the third and fourth degree.

2 For each transfer other than those under the preceding paragraph may freely pass, the statutes contain a blocking scheme.

3rd bequest transfer applies to the application of the blocking scheme as a transfer by the testator.

4 This locking arrangement should be such that the shareholder of the transfer to be valid, requires the approval of a designated institution by the statutes of the company. The transfer must take place within three months after approval is granted. The approval is deemed granted if the institution of the company that the decision is not charged together with the refusal of approval to the applicant indicates to one or more candidates who are willing to purchase all the shares to which the request for approval relates to payment in cash.

5Het paragraph shall not apply insofar as the statutes contain a blocking scheme, under which the shareholder who wants to alienate one or more shares, it must first offer to his fellow shareholders. This scheme can also mean that, if the co-shareholders not accept the offer, the offer must be made to other parties designated by the association therewith responsible organ of the company. The offeror is entitled to withdraw his offer, provided this is done within one month after he announced to the candidates he has the shares to which the offer relates to sell and at what price. If it is determined that not all of the shares to which the offer relates are purchased for cash, the offeror's shares within three months after that adoption may freely transfer.

6 The locking arrangement should be such that the shareholder, if he so desires, of those who as candidates within the meaning of the fourth paragraph shall be given or to whom under the blocking scheme referred to in the fifth paragraph should be offered a price received equal to the value of his share or shares, determined by one or more independent experts.

7 The company itself is only with the consent of the shareholder pursuant to the fourth or fifth paragraph prospective purchaser.

8 Limit of transferability of the shares can not in such a way that such transfer is made impossible or excessively difficult. The same applies for allotment of shares in a community.

9 Provisions in the statutes regarding transfer of shares shall not apply if the holder under the law to transfer his share to a previous holder is required.

Article 195a

1The Regulations may providence tat in cases specified in the statute, the shareholder has held his shares to sacrifice and transfer. The statutes may thereby determining That while shareholder obligations to transfer fails or sacrifice, his voting rights, its right to Participate in the meeting and its right to benefits is suspended.

2nd Regulations may providence That if a shareholder is not within-a reasonable period or its statutory obligations to sacrifice and transfer of its shares outstanding, the Company is irrevocably Authorized to offer shares and transfer. If no candidates to Whom the shareholder will be bootable to transfer all his shares in accor dance with rules in the statutes, Lacks the authority and consent of the shareholder as provided in Paragraph 1 relieved.

3rd Package Should Be Such That the shareholder who so requests will receive a price equal to the value of his share or shares, Determined by one or more independent experts.

Article 195b

1The Regulations may providence That the shareholder who is not or no longer meets the requirements set out in the statutes the vote, the right to Participate in the general assembly and the right to benefits is suspended.

2Indien the shareholder one or more of the rights Mentioned in para graph 1 can not exercise and the shareholder is not obliged to offer its shares and transfer, was irrevocably in the statutes of the requirements relieved When The company Within three months at the request of the shareholder has nominated candidates to Whom he Will Be Able to transfer all his shares in accor dance with rules in the statutes.

3rd Package Should Be Such That the shareholder who so requests will receive a price equal to the value of his share or shares, Determined by one or more independent experts.

Rule 196

1For the issuance and delivery of a share or a limited right to a notarial requirement did in front of a notary did Netherlands, to Which the parties Involved. No separate document is required for the issuance of shares to be placed in the establishment.

2 Acts of issuance or delivery must state:

ade title of the act and how the share or the limited right to it is acquired;

fname, first names, birthdate, birthplace, residence and address of the natural persons who are parties to the transaction;

crechtsvorm, name, residence and address of the persons who are parties to the transaction;

Dhet number and type of shares to All which the act relates to, or

enaam, residence and address of the company in Whose shares the act relates.

Article 196A

1The transfer of a share or the transfer of a right thereto in accor dance with Article 196 para graph 1, co-operation of law against the company. Except in the event That the company Itself is party to the transaction, They may attached to the share rights can only be Exercised after the act has Acknowledged That The Deed has leg served in accor dance with the Provisions of Article 196b, or it Has Been Recognized by registration in the shareholder register as Referred to in para graph 2.

2 The company who has knowledge of the Act Referred to in the first para-graph, as long as its not Their recognition is Requested or notification of the did has leg done, that 'act on its own initiative Recognize the registration of the transferee of the share or reduced the right in the shareholders register. Immediately They do it by registered letter notifying the parties to the transaction with the still request a copy or extract Referred to in Article 196b para graph 1 to submit to her. Following receipt of Such places it in proof of recognition, a note on the piece in the Manner Described in Article 196b of the qualification is Prescribed, the date of acceptance is the date of registration Stated.

3 If an act Referred to in the first para graph has taken place without this has led to a corresponding thing change in the register of shareholders, this Neither the company nor to others who in good faith in the shareholder register person as a shareholder or owner of a limited right to a share Deemed to be invoked.

Article 196b

1Behoudens the Provisions of Article 196A para graph 2 Shall take the acknowledgment in the doing or on the basis of submission of a notarized copy or extract of the doing.

2 In recognition under submission of a notarized copy or extract is a dated statement posted on the document produced.

3 The service is made by a notarial copy or extract of the doing.

Article 197

1The right to Establish a share or usufruct of the statutes can not be excluded cr limited.

2 The shareholder has the right to vote the shares subject to a usufruct.

3 Notwithstanding the preceding para graph, the voting rights to the usufructuary, If That is the establishment of the usufruct and the usufructuary is a person to Whom the shares pursuant to Article 195 para graph 1 of this book may be Freely Transferred. If the usufructuary is not Such a person, comes to his voting rights Exclusively, where Permitted by the establishment of the usufruct and the statutes do not Prohibit, Both That provision provided and - upon transfer of the usufruct - the transfer or voting rights approved by the corporate body designated by the statutes to grant approval to a Proposed transfer of shares, or - in the absence or Such designation - by the general meeting of shareholders. A usufruct Referred to in Articles 19 and 21 of Book 4, the voting rights to the usufructuary Also, unless the establishment of the usufruct by the parties or by the magistrate on the basis of article 23 paragraph in Book 4 4 or other wise.

4 The shareholder who has no voting rights and the usufructuary right to vote Shall have the rights Granted to All which by law are the holders of depositary receipts for shares issued trading energy company. The usufructuary has no voting rights, rights thesis, if the statutes this determination and the establishment or transfer of the usufruct, not other wise.

5 From the Proportion Arising rights, seeking to Acquire Shares Shall be credited to the shareholder with the proviso That he must pay its value to the beneficiary, to the Extent That Entitled under his usufruct thereto.

Article 198

1Based pledge shares may be Established if the statutes other wise providence.

2 The shareholder has voting rights on the pledged shares.

3 Notwithstanding the preceding para graph, the voting rights to the lien holder, If That is the establishment of the pledge and the pledgee is a person to Whom the shares pursuant to Article 195 para graph 1 of this book may be Freely Transferred. If the pledgee is not Such a person, is it the right to vote solely where Permitted by the establishment of the pledge and the establishment of the pledge is approved by the corporate body of the statute is' appropriate to grant approval to a Proposed transfer of shares, or - in the absence or Such designation - by the general meeting of shareholders. Another Occurs in the rights of the pledgee, then only allow him to vote, if the institution Referred to in the preceding sentence or, failing That, the general meeting approves transfer of the franchise. The authority to grant voting rights to the pledgee The statutes Could be excluded.

4 The shareholder who has no voting rights and lien holders who vote Shall have the rights Granted to All which by law are the holders of depositary receipts for shares issued trading energy company. The pledgee who has no voting rights, if the thesis rights statutes this determination and the establishment or transfer of the lien does not other wise providence.

5 Article 195 of this Book and the Statutory Provisions Regarding the disposition and transfer of shares Shall apply to the sale and transfer of shares by the pledgee or verblijving of the shares to the pledgee, the pledgee That provided all Regarding the disposition and transfer to the shareholder rights vested therein, and fulfill its obligations in this respect.

Article 199

1NA transfer or allocation of a share will not be paid any of the previous shareholders for the amount due thereon are jointly and severally Liable Towards the company. The Board may, together with the Supervisory Board of the former shareholders or registered or authenticate pretended Further liability release, All which in the event nonetheless Existed liability for deposits, within-issued trading one year after the date of the authentic instrument or private registered.

2 If a previous shareholder pays, he returns entered into the rights That the company has against Subsequent holders.

Article 200 [repealed on 01/01/1992]

Article 201

1For where the statutes do not other wise specified, all shares in Proportion to Their amount equal rights and obligations.

2 The company, the shareholders or certificate holders who are in similar Circumstances, In The Same Manner treat.

3rd statutes may providence That shares of a child or 'certain special rights as specified in the statute on the control of the company are connected.

Article 201a

1Hij as a shareholder for its own account at least 95% of the issued trading capital of the company provided, be made against the other joint shareholder a claim to transfer Their shares to the plaintiff. The Same applies if two or more group companies this part of the capital together, and together providence set to transfer the claim to one of them.

2 About the application judge at first instance the Enterprise Chamber of the Amsterdam Court. From the statement is only cassation.

3 If one or more defendants against default is Granted, the court of its own motion whether the plaintiff or plaintiffs fulfill the requirements of para graph 1.

4 The court rejects the claim against all defendants off, if a defendant Despite The fee would suffer serious physical injury by the transfer, a defendant is the holder of a share to All which the statutes, a special law on the control of the company or under take a plaintiff against a defendant has waived his claim in the Jurisdiction.

5 If the court finds That Paragraphs 1 and 4 the assignment of the claim does not prevent, he may recommend that one or three experts, messages about the value of the Shares to be Transferred. The first three sentences of Article 350 para graph 3 and Articles 351 and 352 apply. The judge sets the price at Which the shares to be Transferred on a day set by him. Long axis and axis far as the price is not paid, he is plus interest at the statutory rate, from That Day to the transfer, distributions on the shares consistently this period will be payable, stretching on the day of payment or partial payment to the price.

6 The judge who assigns the claim, condemns the transferee to Those to Whom the shares belong or will belong to the set price, with interest payable against delivery of the unencumbered right to the shares. The court indicates That the costs of the proceedings if He Believes That Belongs Such a statement. A defendant who has made no defense, does not pay the costs.

7 State the order to transfer to judicial res fixed, it Shall notify the transferee of the day and place of payment and the price in writing to the holders of the offered shares or Whom know the address. Hey Also Announced in a national newspaper, unless he knows all the address.

8 The buyer can always its obligations under Paragraphs 6 and 7 by ridding the fixed price with interest for all outstanding shares not taken to Consign, Including notice of his known rights and usufruct or pledge and herds known to him. This communication is batter of the shares on the entitlement. By Consign it goes right to the shares Transferred to him and go unencumbered rights of pledge or usufruct on the entitlement. To share and dividend coupons All which after the transition payments are made payable may there after no claim against the company more binding. The buyer makes Consign and the price per share at That time known in the Manner or para-graph 7.

Article 202

Bearer depositary receipts of shares may not be issued trading. If in conflict herewith is not ACTED, as long as bearer certificates outstanding, the rights attached to the share are not Exercised.

Section 3. The ability of the company

Rule 203

1Uit acts ormed On behalf of a prospective private company with limited liability, rights and obligations only for the company Arise When Such acts after its inception, express or implied endorsement or pursuant to Paragraph 4 is connected.

2 Those who perform a legal act on Behalf of a prospective private company with limited liability, except in Relation to That act other wise expressly stipulated, jointly and severally Liable powerful Therefore, until the company after its creation the act ratified.

3 If the company has its obligations under the ratified act fails, Those Who On behalf of the company to be formed ACTED jointly and severally Liable for the damages That the third consequently suffers, When they knew or Could reasonably Know That the company's commitments was the unable to Perform Without prejudice to the liability in respect of the directors Because of the ratification. The Knowledge That the company was the unable to perform its obligations, it is Presumed to exist if the company Within one year after the establishment in a state of bankruptcy.

4 The founders, the company in the memorandum only connect by issuing shares, accepting deposits thereon, to Appoint directors, the appointment of commissioners and perform legal acts Referred to in Article 204 para graph 1. If a founder has not adequately leg diligence, Articles 9 and 248, mutatis mutandis.

Article 203a

1Indien before or at the creation of shares Shall be paid in cash, must comply with the memorandum attached to one or more statements, That was all the amounts on the establishment to place shares must be paid:

ahetzij Immediately after the establishment will be available from the company;

bhetzij all at the sametime not EARLIER than five months before the creation, in a separate account All which were available only after the establishment of the company will stand, if the company accepts deposits in the doing.

2 If foreign money is Deposited must prove the statement against how much money Could be Freely traded in a day When so under Article 191A para graph 3 Could measuring the payment requirement.

3Een Statement Referred to in the first para graph may only be made by a financial 'undertaking under Article 1:1 of the Act on Financial Supervision in the European Union or a State Party to the Agreement on the European Economic Area business or a bank may exercise. The certificate may be issued trading only to a notary.

4 Are the creation of the account Referred to in subparagraph b or para graph 1, Shall be removed, then the founders jointly and severally against the company related to or Reimbursement Such amounts, until the company has endorsed the Explicitly withdrawals.

5th notary, the bank Whose statement he received immediate notification of the establishment. If the establishment does not continue, he must return the bank statement.

6 If after the establishment in a foreign currency is Deposited, Explains the within-company two weeks after the depositary a declaration Referred to in para graph 2, or a bench in the third para-graph at the office of the trade.

Article 204

1Rechtshandelingen:

ain relationelle to the acquisition of shares with special obligations to the company be placed,

bstrekkende for any advantage to ensure a founder of the company or a third in the establishment,

cbetreffende for shares other than cash,

in its Entirety Should Be included in the memorandum or in a document Given to it in original or certified copy is attached to and All which the memorandum refers. If the preceding sentence not with bone compaction song, can the company from Such acts no rights or obligations.

2 After the founding, in the preceding para graph, legal transactions without prior approval of the general meeting may be made only if and insofar as the government the powers expressly Necessary Granted by the statutes.

Article 204A

Establishing 1Indien in payment for shares other than in cash is agreed, the founders make a description of the contribution, stating the value and the Assigned Applied valuation methods. These methods must be according to standards in society Considered acceptable. The description refers to the condition of the contribution on a day not EARLIER than five months before either the establishment or a month before the ministerial declaration of no objection is required for establishment not later than one month after the declaration of no objection made. The description Shall Be signed by all incorporators. The company Explains this on its premises for inspection by the holders of its shares or depositary receipts issued trading with its cooperation.

2 About the description of the contribution must be a chartered accountant or an accounting consultant to make a statement. If it is introduced into a company Whose financial statements must be Examined, only he who is Authorized to mandatory review of financial statements, the statement on the application description. The Same applies if the value of all assets to transfer, without deduction or liabilities, at least? Amounts to 3.6 million. The statement implies That the value of the contribution, in applying Applying society accepted accounting methods, at least, amounts in the statement the amount of the payment obligation ', Expressed in money, to Which the contribution must be with. The statement must be attached to the memorandum. If it is known That the value after the description has reduced bone Significantly, a second explanation is required.

3 The description and auditors are not required if all or thesis founders have waived and a person who has acquired shares or shares with a group company has taken the following requirements:

ade legal person in the commercial where the company is registered a statement That he fi ed jointly and severally Liable for the acts of the company from debts Incurred;

Bkeys last adopted balance sheet with explanatory notes under Applicable law Identified and Investigated in accor dance with the Fourth Directive of the European Communities on the company, one in Dutch, French, German or English copy thereof and of the auditors thereon in accor dance with That Act Deposited at the office of the trade and since the balance sheet date are not yet eighteen months have elapsed;

cblijkens Referred to under b Balance Exceeds the equity of the corporation the nominal amount of the shares after the balance sheet date Entered pursuant to this para-graph in companies for All which the corporation has a declaration as specified in a

4 Article 404 Shall apply mutatis mutandis with the proviso That the declaration may not be with drawn within-two years after the contribution.

Article 204B

1Indien after the establishment for shares other than in cash is agreed, the company pursuant to Article 204A para graph 1 a description of the contribution. The description refers to the state on a day not EARLIER than five months before the date the shares are acquired or subject to an additional payment is issued trading or on Which They agreed. The directors sign the description, if the signature of one or more of them Shall Be Stated and Reasons Given.

2 Article 204A para graph 2 Shall apply mutatis mutandis.

3 The Paragraphs 3 and 4 or Article 204A Shall apply, except That the founders but not all shareholders have waived the preparation of the description and the audit report.

4 The company Shall, within-eight days after the day the shares are acquired or on All which the additional payment Became due, the auditor's contribution or a copy thereof at the office of the register stating the names of the contributors and the amount Galanthus paid part or the capital.

5 This Article Shall not apply where the contribution Consists of shares, share certificates, containing convertible rights or profit shares or another legal entity, All which the company a public bid, provided Such securities or any part thereof are Admitted to trading on a regulated market or multilateral trading facility, as defined in Article 1:1 of the Act on financial supervision or with a regulated market or multilateral trading facility from a State not a Member State.

Article 204c

1one act the company has done without the approval of the general meeting of shareholders or without the declaration referred to in paragraph 3, for the benefit of the company be destroyed, if the transaction:

astrekt to obtain goods, including claims that are settled, that a year before the incorporation or subsequently belonged to a founder or shareholder, and

ba done before two years have elapsed since the registration of the company in the commercial.

2 If the approval is requested, the company should include a description of the available goods and the consideration. The description refers to the condition of the described on a day which are not affect the setting lies. In describing the values that have to return the goods and be granted, the valuation methods

applied. These methods must conform to standards in society be considered acceptable. The directors sign the description, if the signature of one or more of them shall be stated and reasons given.

3 Article 204A paragraph 2 shall apply, except that the statement must include the value of the goods to obtain, by applying in society accepted accounting methods, corresponding to at least the value of the consideration.

4 On the availability for inspection and copy at the disposal of the documents referred to in the preceding paragraphs is Article 212 shall apply mutatis mutandis.

5 The company shall, within eight days after the act or after the approval, if granted afterwards, in the third paragraph statement or a copy thereof at the office of the trade.

6 For the purposes of this article are excluded:

averkrijgingen at public auction or exchange,

bverkrijgingen under the stipulated conditions for the ordinary operations of the company belong

cverkrijgingen which an auditor referred to in Article 204A has been made, and

dverkrijgingen due to merger or division.

7 The paragraphs 3 and 4 of Article 204A shall apply accordingly, provided that not the founders but all shareholders have waived the preparation of the description and the audit and that the value of any quid which that is done, it is surpassed by the equity of the co-liable legal.

Article 205

The company may not own shares.

Article 206

1The company can only pursuant to a resolution of the General Assembly after the establishment shares, provided by the statutes no other body has been designated. The general meeting may delegate its authority to do so to another body and can revoke this transfer.

2 The preceding paragraph shall apply mutatis mutandis to the granting of rights to subscribe for shares, but shall not apply to the issuance of shares to a person who exercises a previously acquired right to subscribe for shares.

Article 206a

1For the extent that the statutes provide otherwise, each shareholder a preferential issue of shares in proportion to the aggregate amount of his shares, the two following paragraphs. He has no respect of shares issued to employees of the company or its group companies. The shares may, each single issue, be limited or excluded by the general meeting, where the statutes provide otherwise.

2 Where the statutes provide otherwise, shareholders who have

aniet above a certain percentage of the nominal amount or only slightly above the share in profits, or

bniet above the nominal amount or only slightly above share in a liquidation surplus, no pre-emptive shares to be issued.

3 To the extent the statutes provide otherwise, the shareholders have no pre-emptive shares to be issued in one of the preceding paragraph a and b defined types.

4 The company announces the issuance of pre-emption rights and the time that can be exercised in a written notice to all shareholders at the address stated by them.

5 The preferential right may be exercised for at least four weeks after the date cf dispatch of this notice.

6 As far as the statutes provide otherwise, the shareholders have a preferential right to grant rights to subscribe for shares other than in paragraph 2 a and b defined types; the preceding paragraphs shall apply mutatis mutandis. Shareholders do not have shares that are issued to a person who exercises a previously acquired right to subscribe for shares.

Article 207

1Verkrijging by the company of partly paid shares in its capital is void.

2 Fully paid shares, the company may only acquire or if:

aThe equity less the acquisition price is not less than the paid-up capital plus the reserves required by law or the statutes must be maintained

BThe nominal amount of the available and already in the company and its subsidiaries collectively held shares in its capital not more than half of the issued capital,

cde statutes authorize the acquisition and

dmachtiging to the acquisition was granted by the general meeting of shareholders or another corporate body for that purpose by the statutes or by the general meeting of shareholders is appropriate.

3 For the validity of the acquisition, the amount of equity according to the last balance sheet, less the purchase price for shares in the capital of the company and distributions of profits or reserves to others, it and its subsidiaries after the balance sheet date were owed. Is a more than six months without the financial statements were adopted, then an acquisition under paragraph 2 is not allowed

4 The preceding paragraphs do not apply to shares held by the Company under the overall title.

5 Under the concept of equity in this article includes depositary receipts.

Article 207a

1Verkrijging of shares contrary to the second paragraph of the preceding Article shall be void. The directors are jointly and severally liable to the vendor in good faith by the nullity damage.

2 The company shall not exceed three years after they own shares for no consideration or under general title has been obtained, together with its subsidiaries hold shares in its capital more than half of the issued capital. The directors are severally liable for compensation to the company the value of the shares it holds or does too much love at the end of the last day of those years, with legal interest from that date. Payment of compensation made against transfer of the shares.

3 Paragraph 2 shall not apply to any fully paid shares of the company under the general title has been obtained and within three years since then, disposed of or withdrawn.

4 Under the concept of equity in this article includes depositary receipts.

Article 207b

If a different name in own shares in the capital of the company or depositary receipts takes or obtains on behalf of the company itself, he considered this for his own account or to obtain.

Article 207c

1The company may not, with a view to taking or acquisition by others of shares in its capital or depositary receipts, provide security, a price guarantee, is any other way or be severally or otherwise next to or for others. This prohibition also applies to its subsidiaries.

2 Loans for the purpose of taking or acquiring shares in its capital or depositary receipts, the company may only provide up to the amount of distributable reserves and insofar as the statutes allow.

3 The Company maintains a non-distributable reserve until the outstanding amount of loans in the previous paragraph.

Article 207d

1one subsidiary may own account or ensure that no shares in the capital of the company. Such shares may subsidiaries for its own account under a special title only obtain or do obtain, if the company itself under paragraphs 1-3 of Article 207 may acquire own shares.

2 If any breach of the previous paragraph, the directors of the company jointly and severally liable to pay compensation to the subsidiary of the purchase price with legal interest thereon from the time when the shares have been taken or obtained. Payment of compensation made against transfer of such shares. A director need not reimburse the purchase price, if he proves that the subscription or acquisition does not meet the company is due.

3 A subsidiary may, after it has become a subsidiary or as a subsidiary after shares in the capital of the company for no consideration or under general title has been granted for no longer than three years with the company and its other subsidiaries of these shares for own account or do keep half the subscribed capital. The directors of the company are jointly liable for compensation to the subsidiary of the value of the shares it holds or does too much love at the end of the last day of those years, with legal interest from that date. Payment of compensation made against transfer of the shares. A director need not pay compensation if he proves that it is due to the company that the shares still held.

4 Under the concept of equity in this article includes depositary receipts.

Article 208

1The general meeting of shareholders may decide to reduce the issued capital by canceling shares or by the amount of shares by reducing. In this decision the shares to which the decision relates shall be designated and must implement the decision governs. The paid-up capital must not be smaller than at the time of the decision required minimum capital.

2 A decision to withdraw may only relate to shares that the company itself or for which they hold certificates or all shares of a class where all shareholders agree or that the issuance of the Constitution states that they can be withdrawn with reimbursement, either the uitgelote shares of a class for which the issuance of the Constitution states that they can be chosen at random with repayment.

3 Reducing the amount of shares without repayment and without waiver of the obligation to pay must be in proportion to all shares of the same class. The requirement of proportionality may be waived by agreement of all shareholders involved.

4 Partial repayment on shares or exemption from the obligation to pay is only possible to implement a decision to reduce the amount of the shares. Such repayment or release must be in proportion to all shares, except for the issuance of a particular class of shares in the statutes provide that reimbursement or exemption may be made only to those shares for which shares are subject to the requirement of proportionality. The requirement of proportionality may be waived by agreement of all shareholders involved.

5 The notice convening a meeting where a decision mentioned in this article is taken, state the purpose of capital reduction and the manner of implementation. The second, third and fourth paragraph of Article 233 shall apply mutatis mutandis.

Article 209

1The company puts in the previous decisions referred to at the office of the Company Registry and announced the filing in a national newspaper.

2 The company must, on pain of a statement founded objection referred to in the following paragraph, for each creditor who requires collateral or make him give any other guarantee for the satisfaction of his claim. This does not apply if the creditor has adequate safeguards or the assets of the company provide sufficient assurance that the claim will be met.

3 Within two months after the notice mentioned in the first paragraph, any creditor by a petition to the court against the decision to reduce capital in revolt, indicating the guarantee that is sought.

4 Before the court decides, he can the company the opportunity to complete it within a deadline set by him to give security. On a legal remedy he may, if the capital has already been reduced, the lodging of a deposit plus a penalty recommended link.

5 A resolution to reduce the subscribed capital shall not take effect until resistance can be done. If timely objection is made, the decision will take effect once the application has been withdrawn or the elimination of the resistance is feasible. A reduction of the capital requirement deed of amendment can not be earlier past.

6 If the company reduces its capital because of losses to an amount not lower than that of its own funds, it shall not guarantee to give the decision immediately.

Article 210

1Jaarlijks within five months of the year the company, subject to extension of this deadline by up to six months by the general meeting under special circumstances, the Board shall prepare annual accounts and submit them to shareholders for inspection at the offices of the company. Within this period the board also the annual report for inspection by the shareholders unless the Articles 396 paragraph 7, or 403 for the company funds. The board of the company to which Articles 268 to 271 and 274 apply, send annual accounts to in Article 268 paragraph 11 referred to council.

2 The accounts shall be signed by the directors and the auditors; if the signature of one or more of them shall be stated and reasons given.

3rd annual accounts are adopted by the General Assembly. Adoption of the annual discharge shall not serve as a director respectively commissioner.

4Besluiten which the accounts are established by the statutes are not subject to the approval of an organ of the company or third parties.

5th statutes contain no provisions that allow binding rules or proposals for the accounts or any item shall be given.

6th statutes may provide that a body other than the company's general meeting has the power to determine what part of the profit for the year is set aside or how the loss is processed.

7 Our Minister of Economic Affairs may upon request, compelling reasons to waive the obligation to draw up, discuss it and adopt the financial statements.

Article 211 [repealed on 01/01/1984]

Article 212

The company ensures that its annual accounts, annual report and pursuant to Article 392 paragraph 1 to add data from the call for the general meeting, for their treatment, its premises are present. The holders of its shares or its participation certificates issued on its behalf, the documents there and there is no charge obtain a copy.

Article 213 [repealed on 01/01/1984]

Article 214 [repealed on 01/01/1984]

Article 215

Charged by the statutory reserves A deficit may only be extinguished to the extent permitted by law.

Article 216

1For where the statutes do not provide otherwise, the profit the shareholders benefit.

2 The company may pay shareholders and others entitled to the distributable profits only for payment if the equity exceeds the paid-up capital plus the reserves required by law or regulations must be observed.

3 Payment of profits made after adoption of the annual accounts showing that this is permissible.

4 The Company may make interim distributions, if the rules permit and the requirement of the second paragraph.

5 In calculating the distribution of profits the shares that the company in its own capital, in part, unless the statute otherwise.

6 In calculating the amount of profit that each share will be paid, is only the amount of the payments due to the nominal amount of the shares eligible, unless the statute otherwise.

7 The statutes may provide that the claim of a shareholder is not barred by lapse of five years, but only after a longer term expires. Such determination shall then apply mutatis mutandis to the claim of the holder of a certificate of a share of the shareholder.

8Geen of shareholders may be entirely excluded from sharing in the profits.

9th Regulations may provide that the profits to which holders of shares of a certain kind of entitled wholly or partly for their benefit will be reserved.

Section 4. The general meeting of shareholders

Article 217

1Aan the general meeting of shareholders, within the law and the Articles of powers within the limits, not to the Board or assigned to others.

2 The board and the supervisory board shall provide it with all requested information, unless an overriding interest of the company opposes.

Article 218

1Jaarlijks at least one general meeting.

2 When the statutes are not a shorter period is prescribed, the annual meeting held within six months of the year the company.

Article 219

The Board and the Supervisory Board are authorized to convene a general meeting in the statutes may be granted authority to others.

Article 220

1one or more shareholders who together hold at least one tenth of the issued capital, or such lesser amount as the statute, can the judge of the court at their request, be authorized to convene a general meeting . The court rejects the application if it does not appear that the applicants before the Board and the Supervisory Board, in writing, stating specifically the items to be discussed this request, addressed a general meeting be convened, and that neither the board or the supervisory board - so in this case equally competent - the necessary measures are taken to ensure that the general meeting within six weeks of the request could be held.

2 For the purposes of this article with holders of shares equivalent to the holders of the certificates in the name of equity, with the cooperation of the company are issued.

3Tenzij the articles otherwise provide, to the requirement of written form of the request referred to in paragraph 1 are met if the request is recorded electronically.

Article 221

1The judge of the court shall, after hearing or notice of the company, the requested authorization, if the applicant summarily have do show that in the previous article have been fulfilled, and that they have a legitimate interest in keeping the meeting. The judge of the court shall determine the form and the deadlines for convening the general meeting. He may also appoint someone who with the guidance of the general meeting shall be responsible.

2 When the notice under paragraph stated that, under court authorization shall. The notice made in this way is valid, even if it appears that the authorization was wrongly granted.

3 Against the decision of the judge is no provision allowed, subject to cassation in the interest of the law.

Article 222

If they are, under Article 219 to the convening jurisdiction, have failed by Article 218 or the Statute, General Assembly to hold, each shareholder by the judge of the court be empowered to do so themselves. Article 220 paragraph 2 and Article 221 shall apply mutatis mutandis.

Article 223

1The notice convening a general meeting of shareholders shall be by means of written notices sent to the addresses of shareholders, as stated in the register of shareholders.

2 Are there certificates with the cooperation of the company on behalf of its shares, the holders thereof will be called by publication in a national newspaper. The statutes may otherwise regulate this notice.

3Tenzij the statutes provide otherwise, if the holder of shares and the holder of the share certificates issued with the cooperation of the company are issued, consent, the notice made by an electronically readable and reproducible message sent to the address provided by him for this purpose the company has announced.

Article 224

1 The notice shall state the subjects to be discussed. In the notice in a daily newspaper or the business to be transacted or is informed that the holders of depositary receipts issued by the Company of its shares at the offices of the company unable to examine.

2 With respect to subjects whose treatment was not stated in the notice or in the same fashion, with due observance of the notice period, can not lawfully be taken, unless the decision is taken unanimously at a meeting at which the entire issued capital is represented .

3 Notice that under the law or the statutes to the General Assembly should be directed, may be included in the notice and, where appropriate, either in the notice in a daily newspaper or either in the document for inspection at the office of the company is filed, provided in the notice thereof is reported.

Article 224a

1one item, which requested in writing by one or more shareholders who individually or collectively at least one hundredth of the issued share capital is included in the notice or in the same way if the company has announced the request no later than the thirtieth day before the meeting and provided no major interest of the company opposes. In the statutes, the required portion of the capital be reduced by and the deadline for submission of the request be shortened.

2for the purposes of this article with the holders of shares equivalent to the holders of certificates representing shares with the cooperation of the company are issued.

3Tenzij the articles otherwise provide, to the requirement of written form of the request referred to in paragraph 1 are met if the request is recorded electronically.

Article 225

Subject to the second sentence of the first paragraph of Article 221 shall be the notice not later than the fifteenth day before the meeting. That period was shorter or if the notice did not take place, then no valid resolutions may be adopted unless unanimously at a meeting at which the entire issued capital is represented.

Article 226

The general meetings are held in the Netherlands spot in the bylaws, or otherwise in the municipality where the company is domiciled. In a general meeting, held elsewhere than one may legitimately decide only be adopted if the entire issued capital is represented.

Article 227

1Iedere shareholder is entitled, in person or by written proxy, the general meeting of shareholders to attend, to speak and to vote. The statutes, the power of shareholders to be represented should be imited. The power of shareholders to be represented by a lawyer, notary, notary, accountant or accounting consultant can not be excluded.

2 Each holder of a cooperation of the company certificate issued in the name of a share shall, in person or by written proxy, the general meeting to attend and to speak. The last sentence of paragraph 1 shall apply mutatis mutandis.

3rd statutes may provide that a shareholder is not entitled to participate in the meeting as long as he fails to comply with a legal or statutory obligation. The bylaws may provide that for attending the meeting is required, the shareholder of its intention known to the directors of the company. The convocation of the meeting shall then state the date on which notification must be made no later. This date can not be earlier than the third day of the meeting. Where the statutes a requirement under the foregoing provisions of this paragraph for the shareholders contain true that the co-holders of the certificates in the name of equity, with support from the company are issued.

4 The directors and auditors as such in the general meetings in an advisory capacity.

5Aan the requirement of a written power of attorney is met if the proxy is recorded electronically.

Article 227a

1The Regulations may provide that each shareholder is entitled to, in person or by written proxy, by means of electronic communication to the General Assembly to participate in it to speak and to vote.

2for the purposes of paragraph 1 requires that the shareholder via the electronic communication can be identified, directly take note of the proceedings of the meeting and exercise his voting rights. The bylaws may provide that additional requirement that the shareholder by electronic communication may participate in the deliberations.

° 3 or pursuant to the statutes may impose conditions on the use of electronic communication. If these conditions are made under the Statute, those disclosed in the notice.

4Lid 1 to 3 shall apply mutatis mutandis to the rights of a cooperation of the company issued a share certificate.

5Aan the requirement of a written power of attorney is met if the proxy is recorded electronically.

Article 227b

Regulations may provide that votes cast at the general meeting by electronic communication may be released not earlier than the thirtieth day of the meeting, be equated with the votes cast at the meeting.

Article 228

1Slechts shareholders have voting rights. Each shareholder has at least one vote. The bylaws may provide that a shareholder is not entitled to voting rights as long as he fails to comply with a legal or statutory obligation.

2 If the share capital into shares of the same figure was divided, each shareholder brings many voices as he shares.

3 If the share capital into shares of different amount is divided, the number of votes each shareholder equal to the number of times that the amount of the smallest share is included in the aggregate amount of his shares, fractional votes shall be disregarded.

4 However, the same by a shareholder to bring vote on the statute be limited, provided that shareholders whose shares amount to equal the same number of votes and the restriction for the holders of a larger amount of shares is not more favorable than is provided for Holders of a smaller amount of shares.

5 From the provisions of the second and third paragraph, the statutes in other ways be waived, subject to the same shareholder not more than six votes are awarded if the share capital is divided into one hundred shares or more, and no more than three vote if the capital in less than one hundred shares is divided.

6 For a share belonging to the company or a subsidiary in general meeting may not exercise voting rights, nor for a share for which one of them holds. Usufructuaries and pledgees of shares to the company and its accessories, are not excluded from voting if the usufruct or pledge was established before the shares to the Company or a subsidiary. The company or a subsidiary can not vote for a share which it has a right of usufruct or pledge.

Article 229 [repealed on 01/01/1992]

Article 230

1All decisions whereof the statutes do not prescribe a larger majority, are taken by absolute majority of votes cast. If the votes in an election of persons, decided by lot, crossed the votes in a vote other than the proposal is rejected, all to the extent that the statutes are another solution is indicated. This solution can be to entrust the decision to a third party.

2 Unless otherwise specified in the statutes, the validity of acts not represented at the meeting depends on the proportion of the capital.

3 If the statute provides that the validity of an act depends on the represented at the meeting portion of the capital and this part at the meeting was not represented, may, unless the articles provide otherwise, a new meeting be convened at which the decision can be taken independently of the represented at the meeting portion of the capital. The notice to the new meeting must state that and why a decision can be taken independently of the meeting represented part of the capital.

4 The management of the company likes the resolutions passed. The records office of the company for inspection by the shareholders and the holders with the cooperation of the company issued certificates for its shares. Each of them will request a copy or extract of such record at the maximum cost.

Article 231

1The general meeting is authorized to amend the statutes, insofar as the statutes the power to amend should have been excluded, is nevertheless possible amendment unanimously in a meeting where the entire issued capital is represented.

2 A provision in the statutes, which the authority to amend any other provisions of the statutes is limited, may only be amended in accordance with the same restriction.

3 A provision in the statutes, that the power to change one or more other rules, may only be amended unanimously in a meeting where the entire issued capital is represented.

Article 231A

1The decision to increase the amount of the shares and the share capital in accordance with Article 178A is taken by an absolute majority. The decision to reduce the amount of the shares and the capital is taken by a majority of at least two-thirds of the votes cast if less than half of the issued capital is represented. Are there different types of shares, then in addition to the decision to increase or decrease a prior or simultaneous approval decision is required from each group of shareholders which affects the conversion.

2for the application of this provision, shares of a particular species also include stocks with a distinct denomination.

Article 232

Amendment of a provision of the statute, where a party other than shareholders of the company as such any right is awarded, if the recipient in the change not consent, his right not prejudicial, unless at the time of the granting of the right ability to change to that provision was expressly reserved.

Article 233

1When to the General Assembly a proposal to amend the statutes will be made, this must always be in the notice convening the general meeting shall be stated.

2 Those who have done such a notice must be simultaneously a copy of the proposal which the proposed amendment verbatim, at the offices of the company deposit for inspection by any shareholder until the end of the meeting. Article 224 paragraph 2 shall apply mutatis mutandis.

3 The shareholders must be given the opportunity of the day of deposit to that of the general meeting a copy of the proposal, as in the previous paragraph, to obtain. These copies shall be provided free of charge.

4 The provisions in this article relating to shareholders is determined, shall apply to holders of depositary receipts issued in the name of the company shares.

Article 234

1of a change in the statutes, under penalty of nullity, a notarial deed. The deed is executed in the Dutch language.

2 The deed may consist of a notarial record of the general meeting at which the amendment is adopted, or at a later notarial deed. The board is authorized the deed, without purpose by the general meeting to be authorized. The general meeting, the board or one or more other persons authorized to make the changes, necessary to prove the statement referred to in the following article available.

3 If the share capital changed, please state what part of the instrument is placed.

Article 235

1The change in the statutes shall not take effect, until by the Minister of Justice stated that his objections are not shown.

2nd statement referred to in paragraph one shall be refused on the grounds that by amending the company would acquire a prohibited character or that there is a danger that by amending the company will be used for illicit purposes.

3b obtaining this statement must meet the Minister of Justice with all the information are necessary to assess the application. Our Minister should also benefit from the State Funds amounting to? 90.76 are met. We may by order increase the amount of administration associated with the increase in wages and prices.

4th statement is not required for conversion of the amounts of the shares or the share or the issued capital in euro under Article 178A.

Article 236

The Directors are required to deposit an authentic copy of the amendment and the amended statute to deposit at the office of the Trade.

Article 237

During the bankruptcy the company may in its constitution not be altered without the consent of the trustee.

Article 238

1The Regulations may provide that decisions of shareholders other than in a meeting can take place except with the cooperation of the company name on certificates of shares issued. If the statutes contain such a scheme, such a decision is possible only with the unanimous vote of the voting shareholders. The votes will be made in writing.

2Tenzij the statutes provide otherwise, the vote also electronically delivered.

Section 5. The board of the company and supervision of the Board

Article 239

1Behoudens restrictions under the statutes, the board is charged with the management of the company.

2nd Regulations may provide that a particular function or designated driver more than one vote is granted. A director may not cast more votes than the other drivers combined.

3Besluiten of the Board may by or under the statutes are subject to the approval of another body of the company.

4th Regulations may provide that the board should behave to the instructions of an organ of the company that the general lines of the policy in more detail in the articles relate to the areas identified.

Article 240

1The board represents the company, insofar as the law provides otherwise.

2 The power of representation is partly to allow each driver. The bylaws may provide to the board except that it only belongs to one or more directors. They may also provide that a director the company only with the cooperation of one or more others may represent.

3 Entitlement to representation at the board or to an operator belongs to, indefinitely and unconditionally, to the extent the law provides otherwise. A legally permitted or prescribed restriction or requirement for the power of representation can only be invoked by the company.

4 The statutes can to persons other than directors power to grant representation.

Article 241

The court, within whose jurisdiction the company is domiciled, take note of all legal actions relating to the agreement between the company and the driver, including the claim referred to in Article 248 of the Book, whose amount is indefinite or? 5000 to beyond. The same court took note of requests under Article 685 of Book 7 on the first sentence in the said agreement.

Article 242

1The appointment of directors shall be for the first time in the memorandum and later by the general meeting of shareholders, unless in accordance with Article 272 of this Book by the superv sory board is made.

2The Association, the group of eligible individuals by limiting requirements which the directors must meet. The requirements may be refused by a decision of the General Assembly require two-thirds of the votes cast representing more than half of the issued capital.

Article 243

1When the statutes may provide that the appointment by the general meeting will take place from a list of at least two persons for each vacancy to be filled contains.

2 The general meeting may, to such nomination of its binding nature of a resolution passed by two thirds of the votes cast, representing more than half of the issued capital.

3 The preceding paragraphs shall not apply if the appointment is made by the supervisory board.

Article 244

1Iedere director may at any time be suspended or dismissed by a person authorized to appoint.

2 Where the statute provides that the decision to suspend or dismiss may only be taken with a strengthened majority in a general meeting at which a certain portion of the capital is represented, should this enhanced two-thirds majority of votes cast, representing more than half of the capital, not to exceed.

3 A conviction for the recovery of the employment contract between the company and driver can not be pronounced by the court.

4 The statutes must contain provisions concerning the manner in which the directors of the company is provisionally in the event of absence or inability of directors.

Article 245

As far as the statutes do not provide otherwise, the remuneration of directors by the general meeting.

Article 246

Unless the statutes provide otherwise, the board is without command of the general meeting has no power to declare the bankruptcy of the company.

Article 247

1Rechtshandelingen of the company against the holder of all shares in the capital of the company or against a partner in a marriage community or a community of a registered partnership which all shares in the capital of the company include, where the company is represented by such shareholder or by one of the partners, be recorded in writing. For the purposes of the preceding sentence, shares held by the company or its subsidiaries are not counted. If the first sentence not been complied with, the legal act on behalf of the company be destroyed.

2 Paragraph 1 shall not apply to operations under the stipulated conditions for the ordinary operations of the company properly.

Article 248

1In the case of bankruptcy of the company, each director against the estate liable for the amount of the debt to the extent not by liquidation of the remaining benefits will be satisfied if the board task manifestly improper has fulfilled and it is plausible that this is a major cause of bankruptcy.

2 If the board has not fulfilled its obligations under Articles 10 or 394, it has fulfilled its task improperly and suspected improper performance of duties is an important cause of bankruptcy. The same applies if the company fully liable partner of a partnership or limited partnership and not fulfilled the obligations under Article 15i of Book 3. An important omission is not taken into account.

3 Do not liable, the director who proves that the improper performance of duties by the board not attributable to him and that he was not negligent in taking measures to avert the consequences.

4 The court may the amount for which the directors are liable if it this reduce excessive songs, given the nature and seriousness of the improper performance of duties by the board, the other causes of bankruptcy, and how this is settled. The judge may also, the amount of the liability of an individual driver reducing this excessive if it occurs, given the time during which the driver has been in office as such in the period in which the improper performance of duties took place.

5 Is the size of the deficit is not yet known, the court may, with or without application of the fourth paragraph, provide that the deficit for the payment of which they are directors condemning a state is prepared in accordance with the provisions of the sixth title of the second book of the Code of Civil Procedure.

6 The claim may be brought only on the basis of improper performance of duties during the period of three years preceding the bankruptcy. A discharge is granted to the driver to adjust the claim is not in the way.

7 With a driver, for the purposes of this article, the one who equated the policy of the Company has determined whether co has determined, as if he was a director. The claim can not be brought against the trustee appointed by the court.

8 This article shall affect the jurisdiction of the bankruptcy trustee to bring a claim under the agreement with the director or pursuant to Article 9.

9 If a director under this section is liable and is unable to pay his debt matter, the trustee by that driver voluntarily performed acts which means that the story on him is reduced to the benefit of the estate by an extrajudicial statement destroy, if it is likely that entirely or almost entirely for the purpose of reduction of that story have been made. Article 45 paragraphs 4 and 5 of Book 3 shall apply mutatis mutandis.

10 Article 138 paragraph 10 shall apply.

Article 249

If the financial statements, interim financial statements by or through the annual report where they are announced, a misleading representation is given the status of the company, the directors against third parties liable for the damages suffered by them as a result. The director who proves that this is not due to him, is not liable.

Article 250

1When the statutes may provide that a board of commissioners will be. The board consists of one or more natural persons.

2 The supervisory board is responsible for supervising the policy of the government and the general affairs of the company and its business. He is the Board with advice. In the performance of their duties, the commissioners themselves to the interests of the company and its business.

3 The articles may contain additional provisions regarding the duties and powers of the board and its members include.

4th statutes may provide for a particular function or designated commissioner more than one vote is granted. A member may not cast more votes than the other commissioners together.

Article 251

1The Board provides the Supervisory Board in time for the performance of its duties.

2The Board shall at least once a year the Supervisory Board in writing of the outline of the strategic policy, the general and financial risks and the management and control of the company.

Article 252

1The commissioners who are not already in the memorandum have been designated, appointed by the general meeting of shareholders. The statutes may the circle of eligible persons limited by requirements which the Board must comply. The requirements may be refused by a decision of the General Assembly require two-thirds of the votes cast representing more than half of the issued capital.

2 The first two paragraphs of Article 243 of this Book shall apply mutatis mutandis, if the appointment by the shareholders' meeting place.

3 In a recommendation or nomination of a Commissioner from the candidate's age, occupation, the amount of shares held by him in the capital of the company and the positions he holds or has held to the extent of interest in connection with the performance of the duties of a commissioner. It also sets out the legal, he is already a; if these include legal persons, belonging to the same group, can refer to that group will be sufficient. The recommendation and the recommendation for appointment or reappointment shall be justified. For reappointment, with the way the candidate has fulfilled his duties as commissioner.

Article 253

The statutes may provide that one or more commissioners, but not more than a third of the whole number, will be appointed other than by the general meeting. Is the appointment of commissioners resolved in accordance with Articles 268 and 269 of this book, then find the preceding sentence shall not apply.

Article 254

1one Board may be suspended or dismissed by a person authorized to appoint unless Article 271 paragraphs 2 and 3 of Article 271a of this book is applicable.

2The second and third paragraph of Article 244 of this Book shall apply mutatis mutandis.

Article 255

The general meeting may grant a remuneration to the auditors.

Article 256

Unless the statutes provide otherwise, the company is in all cases where a conflict of interest with one or more directors, represented by Commissioners. The general meeting is authorized one or more other persons to be appointed.

Article 257

1Tenzij the statutes provide otherwise, the Board of Commissioners authorized any driver at all times be suspended.

2 The suspension may at any time by the general meeting may be canceled, unless the power to appoint directors to the Board of Commissioners based.

Article 258 [repealed on 01/01/1984]

Article 259

The provisions of Articles 9, 241 and 248 shall apply mutatis mutandis with respect to the performance of duties by the Board of Commissioners.

Article 260

If the published financial statements misleading representation is given the status of the company, the board next to the drivers against third parties liable for the damages suffered by them as a result. The Commissioner proves that this is not a shortcoming on his part in the supervision is due, is not liable.

Article 261

1Allen, auditors or others who, without being part of the board of the company, under any provision of the constitution or by resolution of the general assembly, for a certain time or under certain conditions, acts of governing conduct in this respect are, what their rights and obligations towards the company and third parties, as designated drivers.

2 The approval of certain administrative acts or mandate to do this does not count as performing acts of directors.

Section 6. The Board of Commissioners in the large private company with limited liability

Article 262

In this section, a dependent company means:

aa legal entity which the Company or one or more dependent companies, alone or together for their own account at least half of the issued capital;

leg partnership, a company is incorporated and for which the Company or a dependent company as a partner towards third parties fully liable for all debts.

Article 263

1one private company with limited liability, if the following paragraph shall apply to her, within two months after the adoption of its financial statements by the general meeting at the offices of the trade 'declarations that they meet the conditions laid down in that paragraph. Until Article 264 paragraph 3 of this book has been applied, the board shall in each subsequent annual report if the statement is made, the statement is deleted, it will be recorded in the first annual report after the date of such cancellation is made.

2 The obligation to make the statement applies if:

aThe issued capital of the company together with the reserves of the balance sheet and notes at least one established by Royal Decree threshold amount,

bde company or a dependent company under a legal obligation Works has set, and

cbij the company and its dependent companies, together usually at least one hundred employees working in the Netherlands.

3 The obligation to make a statement does not apply to:

aa company dependent company is a legal entity which Articles 63f to 63j, Articles 158 to 161 and 164 or Articles 268 to 271 and 274 apply,

leg company whose activity is exclusively or almost exclusively limited to the management and financing of group companies and its and their shareholdings in other entities, provided that the employees of the company and group companies outside the Netherlands are in majority,

ceen company owned exclusively or almost exclusively to a company referred to in Article 153 b of paragraph 3 b, and the provisions mentioned in that group companies and legal services for the management and funding grants, and

deen company in which at least half the subscribed capital in accordance with a mutual cooperation arrangement brings together two or more persons covered by Articles 63f to 63j, Articles 158 to 161 and 164 or Articles 268 to 271 and 274 applies or who are dependent company of such corporation.

4 The in subparagraph a of paragraph 2 above limit shall be no more than once in two years increased or decreased in proportion to the development of a by general government to designate price index since a bee that measure date to be determined, it is then completed to the nearest multiple of one million. The amount will not be re-established as long as the unrounded amount less than one million differs from the previously fixed amount.

5 Under the issued capital and reserves are included in paragraph 2 under a joint made and yet to be input from members by way of guarantee or in dependent companies which are limited partnerships, where this does not lead to double counting.

Article 264

1The Articles 268-274 of this book are applicable to a company on which a statement referred to in the previous article for three years continuously enrolled, this period shall be deemed not to be interrupted if a cancellation of the statement, which during that period wrongly held, is canceled.

2 The cancellation of the registration by virtue of the fact that the company no longer meets the conditions specified in the second paragraph of the preceding Article, the applicability of Sections 268-274 of the Book terminate only if three years after the cancellation has expired and the company during that period was not re-doing the giving has been required.

3 The company markets its statutes in accordance with Articles 268-274 for which its funds, the latest from the date of such items pursuant to paragraph 1 of its operation.

4In the next meeting after the company which Articles 268 to 274 or 268 to 271 and 274 applies are going to meet the conditions referred to in Articles 263 paragraph 3, 264 paragraph 2, 265 or 265a, does the board to the General Assembly the proposal in the statutes the manner of appointment and dismissal of auditors and the duties and powers of the supervisory board to regulate without application of Articles 268 to 274 respectively in Articles 268 to 271 and 274, or the proposal in whole or in these articles except Article 272 continue to apply. The decision is taken by an absolute majority. The competence of the General Assembly to take a decision pursuant to this Article may not be limited.

5Uiterlijk twelve months after the decision referred to in paragraph 4 is taken, the board shall submit to the General Assembly a proposal to amend the statutes. If the Assembly decides not to amend shall notify the Enterprise Chamber of the Amsterdam Court at the request of the person appointed under the following paragraph has jurisdiction, the statutes. The last two sentences of paragraph 4 shall apply mutatis mutandis.

6One request for adoption of the statutes can be submitted by a designated representative of the board or the supervisory board and the person who is authorized for inclusion under Article 224a.

7th Enterprise controls as necessary consequences of its decision. The clerk of the Enterprise is doing at the office of the commercial where the company is registered a copy of the decision of the Enterprise deposit.

Article 265

1In Notwithstanding Article 264 Article 272 shall not apply to a company in which a participation of at least half of the issued share capital is held:

Adoor a legal entity whose majority of employees work outside the Netherlands, or by dependent companies thereof

bvolgens a mutual cooperation arrangement by a number of such entities or companies, or

cvolgens a mutual cooperation arrangement by one or more of such entities, and one or more legal entities for which Article 153 paragraph 3, under a or Article 263 paragraph 3 under a force or which Articles 63f to 63j, Articles 158 to 161 and 164 or Articles 268 to 271 and 274 apply.

2 The exception under the preceding paragraph shall not apply if the employees of the company, together with those employed by the entity or entities, the majority working in the Netherlands.

3 For the purposes of this Article, employees, employed by a corporation, include the employees of group companies.

Article 265a

1In Notwithstanding Article 264 Article 272 shall not apply to a company in which:

aa natural person or the entire issued capital does provide, or two or more natural persons according to a mutual agreement to cooperate the entire issued capital or do provide;

bone foundation, association or legal entity referred to in Article 1, the entire issued capital for their own account provided or does provide, or two or more of such entities, according to a mutual agreement to cooperate the entire issued capital to provide for its own account or do provide.

2 Using the natural person referred to in paragraph 1 shall be treated as the spouse and registered partner. Also be equated to relatives in a straight line, provided that they are within six months after the death of the individual is a mutual cooperation arrangement entered into.

Article 266

Our Minister of Justice, having heard the Economic and Social Council, to a company at its request to waive one or more of Articles 268-274 of the Book, the exemption may be granted under restrictions and conditions may be attached thereto, which may also be amended or withdrawn.

Article 267

1one company to which Article 264 of this book does not apply, may by its statutes the manner of appointment and dismissal of auditors and the duties and powers of the supervisory control in accordance with Articles 268-274 of this book if they or a dependent society is a Works set to which the provisions of the Works Councils Act apply. She may refrain from applying Article 272. The rules in this paragraph in the statutes loses its validity when the council ceases to exist or no longer works on the provisions of the Works Councils Act apply.

2A company to which Article 265 or 265a applies, the authority to regulate the appointment and dismissal of directors under Article 272.

Article 268

1The company has a supervisory board.

2nd supervisory board consists of at least three members. Is the number of commissioners less than three, the Board takes immediate measures to supplement its membership.

3rd Board of Commissioners adopt a profile of its size and composition, taking into account the nature of the business, its activities and the desired expertise and background of the board. The board discusses the profile for the first down and then for any change in the general meeting and with the works.

4The Board shall, subject to paragraph 9, on the recommendation of the Supervisory Board appointed by the general meeting, provided the appointment has not already been done with the memorandum or before this article on the company became applicable. The nomination is reasoned. Without prejudice to Article 270 the statutes the circle of eligible persons is not limited.

5th general meeting and the council may participate in the Supervisory Board recommend persons to be nominated Commissioner. The Board shall inform them in due time when, as a result and according to which profile a vacancy to be filled. If the place referred to in paragraph 6 enhanced right of recommendation applies, the Board of Commissioners also notice thereof. The Supervisory Board makes recommendations simultaneously to the General Assembly and the Works. The proposal shall be reasoned.

6for a third of the members of the supervisory board is that the supervisory board by the council person recommended the nomination, unless the Supervisory Board objects to the recommendation under the expectation that the recommended person would be unfit for the performance of the duties of Commissioner or the supervisory board appointed pursuant to the recommendation will not properly constituted. If the number of members of the Supervisory Board can not be divided by three, the next lower number that can be divided by three is taken into account for determining the number of members to which this enhanced right of recommendation applies.

7Indien the supervisory objection, it shall inform the works council objection and the reasons for it. The Board shall immediately consult with the works with a view to reaching agreement on the nomination. If the Supervisory Board finds that no agreement can be reached, a designated representative of the board of the Enterprise Chamber of the Amsterdam Court of the objection well founded. The request shall not be filed until four weeks have elapsed after the start of the consultation with the council. The board shall place the person recommended the nomination if the Enterprise's objection unfounded. The Enterprise Division upholds the objection, the works council can make a new recommendation in accordance with paragraph 6.

8The Enterprise, the council calls. The decision of the Enterprise can not be appealed. The Enterprise can not express condemnation of the proceedings.

9th general meeting may by an absolute majority of votes cast, representing at least one third of the issued capital, reject the nomination. If the shareholders by an absolute majority of votes their support to the candidate remember, but this majority is not at least one third of the issued capital, a new meeting may be convened at which the nomination may be rejected by an absolute majority. Then, the board shall make a new nomination. The members 5 to 8 are applied. If the Assembly does not appoint the nominated person and does not decide to reject the nomination, appoints the Supervisory Board of the nominated person.

10th General Assembly, the power conferred by paragraph 5 is due for a to be determined by duration of not more than two consecutive years, transfer to a committee of shareholders, it enables members to designate, in which case the supervisory board to the committee the notification in paragraph 5. The general meeting may at any time undo the transfer.

11Voor the purposes of this section, the council means the council of the business of the company or the company of a dependent society. If more than one works, the powers of this article by these councils separately exercised, if there is a nomination referred to in paragraph 6, the powers of this paragraph by these councils jointly. Does the company or companies concerned a central works council, then the powers of the council under this section to the Central Works Council.

12In the statutes may be made to paragraphs 2, 4 to 7 and 9, except that no derogation from the first two sentences of paragraph 9. The decision to amend the statutes require the prior approval of the Supervisory Board and the consent of the works required.

Article 269

1Ontbreken all Commissioners, other than pursuant to Article 271a, the appointment shall be by the general meeting.

2nd council may recommend persons for appointment as Commissioner. Whoever the general meeting convenes, shall notify the council in a timely manner that the appointment of commissioners subject of treatment in the general meeting will be, whether the appointment is taking place under the right of recommendation of the council pursuant to Article 268 paragraph 6.

3rd paragraphs 6, 7, 8, 10 and 11 of the preceding article shall apply mutatis mutandis.

Article 270

Commissioner can not be:

apersonen employed by the company;

bpersonen employed by a dependent society;

cbestuurders and persons in the service of an employee organization that is usually involved in the determination of the conditions of the persons referred to under a and b.

Article 271

1one Commissioner shall not later than if after his appointment last four years has been Commissioner. The deadline may be extended by the statutes to the day of the next general meeting after the fcur years or after the date of this article for the legal person will apply.

2 The Enterprise Chamber of the Amsterdam Court may on a request to dismiss a commissioner for neglecting his duties, for other important reasons or for substantial change of circumstances justifying enforcement as Commissioner of the Company can not reasonably be required. The request may be submitted by the company, represented by the Board, or by a duly designated representative of the general meeting or of the works referred to in paragraph 11 of Article 268. The members 10 and 11 of Article 268 shall apply mutatis mutandis.

3 A member may be suspended by the supervisory board, the suspension shall expire by law, if the company within one month after the commencement of the suspension with a request referred to in the preceding paragraph at the Enterprise Chamber has submitted.

Article 271a

1The general meeting may by an absolute majority of votes cast, representing at least one third of the issued capital, confidence in the supervisory board terminate. The decision is reasoned. The decision can not be taken with regard to commissioners appointed by the Enterprise in accordance with paragraph 3.

2A resolution referred to in paragraph 1 shall be taken before the administration of the council's proposal for decision and the reasons therefore has informed. Such notice shall be at least 30 days before the general meeting at which the proposal is discussed. If the works a position on the proposal, the Board proposes the Supervisory Board and the General Assembly informed of this position. The works can have its position in the General Assembly do explain.

3The decision referred to in paragraph 1, the immediate dismissal of the members of the supervisory board as a result. Then asks the board immediately to the Enterprise Chamber of the Amsterdam Court temporarily one or more commissioners to be appointed. The Enterprise Chamber regulates the consequences of the appointment.

4th Board of Commissioners encourages that, within a deadline set by the Enterprise a new board be composed in accordance with Article 268.

Article 272

The supervisory board appoints the directors of the company, this authority may not be limited by any binding nomination. He gives the general meeting of an intended appointment of a director of the company, he does not absolve a director until after the general meeting on the proposed dismissal. The eleventh paragraph of Article 268 of this Book shall apply mutatis mutandis.

Article 273 [repealed on 01/10/2004]

Article 274

1Aan the approval of the Supervisory Board are subject to the decisions of the Board concerning:

auitgifte and acquisition of shares and debentures of the company or of debentures of a limited partnership or general partnership of which the company fully liable partner;

bmedewerking to the issuance of certificates issued shares;

chet application for admission of the a and b referred debentures respectively certificates to trading on a regulated market or multilateral trading facility, as defined in Article 1:1 of the Act on financia supervision or with a regulated market or multilateral trading facility system from a non-Member State or is requesting a withdrawal of such authorization;

Dhet into or termination of sustained cooperation of the Company or a related company with another entity or company or as fully liable partner in a limited partnership or partnership, if such cooperation or termination of major significance to the company;

ehet taking a stake worth at least a fourth of the amount of the issued capital and reserves according to the balance sheet and notes of the company, by it or a related company in the capital of another company, or any material increase or reducing such participation;

finvesteringen requiring an amount equal to at least one fourth of the issued capital and reserves of the company in its balance sheet with explanatory notes;

No proposal to amend the statutes;

over proposal to dissolve the company;

iaangifte of bankruptcy and application for suspension of payments;

jbeëindiging of the employment of a substantial number of employees of the company or of a dependent company simultaneously or within a short period of time;

tion ripening changes in the employment of a substantial number of employees of the company or of a dependent company;

loan proposal to reduce the issued capital.

2 The lack of approval of the Supervisory Board on a decision as referred to in paragraph 1 affect the authority of the board of directors not to.

Article 275 -284 [repealed on 01/04/1987]

Section 8. The appeal

Article 284a

The applicant may appeal to the Appeals Board against the business:

aa refusal of the request referred to in Article 175, paragraph 3, second sentence;

leg refusal of the declaration referred to in Article 179, paragraph 2;

ceen refusal of the declaration referred to in Article 235, paragraph 2 and

deen decision to refuse, vary or revoke the exemption and a decision to grant an exemption to appropriate and necessary conditions, or limitations thereby imposed in Article 266.

TITLE 6. FOUNDATIONS

Article 285
1one foundation is a legal act by a created entity, which has no members and aims at using a specially designed power in the statutes stated goal.

2 If the articles one or more persons the power to fill the vacancies in the organ of the foundation to provide, she is not on that account regarded members to know.
3 The aim of the foundation may not include the making of distributions to founders or to those who are part of its organs or to others, except that the latter concerns the benefits of a philanthropic or social scope.

Article 286
1one foundation must be established by notarial deed.
2nd deed must be executed in the Dutch language. If the foundation has its headquarters in the province of Friesland, the Frisian language in the deed be executed. A power of attorney to cooperate with the act must be in writing granted. The foundation may be established by public testament that in other than the Dutch or Frisian is past, the statutes of the foundation must also then in the Dutch or Frisian denominated.
3 The document sets out the statutes of the foundation.
4 The statute should include:
ade name of the foundation, with the word foundation as part of the name;
BThe goal of the foundation;
cde manner of appointment and dismissal of directors;
dde municipality in the Netherlands where it has its seat;
oath appropriation of the surplus after liquidation of the foundation in case of dissolution, or the manner in which the destination will be determined.
5 The notary, in front of whom the instrument is executed, shall ensure that the articles contain what is called in paragraphs 2-4. If he fails, he is personally against those who damaged thereby, liable.

Article 287
In the absence of a designation of a seat in the statutes, the foundation has its seat in the municipality where the notary before whom the instrument was drawn, at the time of the execution of the deed had his place.

Article 288 [repealed on 01/01/2003]

Article 289
1The Directors are required to the foundation in addition to the name, the names and residence or last residence of the founder or founders to do in the commercial register and a certified copy or an original extract from the memorandum containing the statutes, at the offices of that register down.
2 As long as the task for initial registration and deposit have not been done, each director for a legal act, which he connects the foundation, besides the foundation liable.

Article 290 [repealed on 01/01/1992]

Article 291
1Behoudens restrictions under the statutes, the board is charged with the management of the foundation.
2 Only if the statute arises, the board is authorized to decide to enter into agreements to acquire, alienate or encumber registered property, and to enter into agreements with the foundation itself as surety or debtor, for a third party strong or provides security for a debt of another party. The bylaws may delegate this power to restrictions and conditions bind. The exclusion, limitations and conditions also apply to the authority to represent the Foundation in respect of such acts, unless the articles provide otherwise.

Article 292
1The Board represents the Foundation, to the extent the law provides otherwise.
2 The statutes may also grant the authority to represent one or more directors. They may provide that a director, the foundation only with the cooperation of one or more others may represent.
3 Entitlement to representation at the board or to an operator belongs to, indefinitely and unconditionally, to the extent the law provides otherwise. A legally permitted or prescribed restriction or requirement for the authority to represent the foundation can only be invoked.
4 The statutes can to persons other than directors power to grant representation.

Article 293
The statutes of the foundation by its organs can only be amended if the association an opportunity to open. The amendment shall be void by notarial deed come. The Directors are required to deposit an authentic copy of the amendment and the amended articles at the office of the Article 289 of this Book shall register.

Article 294

1Indien continuation with the statute would lead to consequences that can not reasonably in setting its demand, and the possibility of amending the statutes do not provide or those who have the power to amend, without fail, the court may on application by a founder , the Board or the prosecution to change the statutes.
2 The court differs while minimizing off of the existing statutes, if a change of the objective, a goal that it points to the existing kin. Subject to the foregoing, the court has jurisdiction, if necessary, the articles otherwise change is requested.
3 With appropriate application of the two preceding paragraphs, the court may amend the articles to dissolve the foundation on a ground mentioned in Article 21 or Article 301 paragraph 1 under a prevent.

Article 295
A resolution amending the Articles of Association may at any time upon request of the foundation of an interested party or the public prosecutor by the court be annulled if the change means that the foundation may be dissolved on grounds provided for in Articles 21 or 301 paragraph 1, and that change does not lead to conversion. Moreover, Article 15 paragraphs 3 and 4 and Article 16 shall apply.

Article 296
In one case, in which dissolution of a foundation on a ground mentioned in Article 21 or 301 para 1 a is requested, the court's powers in the two preceding Articles, the automatic exercise.

Article 297
1The public prosecutor at the tribunal, in serious doubt whether the law or the articles in good faith compliance, or the Board duly served, responsible to the board to request information.
2 In non-or improper fulfillment of the request, the judge of the court, when so requested, recommended that the Public Prosecutor's books, records and other data carriers of the foundation for consultation are made available and the values of the foundation are shown. The decision of the judge is no appeal or cassation.

Article 298
1one director who:
aiets does or does not conflict with the provisions of the law or the statutes, or is guilty of maladministration, or
bniet or not properly comply with by the judge of the court, pursuant to the previous article, given order, the court can be fired. This can be done at the request of the prosecutor or any interested party.
2 The court may, pending the investigation, a preliminary injunction on the board and take the driver's suspension.
3 A driver dismissed by the court for five years after the dismissal is not a director of a foundation are.

Article 299
Whenever the board by the Statutes weak or absent and it is not in accordance with the statutes, the court may, upon application by any interested person or the prosecutor in the fulfillment of the empty place provided. The court shall, wherever possible, the association observed.

Article 299a
A foundation that one or more undertakings which maintains under the Act must be entered in the commercial mentions in the statement of income and expenses, net sales of these companies.

Article 300
1Jaarlijks within six months of the year from a foundation referred to in Article 360 paragraph 3, subject to extension of this deadline by up to five months by the body referred to in paragraph 3 under special circumstances, the Board shall prepare annual accounts and submit them for those who are part of the body referred to in paragraph 3 at the offices of the foundation. Within this period, the board also under Article 392 paragraph 1 to add data for inspection by those who are part of the body referred to in paragraph 3 and the annual report, unless Article 396 paragraph 7 insofar as it concerns the annual report, or section 403 funds for the foundation. Those who are part of the body referred to in paragraph 3 to a free copy of these documents available.
2nd annual accounts are signed by the directors and by those who are part of the supervisory body; if the signature of one or more of them shall be stated and reasons given.
3rd annual accounts within one month after the period fixed by the competent body to do so under the statutes. Where the statutes that power is not any body to grant this power comes to the supervisory body and failing that to the Board.
4Een foundation referred to in Article 360 paragraph 3 may be covered by the statutory reserves amortize a deficit only to the extent permitted by law.

5Onze Minister of Economic Affairs may upon request, compelling reasons to waive the obligation to draw up, discuss it and adopt the financial statements.

Article 300a
Articles 131, 138, 139, 149 and 150 shall apply mutatis mutandis in case of bankruptcy of a foundation on which company tax is subject.

Article 301
1The court dissolves the foundation at the request of any interested person or the public prosecutor if:
aThe ability of the foundation utterly insufficient for the attainment of its objects, and the possibility that a sufficient capacity by contributions or otherwise in the foreseeable future will be obtained, highly unlikely;
BThe goal of the foundation has been reached or can not be achieved, and change of purpose is not eligible.
2 The court may also automatically dissolve the foundation together with the rejection of an application referred to in Article 294.

Article 302
In any final judgments, holding:
deletion, addition or alteration of entries in the register,
amend the statutes of the foundation,
amend or facility in the board or
annulment of a resolution amending the statute,
by the care of the Registrar of the college which the case was last pending registered in the Article 289 of the Book said register.

Article 303
In the event of bankruptcy or receivership of a foundation are the announcements that under the Bankruptcy Act are included in the Dutch Gazette, by him who is entrusted with the disclosure, partly for entry in the register referred to in Article 289 of this Book, stated .

Article 304
1The participants in a pension fund or a fund referred to in Article 631, paragraph 3 c of Book 7, for the purposes of Article 285 of this Book is not regarded as members of a foundation such as a fund operates.
2 For the purposes of Article 285 paragraph 3 of this book are such as distributions to founders of a foundation or to those who are part of its organs, not the benefits arising from a pension or a claim under a contract in which a clause referred to in Article 631, paragraph 3 c of Book 7 is included.

DUTCH CORPORATE GOVERNANCE CODE

THE DUTCH CORPORATE GOVERNANCE CODE

Preamble

The Corporate Governance Code Monitoring Committee (referred to below as the Committee) has amended the Dutch Corporate Governance Code (referred to below as the Code) of December 2003 at the request of the National Federation of Christian Trade Unions in the Netherlands (CNV), Eumedion, the Federation of Dutch Trade Unions (FNV), the Netherlands Centre of Executive and Supervisory Directors (NCD), NYSE Euronext, the Association of Stockholders (VEB), the Association of Securities-Issuing Companies (VEUO) and the Confederation of Netherlands Industry and Employers (VNO-NCW). The government has supported this request. The amended Code replaces the 2003 Code.

The Code applies to all companies whose registered offices are in the Netherlands and whose shares or depositary receipts for shares have been admitted to listing on a stock exchange, or more specifically to trading on a regulated market or a comparable system, and to all large companies whose registered offices are in the Netherlands (balance sheet value > € 500 million) and whose shares or depositary receipts for shares have been admitted to trading on a multilateral trading facility or a comparable system (referred to below as listed companies).[1] The Code does not apply to an investment company that is not a manager within the meaning of Section 1:1 of the Financial Supervision Act *(Wet op het financieel toezicht / Wft).* For the purposes of the Code holders of depositary receipts issued with the cooperation of the company are treated as shareholders.

The Code contains principles and best practice provisions that regulate relations between the management board, the supervisory board and the shareholders (i.e. the general meeting of shareholders). Relations between the company and its employees (staff representatives) are regulated elsewhere. Nonetheless, the interests of the employees should be taken into account when the interests of all stakeholders are weighed in connection with compliance with the Code.

The principles may be regarded as reflecting the general views on good corporate governance, which enjoy wide support. They have been elaborated in the form of specific best practice provisions. These provisions create a set of standards governing the conduct of management board members, supervisory board members and shareholders. They reflect national and international best practices and may be regarded as elaborating the general principles of good corporate governance. Listed companies may depart from the best practice provisions. Departures may be justified in certain circumstances. Shareholders, the media, businesses that specialise in rating the corporate governance structure of listed companies and persons who advise on the exercise of voting rights attaching to shares should carefully assess the reason for each and every departure from the Code's provisions. Both shareholders and the management and supervisory boards should be prepared to enter into a dialogue on the reasons for any departures. The company should state each year in its annual report how it applied the principles and best practice provisions of the Code in the past year and should, where applicable, carefully explain why a provision was not applied. It is up to the shareholders to call the management board and the supervisory board to account for compliance with the Code.

The Code is not an isolated set of rules, but part of a larger system, together with Dutch and European legislation and case law on corporate governance, which must be viewed in its entirety. The particular merit of the Code as an instrument of self-regulation lies above all in its influence on the behaviour of management board members, supervisory board members and shareholders. The strength of the Code is proportionate to the extent to which the company's stakeholders endorse it and try to comply with it.

The amendments to the Code are based on the existing legislation and case law on the external and internal relationships of listed companies and on the case law, and allow for relevant corporate governance trends since the Code's entry into force. For the sake of the Code's readability and its internal coherence the Committee has decided that any overlap between the legislation and the Code is inherent in the Code's function and need not necessarily result in amendments to the Code, also because the Code may contain provisions that supplement the statutory provisions. If a principle or best practice provision corresponds with a statutory rule, this may mean that a company or shareholder is not allowed to depart from the relevant provision, not even when reasons are given. An example is the parts of the Code dealing with the audit committee, which have been elevated to the status of statutory rule.[2]

The Code is based on the principle accepted in the Netherlands that a company is a long-term alliance between the various parties involved in the company. The stakeholders are the groups and individuals who, directly or indirectly, influence – or are influenced by – the attainment of the company's objects: i.e. employees, shareholders and other lenders, suppliers, customers, the public sector and civil society. The management board and the supervisory board have overall responsibility for weighing up these interests, generally with a view to ensuring the continuity of the enterprise, while the company endeavours to create long-term shareholder value.

The management board and the supervisory board should take account of the interests of the various stakeholders, including corporate social responsibility issues that are relevant to the enterprise. If stakeholders are to cooperate within and with the company, it is essential for them to be confident that their interests are represented. Good entrepreneurship, which includes integrity and transparency of the management board's actions, as well as effective supervision of their actions and accountability for such supervision, are essential conditions for stakeholder confidence in management and supervision. These are the two pillars on which good corporate governance is founded and which are the basis of this Code.

[2] Decree of 26 July 2008 implementing Article 41 of Directive 2006/43/EC of the European Parliament and of the Council of 17 May 2006 on statutory audits of financial statements and consolidated financial statements, amending Council Directives 78/660/EEC and 83/349/EEC and repealing Council Directive 84/253/EEC (Bulletin of Acts and Decrees 323).

The management board is responsible for weighing up the different interests with respect to the company's strategy, while the supervisory board must oversee this process. Both these organs are accountable to the general meeting for the performance of their roles. Unlike the management board and the supervisory board, the other stakeholders of the company are not in principle guided exclusively by the interests of the company and its affiliated enterprise. For example, shareholders can give priority to their own interests with due regard for the principle of reasonableness and fairness. The greater the interest which the shareholder has in a company, the greater is his responsibility to the company, the minority shareholders and other stakeholders.

The above principles can cause tension between on the one hand the management and supervisory boards, which have to serve the interests of the company and are accountable for this to the general meeting and, on the other, the shareholders, who are, in principle, free to put their own interests first. How this tension should be resolved will differ from case to case. The Code contains general rules of conduct designed to ensure the careful handling of the processes involving the management board, the supervisory board and the shareholders (in particular, the general meeting of shareholders) and to help the management board and the supervisory board weigh up the different interests correctly. Good relations between the various stakeholders are of great importance in this connection, particularly through a continuous and constructive dialogue.

The tension described above may become especially pronounced in takeover situations. It has been seen in practice that when various alternatives have to be compared during takeover negotiations, the highest price for the shares is often a major factor. However, decision-making should also take account of other relevant interests. Partly in view of the risk that particular interests may gain the upper hand in takeover situations, the special involvement of the supervisory board is required in cases where, for example, the shares are acquired by means of a public bid or where a company makes a substantial acquisition. This involvement does not detract from the responsibility of the management board.

A different sort of tension may also occur between the remuneration policy of companies and their strategy. It is important for the remuneration policy of companies to be closely aligned with the strategy and the related risks. This applies to the remuneration of both the management board and the other levels of the organisation. Remuneration policy, like the other instruments deployed by the company, can help it to achieve its objectives, but it can also seriously jeopardise such efforts. In this respect the supervisory board must play its oversight role. The supervisory board ensures that the right balance is struck for the enterprise between (a) the fixed and variable components of the remuneration and (b)

the short and longer term remuneration. Ultimately, remuneration policy must serve the interests of the company and its affiliated enterprise, in other words be aimed at creating long-term value.

The 2003 Code was designated as a code of conduct within the meaning of Article 2:391, paragraph 5, of the Netherlands Civil Code by order in council of 30 December 2004. This means that since 1 January 2004 listed companies have been obliged to report on compliance with the Code in their annual report and to explain why any of the principles and best practice provisions intended for the management and supervisory boards are not applied. The statutory requirements to be met by this corporate governance statement are being extended in order to implement European (accounting) directives.[3] For example, the chief characteristics of the internal risk management and control systems connected with the company's financial reporting process have to be included in the statement, which must be verified by the auditor. Under Section 5:86 of the Financial Supervision Act, Dutch institutional investors have been obliged from 1 January 2007 to include in their annual report or on their websites a statement about their compliance with the best practice provisions applicable to them.

The Code consists of this preamble, the principles, the best practice provisions and an explanation of and notes to certain terms used in the Code. The Code is divided into five chapters: (I) compliance with and enforcement of the Code; (II) the management board; (III) the supervisory board; (IV) the shareholders and the general meeting of shareholders; and (V) the audit of the financial reporting and the position of the internal audit function and the external auditor. All these chapters contain principles and best practice provisions for listed companies. Chapter IV also contains provisions for shareholders, including institutional investors and trust offices that administer shares for which depositary receipts have been issued. Chapter V contains some provisions for the external auditor.

The Code is based on the system in which a separate supervisory board exists alongside the management board, whether under the statutory two-tier rules (*structuurregime*) or otherwise. Chapter III.8 contains a number of specific provisions for companies that have a one-tier structure. In November 2008, the government presented to the Lower House of Dutch Parliament a bill containing rules for cases in which executive and non-executive directors form part of one board (one-tier board structure)[4]. The bill also proposes a new scheme for resolving conflicts of interest involving management and supervisory board members, which is in keeping with the provisions of the Code.

The amended Code will come into force with effect from the financial year starting on or after 1 January 2009. The Committee recommends that listed companies include a chapter in their annual report on the broad outline of their corporate governance structure and compliance with the amended Code and present this chapter to the general meeting in 2010 for discussion as a separate agenda item.

[3] Bill to amend Book 2 of the Netherlands Civil Code in order to implement Directive 2006/46/EC of the European Parliament and of the Council of 14 June 2006 amending Council Directives 78/660/EEC, 83/349/EEC, 86/635/EEC and 91/674/EEC on the financial statements and consolidated financial statements (OJ EU L 224) (Parliamentary Papers II 2007/08, 31 508, no. 2) [4] Bill to amend Book 2 of the Netherlands Civil Code in connection with the adjustment of the rules governing management and supervision in public and private limited companies (Parliamentary Papers II 2008/09, 31 763, no. 2)

PRINCIPLES AND BEST PRACTICE PROVISIONS

I. COMPLIANCE WITH AND ENFORCEMENT OF THE CODE

Principle The management board and the supervisory board are responsible for the corporate governance structure of the company and for compliance with this code. They are accountable for this to the general meeting and should provide sound reasons for any non-application of the provisions.

Shareholders take careful note and make a thorough assessment of the reasons given by the company for any non-application of the best practice provisions of this code. They should avoid adopting a 'box-ticking approach' when assessing the corporate governance structure of the company and should be prepared to engage in a dialogue if they do not accept the company's explanation. There should be a basic recognition that corporate governance must be tailored to the company-specific situation and that non-application of individual provisions by a company may be justified.

Best practice provisions

I.1 The broad outline of the corporate governance structure of the company shall be explained in a separate chapter of the annual report, partly by reference to the principles mentioned in this code. In this chapter the company shall indicate expressly to what extent it applies the best practice provisions in this code and, if it does not do so, why and to what extent it does not apply them.

I.2 Each substantial change in the corporate governance structure of the company and in the compliance of the company with this code shall be submitted to the general meeting for discussion under a separate agenda item.

II. THE MANAGEMENT BOARD

II.1 Role and procedure

Principle The role of the management board is to manage the company, which means, among other things, that it is responsible for achieving the company's aims, the strategy and associated risk profile, the development of results and corporate social responsibility issues that are relevant to the enterprise. The management board is accountable for this to the supervisory board and to the general meeting. In discharging its role, the management board shall be guided by the interests of the company and its affiliated enterprise, taking into consideration the interests of the company's stakeholders. The management board shall provide the supervisory board in good time with all information necessary for the exercise of the duties of the supervisory board.

The management board is responsible for complying with all relevant primary and secondary legislation, for managing the risks associated with the company activities and for financing the company. The management board shall report related developments to and shall discuss the internal risk management and control systems with the supervisory board and the audit committee.

Best practice provisions

II.1.1 A management board member is appointed for a maximum period of four years. A member may be reappointed for a term of not more than four years at a time.

II.1.2 The management board shall submit to the supervisory board for approval:
a) the operational and financial objectives of the company;
b) the strategy designed to achieve the objectives;
c) the parameters to be applied in relation to the strategy, for example in respect of the financial ratios; and
d) corporate social responsibility issues that are relevant to the enterprise.
The main elements shall be mentioned in the annual report.

II.1.3 The company shall have an internal risk management and control system that is suitable for the company. It shall, in any event, employ as instruments of the internal risk management and control system:
a) risk analyses of the operational and financial objectives of the company;
b) a code of conduct which should be published on the company's website;
c) guides for the layout of the financial reports and the procedures to be followed in drawing up the reports; and
d) a system of monitoring and reporting.

II.1.4 In the annual report the management board shall provide:
a) a description of main risks related to the strategy of the company;
b) a description of the design and effectiveness of the internal risk management and control systems for the main risks during the financial year; and
c) a description of any major failings in the internal risk management and control systems which have been discovered in the financial year, any significant changes made to these systems and any major improvements planned, and a confirmation that these issues have been discussed with the audit committee and the supervisory board.

II.1.5 As regards financial reporting risks the management board states in the annual report that the internal risk management and control systems provide a reasonable assurance that the financial reporting does not contain any errors of material importance and that the risk management and control systems worked properly in the year under review. The management board shall provide clear substantiation of this.

II.1.6 In the annual report, the management board shall describe the sensitivity of the results of the company to external factors and variables.

II.1.7 The management board shall ensure that employees have the possibility of reporting alleged irregularities of a general, operational and financial nature within the company to the chairman of the management board or to an official designated by him, without jeopardising their legal position. Alleged irregularities concerning the functioning of management board members shall be reported to the chairman of the supervisory board. The arrangements for whistleblowers shall be posted on the company's website.

II.1.8 A management board member may not be a member of the supervisory board of more than two listed companies. Nor may a management board member be the chairman of the supervisory board of a listed company. Membership of the supervisory board of other companies within the group to which the company belongs does not count for this purpose. The acceptance by a management board member of membership of the supervisory board of a listed company requires the approval of the supervisory board. Other important positions held by a management board member shall be notified to the supervisory board.

II.1.9 If the management board invokes a response time within the meaning of best practice provision IV.4.4, such period may not exceed 180 days from the moment the management board is informed by one or more shareholders of their intention to put an item on the agenda to the day of the general meeting at which the item is to be dealt with. The management board shall use the response time for further deliberation and constructive consultation. This shall be monitored by the supervisory board. The response time may be invoked only once for any given general meeting and may not apply to an item in respect of which the response time has been previously invoked or meetings where a shareholder holds at least three quarters of the issued capital as a consequence of a successful public bid.

II.1.10 If a takeover bid for the company's shares or for the depositary receipts for the company's shares is being prepared, the management board shall ensure that the supervisory board is closely involved in the takeover process in good time.

II.1.11 If the management board of a company for which a takeover bid has been announced or made receives a request from a competing bidder to inspect the company's records, the management board shall discuss this request with the supervisory board without delay.

II.2 Remuneration

Level and composition of the remuneration

Principle The level and structure of the remuneration which the management board members receive from the company for their work shall be such that qualified and expert managers can be recruited and retained. When the overall remuneration is fixed, its impact on pay differentials within the enterprise shall be taken into account. If the remuneration consists of a fixed component and a variable component, the variable component shall be linked to predetermined, assessable and influenceable targets, which are predominantly of a long-term nature. The variable component of the remuneration must be appropriate in relation to the fixed component.

The remuneration structure, including severance pay, shall be simple and transparent. It shall promote the interests of the company in the medium and long term, may not encourage management board members to act in their own interests or take risks that are not in keeping with the adopted strategy, and may not 'reward' failing board members upon termination of their employment. The supervisory board is responsible for this. The level and structure of remuneration shall be determined by reference to, among other things, the results, the share price performance and non-financial indicators that are relevant to the company's long-term value creation.

The shares held by a management board member in the company on whose board he sits are long-term investments. The amount of compensation which a management board member may receive on termination of his employment may not exceed one year's salary, unless this would be manifestly unreasonable in the circumstances.

Best practice provisions

II.2.1 Before drawing up the remuneration policy and determining the remuneration of individual management board members, the supervisory board shall analyse the possible outcomes of the variable remuneration components and how they may affect the remuneration of the management board members.

II.2.2 The supervisory board shall determine the level and structure of the remuneration of the management board members by reference to the scenario analyses carried out and with due regard for the pay differentials within the enterprise.

II.2.3 In determining the level and structure of the remuneration of management board members, the supervisory board shall take into account, among other things, the results, the share price performance and non-financial indicators relevant to the long

term objectives of the company, with due regard for the risks to which variable remuneration may expose the enterprise.

II.2.4 If options are granted, they shall, in any event, not be exercised in the first three years after the date of granting. The number of options to be granted shall be dependent on the achievement of challenging targets specified beforehand.

II.2.5 Shares granted to management board members without financial consideration shall be retained for a period of at least five years or until at least the end of the employment, if this period is shorter. The number of shares to be granted shall be dependent on the achievement of challenging targets specified beforehand.

II.2.6 The option exercise price may not be fixed at a level lower than a verifiable price or a verifiable price average in accordance with the trading in a regulated market on one or more predetermined days during a period of not more than five trading days prior to and including the day on which the option is granted.

II.2.7 Neither the exercise price of options granted nor the other conditions may be modified during the term of the options, except in so far as prompted by structural changes relating to the shares or the company in accordance with established market practice.

II.2.8 The remuneration in the event of dismissal may not exceed one year's salary (the 'fixed' remuneration component). If the maximum of one year's salary would be manifestly unreasonable for a management board member who is dismissed during his first term of office, such board member shall be eligible for severance pay not exceeding twice the annual salary.

II.2.9 The company may not grant its management board members any personal loans, guarantees or the like unless in the normal course of business and on terms applicable to the personnel as a whole, and after approval of the supervisory board. No remission of loans may be granted.

Determination and disclosure of remuneration

Principle The supervisory board shall determine the remuneration of the individual members of the management board, on a proposal by the remuneration committee, within the scope of the remuneration policy adopted by the general meeting.

The report of the supervisory board shall include the principal points of the remuneration report concerning the remuneration policy of the company. This shall describe transparently and in clear and understandable terms the remuneration policy that has been pursued and give an overview of the remuneration policy to be pursued. The full remuneration of the individual management board members, broken down into its various components, shall be presented in the remuneration report in clear and understandable terms.

Best practice provisions

II.2.10 If a variable remuneration component conditionally awarded in a previous financial year would, in the opinion of the supervisory board, produce an unfair result due to extraordinary circumstances during the period in which the predetermined performance criteria have been or should have been achieved, the supervisory board has the power to adjust the value downwards or upwards.

II.2.11 The supervisory board may recover from the management board members any variable remuneration awarded on the basis of incorrect financial or other data (clawback clause).

II.2.12 The remuneration report of the supervisory board shall contain an account of the manner in which the remuneration policy has been implemented in the past financial year, as well as an overview of the remuneration policy planned by the supervisory board for the next financial year and subsequent years. The report shall explain how the chosen remuneration policy contributes to the achievement of the long-term objectives of the company and its affiliated enterprise in keeping with the risk profile. The report shall be posted on the company's website.

II.2.13 The overview referred to in best practice provision II.2.12 shall in any event contain the following information:

a) an overview of the costs incurred by the company in the financial year in relation to management board remuneration; this overview shall provide a breakdown showing fixed salary, annual cash bonus, shares, options and pension rights that have been awarded and other emoluments; shares, options and pension rights must be recognised in accordance with the accounting standards;

b) a statement that the scenario analyses referred to in best practice provision II.2.1 have been carried out;

c) for each management board member the maximum and minimum numbers of shares conditionally granted in the financial year or other share-based remuneration components that the management board may member acquire if the specified performance criteria are achieved;

d) a table showing the following information for incumbent management board members at year-end for each year in which shares, options and/or other share-based remuneration components have been awarded over which the management board member did not yet have unrestricted control at the start of the financial year:

i) the value and number of shares, options and/or other share-based remuneration components on the date of granting;

ii) the present status of shares, options and/or other share-based remuneration components awarded: whether they are conditional or unconditional and the year in which vesting period and/or lock-up period ends; iii) the value and number of shares, options and/or other share-based remuneration components conditionally awarded under

i) at the time when the management board member obtains ownership of them (end of vesting period), and iv) the value and number of shares, options and/or other share-based remuneration components awarded under i) at the time when the management board member obtains unrestricted control over them (end of lock-up period);

e) if applicable: the composition of the peer group of companies whose remuneration policy determines in part the level and composition of the remuneration of the management board members;

f) a description of the performance criteria on which the performance-related component of the variable remuneration is dependent in so far as disclosure would not be undesirable because the information is competition sensitive, and of the discretionary component of the variable remuneration that can be fixed by the supervisory board as it sees fit;

g) a summary and account of the methods that will be applied in order to determine whether the performance criteria have been fulfilled;

h) an ex-ante and ex-post account of the relationship between the chosen performance criteria and the strategic objectives applied, and of the relationship between remuneration and performance; i) current pension schemes and the related financing costs; and j) agreed arrangements for the early retirement of management board members.

II.2.14 The main elements of the contract of a management board member with the company shall be made public after it has been concluded, and in any event no later than the date of the notice calling the general meeting where the appointment of the management board member will be proposed. These elements shall in any event include the amount of the fixed salary, the structure and amount of the variable remuneration component, any agreed redundancy scheme and/or severance pay, any conditions of a change-of-control clause in the contract with a management board member and any other remuneration components promised to the management board member, pension arrangements and performance criteria to be applied.

II.2.15 If a management board member or former management board member is paid severance pay or other special remuneration during a given financial year, an account and an explanation of this remuneration shall be included in the remuneration report.

II.3 Conflicts of interest

Principle Any conflict of interest or apparent conflict of interest between the company and management board members shall be avoided. Decisions to enter into transactions under which management board members would have conflicts of interest that are of material significance to the company and/or to the relevant management board member require the approval of the supervisory board.

Best practice provisions

II.3.1 A management board member shall: a) not enter into competition with the company; b) not demand or accept (substantial) gifts from the company for himself or for his wife, registered partner or other life companion, foster child or relative by blood or marriage up to the second degree as defined under Dutch law; c) not provide unjustified advantages to third parties to the detriment of the company; and d) not take advantage of business opportunities to which the company is entitled for himself or for his wife, registered partner or other life companion, foster child or relative by blood or marriage up to the second degree as defined under Dutch law.

II.3.2 A management board member shall immediately report any conflict of interest or potential conflict of interest that is of material significance to the company and/or to him, to the chairman of the supervisory board and to the other members of the management board and shall provide all relevant information, including information concerning his wife, registered partner or other life companion, foster child and relatives by blood or marriage up to the second degree as defined under Dutch law. The supervisory board shall decide, without the management board member concerned being present, whether there is a conflict of interest. A conflict of interests exists, in any event, if the company intends to enter into a transaction with a legal entity: i) in which a management board member personally has a material financial interest; ii) which has a management board member who is related under family law to a management board member of the company, or iii) in which a management board member of the company has a management or supervisory position.

II.3.3 A management board member may not take part in any discussion or decision-making that involves a subject or transaction in relation to which he has a conflict of interest with the company.

II.3.4 All transactions in which there are conflicts of interest with management board members shall be agreed on terms that are customary in the sector concerned. Decisions to enter into transactions in which there are conflicts of interest with management board members that are of material significance to the company and/or to the relevant board members require the approval of the supervisory board. Such transactions shall be published in the annual report, together with a statement of the conflict of interest and a declaration that best practice provisions II.3.2 to II.3.4 inclusive have been complied with.

III. THE SUPERVISORY BOARD

III.1 Role and procedure

Principle The role of the supervisory board is to supervise the policies of the management board and the general affairs of the company and its affiliated enterprise, as well as to assist the management board by providing advice. In discharging its role, the supervisory board shall be guided by the interests of the company and its affiliated enterprise, and shall take into account the relevant interests of the company's stakeholders. The supervisory board shall also have due regard for corporate social responsibility issues that are relevant to the enterprise. The supervisory board is responsible for the quality of its own performance.

Best practice provisions

III.1.1 The division of duties within the supervisory board and the procedure of the supervisory board shall be laid down in terms of reference. The supervisory board's terms of reference shall include a paragraph dealing with its relations with the management board, the general meeting and the central works council or works council. The terms of reference shall be posted on the company's website.

III.1.2 The annual statements of the company shall include a report of the supervisory board. In this report the supervisory board describes its activities in the financial year and which includes the specific statements and information required by the provisions of this code.

III.1.3 The following information about each supervisory board member shall be included in the report of the supervisory board: a) gender; b) age; c) profession; d) principal position; e) nationality; f) other positions, in so far as they are relevant to the performance of the duties of the supervisory board member; g) date of initial appointment; and h) current term of office.

III.1.4 A supervisory board member shall retire early in the event of inadequate performance, structural incompatibility of interests, and in other instances in which this is deemed necessary by the supervisory board.

III.1.6	The supervision of the management board by the supervisory board shall include:
	a) achievement of the company's objectives; b) corporate strategy and the risks inherent in the business activities; c) the design and effectiveness of the internal risk management and control systems; d) the financial reporting process; e) compliance with primary and secondary legislation; f) the company-shareholder relationship; and g) corporate social responsibility issues that are relevant to the enterprise.
III.1.7	The supervisory board shall discuss at least once a year on its own, i.e. without the management board being present, its own functioning, the functioning of its committees and its individual members, and the conclusions that must be drawn on

the basis thereof. The desired profile, composition and competence of the supervisory board shall also be discussed. Moreover, the supervisory board shall discuss at least once a year without the management board being present both the functioning of the management board as an organ of the company and the performance of its individual members, and the conclusions that must be drawn on the basis thereof. The report of the supervisory board shall state how the evaluation of the functioning of the supervisory board, the separate committees and the individual supervisory board members has been carried out.

III.1.8 The supervisory board shall discuss at least once a year the corporate strategy and the main risks of the business, the result of the assessment by the management board of the design and effectiveness of the internal risk management and control systems, as well as any significant changes thereto. Reference to these discussions shall be made in the report of the supervisory board.

III.1.9 The supervisory board and its individual members each have their own responsibility for obtaining all information from the management board and the external auditor that the supervisory board needs in order to be able to carry out its duties properly as a supervisory organ. If the supervisory board considers it necessary, it may obtain information from officers and external advisers of the company. The company shall provide the necessary means for this purpose. The supervisory board may require that certain officers and external advisers attend its meetings.

III.2 Independence

Principle The composition of the supervisory board shall be such that the members are able to act critically and independently of one another, the management board and any particular interests.

Best practice provisions

III.2.1 All supervisory board members, with the exception of not more than one person, shall be independent within the meaning of best practice provision III.2.2.

III.2.2 A supervisory board member shall be deemed to be independent if the following criteria of dependence do not apply to him. These criteria are that the supervisory board member concerned or his wife, registered partner or other life companion, foster child or relative by blood or marriage up to the second degree as defined under Dutch law: a) has been an employee or member of the management board of the company (including associated companies as referred to in Section 5:48 of the Financial Supervision Act *(Wet op het financieel toezicht / Wft)* in the five years prior to the appointment; b) receives personal financial compensation from the company, or a company associated with it, other than the compensation received for the work performed as a supervisory board member and in so far as this is not in keeping with the normal course of business; c) has had an important business relationship with the company, or a company associated with it, in the year prior to the appointment. This includes the case where the supervisory board member, or the firm of which he is a shareholder, partner, associate or adviser, has acted as adviser to the company (consultant, external auditor, civil notary and lawyer) and the case where the supervisory board member is a management board member or an employee of any bank with which the company has a lasting and significant relationship; d) is a member of the management board of a company in which a member of the management board of the company which he supervises is a supervisory board member; e) holds at least ten percent of the shares in the company (including the shares held by natural persons or legal entities which cooperate with him under an express or tacit, oral or written agreement); f) is a member of the management board or supervisory board - or is a representative in some other way - of a legal entity which holds at least ten percent of the shares in the company, unless such entity is a member of the same group as the company;

g) has temporarily managed the company during the previous twelve months where management board members have been absent or unable to discharge their duties.

III.2.3 The report of the supervisory board shall state that, in the board's view, best practice provision III.2.1 has been fulfilled, and shall also state which supervisory board member is not considered to be independent, if any.

III.3 Expertise and composition

Principle Each supervisory board member shall be capable of assessing the broad outline of the overall policy. Each supervisory board member shall have the specific expertise required for the fulfilment of the duties assigned to the role designated to him within the framework of the supervisory board profile. The composition of the supervisory board shall be such that it is able to carry out its duties properly. The supervisory board shall aim for a diverse composition in terms of such factors as gender and age. A supervisory board member shall be reappointed only after careful consideration. The profile referred to above shall also be applied in the case of a reappointment.

Best practice provisions

III.3.1 The supervisory board shall prepare a profile of its size and composition, taking account of the nature of the business, its activities and the desired expertise and background of the supervisory board members. The profile shall deal with the aspects of diversity in the composition of the supervisory board that are relevant to the company and shall state what specific objective is pursued by the board in relation to diversity. In so far as the existing situation differs from the intended situation, the supervisory board shall account for this in the report of the supervisory board and shall indicate how and within what period it expects to achieve this aim. The profile shall be made generally available and shall be posted on the company's website.

III.3.2 At least one member of the supervisory board shall be a financial expert with relevant knowledge and experience of financial administration and accounting for listed companies or other large legal entities.

III.3.3 After their appointment, all supervisory board members shall follow an induction programme, which, in any event, covers general financial, social and legal affairs, financial reporting by the company, any specific aspects that are unique to the company and its business activities, and the responsibilities of a supervisory board member. The supervisory board shall conduct an annual review to identify any aspects with regard to which the supervisory board members require further training or education during their period of appointment. The company shall play a facilitating role in this respect.

III.3.4 The number of supervisory boards of Dutch listed companies of which an individual may be a member shall be limited to such an extent that the proper performance of his duties is assured; the maximum number is five, for which purpose the chairmanship of a supervisory board counts double.

III.3.5 A person may be appointed to the supervisory board for a maximum of three 4-year terms.

III.3.6 The supervisory board shall draw up a retirement schedule in order to avoid, as far as possible, a situation in which many supervisory board members retire at the same time. The retirement schedule shall be made generally available and shall be posted on the company's website.

III.4 The chairman of the supervisory board and the company secretary

Principle The chairman of the supervisory board shall ensure the proper functioning of the supervisory board and its committees, and shall act on behalf of the supervisory board as the main contact for the management board and for shareholders regarding the functioning of the management and supervisory board members. In his capacity of chairman, he shall ensure the orderly and efficient conduct of the general meeting.

The chairman of the supervisory board is assisted in his role by the company secretary.

Best practice provisions

III.4.1 The chairman of the supervisory board shall ensure that: a) the supervisory board members follow their induction and education or training programme; b) the supervisory board members receive in good time all information which is necessary for the proper performance of their duties; c) there is sufficient time for consultation and decision-making by the supervisory board; d) the committees of the supervisory board function properly; e) the performance of the management board members and supervisory board members is assessed at least once a year; f) the supervisory board elects a vice-chairman; and g) the supervisory board has proper contact with the management board and the works council (or central works council).

III.4.2 The chairman of the supervisory board may not be a former member of the management board of the company.

III.4.3 The supervisory board shall be assisted by the company secretary. The company secretary shall ensure that correct procedures are followed and that the supervisory board acts in accordance with its statutory obligations and its obligations under the articles of association. He shall assist the chairman of the supervisory board in the actual organisation of the affairs of the supervisory board (information, agenda, evaluation, training programme, etc.). The company secretary shall, either on the recommendation of the supervisory board or otherwise, be appointed and dismissed by the management board, after the approval of the supervisory board has been obtained.

III.4.4 The vice-chairman of the supervisory board shall deputise for the chairman when the occasion arises. By way of addition to best practice provision III.1.7, the vice-chairman shall act as contact for individual supervisory board members and management board members concerning the functioning of the chairman of the supervisory board.

III.5 Composition and role of three key committees of the supervisory board

Principle If the supervisory board consists of more than four members, it shall appoint from among its members an audit committee, a remuneration committee and a selection and appointment committee. The function of the committees is to prepare the decision-making of the supervisory board. If the supervisory board decides not to appoint an audit committee, remuneration committee or selection and appointment committee, best practice provisions III.5.4, III.5.5, III.5.8, III.5.9, III.5.10, III.5.14, V.1.2, V.2.3, V.3.1, V.3.2 and V.3.3 shall apply to the entire supervisory board. In its report, the supervisory board shall report on how the duties of the committees have been carried out in the financial year.

Best practice provisions

III.5.1 The supervisory board shall draw up terms of reference for each committee. The terms of reference shall indicate the role and responsibility of the committee concerned, its composition and the manner in which it discharges its duties. The terms of reference may provide that a maximum of one member of each committee may not be independent within the meaning of best practice provision III.2.2. The terms of reference and the composition of the committees shall be posted on the company's website.

III.5.2 The report of the supervisory board shall state the composition of the committees, the number of committee meetings and the main items discussed.

III.5.3 The supervisory board shall receive from each of the committees a report of its deliberations and findings.

Audit committee

III.5.4 The audit committee shall in any event focus on supervising the activities of the management board with respect to: a) the operation of the internal risk management and control systems, including supervision of the enforcement of relevant primary and secondary legislation, and supervising the operation of codes of conduct;

b) the provision of financial information by the company (choice of accounting policies, application and assessment of the effects of new rules, information about the handling of estimated items in the financial statements, forecasts, work of internal and external auditors, etc.);

c) compliance with recommendations and observations of internal and external auditors;

d) the role and functioning of the internal audit function;

e) the policy of the company on tax planning;

f) relations with the external auditor, including, in particular, his independence, remuneration and any non-audit services for the company;

g) the financing of the company; and

h) the applications of information and communication technology.

III.5.5 The audit committee shall act as the principal contact for the external auditor if he discovers irregularities in the content of financial reporting.

III.5.6 The audit committee may not be chaired by the chairman of the supervisory board or by a former member of the management board of the company.

III.5.7 At least one member of the audit committee shall be a financial expert within the meaning of best practice provision III.3.2.

III.5.8 The audit committee shall decide whether and, if so, when the chairman of the management board (chief executive officer), the chief financial officer, the external auditor and the internal auditor, should attend its meetings.

III.5.9 The audit committee shall meet with the external auditor as often as it considers necessary, but at least once a year, without management board members being present.

Remuneration committee

III.5.10 The remuneration committee shall in any event have the following duties: a) making a proposal to the supervisory board for the remuneration policy to be pursued;

b) making a proposal for the remuneration of the individual members of the management board, for adoption by the supervisory board; such proposal shall, in any event, deal with: (i) the remuneration structure and (ii) the amount of the fixed remuneration, the shares and/or options to be granted and/or other variable remuneration components, pension rights, redundancy pay and other forms of compensation to be awarded, as well as the performance criteria and their application; and

c) preparing the remuneration report as referred to in best practice provision II.2.12.

III.5.11 The remuneration committee may not be chaired by the chairman of the supervisory board or by a former member of the management board of the company, or by a supervisory board member who is a member of the management board of another listed company.

III.5.12 No more than one member of the remuneration committee may be a member of the management board of another Dutch listed company.

III.5.13 If the remuneration committee makes use of the services of a remuneration consultant in carrying out its duties, it shall verify that the consultant concerned does not provide advice to the company's management board members.

Selection and appointment committee

III.5.14 The selection and appointment committee shall in any event focus on: a) drawing up selection criteria and appointment procedures for supervisory board members and management board members;

b) periodically assessing the size and composition of the supervisory board and the management board, and making a proposal for a composition profile of the supervisory board;

c) periodically assessing the functioning of individual supervisory board members and management board members, and reporting on this to the supervisory board;

d) making proposals for appointments and reappointments; and e) supervising the policy of the management board on the selection criteria and appointment procedures for senior management.

III.6 Conflicts of interest

Principle Any conflict of interest or apparent conflict of interest between the company and supervisory board members shall be avoided. Decisions to enter into transactions under which supervisory board members would have conflicts of interest that are of material significance to the company and/or to the relevant supervisory board members require the approval of the supervisory board. The supervisory board is responsible for deciding on how to resolve conflicts of interest between management board members, supervisory board members, major shareholders and the external auditor on the one hand and the company on the other.

Best practice provisions

III.6.1 A supervisory board member shall immediately report any conflict of interest or potential conflict of interest that is of material significance to the company and/or to him, to the chairman of the supervisory board and shall provide all relevant information, including information concerning his wife, registered partner or other life companion, foster child and relatives by blood or marriage up to the second degree as defined under Dutch law. If the chairman of the supervisory board has a conflict of interest or potential conflict of interest that is of material significance to the company and/or to him, he shall report this immediately to the vice-chairman of the supervisory board and shall provide all relevant information, including information concerning his wife, registered partner or other life companion, foster child and relatives by blood or marriage up to the second degree as defined under Dutch law. The supervisory board member concerned may not take part in the assessment by the supervisory board of whether a conflict of interest exists. A conflict of interest exists in any event if the company intends to enter into a transaction with a legal entity: i) in which a supervisory board member personally has a material financial interest; ii) which has a management board member who is related under family law to a member of the supervisory board of the company; or iii) in which a member of the supervisory board of the company has a management or supervisory position.

III.6.2 A supervisory board member may not take part in a discussion and/or decision-making on a subject or transaction in relation to which he has a conflict of interest with the company.

III.6.3 All transactions in which there are conflicts of interest with supervisory board members shall be agreed on terms that are customary in the sector concerned. Decisions to enter into transactions in which there are conflicts of interest with supervisory board members that are of material significance to the company and/or to the relevant supervisory board members require the approval of the supervisory board. Such transactions shall be published in the annual report, together with a statement of the conflict of interest and a declaration that best practice provisions III.6.1 to III.6.3 inclusive have been complied with.

III.6.4 All transactions between the company and legal or natural persons who hold at least ten percent of the shares in the company shall be agreed on terms that are customary in the sector concerned. Decisions to enter into transactions in which there are conflicts of interest with such persons that are of material significance to the company and/or to such persons require the approval of the supervisory board. Such transactions shall be published in the annual report, together with a declaration that best practice provision III.6.4 has been observed.

III.6.5 The terms of reference of the supervisory board shall contain rules on dealing with conflicts of interest and potential conflicts of interest between management board members, supervisory board members and the external auditor on the one hand and the company on the other. The terms of reference shall also stipulate which transactions require the approval of the supervisory board. The company shall draw up regulations governing ownership of and transactions in securities by management or supervisory board members, other than securities issued by their 'own' company.

III.6.6 A delegated supervisory board member is a supervisory board member who has a special duty. The delegation may not extend beyond the duties of the supervisory board itself and may not include the management of the company. It may entail more intensive supervision and advice and more regular consultation with the management board. The delegation shall be of a temporary nature only. The delegation may not detract from the role and power of the supervisory board. The delegated supervisory board member remains a member of the supervisory board.

III.6.7 A supervisory board member who temporarily takes on the management of the company, where the management board members are absent or unable to fulfil their duties, shall resign from the supervisory board.

III.7 Remuneration

Principle The general meeting shall determine the remuneration of supervisory board members. The remuneration of a supervisory board member is not dependent on the results of the company.

Best practice provisions

III.7.1 A supervisory board member may not be granted any shares and/or rights to shares by way of remuneration.

III.7.2 Any shares held by a supervisory board member in the company on whose board he sits are long-term investments.

III.7.3 The company may not grant its supervisory board members any personal loans, guarantees or the like unless in the normal course of business and after approval of the supervisory board. No remission of loans may be granted.

III.8 One-tier management structure

Principle The composition and functioning of a management board comprising both members having responsibility for the day-to-day running of the company (executive directors) and members not having such responsibility (non-executive directors) shall be such that proper and independent supervision by the latter category of members is assured.

Best practice provisions

III.8.1 The chairman of the management board may not also be or have been an executive director.

III.8.2 The chairman of the management board shall check the proper composition and functioning of the entire board.

III.8.3 The management board shall apply chapter III.5 of this code. The committees referred to in chapter III.5 shall consist only of non-executive management board member.

III.8.4 The majority of the members of the management board shall be non-executive directors and are independent within the meaning of best practice provision III.2.2.

IV. THE SHAREHOLDERS AND THE GENERAL MEETING OF SHAREHOLDERS

IV.1 Powers

Principle Good corporate governance requires the fully-fledged participation of shareholders in the decision-making in the general meeting. It is in the interest of the company that as many shareholders as possible take part in the decision-making in the general meeting. The company shall, in so far as possible, give shareholders the opportunity to vote by proxy and to communicate with all other shareholders.

The general meeting should be able to exert such influence on the policy of the management board and the supervisory board of the company that it plays a fully-fledged role in the system of checks and balances in the company.

Management board resolutions on a major change in the identity or character of the company or the enterprise shall be subject to the approval of the general meeting.

Best practice provisions

IV.1.1 The general meeting of shareholders of a company not having statutory two tier status (structuurregime) may pass a resolution to cancel the binding nature of a nomination for the appointment of a member of the management board or of the supervisory board and/or a resolution to dismiss a member of the management board or of the supervisory board by an absolute majority of the votes cast. It may be provided that this majority should represent a given proportion of the issued capital, which proportion may not exceed one third. If this proportion of the capital is not represented at the meeting, but an absolute majority of the votes cast is in favour of a resolution to cancel the binding nature of a nomination, or to dismiss a board member, a new meeting may be convened at which the resolution may be passed by an absolute majority of the votes cast, regardless of the proportion of the capital represented at the meeting.

IV.1.2 The voting right attaching to financing preference shares shall be based on the fair value of the capital contribution. This shall in any event apply to the issue of financing preference shares.

IV.1.3 If a serious private bid is made for a business unit or a participating interest and the value of the bid exceeds the threshold referred to in Article 2:107a, paragraph 1 (c), of the Netherlands Civil Code, and such bid is made public, the management board of the company shall, at its earliest convenience, make public its position on the bid and the reasons for this position.

IV.1.4 The policy of the company on additions to reserves and on dividends (the level and purpose of the addition to reserves, the amount of the dividend and the type of dividend) shall be dealt with and explained as a separate agenda item at the general meeting.

IV.1.5 A resolution to pay a dividend shall be dealt with as a separate agenda item at the general meeting.

IV.1.6 Resolutions to approve the policy of the management board (discharge of management board members from liability) and to approve the supervision exercised by the supervisory board (discharge of supervisory board members from liability) shall be voted on separately in the general meeting. Compliance with the Code shall be accounted for as part of the annual report.

IV.1.7 The company shall determine a registration date for the exercise of the voting rights and the rights relating to meetings.

IV.1.8 The chairman of the general meeting is responsible for ensuring the proper conduct of business at meetings in order to promote a worthwhile discussion at the meeting.

IV.2 Depositary receipts for shares

Principle Depositary receipts for shares are a means of preventing a (chance) majority of shareholders from controlling the decision-making process as a result of absenteeism at a general meeting. Depositary receipts for shares may not be used as an anti-takeover measure. The management of the trust office shall issue proxies in all circumstances and without limitation to the holders of depositary receipts who so request. The holders of depositary receipts thus authorised can exercise the voting right at their discretion. The management of the trust office shall have the confidence of the holders of depositary receipts. Depositary receipt holders shall have the possibility of recommending candidates for the management of the trust office. The company may not disclose to the trust office information which has not been made public.

Best practice provisions

IV.2.1 The management of the trust office shall enjoy the confidence of the depositary receipt holders and operate independently of the company which has issued the depositary receipts. The trust conditions shall specify in what cases and subject to what conditions holders of depositary receipts may request the trust office to call a meeting of holders of depositary receipts.

IV.2.2 The managers of the trust office shall be appointed by the management of the trust office. The meeting of holders of depositary receipts may make recommendations to the management of the trust office for the appointment of persons to the position of manager. No management board members or former management board members, supervisory board members or former supervisory board members, employees or permanent advisers of the company should be part of the management of the trust office.

IV.2.3 A person may be appointed to the management of the trust office for a maximum of three 4-year terms.

IV.2.4 The management of the trust office shall be present at the general meeting and shall, if desired, make a statement about how it proposes to vote at the meeting.

IV.2.5 In exercising its voting rights, the trust office shall be guided primarily by the interests of the depositary receipt holders, taking the interests of the company and its affiliated enterprise into account.

IV.2.6 The trust office shall report periodically, but at least once a year, on its activities. The report shall be posted on the company's website.

IV.2.7 The report referred to in best practice provision IV.2.6 shall, in any event, set out: a) the number of shares for which depositary receipts have been issued and an explanation of changes in this number; b) the work carried out in the year under review; c) the voting behaviour in the general meetings held in the year under review; d) the percentage of votes represented by the trust office during the meetings referred to at c); e) the remuneration of the members of the management of the trust office; f) the number of meetings held by the management and the main items dealt with in them; g) the costs of the activities of the trust office; h) any external advice obtained by the trust office; i) the positions of the managers of the trust office; and j) the contact details of the trust office.

IV.2.8 The trust office shall, without limitation and in all circumstances, issue proxies to depositary receipt holders who so request. Each depositary receipt holder may also issue binding voting instructions to the trust office in respect of the shares which the trust office holds on his behalf.

IV.3 Provision of information to and logistics of the general meeting

Principle The management board or, where appropriate, the supervisory board shall provide all shareholders and other parties in the financial markets with equal and simultaneous information about matters that may influence the share price. The contacts between the management board on the one hand and press and analysts on the other shall be carefully handled and structured, and the company may not engage in any acts that compromise the independence of analysts in relation to the company and vice versa.

The management board and the supervisory board shall provide the general meeting in good time with all information that it requires for the exercise of its powers.

If price-sensitive information is provided during a general meeting, or the answering of shareholders' questions has resulted in the disclosure of price-sensitive information, this information shall be made public without delay.

Best practice provisions

IV.3.1 Meetings with analysts, presentations to analysts, presentations to investors and institutional investors and press conferences shall be announced in advance on the company's website and by means of press releases. Provision shall be made for all shareholders to follow these meetings and presentations in real time, for example by means of webcasting or telephone. After the meetings, the presentations shall be posted on the company's website.

IV.3.2 Analysts' reports and valuations may not be assessed, commented upon or corrected, other than factually, by the company in advance.

IV.3.3 The company may not pay any fee(s) to parties for the carrying out of research for analysts' reports or for the production or publication of analysts' reports, with the exception of credit rating agencies.

IV.3.4 Analysts meetings, presentations to institutional or other investors and direct discussions with the investors may not take place shortly before the publication of the regular financial information (quarterly, half-yearly or annual reports).

IV.3.5 The management board and the supervisory board shall provide the general meeting with all requested information, unless this would be contrary to an overriding interest of the company. If the management board and the supervisory board invoke an overriding interest, they must give reasons.

IV.3.6 The company shall place and update information which is relevant to the shareholders and which it is required to publish or deposit pursuant to the provisions of company law and securities law applicable to it, in a separate section of the company's website.

IV.3.7 The agenda of the general meeting shall list which items are for discussion and which items are to be voted upon.

IV.3.8 A resolution for approval or authorisation to be passed by the general meeting shall be explained in writing. In its explanation the management board shall deal with all facts and circumstances relevant to the approval or authorisation to be granted. The notes to the agenda shall be posted on the company's website.

IV.3.9 Material amendments to the articles of association of the company and resolutions for the appointment of management board members and supervisory board members

	shall be submitted separately to the general meeting.
IV.3.10	The report of the general meeting shall be made available, on request, to shareholders no later than three months after the end of the meeting, after which the shareholders shall have the opportunity to react to the report in the following three months. The report shall then be adopted in the manner provided for in the articles of association.
IV.3.11	The management board shall provide a survey of all existing or potential anti-takeover measures in the annual report and shall also indicate in what circumstances it is expected that these measures may be used.
IV.3.12	The company shall give shareholders and other persons entitled to vote the possibility of issuing voting proxies or voting instructions, respectively, to an independent third party prior to the general meeting.
IV.3.13	The company shall formulate an outline policy on bilateral contacts with the shareholders and publish this policy on its website.

IV.4 Responsibility of shareholders

Responsibility of institutional investors

Principle Institutional investors shall act primarily in the interests of the ultimate beneficiaries or investors and have a responsibility to the ultimate beneficiaries or investors and the companies in which they invest, to decide, in a careful and transparent way, whether they wish to exercise their rights as shareholder of listed companies.

Best practice provisions

IV.4.1 Institutional investors (pension funds, insurers, investment institutions and asset managers) shall publish annually, in any event on their website, their policy on the exercise of the voting rights for shares they hold in listed companies.

IV.4.2 Institutional investors shall report annually, on their website and/or in their annual report, on how they have implemented their policy on the exercise of the voting rights in the year under review.

IV.4.3 Institutional investors shall report at least once a quarter, on their website, on whether and, if so, how they have voted as shareholders at the general meeting.

Responsibility of shareholders

Principle Shareholders shall act in relation to the company, the organs of the company and their fellow shareholders in keeping with the principle of reasonableness and fairness. This includes the willingness to engage in a dialogue with the company and their fellow shareholders.

Best practice provisions

IV.4.4 A shareholder shall exercise the right of putting an item on the agenda only after he consulted the management board about this. If one or more shareholders intend to request that an item be put on the agenda that may result in a change in the company's strategy, for example through the dismissal of one or more management or supervisory board members, the management board shall be given the opportunity to stipulate a reasonable period in which to respond (the response time). This shall also apply to an intention as referred to above for judicial leave to call a general meeting pursuant to Article 2:110 of the Netherlands Civil Code. The shareholder shall respect the response time stipulated by the management board within the meaning of best practice provision II.1.9.

IV.4.5 A shareholder shall vote as he sees fit. A shareholder who makes use of the voting advice of a third party is expected to form his own judgment on the voting policy of this adviser and the voting advice provided by him.

IV.4.6 If a shareholder has arranged for an item to be put on the agenda, he shall explain this at the meeting and, if necessary, answer questions about it.

V. THE AUDIT OF THE FINANCIAL REPORTING AND THE POSITION OF THE INTERNAL AUDIT FUNCTION AND THE EXTERNAL AUDITOR

V.1 Financial reporting

Principle The management board is responsible for the quality and completeness of publicly disclosed financial reports. The supervisory board shall ensure that the management board fulfils this responsibility.

Best practice provisions

V.1.1 The preparation and publication of the annual report, the financial statements, the quarterly and/or half-yearly figures and ad hoc financial information require careful internal procedures. The supervisory board shall supervise compliance with these procedures.

V.1.2 The audit committee shall determine how the external auditor should be involved in the content and publication of financial reports other than the financial statements.

V.1.3 The management board is responsible for establishing and maintaining internal procedures which ensure that all major financial information is known to the management board, so that the timeliness, completeness and correctness of the external financial reporting are assured. For this purpose, the management board ensures that the financial information from business divisions and/or subsidiaries is reported directly to it and that the integrity of the information is not compromised. The supervisory board shall ensure that the internal procedures are established and maintained.

V.2 Role, appointment, remuneration and assessment of the functioning of the external auditor

Principle The external auditor is appointed by the general meeting. The supervisory board shall nominate a candidate for this appointment, while both the audit committee and the management board advise the supervisory board. The remuneration of the external auditor, and instructions to the external auditor to provide non-audit services, shall be approved by the supervisory board on the recommendation of the audit committee and after consultation with the management board.

Best practice provisions

V.2.1 The external auditor may be questioned by the general meeting in relation to his report on the fairness of the financial statements. The external auditor shall for this purpose attend and be entitled to address this meeting.

V.2.2 The management board and the audit committee shall report their dealings with the external auditor to the supervisory board on an annual basis, including his independence in particular (for example, the desirability of rotating the responsible partners of an external audit firm that provides audit services, and the desirability of the same audit firm providing non-audit services to the company). The supervisory board shall take this into account when deciding its nomination for the appointment of an external auditor, which nomination shall be submitted to the general meeting.

V.2.3 At least once every four years, the supervisory board and the audit committee shall conduct a thorough assessment of the functioning of the external auditor within the various entities and in the different capacities in which the external auditor acts. The main conclusions of this assessment shall be communicated to the general meeting for the purposes of assessing the nomination for the appointment of the external auditor.

V.3 Internal audit function

Principle The internal auditor shall operate under the responsibility of the management board.

Best practice provision

V.3.1	The external auditor and the audit committee shall be involved in drawing up the work schedule of the internal auditor. They shall also take cognizance of the findings of the internal auditor.
V.3.2	The internal auditor shall have access to the external auditor and to the chairman of the audit committee.
V.3.3	If there is no internal audit function, the audit committee shall review annually the need for an internal auditor. Based on this review, the supervisory board shall make a recommendation on this to the management board in line with the proposal of the audit committee, and shall include this recommendation in the report of the supervisory board.

V.4 Relationship and communication of the external auditor with the organs of the company

Principle The external auditor shall, in any event, attend the meeting of the supervisory board at which the financial statements are to be adopted or approved. The external auditor shall report his findings in relation to the audit of the financial statements to the management board and the supervisory board simultaneously.

Best practice provisions

V.4.1 The external auditor shall in any event attend the meeting of the supervisory board, at which the report of the external auditor with respect to the audit of the financial statements is discussed, and at which financial statements are to approved or adopted. The external auditor shall receive the financial information underlying the adoption of the quarterly and/or half-yearly figures and other interim financial reports and shall be given the opportunity to respond to all information.

V.4.2 When the need arises, the external auditor may request the chairman of the audit committee for leave to attend the meeting of the audit committee.

V.4.3 The report of the external auditor pursuant to Article 2:393, paragraph 4, of the Netherlands Civil Code shall contain the matters which the external auditor wishes to bring to the attention of the management board and the supervisory board in relation to the audit of the financial statements and the related audits. The following examples can be given:

A. With regard to the audit:

information about matters of importance to the assessment of the independence of the external auditor;

information about the course of events during the audit and cooperation with internal auditors and/or any other external auditors, matters for discussion with the management board, a list of corrections that have not been made, etc.

With regard to the financial figures:

analyses of changes in shareholders' equity and results, which do not appear in the information to be published, and which, in the view of the external auditor, contribute to an understanding of the financial position and results of the company;

comments regarding the processing of one-off items, the effects of estimates and the manner in which they have been arrived at, the choice of accounting policies, when other choices were possible, and special effects of such policies;

comments on the quality of forecasts and budgets.

With regard to the operation of the internal risk management and control systems (including the reliability and continuity of automated data processing) and the quality of the internal provision of information:

points for improvement, gaps and quality assessments;

comments about threats and risks to the company and the manner in which they should be reported in the particulars to be published;

compliance with articles of association, instructions, regulations, loan covenants, requirements of external supervisors, etc.

Explanation of and notes on terms used in the Code

Preamble

Section 2 The Code does not apply to collective investment schemes, which can be treated as 'financial products'. It does apply to the managers of collective investment schemes, unless the managers are members of a centrally managed group.

II. The management board

II.1.1 Management board members are normally reappointed.

II.1.3 The internal risk management and control system must be suitable for the company concerned. This gives smaller listed companies the possibility of using less comprehensive procedures.

II.1.4 Pursuant to a) the company's annual report must include a description of the main risks it encounters in implementing its strategy. Rather than providing an exhaustive list of all possible risks, the company should identify the main risks it faces, i.e. strategic and operational risks, financial risks, legal and regulatory risks and financial reporting risks. The remuneration structure of management board members and other staff can also pose an operational risk. The description should also specify the company's risk profile, in other words its risk appetite and, as far as possible, its risk sensitivity. In certain circumstances quantification of the risks identified can enhance the value of the information. The description of the main risks is in keeping with the 'risk section' prescribed in Article 2:391, paragraph 2, of the Netherlands Civil Code and the description of the essential risks under Section

5:25 (c) of the Financial Supervision Act.

As regards b) it would be logical for the management board to indicate in the description of the design and effectiveness of the internal risk management and control systems what framework or criteria (e.g. the COSO framework for internal control) it used in assessing the internal risk management and control system.

II.1.5 The statement can form part of the management board's report that is required in the context of Section 5:25 (c) of the Financial Supervision Act. Companies whose securities are traded on a system in the

United States comparable to a regulated market or multilateral trading facility are deemed to comply with parts a) and b) if they correctly apply Section 404 of the Sarbanes-Oxley Act.

This concerns a report on the sensitivity of results to external factors and variables in a general sense.

II.1.8 'Other important positions' (i.e. positions that should be notified to the supervisory board) include membership of the supervisory board of a large, unlisted company.

II.2.7 Examples of structural changes are the splitting and consolidation of shares, the consequences of a merger or acquisition in which options are 'rolled over' to shares of the bidder, and the payment of a 'super dividend'.

II.2.8 The fixed remuneration component means periodic pay within the meaning of Article 2:383c, paragraph 1 (a), of the Netherlands Civil Code. A redundancy scheme providing for a maximum of one year's salary could be 'manifestly unreasonable' where a management board member is dismissed during his first term of office and has been in the company's service for a long time prior to his appointment to the board. Compared to the level of the entitlement of an 'ordinary' employee, severance pay of one year's salary could possibly be too low in such circumstances. This upper limit also applies to management board members who leave the company of their own free will, although in such cases it would be appropriate for no remuneration whatever to be paid. This provision does not detract from the principle that failing policy (mismanagement or fraud) on the part of a management board member should not be rewarded.

II.2.9 / III.7.3 The words 'or the like' in any event include an acknowledgement of debt or an obligation to make payment in due course.

II.2.10 This power does not apply to new contracts only; the supervisory board has a responsibility to endeavour to include such a provision in existing contracts as well.

II.2.11 The power of the supervisory board relates both to situations where the remuneration has been awarded but not yet received by the management board member and to situations where the remuneration has already been received. This power does not apply to new contracts only; the supervisory board also has a responsibility to endeavour to include such a provision in existing contracts as well.

The phrase 'an account of the manner in which the remuneration policy has been implemented in the past financial year' means the statement referred to in Article 2:391 of the Netherlands Civil Code. 'The remuneration policy planned by the supervisory board for the next financial year and subsequent years' means the remuneration policy referred to in Article 2:135, paragraph 1, of the Netherlands Civil Code.

II.2.13 Parts c) and d) 'Other share-based remuneration components' in any event include stock appreciation rights and phantom stock.

III. The supervisory board

III.1.2 The 'annual statements' are the entire annual report referred to in Article 2:391 of the Netherlands Civil Code, the financial statements referred to in Article 2:361 of the Netherlands Civil Code, the other information referred to in Article 2:392 of the Netherlands Civil Code, the report of the supervisory board, key figures, multi-year figures, shareholder information and so forth.

III.1.4 Nonetheless, in the case of companies not having statutory two-tier status the general meeting may suspend or dismiss supervisory board members at any time. Under the provisions on companies having statutory two-tier status the general meeting of such companies may pass a resolution of no confidence in the entire supervisory board. The adoption of such a resolution implies the immediate dismissal of all the members of the board.

III.1.7 This provision relates to the annual review by the supervisory board members of their own functioning and that of the management board. The aim of the review is to reflect critically on the functioning of the members of the supervisory board and management board. A periodic review can enhance the quality of the functioning of the supervisory board and the management board and help to ensure that the right choices are made when preparing appointments or reappointments of supervisory and management board members, for example in connection with the appropriate composition of the boards or the appropriate diversity in their composition. How the review is carried out is a matter for the company and may therefore differ from one company to another. The review can take place collectively, on an individual basis between the chairman and the members separately, or through the input of an external adviser. Each supervisory board member should be able to express his views confidentially during the review.

Part d) relates to what are termed 'cross-links'. A supervisory board member of listed company A who is a member of the management board of listed company B is not deemed to be independent if a management board member of company A is also a supervisory board member of company B.

III.3.1 The Code provides that the composition of the supervisory board should be such that the members are able to act independently of one another, the management board and any particular interests. In addition to expertise and personal involvement, independence is a crucial requirement for the proper functioning of a supervisory board. An important means of promoting independent action of the supervisory board is to ensure the diversity of its composition in terms of such factors as age, gender, expertise, social background or nationality.

III.4.3 The activities of the company secretary need not be limited to the provision of support for the supervisory board. He may also work for the management board. The secretary need not necessarily be an employee of the company. The work may also be carried out by, say, a lawyer appointed for this purpose.

III.5.10 The remuneration committee's duty to make proposals for the remuneration policy to be pursued means that it has initial responsibility for formulating the basic remuneration policy principles. This involves determining such matters as the performance criteria, the use and composition of any peer group, the ratio of fixed to variable and short-term to long-term remuneration, the ratio of the chairman's remuneration to that of the other management board members and the ratio of the remuneration of the management board to that of other grades within the company. The remuneration committee also checks whether the existing remuneration policy is still up to date and, if necessary, makes proposals for changes. In carrying out its duties the remuneration committee may make use of the services of a remuneration consultant, but it always remains responsible itself for making proposals for the remuneration policy to be pursued and taking whatever initiatives are necessary for this purpose.

IV. The shareholders and the general meeting of shareholders

IV.1.2 This provision is intended to apply to future issues of financing preference shares. However, the management board and supervisory board may agree with the holders of the existing financing preference shares to adjust the present control of the financing preference shares.

A private bid is not deemed to be 'serious' if it is clear that the bidder does not have sufficient financial resources to finance the bid or if no right-thinking and sensible shareholder would wish the management board to accept the bid, for example because the bid price does not reflect the true value or the market value of the business unit or the participating interest.

IV.1.7 A bill introducing a compulsory registration period of 21 days before the start of the general meeting has been submitted to implement Directive 2007/36/EC on the exercise of certain rights of shareholders in listed companies.[5]

IV.4.5
In so far as a shareholder uses the services of a voting adviser before exercising his voting right, it is logical that he should check that the adviser provides balanced advice based on fair consideration of all the issues.
V.

The audit of the financial reporting and the position of the internal audit function and the external auditor

V.2.1 The presence of the external auditor at the general meeting does not detract from the general duty of the management board and the supervisory board to render account to the general meeting or their duty to provide all requested information to the general meeting (unless there is an important reason for not doing so). The external auditor can be questioned only in respect of his audit and audit report. Primary responsibility for the content of the financial statements rests with the management board. It follows that the external auditor should participate in the preparation of the general meeting. The Committee refers to NIVRA Guideline 780N on the position of the external auditor in the general meeting.

[5] Bill to amend Book 2 of the Netherlands Civil Code and the Financial Supervision Act in order to implement Directive 2007/36/EC of the European Parliament and of the Council of the European Union of 11 July 2007 on the exercise of certain rights of shareholders in listed companies (Parliamentary Papers II 2008/09, 31 746, no. 2).

Recommendations to the legislator

To facilitate compliance with the Code, the Committee recommends to the legislator that this Code be designated by order in council (pursuant to Article 2:391, paragraph 5, of the Netherlands Civil Code) as a code of conduct that obliges listed companies to include a statement in their annual report on compliance with the principles and best practice provisions and that replaces the 2003 Code.

The Committee recommends that a new Monitoring Committee be appointed to monitor compliance with the Code and ensure that its provisions are up to date and practicable. The Committee considers that the terms of the decree of 6 December 2004 establishing the Monitoring Committee can be maintained.

The Committee has taken note of the draft bill introduced following its advisory report dated May 2007. The Committee would observe that it is evidently difficult to formulate the shareholder obligation of notification of intentions in such a way as to actually achieve what is intended, and that such an obligation also entails risks. The Committee considers that a response time is in fact a different way of ensuring that shareholders provide transparency to the company about their intentions. To increase the legal certainty and effectiveness of the response time and to comply with Directive 2007/36/EC[6], the Committee recommends that the basic principle that the management board, when confronted with requests from one or more shareholders to add items to the agenda that could alter the company's strategy, must be given sufficient time to take a considered decision on this, should be embedded in legislation. This principle is elaborated in the Code in best practice provision II.1.9.

The Committee recommends that the legislator examine whether it is possible to amend the Dutch bidding rules in such a way that a company is not subject to takeover speculation for longer than necessary. Consideration could be given in this connection to the possibility of making an addition to the Public Bids Decree (*Besluit openbare biedingen*) giving a bidder (or prospective bidder) the choice in the case of takeover speculation of announcing within a given period either that it intends to make a bid or that it has decided against doing so. In the latter case the party concerned should not be able to make any further bid for the company for some considerable time (i.e. the requirement of 'put up or shut up').

The Monitoring Committee notes that various special interest groups have identified problems in the present squeeze-out procedures and have proposed solutions for them. The Committee recommends that the legislator take note of these views. The Committee does not believe that it is part of its remit to distil a recommendation to the legislator from all these different opinions.

[6] Directive 2007/36/EC on the exercise of certain rights of shareholders in listed companies (OJ EU L 184/17).

Account of the Committee's work

Background and objective of the Committee

1. In the spring of 2008 the National Federation of Christian Trade Unions (CNV), Eumedion, the Federation of Dutch Trade Unions (FNV), the Netherlands Centre of Executive and Supervisory Directors (NCD), NYSE Euronext, the Association of Stockholders (VEB), the Association of Securities-Issuing Companies (VEUO) and the Confederation of Netherlands Industry and Employers (VNO-NCW) requested the Monitoring Committee to update the 2003 Dutch Corporate Governance Code. The government endorsed this request.

Developments since the introduction of the Code in 2003

Since the introduction of the Code, developments have occurred at national and international level in the areas of legislation, codes and case law and in the market. As regards legislation, the changes to Book 2 of the Netherlands Civil Code, parts of the Financial Supervision Act *(Wet op het financieel toezicht)* and the Financial Reporting (Supervision) Act *(Wet toezicht financiële verslaggeving)* are of special importance. In recent years the Enterprise Division of the Amsterdam Court of Appeal and the Supreme Court of the Netherlands issued important rulings on the relationship between the stakeholders of a company. The Code also plays a role in the social debate on corporate governance. Over the years various arguments have been put forward for extending the Code to cover new themes, the most notable of which are diversity / position of women and corporate social responsibility. In addition, levels of executive pay have caused social indignation in some cases.

The activities of some shareholders and the foreign takeovers of leading Dutch companies have also prompted social debate. Since the Code came into force in 2004, Dutch listed companies have increasingly come under the influence of the market for corporate control (mergers and acquisitions). The shares of large Dutch listed companies in particular are to a great extent in the hands of foreign shareholders. Many companies – sometimes under pressure from the market – have dismantled their anti-takeover mechanisms, for example by abolishing certain forms of depositary receipts. Shareholders have adopted a more active approach and exercised their rights to a greater extent. Dutch listed companies have become acquainted with (relatively) new types of shareholder: private equity parties, hedge funds and sovereign funds. In some cases this has resulted in disputes between management board (and supervisory board) and shareholders on corporate strategy. These disputes resulted in rulings by the Enterprise Division of the Amsterdam Court of Appeal and the Supreme Court of the Netherlands.

The procedures and functioning of management and supervisory boards have evolved since the introduction of the Code. Risk control has become more important, an ever larger proportion of executive pay is performance-related and awarded in the form of options and/or shares and the work of the supervisory board has intensified and become more specialised, partly due to the establishment of various committees within the supervisory board.

The principal aim of the 2003 Code was to restore confidence in the private sector, partly in response to accounting scandals. The emphasis was on accountability and transparency. It has emerged that detailed transparency regulations can be instrumental in creating a 'box-ticking' mentality and making the available information even more opaque, particularly in the field of executive pay. This is why the Committee puts even more emphasis in the amended Code on influencing the behaviour of management board members, supervisory board members and shareholders. The principles and best practice provisions are designed to encourage the desired behaviour. In this way the Committee intends to promote real discussion within and between the different organs of a company. The Committee is aware that the Code assigns a heavy responsibility to the supervisory board. This is partly why the Committee considers it desirable for supervisory board members to establish a form of structured consultation. This should enable them to exchange ideas and information and serve as a point of contact for third parties. The Committee calls on supervisory board members to develop initiatives in this respect.

The proposed amendments

6. On 4 June 2008, the Committee published its proposals for updating the Code. Interested parties could comment on the proposals until 15 September 2008. The Committee received a total of 32 reactions from special interest groups, listed companies, accountancy and law firms and private individuals. In addition to these reactions the Committee held two meetings with experts and representatives of various groups to

discuss the proposals in more detail. The Committee wishes to thank all of them for their contributions to the debate and for their commitment to the subject matter. Their comments have led to amendments to the wording of the principles and best practice provisions, thereby helping to improve the Corporate Governance Code and, as the Committee expects, to further broaden the base of support for the Code.

General tenor of the comments

In general the respondents were broadly in favour of the Committee's proposals. Some respondents considered that various proposals were too detailed and not in keeping with the principle-based nature of the Code, particularly in relation to executive pay. The Committee considers that the strength of the Code lies in its principle-based nature. As existing provisions of the Code have failed to produce the desired results to a sufficient extent, particularly as regards executive pay, the Committee has now strengthened and at the same time simplified the wording of the principles. The Committee believes that the aim should be to encourage those concerned to adopt the desired behaviour. There is a perceived need for more detailed best practice provisions in some respects in order to provide more guidance for those concerned.

Some respondents also pointed to the undesirability of an overlap between the Code and existing or future legislation. The point was made on behalf of shareholders that the sheer volume of rules and regulations would curb the influence of shareholders. As against this, some respondents argued that the proposals relating to the relationship between a company and its shareholders did not go far enough and requested additional recommendations to the legislator

in this field. One respondent asked that more attention be given to takeover situations. The Committee deals with the relationship between the Code and existing and future legislation in section 6 of the preamble.

One respondent asked the Committee to try to avoid including social themes in the Code. In the respondent's view, social themes are not directly connected with corporate governance, such as detailed rules on executive pay, diversity and corporate social responsibility. Other respondents considered that the proposals did not go far enough to safeguard the company as a long-term alliance of interests, or wished greater emphasis to be placed on the role of employees (and their representatives) or more attention to be given to integrity. The Committee believes that the fact that the Code is seen as a way of solving issues identified in society is a testament to its strength. The Committee considers that the Code is first and foremost a corporate governance code. The principles and best practice provisions should safeguard and promote good management and supervision of listed companies. In the Committee's view, the amendments reflect widely held views on corporate governance.

One respondent drew attention to the inherent tension in the stakeholder model between, on the one hand, the rule that when taking decisions the management and supervisory boards should be guided by the interests of the company and its stakeholders and, on the other, the fact that these boards are accountable for their actions to shareholders, who are themselves entitled to put their own interests first. The Committee deals with this issue in sections 10 and 11 of the preamble.

Another respondent requested that the scope of the Code should not be limited to listed companies but extended to cover all businesses of a given size and social impact. The Committee held consultations on the scope of the Code in 2007. In its advisory report of May 2007, the Committee recommended to the legislator that compliance with the Code should not be made legally compulsory for trading in shares of small and medium-sized enterprises on alternative trading systems. The Committee sees no reason to reopen the debate on the scope of the Code.

Developments since the amendments proposed in June 2008

A global credit crisis that also affects the Netherlands has developed since the amendments were proposed in June 2008. The Dutch government has become a provider of capital to financial institutions and has agreed to appoint supervisory board members having specific powers. The Committee considers that the Code applies in these cases too.

> Foreign governments have also taken measures affecting the financial sector. On 13 October 2008, the British Financial Services Authority (FSA) wrote a letter to the Chief Executive Officers of the companies under its supervision concerning their pay policy in the light of concerns that inappropriate remuneration schemes might have contributed to the credit crisis. The FSA stated that some remuneration schemes could have given incentives to staff to pursue risky policies, undermining the impact of systems designed to control risk, to the detriment of the companies, their shareholders and stakeholders and, ultimately, the taxpayer. Although the FSA did not wish
>
> to concern itself with levels of executive pay, it did wish to ensure that companies brought their remuneration policy into line with sound risk management and control principles and with their established risk profile. The FSA identified what it termed 'good practices' and 'bad practices' in remuneration policy, for example as regards the measurement of performance for the calculation of bonuses, the composition of the remuneration, deferred performance-related pay and the process, and called on businesses to modify their schemes and adopt good practices.

The Committee considers that it would be sensible for all listed companies to review their remuneration policy in the light of the latest developments, not only as regards executive pay but also as regards their entire organisation. In section 12 of the preamble and principle II.2, the Committee therefore addresses the relationship between remuneration policy and risk control (as regards executive pay see also points 28 to 36 below).

In May 2008, the State Secretary for Economic Affairs established a committee under the chairmanship of Mr A. Burgmans to direct a study into the relationship between corporate social responsibility and corporate governance. This committee presented its findings to the State Secretary on 6 November 2008. Its report contains specific recommendations for supplementing the Code with passages about corporate social responsibility issues relevant to the enterprise.

The Monitoring Committee has held consultations about these recommendations with special interest groups and experts. The Committee considers that the recommendations represent a valuable addition to the Code and are a logical elaboration of the Dutch corporate governance model. This is why the Committee has adopted the recommendations in the preamble and the Code, with the exception of the recommendation concerning institutional investors. In the Committee's view, this is beyond the scope of the Code.

Preamble

The Committee has updated the 2003 preamble while preserving its essence. The preamble has been supplemented by passages that reflect views and ideas that have evolved since 2003 and some of which have already been discussed in previous reports. Section 3 expressly states that the Code does not deal with relations between the company and its employees. Obviously the interests of the employees should be taken into account.

The Committee deals with the overlap between the Code and existing and future legislation in section 6 of the preamble. For the sake of the Code's readability and its internal coherence the Committee has decided that any overlap between the legislation and the Code is inherent in the Code's function and need not necessarily result in amendments to the Code, also because the Code may contain provisions that supplement the statutory provisions. In so far as a principle or best practice provision corresponds with a statutory rule, this may mean that a company or shareholder is not allowed to depart from the relevant provision, not even when reasons are given.

Section 7 contains the essence of the Dutch corporate governance model and has been left unchanged by the Committee. The same applies to section 8, which deals with confidence in management and supervision.

In section 9 the Committee considers the relationship between the management and supervisory boards on the one hand and shareholders on the other in relation to corporate strategy. Reference is also made to the responsibility of shareholders with respect to the principle of reasonableness and fairness that stakeholders must observe towards each other. Sections 10 and 11 deal with the tension between, on the one hand, the duty of the management and supervisory boards to take account of all interests and, on the other, the right of the shareholders to put their own interests first. This applies in particular in takeover situations.

Recommendations to the legislator

Wide support has been expressed for amended the Dutch bidding rules to include the 'put up or shut up' principle. Some respondents have also identified problems concerning squeeze-out procedures and proposed solutions. However, the Committee believes that formulating a recommendation for the legislator on the basis of the different solutions that have been proposed is beyond its remit.

There has also been a widely expressed wish to regulate the response time by law. The Committee has acted on this wish by recommending – as an addition to the provision of the Code – that the basic principle that the management board, when confronted with requests from one or more shareholders that could alter the company's strategy, must be given sufficient time to take a considered decision on this, should be embedded in legislation.

In other respects the Committee sees no wide support for other recommendations to the legislator.

Commentary on individual chapters

Chapter 1 - Compliance with and enforcement of the Code

24. In view of the reactions during the consultation round, the Committee has moved the part of principle IV.4 that relates to non-application of the provisions of the Code, including the proposed amendments, to principle I.

Chapter II – The management board

Internal risk management

In view of the reactions during the consultation round, the Committee has expressed more emphatically in principle II.1 and best practice provision II.1.4 the importance of the management board's responsibility for determining the strategy-related risk profile and the risk management based on it.

The Committee realises that the 'in control' statement in best practice provision II.1.5 goes further than the requirements under European directives. However, it believes that the 'in control' statement has resulted in an increased company focus on risk control and has improved the quality of the reporting. The responsibilities of those concerned are more clearly defined as a result of the 'in control' statement. The compliance reports show that the great majority of listed

companies issue an 'in control' statement. The Committee therefore considers that the 'in control' statement serves a useful function. In the light of the reactions during the consultation round the Committee has dropped the forward-looking statement.

Response time

27. In view of the reactions during the consultation round the Committee has modified the response time in various ways. First of all, a distinction is made between the conduct of the management and supervisory boards on the one hand and that of the shareholders on the other. The response time is therefore now mentioned in two places in the Code, namely in best practice provisions II.1.9 and IV.4.4. Second, it is stated explicitly that no more than 180 days may elapse between the moment the management board is

informed by one or more shareholders of their intention to put an item on the agenda and the day of the general meeting. This includes the statutory period of 60 days for having items put on the agenda. Third, clarity has been provided that the response time may be invoked only once in relation to one and the same item. The possibility of invoking a response time is also excluded in a situation where a shareholder holds 75 per cent or more of the share capital following a successful public bid. In addition to the provisions of the Code, the Committee recommends to the legislator that the basic principle that the management board, when confronted with requests from one or more shareholders that could alter the company's strategy, must be given sufficient time to take a considered decision on this, should be embedded in legislation.

Role of the management board and the supervisory board in takeovers

28. In view of the reactions during the consultation round, the Committee has dropped the proposed chapter VI on takeovers. The essence of the proposed chapter is expressed by best practice provisions II.1.10 and II.1.11, which deal with the role of the management board and the supervisory board in takeovers. As the proposed chapter VI has been dropped, the proposed provision on the fairness opinion has also been cancelled. The Committee believes that there is still no clear practice on this point that qualifies as best practice. Nonetheless, in the opinion of the Committee, this does not affect the responsibility of the management and supervisory boards to assess the bid on its merits and advise the shareholders accordingly.

Remuneration of management board members

The reactions during the consultation round reflected general support for the Committee's proposals on executive pay. One respondent also advocated that the variable part remuneration component should be capped. Another respondent pointed out that much attention had been paid to the level and transparency of the remuneration, while the nature of the performance criteria and the question whether the structure of the remuneration was consistent with the stakeholder model had been given little consideration. In addition, in the debate on the causes of the credit crisis, many people have pointed to the adverse consequences of ill-conceived

remuneration systems on the risk attitudes of the management board and senior executives. An example was the letter from the FSA of 13 October 2008 referred to in point 13 above.

Principle II.2 on the level and composition of the remuneration provides that the remuneration structure, including severance pay, should be such that it promotes the interests of the company in the medium and long term, does not encourage management board members to act in their own interests and does not 'reward' failing board members upon termination of their employment. The Committee considers that this principle is paramount and implicitly reflects the link between remuneration and the company's strategy and interests. The Committee has extended this principle to include an explicit reference to the risk attitude of management board members. Principle II.2 on the level and composition of the remuneration has also been supplemented. When the overall remuneration of the management board members is fixed, its impact on pay differentials within the company should be taken into account. In this way the remuneration process can be subjected to an internal brake that counters any possible leapfrog effect. The right balance should exist between the variable and fixed components of the remuneration. The level and structure of the remuneration should be determined by reference not only to existing factors such as the development of results and share price performance but also to non-financial indicators that are relevant to the company's long-term value creation. The principle concerning the determination and disclosure of remuneration emphasises the importance of clarity and simplicity. The references to statutory requirements and powers have also been dropped for this reason.

The Committee notes that the management board remuneration structure may infringe principle

II.2 in various ways. First of all, the variable remuneration may be focused too much on the short term. Second, the remuneration may be structured in such a way that management board members do not run any real risk of losing all or part of their variable remuneration if their decisions prove ill-judged in the medium or long term. The Committee believes that the amended Code offers supervisory boards and shareholders sufficient ways of combating these risks.

The Committee's amendments provide supervisory boards with instruments for improving the quality of decision-making on remuneration and the transparency of the remuneration structure. The basic concept is that management board members should earn their remuneration on the basis of performance, but that it is ultimately for the supervisory board to determine how much it would be reasonable for a management board member to earn, taking account of all the circumstances. The active involvement of the shareholders is also essential in this connection.

Level and composition of the remuneration

33. The Committee has introduced three new best practice provisions governing the level and composition of the remuneration. Best practice provision II.2.1 provides that before determining the remuneration of management board members, the supervisory board should analyse the possible outcomes of the variable remuneration components. The supervisory board then determines the level and structure of the remuneration by reference to the scenario analyses carried out, taking account not only of results and share price but also of non-financial indicators relevant to the company's long-term objectives. The provisions on options and shares have also been simplified.

Determination and disclosure of remuneration

34. It was pointed out during the consultation round that principle II.2 is unclear and opaque. The Committee recognises that the principle refers to various documents in connection with the disclosure of remuneration policy: the notes to the financial statements, the report of the supervisory board and the remuneration report. The remuneration report contains a more detailed description of the remuneration policy than the report of the supervisory board does. Partly in response to the reactions on this point, the Committee has simplified the principle and the related best practice provisions. Best practice provision II.2.13 (old) has been combined with best practice provision II.2.12. Best practice provision II.2.12 also provides that the remuneration report should indicate how the remuneration policy contributes to the achievement of the long-term objectives, in keeping with the risk profile.

Powers of the supervisory board to adjust the remuneration

35. In view of the reactions during the consultation round, the Committee has introduced separate best practice provisions giving effect to the 'ultimate remedy' power of the supervisory board and the claw-back clause (II.2.11 and II.2.10 respectively). It has also been stated more clearly that the supervisory board should endeavour to have these powers recorded not only in new contracts with management board members but also in existing contracts.

Content of the remuneration report;

36. In view of the reactions during the consultation round, the Committee has made clear in best practice provision II.2.13 b) that although the scenario analyses themselves need not be published, the remuneration report should confirm that the analyses have been carried out. In general the respondents reacted favourably to the remuneration table introduced in best practice provision II.2.13 d). For the sake of clarity the provision states the table relates only to management board members holding office at year-end. In response to a comment from a respondent, the Committee has brought best practice provision II.2.13 g) into line with its previous recommendation in 2005. Parts have also been deleted or combined.

Disclosure of the main elements of the remuneration contract

37. As it was pointed out in reactions during the consultation round that the term 'immediately' is imprecise, the Committee has replaced it in II.2.14 by the wording 'in any event no later than the date of the notice calling the general meeting where the appointment of the management board member will be proposed'. In

the Committee's opinion, the point is that shareholders should be able to take th s information into account when considering how to vote on appointments to the board.

Chapter III – The supervisory board

Diversity

38. Some respondents expressed general support for the manner in which the Committee had worded the provisions on diversity in the Code. A few advocated the inclusion of a target figure in the Code. The Committee has included an explicit provision that companies are expected to apply and disclose a specific objective in relation to diversity. The Committee believes that there is wide support for this amendment,

Maximum of five supervisory board memberships

39. The reactions during the consultation round led the Committee to wonder whether best practice provision III.3.4 should be amended. The Committee considers that this provision has been successful in promoting diversity within supervisory boards. While the Committee acknowledges that the provision is of a somewhat arbitrary nature, it nonetheless considers it is still worthwhile. The idea underlying this provision is also that supervisory board members should make sufficient time available for the performance of their duties, as is apparent from the words 'to such an extent that the proper performance of his duties is assured'.

Position of the chairman of the supervisory board

40. Partly in response to the reactions during the consultation rounds, the Committee has simplified principle III.4 on the role of the chairman of the supervisory board in order to clarify his key responsibilities. The Committee has also extended these responsibilities by adding that the chairman is the person to be contacted by shareholders on matters relating to the functioning of members of the management and supervisory boards.

Duties of remuneration committee

41. In view of the reactions in the consultation round the Committee has dropped the proposed provisions III.5.12 (a) and III.5.12 (b). The idea behind these provisions was to emphasise that the remuneration committee itself should take the initiative in proposing the remuneration policy to be pursued and should not rely unduly on the remuneration consultant. Upon reflection the Committee considers that it is not necessary to record this expressly in the Code.

Chapter IV - The shareholders and the general meeting of shareholders

Report on compliance with the Code

42. In view of the reactions during the consultation round, the Committee has clarified in best practice provision IV.1.5 that compliance with the Code should be accounted for as part of the annual report. This ensures that the items are dealt with in the right order and, in so far as the compliance remains largely unchanged, need not be included as a separate agenda item every year. Nonetheless, shareholders are free to ask questions about matters relating to the Code in the general meeting.

Decision-making in the general meeting

In view of the reactions during the consultation round, the Committee has qualified best practice provision IV.1.7 concerning the responsibility of the chairman for the proper conduct of business at meetings. It is now provided that the chairman of the general meeting is responsible for ensuring the proper conduct of business at meetings in order to promote a worthwhile discussion at the meeting.

In view of the reactions during the consultation round, the Committee has added two new best practice provisions in order to improve the provision of information to shareholders about the agenda. Best practice provision IV.3.7 states that agenda should list which items are for discussion and which are to be voted upon. Best practice provision IV.3.9 states that material amendments to the articles of association and resolutions for the appointment of management and supervisory board members should be submitted separately to the general meeting.

Responsibility of shareholders

Principle IV.4 no longer focuses exclusively on institutional investors. The principle is subdivided into *responsibility of institutional investors* and *responsibility of shareholders*. In addition, part of the second paragraph of principle IV.4 (old) has been moved to principle I.1. Principle IV.4 on the responsibility of shareholders expresses the fact that shareholders are also bound by the principle of reasonableness and fairness, including the willingness to enter into a dialogue with the company and fellow shareholders. If the dialogue fails to produce a result, shareholders are naturally entitled to exercise their statutory rights (right to put items on the agenda and right to call an extraordinary meeting of shareholders) in order to express the views they have on the strategy.

The Committee considers that the increase in the powers of the general meeting in the 2003 Code was prompted by the need to strengthen the checks and balances within the company and improve the quality of corporate governance. It is now apparent that an increase in shareholder rights has also resulted in greater emphasis being put on the interests of shareholders both individually and collectively. The Committee considers that requiring shareholders to act in accordance with the principle of reasonableness and fairness will help to strengthen the checks and balances within the company.

Institutional investors are a special category of shareholders, who act primarily in the interests of the ultimate beneficiary owners or investors. As such, they are obliged vis-à-vis these ultimate beneficiary owners or investors, and the listed companies in which they invest, to decide in a careful and transparent manner whether they wish to exercise their rights as shareholder in these companies. Owing to this special position, best practice provisions IV.4.1 to IV.4.3 (inclusive) relate exclusively to institutional investors.

Chapter V - The audit of the financial reporting and the position of the internal audit function and the external auditor

48. The reactions to the consultation round included suggestions for the internal audit function to be given a higher profile in the Code. In the Committee's view, every listed company should, in principle, have an internal auditor under best practice provision V.3.1. The Committee has amended principle V.3 to record categorically that the internal auditor operates under the responsibility of the management board. The Committee believes it is necessary to prevent a situation in which an internal auditor is regarded as an outsider in his own company. The audit committee, in particular its chairman, is responsible for communication between the audit committee and the internal auditor. This is apparent from best practice provisions V.3.1 and

III.5.4. In addition, a new best practice provision V.3.2 explicitly states that in carrying out his duties an internal auditor should have access to the external auditor and the chairman of the audit committee. The Committee has noted in its compliance reports that local listed companies in particular are likely not to have an internal audit function. The Committee has therefore provided in V.3.3 that if there is no internal audit function, the audit committee should review annually whether there is a need for an internal auditor. Based on this review, the supervisory board makes a recommendation to the management board and includes a note of this in its report. Finally, in the light of the reactions in the consultation round, the term 'internal accountant' has been replaced by 'internal auditor'.

TRADE NAMES ACT

Article 1

Under this law means the trade name under which a company is driven.

Article 2

The trade passes by succession and is subject to transfer, but only one and the other in connection with the company, which is driven by that name.

Article 3

1
It is owned energy company forbidden to enter a trade, which falsely indicates, that the company, in whole or in part, to another would be accessories.
2
The first paragraph also applies if the common name in the trade just so little of the name of that person departs, that therefore the public is confused by the owner of this company is to be feared.
3
The first paragraph does not apply if the trade and business from someone who has carried that name does not conflict with this Act.

Article 4

1
It is forbidden to a trade to be carried, which falsely indicates, that the company would belong to one or more persons, acting as a company under a firm, as a partnership en commandite or a company, either to a limited company , a private limited liability company, a mutual association, a cooperative, an association or a foundation.
2
In the trade marks the entry of more than one person, even if their names are not mentioned, to which the company belongs to any person, acting as a company under a firm, the words "and company", which the company belongs to people , acting as a company under a firm or to one or more persons, acting as a partnership en commandite, the word "society", which the company belongs to a limited liability company to a private company with limited liability or a club, and the word "fund" to a foundation, if not all of the trade in its entirety to the contrary.
3
The first paragraph does not apply if the trade is conducted by a person without partners, and that name and the company from a company under a company or a partnership en commandite, which has conducted that trade not in conflict with these laws.

Article 5

It is forbidden to a trade to be carried, which, before the company under that name was driven already by another lawfully waged, or those of its trading only slightly different, and any other points where, consequently, in connection with the nature of both companies and the place where they are located, the public is confused between these companies is to be feared.

Article 5a

It is forbidden a trade name to be carried, which the mark comprises, on which another to distinguish it from their technical or commercial were straight, or of an indication, which is of such a mark is only slightly different, in so far as, consequently, in the public confusion as to the origin of the goods is to be feared.

Item 5b

It is forbidden to enter a trade, which is an incorrect impression of the business carried on under that name, where consequently misleading the public is to be feared.

Article 6

1
If a trade is conducted in contravention of this Act, any interested party, without prejudice to his claim under Title 3 of Book 6 of the Civil Code, joined a petition to the subdistrict court judge's request, the person who performs the forbidden trade, convict, containing such by the court to determine, to amend that the alleged illegality is removed.
2
The petition is addressed to the court of the district where the company is established under the prohibited trade is driven. Is the company outside the empire based in Europe, but was in that realm a subsidiary or branch, or are they there represented by a proxy agent, the court of the district in which such branch or branch or agent is established, authorized . Where the above provisions no court has jurisdiction, the court of the district where the residence of the applicant's jurisdiction is located. Is the company located in more than one district, the court has jurisdiction of each of these districts, at the discretion of the applicant. The same applies if the company outside the realm located in Europe, but in more than one district branch or branch or by an authorized agent represented. The petition is heard by the court.
3
The application is to the opposite party. The subdistrict has not then the petition after hearing or proper summons of the parties.
4
The Registrar shall send a copy of the decision of the magistrate to the parties. Within one month after the date of dispatch of this copy can by him, which can completely or partially unsuccessful, to appeal to the court that decides in chambers. The third paragraph shall apply mutatis mutandis.
5
The Registrar shall send a copy of the decision of the court to the parties. Within one month after the date of dispatch of this copy can by him, which can completely or partially unsuccessful, appeal in cassation. The adoption of such a petition to the opposite party.
6
The court may order provisional enforcement of its order.

Article 6a

1
The request referred to in the first paragraph of the preceding Article may also be done by the Chamber of Commerce and Industry.
2
The Chamber of Commerce and Industry, within whose jurisdiction under Article 6, paragraph competent court sits, is to make the request authorized.
3
The petition by the Registrar sent to the owner of the company, of any change in the trade is requested and where appropriate to other stakeholders. The Cantonal Court decided only after proper notice of hearing or those to whom the application is sent.
4
The fourth, fifth and sixth paragraphs of the preceding Article shall apply mutatis mutandis.

Article 6b

The court may on application of plaintiff temporary continuation of the alleged breach of Articles 5 and 5a permit on condition that defendant security for compensation for the plaintiff suffered.

Article 6c

1
If a trade is conducted in violation of Articles 5 and 5a, the court may in appropriate cases the damages as a lump sum.
2
The court may, upon application by the person who conducts the trade order at the expense of the person who has acted in breach of Articles 3 to 5b appropriate measures to disseminate information about the ruling.

Article 7

1
He argues that a trade in contravention of this Act, shall be punished by a fine of the second category.
2
The fact is regarded as an offense.
3
If during the commission of the offense less than two years have elapsed since a previous conviction of the guilty because the same offense has become final, may be imprisonment not exceeding fourteen days or a fine of the second category are imposed.
4
An official of the prosecution may, prior to prosecute the offense to pass, the one who banned trade leads, changes state, the officer need occurs to the illegality of the trade to lift, it being a competent term made to change to that. That change within the time provided, then the right to prosecute expired.

Article 8 [repealed on 10/01/1954]

Article 9

[Contains amendments to other legislation.]
Final and transitional provisions

Article 10

This Act may be cited as the "Handelsnaamwet".

Article 11

1
This Act shall enter into force on a date to be determined by Us.
2
If the entry into force of this law a trade is conducted in contravention of this Act in respect thereof may for four months after that time no appeal be lodged.
3
When the phrase "not inconsistent with this Act" at the end of Articles 3 and 4 will consist of a trade before the entry into force of this law, it means: not in conflict with this Act, if they are keeping the trade effect was true.
And ordain that it shall be published in the Gazette, and that all ministerial departments, authorities, bodies and officials whom it may concern shall diligently implement it will keep.

STRATEGIC INFORMATION FOR CONDUCTING BUSINESS[2]

STARTING UP BUSINESS IN THE NETHERLANDS

In preparing to conduct business activities in the Netherlands, a company is presented with several choices of how to go about it as well as a slew of legal requirements to be complied with. From a legal and tax point of view, the first priority is deciding on which legal form to use 'to house' the proposed Dutch-based activities.

LEGAL BUSINESS FORM

Compared to other EU countries, the Netherlands has a flexible and liberal legal framework for the organization of enterprises by non-resident companies or individuals. There are no special restrictions on foreign-owned companies that wish to start a business in the Netherlands. Business operations can be set up as having either legal personality or not. If a legal entity has legal personality, the entrepreneur cannot be held liable for more than the sum he contributed to the company's capital. A private limited liability company - 'Besloten Vennootschap' (BV) - and a public limited liability company - 'Naamloze Vennootschap' (NV) - are examples of limited liability companies with legal personality.

Most foreign investors in the Netherlands conduct their business activities there in the form of a private company with limited liability (BV). The BV is commonly used for all types of business ventures. However, a public limited liability company (NV) is the usual form of business enterprise adopted when capital is to be acquired through public offerings. When incorporating a BV or an NV, the foreign investor must submit a notarial deed of incorporation, which this must contain the articles of association. The incorporators of a BV must provide a minimum of EUR 18,000 of the share capital, whereas for the incorporators of an NV the amount is EUR 45,000.
To complete the incorporation procedure, the founders have to register the new company in the Commercial Register at the Chamber of Commerce of the district in which its main business will be located.

Sole traders, partnerships and limited partnerships are examples of legal forms without legal personality, wherein the guiding principle is that the entrepreneur remains personally liable for the company's debts. A partnership format can be used when two or more partners wish to do business jointly and under a joint name without having to meet all the legal requirements that a BV or NV would entail.

If the foreign investor prefers not to set up a legal entity in the Netherlands, a branch might be a better option. A branch is easier and less expensive to establish than a subsidiary. However, a branch is not a separate legal entity, so branch's foreign parent is fully liable for all of its obligations.

PERMIT REQUIREMENTS

Usually, an establishment permit is not required to register a new business in the Commercial Register of the Chamber of Commerce. However, permits are required for more complex businesses that place extra demands on the entrepreneur. Examples are enterprises in the construction, automotive and food sectors.

Dutch environmental law calls for an environmental permit for all new (industrial) plants in the Netherlands. In order to obtain this permit, an application has to be filed with the competent authority, which is usually local or provincial governments.
A regular building permit is required for the construction of new businesses or industrial premises. A building permit application has to be filed with the local government, which must decide on the application within 12 weeks of its receipt. However, should a company require both a building and an environmental permit, the former will not be issued before the application for the latter has been approved.

In principle, every employer planning to employ a citizen of a country from outside the European Economic Area (EEA) must apply for a permit for this purpose. Application for such a work permit is made at the Centers of Work and Income - 'Centrum voor Werk en Inkomen' (CWI) - in the municipality where the company is or will be located, and this must be done before the applicant moves to the Netherlands.

[2] This section based in part on the materials of the US Department of Commerce

CHOOSING A TRADE NAME

In the preliminary stages of forming a company, the founders must check that its proposed name is not identical to or too closely resembles that of an existing company. This is normally done by the public notary through the Chamber of Commerce, which maintains a Register of Trade Names. A general search will carried out to determine if there is already a business with that name in that region. Beyond the region, the Chamber of Commerce may conduct a nationwide business name search on request.
For a BV or NV, the name must begin or end with the initials BV or NV, or the equivalent words spelled out.

INTERNET DOMAIN NAME REGISTRATION

The Foundation Internet Domain Registration the Netherlands (SIDN) is responsible for the registration of domain names ending in .nl. Apart from the technical requirements, SIDN's only criterion is whether the name is unique and does not concern itself with content. Nor is a potential domain name holder prevented from registering multiple names. In fact, there is no limitation on the number.
There is no requirement for the applicant to be based in the Netherlands for an ' nl' domain name. However, if the applicant is based outside the Netherlands, an address in the Netherlands does have to be given, to which formal correspondence can be sent.

CONTACTING THE DUTCH TAX DEPARTMENT

The entrepreneur should notify the Dutch Tax Department as soon as it is known when the company plans to start business. The relevant form, 'Opgaaf Gegevens Startende Onderneming' (statement of information for starting up a new business), is available from the Dutch Tax Department, which uses it as a basis to decide for which taxes the entrepreneur will be liable.

PERSONNEL MATTERS

New personnel must be reported to and recorded by the following organisations:

- *Tax Department* - In addition to reporting the names and related statistics of new employees, all employers in the Netherlands are required to withhold income tax from wages and remit it to the tax collector periodically. The tax is levied on employment income of non-resident as well as resident employees.
- *National Institute for Social Security (UWV)* - Information on employees must be sent to the UWV within 14 days of their joining the company. The UWV collects contributions for employee insurance schemes.
- *Health Insurance Fund* - A Health Insurance Fund is notified of a new employee only if he or she is hired for more than three months and earns less than EUR 31,750 per year.
- *Risk Management Service ('Arbo Dienst')* - Each employer has to report new staff to a certified Risk Management Service, which provides counseling services to reduce absenteeism. In all branches of industry this 'Arbo' service is obligatory.

PREPARATIONS IN HOME COUNTRY

For incorporating a subsidiary, the following data and documents need to be submitted:

- Name of the company
- Statutory seat
- Incorporators (incl. addresses, dates and places of birth, nationalities, annual report for corporate incorporator)
- Members of the board of management (same information as above)
- Members of the supervisory board (same information as above) (if applicable)
- Authorized, issued and paid-in capital (min. EUR 18,000)
- Power of attorney authorizing the manager
- Dutch articles of association (together with Dutch civil notary)

For registering a branch:

- Certified articles of association
- Certified translation of articles of association
- Copy of annual report
- Extract of commercial register of the foreign company
- Notarized decision of board of directors resolving:
  - to establish the foreign branch
  - to appoint the branch manager
  - to determine his powers
- Power of attorney authorizing the branch manager

For expatriate employees:

- Certificate from foreign employer explicitly stating expatriation and effective date
- E101/102 forms (only for EU countries)

ACTIONS IN THE NETHERLANDS

The actions to be taken by an investor in the Netherlands depend on the business form chosen and on the type of activity that will be undertaken in the Netherlands.

ONLY FOR A SUBSIDIARY

Activity	Contact	Estimated timeframe
Incorporation of subsidiary	Public notary	1 month
Payment of capital tax	Revenue tax inspector	1 month

ADMINISTRATIVE ISSUES FOR SUBSIDIARY AND BRANCH

Activity	Contact	Estimated timeframe
Registration with Chamber of Commerce	Commercial Register of local Chamber of Commerce	1 day
Opening of bank account	Commercial bank	2-3 days
Registration with Tax Department	Tax Inspectorate for Enterprises	4 weeks
Registration with National Institute for Social Security (UWV)	UWV (Contact for foreign enterprises) Prinses Beatrixstraat 9/15 7551 BK Hengelo Tel: 074-7502004 Contacts: Mr Vink - 074-7503814 Ms Dekker-Aarten - 074-7503813 Mr de Mare - 074- 7503812	1 month
Arrangement of the necessary insurance cover: • Liability insurance • Insurance of business assets • Legal assistance insurance	Insurance company	

PERSONNEL ISSUES

Activity	Contact	Estimated timeframe
Drawing up terms and conditions for employment	Employers' organization for applicable Collective Labor Contract (CAO)	
Work permit application	Local Center of Work and Income (CWI)	6 weeks
30% tax rule application	Belastingdienst Particulieren Buitenland Postbus 2865, 6401 DJ Heerlen Schakelweg 5, 6411 NX Heerlen Tel: 045-5779000	3-4 weeks

LEGAL ISSUES

Activity	Contact	Estimated timeframe
Environmental permit application	Local or provincial government	6 months
Building permit* application	Local government	3 months
Trademark registration	Benelux Trademarks Office Bordewijklaan 15 2591 XR The Hague The Netherlands Tel.: 070-3491111	10 working days to a few months (depends on whether a quick search is requested by applicant)
Patent application	Patents Council Patentlaan 2288 EE Rijswijk The Netherlands Tel.: 070-3986655	None (applicant may have process start immediately after filing).
Import certificates, export licenses application	Belastingdienst/Douane Centrale dienst in- en uitvoer Engelse Kamp 2 P.O. box: 30003 9700 RD Groningen The Netherlands Tel.: 050-5239111	

*If the construction of the building requires an environmental permit, the building permit will not be granted until it becomes sufficiently clear whether the environmental permit can be granted and what conditions will be attached to it.

FORMATION OF A BV

A BV is established by one or more individuals or companies that sign the articles of incorporation ('akte van oprichting') before a public notary. (A notary in the Netherlands is a public official appointed by Royal Decree whose legally prescribed functions include drawing up articles of incorporation and deeds for the transfer of property and mortgages. He may also act as legal advisor in certain matters.)
The articles of incorporation should include the company's articles of association, which state the company's official name and the registered office, which is required to be in the Netherlands (the registered office need not necessarily be at the company's principal place of business). The company's objectives stated quite briefly are included. The articles of incorporation should be in the Dutch language. This also applies to the articles of association, as these are a subset of the articles of incorporation. The public notary is completely responsible for ensuring that the articles of association comply with relevant legislation.

A founder need not be present at the signing of the articles of incorporation as long as he has given power of attorney to his representative or acts through a nominee. In addition, a founder need not necessarily be a Dutch resident or citizen. As a group, the founders are required to make a minimum capital contribution of EUR 18,000. Payment of capital may be made in cash or in other assets. For each form of payment, there are different formal requirements.

Prior to the incorporation of a BV, a declaration of no objection ('verklaring van geen bezwaar') issued by the Ministry of Justice is required. This declaration may be refused only if:

- The background of the persons who will control the company indicates a risk that it will be used for improper purposes or for activities that may harm its creditors;
- The fee due to the Ministry of Justice for obtaining the declaration has not been paid.

When the 'declaration of no objection' is obtained and the deed of incorporation is certified by the public notary, the new BV comes into existence as a legal entity with full rights. The founders then complete the incorporation process by registering the new company in the Commercial Register at the Chamber of Commerce of the district where its main business will be located. At this time, the total cost of incorporation must be disclosed.

The formalities required for incorporation usually take about two months. In the meantime, before the 'declaration of no objection' is obtained, a company is allowed to function on a provisional basis, but must signify this by adding the initials i.o. (for 'in oprichting' which means 'formation in progress') to the initials BV after its name.
During the pre-incorporation period, the BV i.o. must be registered with the Commercial Register at the Chamber of Commerce, if it intends to conduct any business prior to incorporation. The executives acting on behalf of the BV i.o. are personally liable until the formalities concerning registration and contribution of capital have been completed and the BV has, either expressly or implicitly, ratified the actions performed on its behalf during the pre-incorporation period.

Registration in the Commercial Register is automatically reported in the Official Gazette ('Nederlandse Staatscourant').

ARTICLES OF ASSOCIATION

These articles set out the mission and objectives of the company and its internal regulations. No separate document containing by-laws is required. Apart from the name, the registered office and the company's objectives, the articles should contain at least the following items, some of which some are prescribed by law while others represent general good practice:

- The authorized, issued and paid-in capital, by number and nominal value of shares, and expressed in EUR including the amount of issued share capital of each type (if there are several types of shares) for each founder.
- Rules regarding the restriction on the transfer of shares. A BV must have "blocking clauses," clauses which prevent the transfer of its shares without either (i) approval by the Board of Directors, or (ii) having followed a certain offering system to the other shareholders.
- The powers of the managing director(s) and procedures to be followed if no managing directors are available for any reason.
- Provisions regarding supervisory boards (for companies that have such boards)
- The date of the financial year-end and rules as to the preparation of financial statements and audits
- Rules for general meetings of shareholders
- Shareholders' voting rights
- Provisions for the distribution of profits or treatment of losses
- Dissolution procedures
- Details of all pre-incorporation agreements that the new company will be required to assume (for example, those concerning the rights of the founders or contributions to capital other than in cash.)

NAME

In the preliminary stages of forming a company, the founders must check that its proposed name is not identical to or too closely resembles that of an existing company. This is normally done by the public notary through the Chamber of Commerce which maintains a Register of Trade Names.

The name must begin or end with the initials BV or the equivalent words spelled out, but otherwise need not be in Dutch.

For foreign enterprises operating in the Netherlands through subsidiaries, the Ministry of Justice reviews their names and often requires that 'Netherlands', 'Nederland' or 'Holland' be added in brackets to avoid confusion between the parent company and its Dutch subsidiary.

COSTS OF INCORPORATION

The chief expenses incurred in forming a company are:

- Capital issue tax, which is charged at 0.55% on the amount of paid-in capital. Where capital is contributed other than in cash, the tax is payable on the value of the assets introduced. The contribution of services that cannot be valued as consideration for shares is not allowed;
- The public notary's fee charged for drawing up and executing the articles of incorporation. Additional fees are charged when difficult problems necessitate much correspondence, translation or discussion. If other professional advisors have been engaged, provision for their fees should not be overlooked. The notary cost of setting up a BV depends on the notary and varies between EUR 850 and EUR 1,400 (excl VAT).
- Chamber of Commerce fee charged for filing the company's documents in the Commercial Register. This fee is based on the legal form of the company and the location. Registration at the Commercial Register will cost around EUR 180.
- Ministry of Justice fee charged for issuing the Declaration of No Objection is approximately EUR 90.

SUBSIDIARY VERSUS BRANCH

Each company's unique circumstances will steer it toward one or the other means of starting up activities in the Netherlands: via a Dutch branch (possibly creating a taxable permanent establishment in the Netherlands) or via a Dutch subsidiary. In making this decision, not only the tax consequences should be considered, but also the operational consequences.

Bilateral tax treaties concluded by the Netherlands with many countries generally provide that withholding tax on dividends from a Dutch subsidiary to its foreign parent is in many cases reduced to 5%, sometimes even 0%. Assuming the 5% rate applies, total effective Dutch income tax on remitted earnings would be 34.93% (e.g. Profit = 100, after corporate tax of 31.5%: profit = 68.5. A 5% withholding tax on 68.5 = 3.43. Total effective income tax = 31.5% + 3.43% = 34.93%). In the absence of a treaty, the dividend withholding tax rate is 25%.

No withholding tax is levied on the distribution of dividends by a subsidiary established in an EU member state to its parent company in another EU member state, provided the parent company holds at least 25% of the subsidiary's capital (or, in certain cases, voting rights). For certain countries the threshold is reduced to 10% on the basis of reciprocity. A waiting period (the time the shares must be held by the parent company before the exemption of withholding tax applies) of one year is applicable in the Netherlands. (The waiting period in other EU countries can be up to two years). If the one-year period has not expired, a provisional withholding tax exemption in the Netherlands will apply. The exemption will be cancelled retrospectively if, following the dividend distribution, the one-year holding requirement is not met.

A Dutch branch of a foreign company is subject to the normal corporate income tax rate of 29%-31.5%. However, no withholding tax on remitted earnings is due. Therefore, the initial advantage of a branch is that the total Dutch effective income tax rate on remitted earnings can be limited to 29%-31.5% rather than 34.93%.

If initial losses are anticipated, the Dutch branch of a foreign company has another advantage over a subsidiary. For Dutch tax purposes, losses can be offset against future Dutch profits. For foreign tax purposes, the losses can often be utilized by the head office on its current-year tax return.

Use of a Dutch branch may not be an advantage in situations where it is anticipated that the operation will only break even at first, or both the Dutch branch and the foreign head office will be profitable. This is because the branch's income is subject to current taxation in the foreign country. In many cases, however, the Dutch source income will be tax-exempt in the other country by virtue of applicable Tax Treaties. Alternatively, having a Dutch subsidiary, may enable a company to avoid or defer taxation in its home country, simply by not paying dividends to the foreign parent and instead reinvesting the Dutch subsidiary's earnings.

A disadvantage of a corporation in comparison to a branch is the (0.55%) Dutch capital registration tax, which becomes due when capital is contributed to a corporation. The transfer of equity to a Dutch branch is not subject to Dutch capital registration tax.
Another advantage of a Dutch subsidiary is the amortization of intangible assets (e.g. technology) over its economic life, generally five to ten years. If intangible assets are transferred (and contributed as equity) by the parent company to its Dutch subsidiary, such assets can be amortized for Dutch tax purposes. Note that a 0.55% Netherlands capital tax is due on the value of the capital contribution. If intangibles are transferred in exchange for shares in the Dutch subsidiary, the parent company is often not subject to taxation in its home country upon receipt of such shares. Thus, depending on dividend policy, a tax deferral of up to 31.5% of the intangible asset value can be achieved. A branch of a foreign corporation is in essence entitled to the same tax treatment for intangibles, under the condition however, that the intangibles are allocable to the business activities of the branch.

Issues concerning the amortization of intangible assets can be discussed with the tax inspector and require justification of the amounts involved.

SUBSIDIARY COMPARISON

Pros	Cons
Liability of shareholders is limited to the extent of their capital contribution.	More expensive, complicated and time-consuming.
Unless agreed otherwise by contract, foreign parent company is not responsible for debts, obligations and liabilities of the Dutch subsidiary.	Withholding tax on remitted earnings (usually 5% on dividends).
Dutch nationals prefer dealing with a Dutch subsidiary as opposed to a foreign branch office.	Publication of financial statements in full is mandatory for a medium-sized or large company.
If no remittance of profits to the parent is necessary, further taxation can be deferred by reinvesting the subsidiary's earnings.	Liability to various Dutch taxes may arise when the company liquidates and the shareholders have not acted in good faith.
Intangible assets can be amortized for Dutch tax purposes regardless the business activities of the company	A capital registration tax of 0.55% is payable on the (value of) capital contributions.
	Appointment of at least one director is required by law.

BRANCH COMPARISON

Pros	Cons
Relatively easy to set up and costs are generally lower.	Operates as a foreign company and has no Dutch identity, so acceptance by Dutch nationals may be affected.
No withholding tax on remitted earnings.	Foreign parent company is fully responsible for debts, obligations and liabilities of the Dutch branch.
No requirement to publish the financial result of the branch (except foreign insurance companies and banks).	
Losses of Dutch branch may be offset against taxes/profits of the foreign head office.	
No capital registration tax is due.	

INVESTMENT CLIMATE

OPENNESS TO FOREIGN INVESTMENT

The Netherlands' trade and investment policy is among the most open in the world. With merchandise exports and imports combined accounting for more than two-thirds of GDP, the Dutch economy is one of the most internationally oriented in the world. The Netherlands is one of the world's largest suppliers of investment capital and currently ranks number six among the ten largest foreign investors in the world (fourth position if FDI is related to GDP). The Netherlands currently also ranks number eight among global recipients of FDI. The Dutch government maintains liberal policies toward foreign direct investment, and adheres to the OECD investment codes.

The only Dutch exceptions to national treatment are in air transport and maritime transport. In air transport, nationality and ownership requirements apply for licenses to operate an airline and cabotage is reserved to national airlines. With the exception of a few public and private monopolies from which foreign and domestic private investment is banned (the Netherlands Central Bank, Netherlands Railways, and public broadcasting)foreign firms are able to invest in any sector and are entitled under the law to equal treatment with domestic firms. The Dutch are also bound by European Union reciprocity provisions in banking, investment services and a few other areas. Provision of government incentives, national rules of incorporation, access to the capital market, etc., are all non-discriminatory.

Structural and regulatory reforms have been an integral part of a major reorientation of Dutch economic policy since the early eighties. Product market competition is strengthened by way of the Market Forces, Deregulation and Legislative Quality (MDW) project combined with tightening of competition policy. The government has reduced its role in the economy by introducing market forces in formerly public utilities sector. While the gas and electricity sector is gradually being opened up for foreign competition, the government maintains its dominant position in rail transport, public utilities and continues to play a large role in aviation, and telecommunications.

Despite relatively high labor costs, foreign investors favor the Netherlands for their European investment projects because of the country's stable political and macro economic climate; a highly developed financial sector; the presence of a well educated, flexible and productive labor force, and the high quality of its physical and communication infrastructure.

The Netherlands is also known for its favorable fiscal climate. Precise tax guidance given to foreign investors provides transparency with regard to investors' long-term tax obligations. The business climate in the Netherlands ranked highly in surveys by various international institutions. The Swiss based International Institute for Management Development (IMD) 2004 world competitive project ranks the Netherlands number four in the world's most competitive economies, behind the U.S., Finland and Singapore.

The Economist Intelligence Unit's 2004 survey of global business environment singled out the Netherlands as the country with the most favorable business climate for the next four-year period up to 2004. The International Location Advisory Service (ILAS) subscribes to the Economist's observation but flags recruitment problems (particularly in ICT) in a tight labor market and a shortage of industrial sites as potential bottlenecks in attracting foreign direct investment to the Netherlands. Erosion of the fiscal climate due to sharper tax competition among EU member states is likely to also cloud the Dutch investment climate.

The Dutch actively recruit foreign investment through the Netherlands Foreign Investment Agency (NFIA), and regional economic development companies. More than 25 percent of total FDI in the European Union is in the Netherlands. Foreign direct investment is concentrated in growth areas including information technology hardware, software and services, biotechnology, medical technology, and in food processing.

Investment projects are predominantly in contract manufacturing (high-tech assembly), distribution, and value-added logistics. The Netherlands is particularly attractive for the establishment of European headquarters, distribution centers, call centers and shared services centers. Investment surveys indicate that U.S. investors in particular favor the Netherlands as a location for European Distribution Centers (EDCs). An estimated 60 percent of U.S. companies in Europe have located their (self-operated or out-sourced) EDCs in the Netherlands.

The Dutch government and the EU give certain regional preferences in the form of grants for investment in economically depressed regions of the country. These incentives are available to foreign investors on the same terms as to Dutch investors. The Investment Premium Regulation (IPR), the only major investment incentive currently available from the central government, aims to encourage investment in areas with relatively high unemployment (predominantly in the North-East) with subsidies for new investments (industrial buildings and fixed assets). The IPR applies to investments of which at least 25 percent is the investor's own capital. Investment grants range from 15 percent for expansion projects, to 20 percent of new investment in buildings and equipment, and sometimes land. Local investment subsidies are sometimes also available from regional development companies. Regional restrictions apply to certain EU subsidies.

There are no apparent foreign investment screening mechanisms, and 100 percent foreign ownership is permitted in those sectors open to foreign investment. The rules on acquisition, mergers, takeovers, and reinvestment are nondiscriminatory. All firms must conform to certain rules of conduct on mergers and takeovers. These rules are administered by the Socio-Economic Council (SER), an official advisory body composed of representatives of government, business and labor. The SER rules are intended to protect the interests of stakeholders and employees. They include requirements for timely announcement of merger and takeover plans and for discussions with trade unions. A recent survey among European companies by Heidrick & Struggles ranks The Netherlands second after the UK as country with the most transparent corporate governance practices.

Despite the de jure open policy, elaborate corporate protective measures against hostile takeovers may de facto block acquisitions or takeovers by Dutch and foreign investors. Legislation and an industry code of conduct providing for a marginal restriction of takeover defenses took effect in 1997. A further move towards even more open merger and takeover practices is expected when by 2009 the EU takeover directive takes effect.

The Netherlands maintains no preferential or discriminatory export or import policies with the exception of those which result from its membership in the European Union. The Dutch also abide by all internationally agreed strategic trade controls e.g. Wassenaar Agreement. In summary, Dutch domestic restrictions on foreign investment remain minimal and no new ones are being planned. The Dutch investment climate should continue as it is, but may be influenced in the future by EU policies.

RIGHT TO PRIVATE OWNERSHIP AND ESTABLISHMENT

There are full rights of private ownership and establishment of business enterprises in the Netherlands, except in the monopoly sectors as noted in the introduction. Numerous enterprises in the Netherlands are 100 percent owned by foreign firms, including many from the U.S. Licenses are granted on the basis of competitive equality.

PROTECTION OF PROPERTY RIGHTS

The Netherlands has a generally good record on IPR protection, with the exception of the enforcement of anti-piracy laws (see below). It belongs to the World Intellectual Property Organization (WIPO), is a signatory of the Paris Convention for the Protection of Industrial Property, and conforms to accepted international practice for protection of technology and trademarks. Patents for foreign investors are granted retroactively to the date of original filing in the home country, provided the application is made through a Dutch patent lawyer within one year of the original filing date. Patents are valid for 20 years. Legal procedures exist for compulsory licensing if the patent is determined to be inadequately used after a period of three years, but these procedures have rarely been invoked.

Since the Netherlands and the United States are both parties to the Patent Cooperation Treaty (PCT) of 1970, patent rights in the Netherlands may be obtained if PCT application is used. The Netherlands is a signatory of the European Patent Convention, which provides for a centralized Europe-wide patent protection system. This convention has simplified the process for obtaining patent protection in the member states. Infringement proceedings remain within the jurisdiction of the national courts, which could result in divergent interpretations detrimental to U.S. investors and exporters.

The enforcement of anti-piracy laws remains a concern to U.S. producers of software, audio and videotapes, and textbooks. The Netherlands allegedly is one of Europe's worst piracy offenders with as much as half of software used in the country illegally copied. The Dutch government has recognized the need to protect intellectual property rights and law enforcement personnel have worked with industry associations to find and seize pirated software. Dutch IP legislation explicitly includes computer software as intellectual property under the copyright statutes.

LAWS AND REGULATIONS FOR COMMERCIAL TRANSACTIONS

Dutch laws and regulations governing commercial transactions are transparent and in accordance with international legal practices and standards. Business laws and regulations are non-discriminatory and apply equally to foreign and Dutch domestic companies operating in the Netherlands.

FOREIGN TRADE ZONES/FREE PORTS

The Netherlands has no free trade zones or free ports in the sense of territorial enclaves where commodities can be processed or reprocessed tax-free. There are, however, a large number of customs warehouses (EU category A through E, but no category A and F or "Free Zones") and free warehouses at designated places and international airports where goods in transit may be temporarily stored under customs supervision. Goods may be repacked, sorted or relabeled.

TAXATION ISSUES AFFECTING BUSINESS

The Dutch recently took the first step towards a fundamental reform of the tax system, partly with a view to further EU integration. The new tax system for the 21st century entails a substantial reduction in wage and individual income taxes, and simultaneous broadening of the tax base, as well as increasing VAT rates. As of 2001, the highest marginal tax rate on wage and salary income will be reduced from 60 percent to 52 percent.

When implemented, the new tax plan will yield a more transparent and equitable tax system and result in an appreciable shift from taxation of labor to taxation of consumption. The Dutch corporate tax rate is among the lowest in the EU. Effective January 1, 2003, corporations (including foreign-owned corporations) pay a standard corporate tax rate of 35 percent on all taxable profits. A possible reduction of the corporate tax rate to 30 percent over the first $25,000 of taxable profits by the year 2002 is being studied.

In recent years, Dutch and Foreign Multinationals have increasingly established their group financing activities outside the Netherlands due to attractive tax regimes elsewhere. In an attempt to reverse this trend, a bill became effective in 1997 offering finance companies of multinational companies a more friendly tax regime. Under certain conditions, companies conducting group financing activities are allowed to establish an international financial services reserve for tax purposes of up to 80 percent of their annual profits. The reduced profits are subject to the standard corporate tax rate.

PERFORMANCE REQUIREMENTS/INCENTIVES

There are no trade-related investment performance requirements in the Netherlands. General requirements to qualify for investment subsidy schemes apply equally to domestic and foreign investors. There are no requirements for employment of local capital or managerial personnel. However in practice most chief executives of major U.S. subsidiaries in the Netherlands are Dutch or other EU nationals because skilled managers are available at a cost less than that of posting an American abroad. In the case of staff personnel, moreover, Dutch nationals must be employed unless firms can demonstrate that the job in question cannot be performed by a Dutch national. This burden is eased by an existing provision that prior employment with the firm of at least two and a half years amounts to a presumption of unique qualifications for the job.

Limited, targeted investment incentives have long been a well-publicized tool of Dutch economic policy to facilitate economic restructuring and to promote energy conservation, regional development, environmental protection, R&D, and other national socio-economic goals. Subsidies and incentives are available to foreign and domestic firms alike and are spelled out in detailed regulations. Subsidies are in the form of tax credits which are usually disbursed through corporate tax rebates, or direct cash payments in the event of no tax liability. The investment premium regulation (IPR), the only major investment incentive still available to investors, aims to encourage corporate investment in parts of the country with a high unemployment rate by giving an investment subsidy for new investments (industrial buildings and fixed assets). Sharply falling unemployment(a major criteria for Brussels approval of national investment subsidies)is likely to reduce the significance of the IPR as an investment stimulating instrument over time.

The IPR subsidy applies to capital investment, of which at least 25 percent is the investor's own capital. Grants ranging from 20 percent of the investment up to 18 million guilders ($9 million) per project for new investment and expansion in buildings and equipment, and sometimes land, to 15 percent in case of new investment or expansion of up to 8 million guilders ($4 million) made five years after establishing apply to the Northern provinces of Groningen, Friesland, and Drenthe. IPR grants ranging for new investment and expansions in the Twenthe region in the East and the province of Limburg in the South are determined on an ad hoc basis. Local investment subsidies are sometimes also available from regional development companies. Regional non-tax incentives are available in the form of cash grants, low-interest loans, local government participation, and export guarantees for selected areas.

The growing number of tax incentives offered to investors in other EU countries has prompted the government to look into the possibilities of expanding existing tax instruments to aggressively improve the Dutch tax climate vis-a-vis that in competitor countries like Belgium, Germany and Ireland.

TRANSPARENCY OF THE REGULATORY SYSTEM

Laws and regulations which affect direct investment, such as environmental rules, health and safety regulations, etc., are non-discriminatory and apply equally to foreign and domestic firms. Dutch tax law facilitates attracting non-Dutch personnel to live and work in the Netherlands. Currently, the expatriate transferred to the Netherlands on a temporary contract can make use of the 35 percent ruling, which provides that 35 percent of his/her gross employment income in the Netherlands is not taxable under Dutch personal income tax laws. This treatment is granted for 4 years, with another 4 years possible upon application. Furthermore, the expatriate is considered a non-resident, meaning that only income from Dutch sources is taxed in the Netherlands.

Effective January 1, 2003, Dutch corporations and branches of foreign corporations are subject to a corporate tax rate of 35 percent on taxable profits, which puts the Netherlands in the middle bracket of the EU. Dutch corporate taxation generally allows for the exemption of dividends and capital gains derived from a foreign subsidiary (participation exemption). No local Dutch income taxes are levied on corporations. Furthermore, the Netherlands maintains an extensive network of tax treaties with a large number of countries. A new tax treaty with the U.S. took effect on January 1, 1994.

CORRUPTION

Dutch implementation of the 1997 OECD anti-bribery convention is moving more slowly than officials had hoped, due to technical drafting problems and the labyrinthine process for approval of legislation. Although the Dutch have signed the 1997 OECD anti-bribery convention, the domestic process which will allow the Dutch to deposit instruments of ratification has still not been completed. The Ministry of Justice (MOJ), with the assistance of the Ministry of Interior, is responsible for drafting amendments to the Dutch penal code to meet the requirements of the convention.

The MOJ has been wrestling with technical problems related to the need to reconcile the language of the convention with the EU fraud directive and the COE convention on fraud. Corruption in the Netherlands is, therefore, not expected to become a penal offense until new anti-bribery legislation will become effective. Likewise, bribes paid by Dutch businesses in landing contracts abroad will continue to be deductible for corporate tax purposes until the Dutch have deposited instruments of ratification with the OECD sometime in late 2004. At a national level, Dutch justice and interior ministries have taken steps to sharpen regulations which seek to combat bribery in public procurement and in the issuance of permits and subsidies.

LABOR

The Dutch workforce is largely well-educated and multilingual with the skills needed in a sophisticated, high-tech economy. Because employment in the Netherlands rose more than the labor force did in the past few years, the official unemployment rate currently ranks among the lowest in the European Union. Unemployment is forecast to fall from an average 7 percent of the labor force in 1997, to less than 3 percent in 2004 and 2001, which is well below the EU-15 average. Despite favorable labor market developments, structural unemployment, particularly long-term unemployment, is still considered too high. The Dutch government, therefore, continues to give the highest priority to job creation.

The Netherlands currently has the highest level of part-time work in the EU. The substantial increase in the participation of women in the workforce resulted in the significant rise in part-time work. More than 40 percent of the working population is currently employed part-time, which has significantly improved labor market flexibility.

The Dutch government's job creation policy is focused on the following elements: reducing the tax burden and social security contributions, moderate growth in wage levels, redistribution of work, and strengthening the economic structure. In addition, the Dutch government has taken measures to improve labor market flexibility. This combination of greater (but not full) labor market flexibility, consensual wage restraint, and lowering of the tax burden and social security contributions has received praise as the "Dutch Model."

A 1999 benchmark report by the European industry federation Unice observed that, despite relatively high wage costs, the Netherlands has one of the highest levels of labor productivity in the manufacturing industry. In order to reduce the gap between productivity and wage costs, the Dutch government has significantly reduced employers' costs for workers who earn or are just above the minimum wage level.

It has also called on organizations of employers and workers to create jobs at the lowest end of the wage scale. Currently, the lowest wage established by collective labor agreements (CAO's) is about 8 percent higher than the statutory minimum wage ($1,021 per month during the first quarter of 2004). Most recent collective labor agreements (CAO's) do indeed provide for lower wage scales.

Labor/management relations in both the public and private sectors are generally good in a system which emphasizes the concept of social partnership. Although wage bargaining in the Netherlands is increasingly decentralized, there still exists a central bargaining apparatus where labor contract guidelines are established. About 75 percent of all Dutch workers are covered by union contracts which are negotiated on a sectoral basis with employers associations and, if accepted by the government, are extended by law to the entire sector. Some sector labor contracts (e.g. road transport and haulage) are relatively cheap, others (e.g. metal) are more costly.

To avoid surprises, potential investors are advised to consult with local trade unions to determine which (if any) labor contracts apply to workers in their business sector prior to making an investment decision. Collective bargaining agreements negotiated in the past few years have, by and large, been accepted by the rank and file without much protest, despite only moderate wage rises, and days lost to strikes are relatively low.

The contract wages rise in 2004 is expected to accelerate to slightly over three percent from a contract wage increase of 2.5 percent in 1999. Counting on the impact of a tax burden cut under the 2001 tax reform, official estimates optimistically expect the negotiated contract wage rise in 2001 to stay just below three percent. Tight labor market conditions make an increase of close to four percent more likely.

The average per unit wage costs increase in 2004 and 2001 is forecast to remain virtually unchanged from 1999 at 3.6 percent. This is in excess of an average three percent wage costs rise predicted for Euroland. A 1999 survey on average annual labor costs (base pay plus employers' social security costs, mandatory benefits and voluntary benefits) across the EU by International Consulting Practice William Mercer ranks the Netherlands number nine after countries such as the UK, Germany, France, Sweden and Denmark.

Workers may be found through government-operated labor exchanges, a rapidly growing number of private employment firms or directly through, for example, newspaper ads. The official average workweek currently averages 37 hours, but work-shortening programs (ADV) effectively reduce the average workweek to 36 hour. There is a trend to cut working hours further in order to create jobs or avoid layoffs. Recently concluded wage contracts include provisions for a 36-hour workweek. Also, the American business community in the Netherlands has given a cautious thumbs up to calls to split the average 37-hour working week over four instead of five days, and treat Saturday as a normal working day. This would help ease the country's traffic-choked roads and allow companies to better utilize their machinery. On the other hand, new legislation has been adopted increasing the flexibility in the operating hours of companies and shops.

The Dutch have always had a trade-dependent economy which derives its strength from free trade and a stable industrial climate fostered by partnership between unions, employers organizations and the government. There is substantial labor involvement in corporate decision-making on matters affecting workers. Each company in the Netherlands with at least 50 workers is required by law to institute a Works Council with which management must consult on a range of issues including investment decisions. Legislation implementing an EU Work Council directive came into effect in March of 2003. Trade unions and management are generally receptive to foreign investment, especially where this leads to improved employment possibilities and related benefits. U.S. companies generally perceive Works Councils as contributing to management-worker relations and a benefit to the company.

EFFICIENCY OF CAPITAL MARKETS AND PORTFOLIO INVESTMENT

Dutch financial markets are fully developed and operate at market rates, facilitating the free flow of financial resources. The Netherlands is an international financial center for the foreign exchange market and for Eurobonds and bullion trade. The flexibility that foreign companies enjoy in conducting business in the Netherlands extends into the area of currency and foreign exchange. There are no restrictions on foreign investors' access to sources of local finance.

CONVERSION AND TRANSFER POLICIES

There are no restrictions on the conversion or repatriation of capital and earnings, including branch profits, dividends, interest, royalties, or management and technical service fees, with the exception of the nominal exchange license requirement for non-resident firms.

EXPROPRIATION AND COMPENSATION

The Netherlands maintains strong protection on all types of property, including private property, and the right of citizens to own and use property. Expropriation would only take place in the public interest and with adequate compensation. We have no reason to believe that it would be undertaken in a discriminatory manner or in violation of established principles of international law. The Embassy is unaware of any recent expropriation claims involving the Dutch government and U.S. or other foreign-owned property.

DISPUTE SETTLEMENT

The Embassy is not aware of any investment dispute involving the Dutch government and U.S. or other foreign companies. The Netherlands is a signatory to the international convention on investment disputes and a member of the International Center for the Settlement of Investment Disputes (ICSID). Although the central government has no rules regarding withdrawals of investment, occasionally trade unions go to court over company closures. This has occurred in the case of both domestic and foreign-owned firms.

POLITICAL VIOLENCE

The Netherlands is noted for its stable political environment. In the highly consensus-oriented Dutch society, political violence is nonexistent. The Dutch economy derives much of its strength from a stable industrial climate fostered by partnership between unions, employer organizations, and the government. Strikes are rarely regarded as the primary means to settle labor disputes, and labor strikes in recent decades have been very rare.

BILATERAL INVESTMENT AGREEMENTS

The Netherlands has signed bilateral investment agreements with a large number of countries including: Albania, Argentina, Bangladesh, Belarus, Bolivia, Bosnia-Herzegovina, Brazil, Bulgaria, Cameroon, Cape Verde (Republic of), Chili, China, Croatia, Czech Republic, Egypt, Estonia, Georgia, Ghana, Hong Kong, Hungary, India, Indonesia, Ivory Coast, Jamaica, Jordan, Kenya, Korea (Republic of), Latvia, Lithuania, Macedonia, Malaysia, Malta, Mexico, Moldova (Republic of), Mongolia, Morocco, Nigeria, Oman, Pakistan, Paraguay, Peru, Philippines, Poland, Romania, Russian Federation, Senegal, Singapore, Slovenia, Slovak Republic, South Africa, Sri Lanka, Sudan, Tanzania, Thailand, Tunisia, Turkey, Uganda, Ukraine, Uruguay, USSR, Uzbekistan, Venezuela, Vietnam, Yemen, Yugoslavia and Zimbabwe. The Netherlands adheres to the OECD codes on capital movements and invisible transactions, with the exceptions mentioned earlier, and has a treaty of friendship, commerce and navigation with the U.S. which generally provides for national treatment and free entry for foreign investors, with certain exceptions. The Netherlands is also a member of the EU single market.

OPIC AND OTHER INVESTMENT INSURANCE PROGRAMS

The Netherlands has no investment insurance agreements like OPIC's. However, Dutch companies investing in developing countries through the establishment of subsidiaries or joint ventures can insure their investment against non-commercial risks with the privately-owned Netherlands Credit Insurance Company (NCM) under the 1969 Investment Reinsurance Act (WHI). The NCM reinsures its political risks with the Ministry of Finance. This insurance program has not been heavily utilized by Dutch investors, however, and efforts are underway to find ways of making the program more effective.

According to article 7b of the Investment Reinsurance Act (WHI)of 1969, reinsurance of investment in LDC's can be provided only if a satisfactory agreement has been reached with the recipient country regarding regulations which will apply to Dutch investment in that country.

The Act covers procedures which will be followed in the case of a dispute between the investor and the host country on recovery of indemnity resulting from the insurance of the investment. A temporary program covering the insurance of investment in all Eastern and Central European countries, with the exception of the former Yugoslavia and the Asian republics of the CIS (THRIO) was introduced in 1991. In 1997, the WHI and THRIO programs were merged with similar programs for developing countries into the Investment Reinsurance Arrangement (IRA). Investments in countries with which the Netherlands has concluded a bilateral investment treaty are eligible for coverage under the IRA. The Netherlands is a member of the Multilateral Investment Guarantee Agency (MIGA).

FOREIGN DIRECT INVESTMENT STATISTICS

Data on the stock of foreign direct investment in the Netherlands (by country of origin and industry sector) and comparable data covering the stock of Dutch direct investment abroad are compiled by the Netherlands Central Bank (NB) on an ad hoc basis. Netherlands Central Bank investment statistics reveal that the total FDI stock in the Netherlands at the end of 1999 equaled more than 50 percent of GDP, while FDI inflows in 1999 fell to slightly over eight percent of GDP. The FDI stock in the Netherlands is among the highest in the European Union.

Foreign direct investment statistics in the Netherlands are based on sources of capital inflows and not on actual "by country" investment outlays. Official Economic Ministry statistics based on actual investment outlays by country of origin and by industry sector are protected for commercial reasons.

During the last decade the number of foreign companies with establishments in the Netherlands has grown to over 6,400, employing more than 357,000 workers. Included are more than 1,600 U.S. companies which account for 150,000 jobs. In 1999, the number of foreign direct investment projects established though the official Foreign Investment Agency (NFIA) totaled 85 (108 projects in 2003), with a value of 1.1 billion guilders (roughly $531 million), and creating roughly 5,000 new jobs.

The bulk (65 percent) were U.S. investments worth 873 million guilders ($439 million), concentrated predominantly in ICT related investment (50 percent), European headquarters and call centers. Investment projects from the U.S. accounted for more than 80 percent of total investment outlays and jobs created. Direct investment and capital movements by non-bank financial enterprises, raised the stock of U.S. direct investment in the Netherlands to $41.97 billion in 1999 ($106.4 billion according to USDOC statistics). This ranked the Netherlands in 1999 as the third largest recipient of U.S. direct investment worldwide, up from fifth position in 1995, and moving ahead of countries like France and Switzerland. There is no compulsory registration of foreign investment projects in the Netherlands. Since there is a considerable amount of regional investment acquisition, the total volume and value of direct investment projects in 1999 (NFIA sponsored projects plus independent projects) is unknown but estimated to be considerably higher than the official number.

Foreign companies in the Netherlands account for roughly a quarter of industrial production and employment in industry. At the end of 2003, an estimated one-quarter of foreign establishments in the Netherlands was of U.S. origin, with 4 percent Japanese, 51 percent from the EU, 10 percent from other European countries, and the remaining 12 percent from non-OECD and non-EU countries. During the past few years, investment from the U.S. has seen a sharp increase in both manufacturing and services. The Economics Ministry is confident that with the completion of the EU internal market and the creation of an Economic and Monetary Union (EMU), investment from the U.S. will continue to play a dominant role in overall foreign investment. Special efforts are being made to attract investments in value-added logistics, shared service centers, call centers, and European headquarters.

MAJOR FOREIGN INVESTORS

During the period 1987 through 1999, the Netherlands Foreign Investment Agency (NFIA) was involved in the establishment of 521 U.S. investment projects in the Netherlands with a total investment value of 10.4 billion guilders ($5 billion). The most important U.S. investment projects in the Netherlands include: Abbott, Albany International B.V., Amazon, Amgen Inc., APM-Holland, American Saw & Mfg. Company Int., Amresco, Arco Chemicals, Airtouch Communications, Arrow International, BF Goodrich, Bruce Foods Inc., Caddock Europe B.V., Campbell, Cargill, Davidson/Marley, Cisco Systems Inc., Datastream Inc., DHL, Distribution Services International, Dow Chemical, Du Pont de Nemours, Engelhard Terneuzen B.V., Eastman Chemicals, Euramax Castings, General Electric Plastics, IAMS Pet-food Company, Ingram Micro, Intec Engineering, Hewlett-Packard (SCI Systems), Kelsey Hayes, Lucent Technologies, Malden Mills, Mattel, Medarex Inc., Media Cybernetics, Memorex-Telex, Metrix, Metromedia Technologies International Inc., Morton International, Nike, Oasis, Pemstar, Perkin-Elmer, Phillip Morris Holland B.V., Plantronics, Prime Computers, Reebok International, Seagate Technology, SC Johnson Polymer, Silicon Graphics Inc., Spechem B.V., SPX Power Team (O.T.C.), Tandem Computers, Tessco Technologies, Vitalink Europe B.V., Western Digital Corporation, Packard Bell, Mobil Chemical Company, Nike, Scholle Corporation, and Texas Instruments.

The Netherlands is regarded as one of the most attractive countries for setting up European headquarters, call centers, shared services centers (SSC's), and European distribution centers (EDC's). Of all foreign headquarters established in Europe, close to sixty percent are located in the Netherlands. An estimated 25 percent of SSC's in Europe have chosen to come to the Netherlands. The Netherlands currently also has some 200 call centers within its borders. The Dutch also lead Europe in attracting distribution centers. An estimated 42 percent of U.S. multinational companies have established a European distribution center in the Netherlands. U.S. companies investing in the Netherlands have also been expanding strongly in the micro-electronics field, value-added logistics and the establishment of European headquarters.

According to the NFIA, computer manufacturers in particular are looking to northern Europe to establish an assembly, maintenance and distribution center. To this end Packard Bell is currently successfully operating a distribution center in the city of Nijmegen in the east employing 500 workers. PC manufacturer, Ingram Micro established a multi-million dollar regional distribution center in the province of Limburg in the south. Ingram Micro recently acquired Dutch PC producer Tulip. SCI Systems (contract manufacturer for Hewlett Packard) established a production facility in Heerenveen in the North employing 400 workers Other large U.S. electronics firms with establishments in the Netherlands are AT&T, Rank Xerox, IBM, and Honeywell.

During the period 1987 through 1999 the NFIA attracted 424 non-U.S. investment projects valued at 6 billion guilders ($2.9 billion), notably from Japan, South Korea and Taiwan, and including: British Oxygen Company, British Steel, Ericsson, Fuji Photo, Hoechst Holland, Kyowa Chemica Industry, Marley Foam, M&T Chemical, Mead, Metallverken, Mita Europe, Mitsubishi, Mitsubishi Motors, Mitutoyo, Nissin Food, Nissan, Omron, Outokumpu, Plalloy, Rexham UK, Roth Frere, and Supertron.

The top fifteen U.S. investors in the Netherlands - based on the number of employees, are listed below:

1. Sara Lee/Douwe Egberts NV
P.O. Box 2
3500 CA Utrecht
Phone: (31) 30 292 7311
Fax: (31) 30 293 7646
Manufacturing, sales and marketing of coffee and groceries, and household and personal care products.

2. AT&T Network Systems International BV
P.O. Box 1168
1200 BD Hilversum
Phone: (31) 35 687 3111
Fax: (31) 35 687 1748
Telecommunications equipment and systems.

3. Philip Morris Holland BV
P.O. Box 205
4600 AE Bergen op Zoom
Phone: (31) 164 279 911
Fax: (31) 164 279 335
Manufacturing, sales and marketing of cigarettes and tobaccos.

4. Ernst & Young
G.H. Betzweg 1
3068 AZ Rotterdam
Phone: (31) 10 407 4444
Fax: (31) 10 455 6440
Accountants and auditors, tax advisers, and management consultants.

5. IBM Nederland NV
P.O. Box 9999
1006 CE Amsterdam
Phone: (31) 20 513 3111
Fax: (31) 20 513 3634
Development, production, maintenance and sales of word processing, data processing and telecommunications equipment and services.

6. Alcoa Nederland Holding
P.O. Box 21
5150 BA Drunen
Phone: (31) 416 386 100
Fax: (31) 416 386 210
Manufacturing and sales of aluminum rolling and extrusion and end products.

7. General Electric Plastics Europe BV
P.O. Box 117
4600 AC Bergen op Zoom
Phone: (31) 164 232 911
Fax: (31) 164 232 940
Manufacturing, sales and marketing of thermoplastic resins.

8. Coopers & Lybrand Dijker van Dien
P.O. Box 94200
1097 GE Amsterdam
Phone: (31) 20 568 6666
Fax: (31) 20 568 6888
Accounting and auditing services, tax and management consultancy.

9. Deloitte & Touche
P.O. Box 90721
2509 LS The Hague
Phone: (31) 70 326 4701
Fax: (31) 70 324 4482
Public accountants, tax advisors and related services.

10. Dow Benelux NV
P.O. Box 48
4530 AA Terneuzen
Phone: (31) 115 671 234
Fax: (31) 115 672 423
Production of chemicals and plastics.

11. Digital Equipment BV
P.O. Box 9064
3506 GB Utrecht
Phone: (31) 30 283 9111
Fax: (31) 30 289 0623
Electronics

12. Rank Xerox Manufacturing (Nederland) BV
P.O. Box 43
5800 MA Venray
Phone: (31) 478 525 000
Fax: (31) 478 588 159
Manufacturing of copying equipment and supplies.

13. Du Pont de Nemours (Nederland) BV
P.O. Box 145
3300 AC Dordrecht
Phone: (31) 78 621 8911
Fax: (31) 78 616 3737
Manufacturing and sales of plastics, synthetic fibers and industrial organic chemicals.

14. Cargill
P.O. Box 8074
1005 AB Amsterdam
Phone: (31) 20 580 1911
Fax: (31) 20 682 0193
Agricultural products.

15. Honeywell BV
P.O. Box 12683
1100 AR Amsterdam
Phone: (31) 20 565 6911
Fax: (31) 20 565 6600
Manufacturing and sales of low pressure regulators for gas burners, micro switch precision components, control apparatus for heating, ventilating, air-conditioning controls, instruments and systems for process automation, safety controls for steam boilers, hot water boilers and special liquid level application and flow switches.

CONTACT INFORMATION FOR INVESTMENT RELATED INQUIRIES

Netherlands Foreign Investment Agency (NFIA)
P.O. Box 20101
2500 EC The Hague
The Netherlands
Phone: (31) 70 379 8818
Fax: (31) 70 379 6322

STARTING A BUSINESS IN THE NETHERLANDS FUNDUMENTALS

The Netherlands has a long trading history with the UK and is one of our major trading and investment partners. It is our 4th largest export market accounting for over 9% of the UK's world trade. The UK is The Netherlands 2nd largest investor. The Netherlands is the second major location for UK direct investment after the USA with about 1,000 UK companies or subsidiaries established there. Half of our direct investment in the EU is in The Netherlands.

The UK's share of invisible earnings is not known but it is very significant. Activities range widely across all sectors. Banks, insurance companies, transport firms, software houses and others in the service sectors are all well represented.

The Netherlands' trade and investment policy is among the most open in the world. Foreign investment is actively encouraged. Its stable political and economic environment makes it a favoured nation for foreign investors in certain sectors, with about 7,000 foreign companies present in The Netherlands. Most of the investment activity is in assembly, distribution, sales offices, call centres and shared service centres, although there are several British retail operations in The Netherlands: e.g. Body Shop and Kwik Fit.

Registration Requirements:

No:	Procedure	Time to complete:	Cost to complete:
1	Deposit the minimum capital required in the bank	1 day	no charge
2	Check the company name for appropriateness and validity at the Chamber of Commerce.	3 days	about EUR 90
3	Submit details of the incorporator(s) and first managing director(s) to the Ministry of Justice for approval or “declaration of no objection”	3 days	EUR 91
4	Draft and sign the company's deed of incorporation, executed by a civil law notary	1 day	EUR 1,750
5	Enter the company in the commercial register at the local chamber of commerce and obtain a registration number.	1 day	EUR 123.34
6	Register with the local tax authorities (at the same office register for social security authorities)	1 day	no charge

Procedure 1.
Deposit the minimum capital required in the bank
Time to complete:
1 day
Cost to complete:
no charge
Comment:
Procedure 2.
Check the company name for appropriateness and validity at the Chamber of Commerce.
Time to complete:
3 days
Cost to complete:
about EUR 90
Comment:

One or two alternative names may be submitted at the same time. The response arrives by mail. The cost may vary among different chambers of commerce.

Procedure 3.

Submit details of the incorporator(s) and first managing director(s) to the Ministry of Justice for approval or "declaration of no objection"

Time to complete:

3 days

Cost to complete:

EUR 91

Comment:

Until executing the deed of incorporation, the firm can operate as a BV "in the process of incorporation." The civil law notary cannot execute the deed of incorporation without prior approval of the Ministry of Justice, which is indicated by a declaration of no-objection. The deed also includes the amounts of authorized, issued and paid-up share capital and the names of the incorporators, shareholders, managing directors, and members of the supervisory board. If any of these parties (natural persons or legal entities, in principle apart from members of the supervisory board) are not Dutch citizens, more detailed information is possibly required for the approval. Acquiring a declaration of no-objection from the Ministry of Justice takes from 48 hours (for an urgent application) up to about 2 weeks, depending on the time the Ministry of Justice needs for its investigation of the antecedents of the parties.

Procedure 4.

Draft and sign the company's deed of incorporation, executed by a civil law notary

Time to complete:

1 day

Cost to complete:

EUR 1,750

Comment:

Notary rates are negotiable and can be billed on the basis of an hourly rate, or a fixed fee. This varies between notaries. The deed can be signed with a power of attorney of one of the employees of the notary.

Procedure 5.

Enter the company in the commercial register at the local chamber of commerce and obtain a registration number.

Time to complete:

1 day

Cost to complete:

EUR 123.34

Comment:

If the Chamber of Commerce is visited in person, it takes several hours to receive a registration number. If the documents are filed by mail, it takes a week. Membership in the local chamber of commerce is mandatory. Initial and annual fees depend on the number of employees and the authorized share capital of the firm. The initial annual fee for a small firm (fewer than 50 employees and authorized capital of no more than EUR 90.000) is EUR 115.80. A medium-size firm (50–250 employees and authorized capital of EUR 2.5–10 million pays EUR 299.80. A large firm (more than 250 employees and more than EUR 10 million authorized share capital) pays EUR 760.30. The payment of the fee can be in cash, wire transfer, bank draft, and the like. Usually an invoice arrives by mail from the Chamber, and the preferred method of payment is by wire transfer.

After incorporation of the company, the founders of the company are jointly and severally liable for each legal act performed during their management and which binds the company in the period before (a) the registration has been effected and (b) the minimum required capital is paid up. Publication in the Netherlands Official Gazette (Staatscourant) of the first registration and certain subsequent registrations is required and will be made by the Chamber. Companies with more than 50 employees must have a properly constituted workers council. The workers council representatives are entitled to participate in discussions and give advice on important company matters.

Procedure 6.

Register with the local tax authorities (at the same office register for social security authorities)

Time to complete:

1 day

Cost to complete:

no charge

Comment:

The registration form can be filed in a day but it will take the tax office 4–6 weeks to provide the required tax numbers. For income tax a separate registration form must be filed and this can also take 4 weeks.

REGISTERING PROPERTY

Registration Requirements:

No:	Procedure	Time to complete:	Cost to complete:
1	The civil law notary conducts a title search at the Land Registry, conducts research regarding the representation of the involved parties, drafts the deed of the transfer, and carries out the final check for liens/attachments before executing the deed	up to 4 days	Title search: (disbursements, charged by the Land Registry) (subject to 19% VAT): EUR 1.4 per registered title; EUR 1.4 per cadastral map; EUR 1.4 per cadastral extract (x4). (per cadastral parcel two extracts are required, one regarding the ownership and one regarding the mortgages and attachments – even if the property has no mortgages). Research regarding the representation of the buyer and purchaser: (disbursements, charged by the Chamber of Commerce) total EUR 49.00: EUR 11.00 for the articles of association (of each company); EUR 11.00 for an authenticated commercial extract (of each company); EUR 2.50 per on-line review of the details of the companies involved (commercial extract) (of each company). Notarial fee (inter alia including the work mentioned above under procedure 1): EUR 1,000-3,500 (subject to 19% VAT) Final check: no cost
2	Execution of the transfer deed, registration of deed and post-registration check	1 day	Transfer Tax: 6% of property value (Transfer Tax) Land Registry: + EUR 70 for registration (free of VAT) + EUR 2.8 for post-registration check (free of VAT)

Procedure 1.

The civil law notary conducts a title search at the Land Registry, conducts research regarding the representation of the involved parties, drafts the deed of the transfer, and carries out the final check for liens/attachments before executing the deed

Time to complete:

up to 4 days

Cost to complete:

Title search:
(disbursements, charged by the Land Registry) (subject to 19% VAT):
EUR 1.4 per registered title;
EUR 1.4 per cadastral map;
EUR 1.4 per cadastral extract (x4).
(per cadastral parcel two extracts are required, one regarding the ownership and one regarding the mortgages and attachments – even if the property has no mortgages).
Research regarding the representation of the buyer and purchaser:
(disbursements, charged by the Chamber of Commerce)
total EUR 49.00:
EUR 11.00 for the articles of association (of each company);
EUR 11.00 for an authenticated commercial extract (of each company);
EUR 2.50 per on-line review of the details of the companies involved (commercial extract) (of each company).
Notarial fee (inter alia including the work mentioned above under procedure 1):
EUR 1,000-3,500 (subject to 19% VAT)
Final check: no cost

Comment:

According to Dutch law it is mandatory to hire a civil law notary to perform the registration process of property in the Netherlands. The civil law notary will conduct a title search at the Land Registry, verify the authority of the seller to dispose of the property, conduct research regarding the representation of the involved parties, draft the deed of the transfer, provide for a transfer of the property free of mortgages and attachments, and carry out the final check for attachments before executing the deed.

Notaries can consult the land register by an on-line system, called the Automatic Cadastral Registration (AKR), but only regarding some aspects. The deeds and other registered documents from 1998 onwards are online accessible. Older deeds and documents are scanned on demand and are sent immediately by email. Extracts from the cadastral map showing the relevant properties are also available online. To obtain all relevant information takes a few minutes.

A notary can ask the Land Registry Office to find out the history and numbers of a parcel. If a cadastral parcel has been changed (e.g. a parcel is divided in 2 new parcels), the parcel will be given a new, unique parcel number. For companies the notary must conduct an on-line research with the Trade Register with respect to specific information of the company (such as address, managing directors). The articles of association can not be checked on-line. The civil law notary can have these sent to him by mail or fax. The civil law notary then drafts the deed of transfer. Some notaries charge by the hours of work they spend on the case, others charge as a percentage on the value of the property. An average fee is estimated between EUR 1,000 and 3,500.
Due to the need for the notary to draft the deed of transfer and provide for a transfer free of mortgages and attachments, this requires the cooperation of third parties and the retrieval of information other than that provided by the Land Registry.

Procedure 2.

Execution of the transfer deed, registration of deed and post-registration check

Time to complete:

1 day

Cost to complete:

Transfer Tax:
6% of property value (Transfer Tax)
Land Registry:
+ EUR 70 for registration (free of VAT)
+ EUR 2.8 for post-registration check (free of VAT)

Comment:

The notary executes the transfer deed. The authorized persons will either have to appear before the notary or must have granted power of attorney. The transfer tax is paid to the civil law notary, who will pay this tax to the Tax Authorities after registration. The transfer tax is 6% of the total purchase price or the market value, if that is higher. Also, or instead of transfer tax, sometimes VAT is applicable. It is 19% regarding property. This depends, inter alia, on the status of the property and the fact if the seller is a VAT-entrepreneur.
Each notarial deed has to be registered within 10 days with the Tax Authority who checks the deed for taxable aspects. They do not keep a copy but give a statement that the deed involved is checked on a certain date. The deed itself is then returned with that statement to the civil law notary. A true copy of the deed is registered at the relevant Land Registry Office. Such registration takes place immediately after the execution by submitting the deed to the Land Registry by internet. The civil law notary will receive a receipt from the internet within a few minutes of providing evidence of registration. An adaptation of the Cadastre Act making this an official procedure was endorsed by the Parliament per 1 February 2005.

The registration fee of the Land Registry depends on the kind of deed or document registered, and the number of cadastral parcels and purchasers involved. For example, the registration fee for a deed of transfer of a property that forms 1 cadastral parcel to 1 new owner costs EUR 70. The registration fee is paid to the Land Registry Office.

After the deed has been registered with the Land Registry Office, a civil law notary must carry out the post registration check in order to detect any potential change between the execution and the registration of the deed. As the evidence of the registration is sent by internet, just after the electronic submission following execution of the transfer deed, this check can be done immediately.

PAYING TAXES

Tax or mandatory contribution	Payments (number)	Notes on Payments	Time (hours)	Statutory tax rate	Tax base	Total tax rate (% profit)	Notes on TTR
Corporate income tax	1	online filing	40	25.5% (EUR 0 - 25,000 20%; 25,000-60,000 23.5%)	taxable profit	21.8	
Disablement act contribution	0	paid jointly	-	6.4%	gross salaries	6.4	
Health insurance contribution	1	online filing	80	6.5%	gross salaries	6.2	
Unemployment contribution	0	paid jointly	-	3.5%	gross salaries	1.9	
Special employment insurance contribution	0	paid jointly	-	1.2%	gross salaries	1.4	
Fuel tax	1		-	19% VAT and 0,376 Excise duty per liter Diesel	fuel consumption	1.2	
Property tax	1		-	EUR 4,17 per EUR 2,500 tax base	assessed property value	0.1	
Tax on insurance contracts	1		-	7.0%	insurance premium	0.1	
Road tax	1		-	various rates	vehicle weight	0	
Sewage charges	1		-	EUR 115	fixed fee	0	
Polder Board Taxes	1		-	EUR 0,17 per EUR 2,500tax base	assessed property value	0	
Value added tax (VAT)	1	online filing	60	19.0%	value added		not included
Totals:	9		180			39.1	

Notes:

Name of taxes have been standardized. For instance income tax, profit tax, tax on company's income are all named corporate income tax in this table.

The hours for VAT include all the VAT and sales taxes applicable.

The hours for Social Security include all the hours for labor taxes and mandatory contributions in general.

SETTING UP IN BUSINESS

The Netherlands Foreign Investment Agency (NFIA), part of the Ministry of Economic Affairs, is the Dutch government agency tasked specifically with assisting foreign investors. It has offices in London and should be contacted at the earliest opportunity. Contact details: 38 Hyde Park Gate, London SW7 5DP, Tel : 020 7225 1074 Fax : 020 7584 3396.

The NFIA is responsible for foreign direct investment, and within The Netherlands there are regional and local development organisations. The NFIA provides companies with a range of basic economic, financial, statistical and technical information on which to decide if The Netherlands is a suitable location. It maintains a computerised database of all suitable Dutch industrial sites with descriptions, and will organise fact finding trips to selected sites. Its services are confidential and free of charge.

Chambers of Commerce can also help. There are 21 Chambers of Commerce in The Netherlands. All commercial organisations, with the exception of some small businesses, must register with the local Chamber of Commerce. The particulars to be recorded are name, address, place of establishment, business activities, legal form (public or private company) and management (members of the board of management, authorised representatives). More details are available on the English pages of Chambers of Commerce website: www.kvk.nl.

The most common legal structures which foreign investors choose to conduct their business in The Netherlands is either as a public company (Naamloze Vennootschap (NV)) or a private company (Besloten Vennootschap met Beperkte Aansprkelijkheid (BV)). Other types of company are: General Partnership (Vennootschap onder firma (VOF)); Limited partnership (Commanditaire Vennootschap (CV)); Cooperative Society (Cooperative Vereninging (CV)).

An NV can be formed by one or more founders. A minimum paid-in capital of DFl 100,000 is required and at least 20% of the authorised share capital must be issued. Shares issued must amount to 25% paid for on subscription and a company may not purchase more than 10% of its own shares. There are no restrictions on the issue or transfer of shares or notes. A BV requires a minimum of DFl 40,000. Shares cannot be transferred freely.

Branches of foreign companies are subject to the same commercial registry requirements as a foreign owned Dutch company. The foreign parent is responsible for all liabilities and obligations of The Netherlands branch. The cost of establishing a branch is minimal.

STAFFING

The Netherlands has one of the lowest unemployment rates in Europe. Unemployment is currently about 2.4% of the working population. This has resulted in staff shortages in some areas.

The Netherlands has a well educated multi-lingual population. English is widely spoken. Companies wishing to set up in The Netherlands will benefit from the incomparable language skills. Sales, secretarial and admin staff bring at least one other language with them, and often more, without the additional costs such skills would attract in the UK. Dutch salaries are relatively high. Dutch workers are covered by a social security programme, the cost of which is shared by employers, employees and government.

Labour law is complex and favours the employee. It is strongly recommended that legal advice is taken before entering into any contractual agreement. British nationals and other EU nationals benefit from the Single Market and do not require work permits. But a residence permit is necessary for all foreigners residing in The Netherlands for more than 6 months. An application can be made at the Dutch embassy or consulate before departure. Registration is required with the police and the local authority where the employee lives. Expatriate staff can benefit from the Dutch 35% tax rule, whereby 35% of income is non-taxable. Staff may be recruited through a large number of recruitment agencies, government organisations, or via newspaper advertisements.

Companies employing more than 35 workers are legally required to institute a works council which must be consulted on a wide range of issues.

There are several international schools in the Netherlands.

LOCAL REGULATIONS

What are the local and regulatory considerations?

The Netherlands has a well developed legal and regulatory system. Rules on health and safety, environment, etc are applicable. Foreign ownership is permitted in most sectors.

It is recommended that legal advice is sought before taking investment decisions. The major accountancy companies Ernst & Young, KPMG, Pricewaterhouse Coopers, Deloitte Touche, Arthur Andersen are all represented in The Netherlands. Several British law firms have set up operations in The Netherlands including Evershes and Freshfields, A list of local lawyers and accountants experienced in UK and Dutch law can be obtained from British Trade International's Europe Directorate.

FINANCIAL ASSISTANCE

Is finance available for a start-up operation?

Amsterdam is a top international financial centre. The Dutch banking system is open, with a high concentration of domestic and foreign banks, and financial advisers. The largest Dutch banks have offices world-wide. There are over 50 foreign banks with offices in The Netherlands. The financial markets operate at market rates and it is claimed that the cost of Dutch financial services are amongst the lowest in Europe.

In some areas EU, Dutch government and local authority grants and subsidies may be available. In certain circumstances special incentives are also available. The regional development corporations, established by the government to stimulate development in the less active regions, can help set up enterprises and also act as risk bearing partners. The Netherlands Foreign Investment Agency will have details.

In addition to commercial banks there are a number of specialised institutions providing industrial funding. The National Investment Bank specialises in medium and long term lending, equity investment and capital market activities. The Industrial Fund (Industriefonds) is a joint venture between the Ministry of Economic Affairs, banks, insurance companies and pension funds. Its aim is to provide risk bearing capital to the larger high-tech companies. There are also venture capital funds available.

CULTURE

Are there any special cultural or language issues I should be aware of? The Dutch are governed by consensus in most areas of work. The work structure tends to be less hierarchical than in the UK.

REPRESENTATIVES IN THE MARKET - WHOM SHOULD I SEND?

It depends on the nature of business. Long term relationships built on mutual respect are important to the Dutch. Someone with good interpersonal skills, able to make decisions locally and to inspire confidence in staff and customers would be the ideal person.

PRACTICAL INFORMATION FOR CONDUCTING BUSINESS

STARTING BUSINESS IN THE NETHERLANDS

MARKET OVERVIEW

- The United States' partnership with the Netherlands is its oldest continuous relationship and dates back to the American Revolution.
- The Netherlands is a geographically small (approximately the size of the State of Maryland), densely populated (16.5 million people) country occupying a highly strategic commercial location, with Europe's largest Port, that makes it the "Gateway to Europe".
- Over 160 million consumers (roughly one third of the population of the expanded European Union of 27 Member States) reside within a 300-mile radius of Rotterdam.
- More than sixty percent of the Netherlands' GDP is generated by foreign trade in goods and services.
- The Netherlands is a key center within the global business network with an advanced infrastructure geared towards the transportation of goods, people, and electronic data.
- Its core distribution points include Rotterdam, Europe's largest port, and Amsterdam Schiphol Airport, the fourth largest in Europe.
- The Netherlands has capitalized on its location and advanced economy to become one of the top dozen trading countries in the world.
- It is currently ranked 16th in GDP in the world, eighth in imports of goods and services from the United States, and fourth in direct investment in the United States.
- The United States is the largest foreign investor in the Netherlands and has its largest bilateral trade surplus in the world with this country (est. $13 billion in 2007).

MARKET CHALLENGES

- Except for EU-wide impediments, there are no significant trade barriers.
- Because of the size, accessibility, and competitive nature of the Dutch market, importers usually insist on an exclusive distributorship.
- Exporters may need to adapt their products and documentation for the Dutch market.

MARKET OPPORTUNITIES

European Union rules have opened public procurement to U.S. firms, and there may be attractive opportunities for U.S. companies to participate in the renewal of the Dutch transport infrastructure, specifically, projects resulting from the development of the European high-speed railway network (HSL). Six "New Key Projects" (NSPs) have been launched to develop train stations and surrounding areas in Amsterdam, Rotterdam, The Hague, Breda, Utrecht, and Arnhem. For more information, go to: http://international.vrom.nl/pagina.html?id=7347

The Netherlands strategic location, the relative ease of doing business, the high level of proficiency in English, and its world-class and user-friendly transportation and distribution infrastructure make it an ideal market and European operations location for American companies. Best prospects are listed in Chapter 4 in this report. A rule of thumb is that products selling well in the U.S. market will generally have market potential in the Netherlands.

MARKET ENTRY STRATEGY

- The Dutch market is highly competitive -the "golden key" of customary business is courtesy, especially replying promptly to requests for price quotations and to orders.
- Dutch business executives are generally more conservative than their American counterparts; therefore, it is best to refrain from using first names until a firm relationship has been formed.
- Friendship and mutual trust are highly valued, and once trust has been earned, a productive working relationship can usually be counted upon.
- Dutch buyers appreciate quality and service and are also interested in delivery price. Care must be taken to assure that delivery dates will be met and that after-sales service will be promptly honored.
- U.S. exporters should maintain close liaison with distributors and customers to exchange information. Understanding developed through periodic personal visits is the best way to keep distributors apprised of new developments and to resolve problems quickly.
- U.S. exporters should consider warehousing in the Netherlands for speedy supply and service of their Dutch and European customers.
- A vigorous and sustained promotion is often needed to launch products because buying habits are generally strong. Products must be adapted to both technical requirements and to consumer preferences. It is not sufficient to merely label a product in conformity to national requirements for the development of the full market potential. Consumers must also be attracted to the product by label and packaging as well as ease of use.
- Most Dutch speak their minds and will not waste your time or their own if they are not interested in your product.

BUSINESS LAW

The Netherlands is well known for its open economy. It is in favor of international trade without national and/or regional barriers and it welcomes foreign investments. Therefore, an indispensable feature of Dutch legislation is, among other things, that company law does not make a difference between Dutch nationals and foreigners. Additionally, companies created under foreign law are free to operate in the Netherlands. For instance, they can be party to a contract, they can participate in partnerships and they can establish a legal entity. Also, it should be noted that there are usually no objections to the employment of skilled foreign managers or specialist staff in the Netherlands.
Dutch legal entities are internationally regarded as sound and generally respected. This reputation is ensured by Dutch business law, fine-tuned by case law, which governs the institution, running and liquidation of legal entities. For foreign investors the most important entities include a private limited liability company or Besloten Vennootschap (BV), a public limited liability company or Naamloze Vennootschap (NV), some forms of partnerships.
With effect from 8 October 2004, it will be possible to incorporate a European company (SE) within the European community.
Business activities can also be conducted in the form of a branch. A branch is a long-lasting business operation that is owned by a foreign entity resident outside the Netherlands.

A special way for a foreign company to carry out activities in the Netherlands or in Europe with the Netherlands as its base, is the conclusion of a joint venture with a Dutch party. Another possibility is to merge with or acquire another company. A joint venture can take the form of, for instance, a partnership or a BV. The selection of a potential joint venture partner and the structuring of a joint venture is a very complicated process. Therefore, it would be advisable to contact one of the competent advisors in this field, available in The Netherlands.

The introduction of products into the Dutch market is relatively uncomplicated and may be achieved using several methods. Sales agents and distributors can often provide a good starting point in exporting to the Netherlands.
A separate, but very important, subject is formed by the enhancement of free competition in the Netherlands by the Competition Act.

REGISTRATION OF NEW BUSINESS ENTITIES

All new businesses should be registered with the Commercial Register, which is kept at the office of the local or regional Chamber of Commerce. This registration, which will be open to public inspection, will have to be accompanied by specific information, the nature of which depends on the type of the selected business entity. Often this information includes:

- A copy of the articles of association, showing the entity's name, its business objectives and address.
- Statement of issued and paid-in share capital in the case of BV's and NV's. Annually, all changes in issued and paid-in capital will be filed. In case issued shares are not fully paid in, annually a list will be filed, containing names and addresses of shareholders, number of shares and the amount already paid in.
- An overview of names, addresses, nationalities and other details of all supervisory and managing directors. A company held by a single shareholder, be it an individual or a legal entity, must disclose name and address/office registration.
- In case of a general partnership similar information must be filed. The same applies in case of general partners in a limited partnership, while with regard to limited partners their number, nationality, country of residence and their capital contributions (not their names) have to be filed.
- A description of each managing director's authority to represent and bind the company. For example, in case there are two or more of such directors, whether one may act alone or only in combination with the other.

All subsequent changes in the company must be filed with the Commercial Register. Fees are charged to cover registration costs.

Registration of companies at the Chamber of Commerce can only be done with the Dutch forms. However, for foreign companies these forms are translated in English. The English forms can be used to fill in the Dutch ones. The NFIA can provide these forms on request.

Other important formalities may include the application for licenses, such as an environmental permit or a building permit, both issued by local government.

THE DUTCH CORPORATE GOVERNANCE CODE

To strenghten the international image of Dutch companies and to restore public confidence in the honesty, integrity and transparancy of the conduct of affairs within Dutch listed companies a new Dutch corporate goverrnance code was introduced on December 9, 2009 and is effective as of January first, 2004. For more in-depth information on the code go to: www.corpgov.nl

THE BV - A PRIVATE LIMITED LIABILITY COMPANY

The BV is a suitable vehicle for an individual or a small number of interested parties, who wish to operate with limited liability, to carry out a business. Also, it is often used when a company decides to establish a holding company in the Netherlands for tax purposes. Similar legal entities exist in the form of an Inc. in the US, the Sarl in France and the GmbH in Germany. It often concerns closely held small or medium sized companies, including many foreign subsidiaries. An important feature of the BV is that it cannot raise public funding. Furthermore, the transfer of shares of a BV is restricted.

INCORPORATION

Before the actual incorporation takes place, the Dutch Ministry of Justice must agree with the contents of the deed of incorporation by issuing a "statement of no objection." This procedure may take up to 4 weeks. Next the deed of incorporation in the Dutch language must be executed before a Dutch civil law notary. This deed must contain

- The articles of association.
- The amounts of issued and paid-up share capital.
- The names of the (first) managing (and supervisory) directors.

ARTICLES OF ASSOCIATION

After having obtained the deed of incorporation, the articles of association must be filed with the Commercial Register of the appropriate Chamber of Commerce. The articles of association must contain, among other things:

- The business objectives
- The financial structure and
- The location of the company seat.

PAID-UP CAPITAL

The authorized, issued and paid-up capital of a BV must at least amount to EUR 18,000.

LEGAL ACTS

An important issue is, whether the company is bound by legal acts, carried out in its name before the above mentioned incorporation procedure has been finalized. Dutch company law allows for ratification after completion. Until ratification the persons performing such legal acts before incorporation are personally and jointly liable. Also those acts are binding, which are based on and directly refer to the articles of association.

LIABILITY OF SHAREHOLDERS

In case of an established BV the liability of a shareholder is restricted to the amount of issued share capital. However, under certain circumstances managing directors of the BV may face personal liability.

SHAREHOLDER'S MEETING

At least one shareholder's meeting should be held each year. This meeting must be scheduled within a period of six months after the end of the company's financial year, in order to adopt or approve the annual accounts.

SUPERVISORY BOARD

The articles of association of a BV may stipulate the formation of a supervisory board next to the board of management. In case of large companies the law requires the establishment of a supervisory board. A large company is a company, of which the issued share capital and reserves amount to at least EUR 13 million, which qualifies for the establishment of a work council and which employs 100 or more employees in the Netherlands (including those employed through subsidiaries). If a small company decides to establish a supervisory board it may attribute to this board whatever powers and duties it may decide. In case of large companies, a number of decisions, spelled out by law, which may influence the continuity of the company needs approval by the supervisory board.

FINANCIAL STATEMENT

A BV must file all or parts of its annual financial statements with the Commercial Register, depending on its size.

IMPORTANT DIFFERENCES BETWEEN A BV AND NV

Finally, as stated earlier in the introduction, the BV has most features in common with the NV. Nevertheless, there are some important differences:

- The NV is the only legal entity to be able to issue bearer shares. Like the BV it can also issue registered shares.
- It should be noted that the bearer shares of a NV are the only shares which can be traded on the stock exchange. Consequently, trading of shares of a BV is excluded in any event.
- As said before, the transferability of shares of a BV is necessarily restricted by the articles of association. In the case of a NV transferability is only restricted if the articles of association provide for it.

THE NV - A PUBLIC LIMITED LIABILITY COMPANY

The NV is the usual form of business enterprise adopted, when capital is to be acquired through public offerings. Its general characteristics are similar to those of a public limited liability company elsewhere. Similar entities exist in the form of a Corp. in the US, the SA in France and the AG in Germany. There is no restriction on the amount of capital to be raised and its shares are freely transferable, although subject to any restriction incorporated in the articles of association.

INCORPORATION

Before the actual incorporation takes place the Dutch Ministry of Justice must agree with the contents of the deed of incorporation by issuing a "statement of no objection." This procedure may take up to 8-10 weeks. Next, the deed of incorporation in the Dutch language must be executed before a Dutch civil law notary. This deed must contain:

- The articles of association.
- The amounts of issued and paid-up share capital.
- The names of the (first) managing (and supervisory) directors.

ARTICLES OF ASSOCIATION

After having obtained the deed of incorporation, the articles of association must be filed with the Commercial Register of the appropriate Chamber of Commerce. The articles of association must contain, among other things,

- The business objectives.
- The financial structure.
- The location of the company seat.

PAID-UP CAPITAL

The authorized, issued and paid-up capital of a NV must at least amount to EUR 45,000.

LEGAL ACTS

An important issue is, whether the company is bound by legal acts, carried out in its name before the above mentioned incorporation procedure has been finalized. Dutch company law allows for ratification after completion. Until ratification the persons performing such legal acts before incorporation are personally and jointly liable. Also those acts are binding, which are based on and directly refer to the articles of association.

LIABILITY OF SHAREHOLDERS

In case of an established NV, the liability of a shareholder is restricted to the amount of issued share capital. However, under certain circumstances managing directors of the NV may face personal liability.

SHAREHOLDERS' MEETING

At least one shareholder's meeting should be held each year. This meeting must be scheduled within a period of six months after the end of the company's financial year, in order to adopt or approve the annual accounts.

SUPERVISORY BOARD

The articles of association of a NV may stipulate the formation of a supervisory board next to the board of management. In case of large companies the law requires the establishment of a supervisory board. A large company is a company, of which the issued share capital and reserves amount to at least EUR 11.3 million, which qualifies for the establishment of a work council and which employs 100 or more employees in the Netherlands (including those employed through subsidiaries). If a small company decides to establish a supervisory board it may attribute to this board whatever powers and duties it may decide. In the case of large companies a number of decisions, spelled out by law, which may influence the continuity of the company needs approval by the supervisory board.

FINANCIAL STATEMENT

A NV must file all or parts of its annual financial statements with the Commercial Register, depending on its size.

MAJOR DIFFERENCES BETWEEN BV AND NV

The NV has most features in common with the BV. Nevertheless, there are some important differences:

- It should be noted that shares of a BV cannot be traded on the stock exchange. Trading is limited to bearer shares of a NV.
- Contrary to the NV, the BV cannot issue bearer shares, but only registered shares. The NV can also issue registered shares.
- As stated earlier, the transferability of shares of a BV is necessarily restricted by the articles of association. In case of a NV, transferability is only restricted, if the articles of association provide for this.

BRANCHES AND REP OFFICES

As part of the parent company, a branch (Dutch: "filiaal" or "nevenvestiging") is not a separate legal entity. However, like other business entities, a branch of a foreign company must be entered in the Commercial Register of the Chamber of Commerce. Information to be filed must include:

- Name and address of the foreign legal entity or partnership, its legal form, details about the registration in its home country (such as name register and registering body, city and country of registration, registration number).
- A proof of registration, not older than one month, issued by the foreign registering body.
- In the case of a foreign *legal entity*, a copy of the articles of incorporation and articles of association (if these last are a separate act). These documents must be original or certified copies. All these documents should be in Dutch, English, French or German or have been translated into any of these languages.
- The identities and addresses of its directors and the identity of the branch manager, empowered to legally bind the company.
- The office address of the branch in the Netherlands, which is to be considered its legal domicile.
- The trade name and a description of the business.

Generally speaking, all the information that the foreign company needs for registration in its own country should be filed with the Commercial Register.
As a rule, no financial accounts need be published.
For a foreign company, a branch may be useful in the early stages of having a presence in the Netherlands. Also the speedy formation and the relative privacy of the branch can be advantageous. On the other hand, a disadvantage of the branch is the full liability of its parent for claims caused by actions carried out by the branch. Usually, foreign investors prefer to operate through a BV or NV.
In principle, branches are subject to Dutch corporate income tax at the same rate as an NV or BV.

REP OFFICES

In contrast to a branch, which is a permanent establishment from which business operations are carried on, a liaison or representative office may not engage in actual business and cannot sign contracts or generate income. Its sole function is to gather market information or serve as a local communication channel. Legally, a representative office is not defined or regulated.

As the representative office does not generate income, it is not subject to corporate tax. The representative(s), however, must register for personal income tax. A work permit and residence permit are, of course, also required. When hiring staff the representative office must observe the normal rules of labor law.
If the activities of the liaison office change into those of a branch, the appropriate registration/amendment of registration in the trade register will have to be made. At the same time, the new entity must register for corporate tax, VAT etc.

SUBSIDIARY VERSUS BRANCH

Each company's unique circumstances will steer it toward one or the other means of starting up activities in the Netherlands: via a Dutch branch (possibly creating a taxable permanent establishment in the Netherlands) or via a Dutch subsidiary. In making this decision, not only the tax consequences should be considered, but also the operational consequences.

Bilateral tax treaties concluded by the Netherlands with many countries generally provide that withholding tax on dividends from a Dutch subsidiary to its foreign parent is in many cases reduced to 5%, sometimes even 0%. Assuming the 5% rate applies, total effective Dutch income tax on remitted earnings would be 34.93% (e.g. Profit = 100, after corporate tax of 31.5%: profit = 68.5. A 5% withholding tax on 68.5 = 3.43. Total effective income tax = 31.5% + 3.43% = 34.93%). In the absence of a treaty, the dividend withholding tax rate is 25%.
No withholding tax is levied on the distribution of dividends by a subsidiary established in an EU member state to its parent company in another EU member state, provided the parent company holds at least 25% of the subsidiary's capital (or, in certain cases, voting rights). For certain countries the threshold is reduced to 10% on the basis of reciprocity. A waiting period (the time the shares must be held by the parent company before the exemption of withholding tax applies) of one year is applicable in the Netherlands. (The waiting period in other EU countries can be up to two years). If the one-year period has not expired, a provisional withholding tax exemption in the Netherlands will apply. The exemption will be cancelled retrospectively if, following the dividend distribution, the one-year holding requirement is not met.

A Dutch branch of a foreign company is subject to the normal corporate income tax rate of 29%-31.5%. However, no withholding tax on remitted earnings is due. Therefore, the initial advantage of a branch is that the total Dutch effective income tax rate on remitted earnings can be limited to 29%-31.5% rather than 34.93%.
If initial losses are anticipated, the Dutch branch of a foreign company has another advantage over a subsidiary. For Dutch tax purposes, losses can be offset against future Dutch profits. For foreign tax purposes, the losses can often be utilized by the head office on its current-year tax return.

Use of a Dutch branch may not be an advantage in situations where it is anticipated that the operation will only break even at first, or both the Dutch branch and the foreign head office will be profitable. This is because the branch's income is subject to current taxation in the foreign country. In many cases, however, the Dutch source income will be tax-exempt in the other country by virtue of applicable Tax Treaties. Alternatively, having a Dutch subsidiary, may enable a company to avoid or defer taxation in its home country, simply by not paying dividends to the foreign parent and instead reinvesting the Dutch subsidiary's earnings.

A disadvantage of a corporation in comparison to a branch is the (0.55%) Dutch capital registration tax, which becomes due when capital is contributed to a corporation. The transfer of equity to a Dutch branch is not subject to Dutch capital registration tax.
Another advantage of a Dutch subsidiary is the amortization of intangible assets (e.g. technology) over its economic life, generally five to ten years. If intangible assets are transferred (and contributed as equity) by the parent company to its Dutch subsidiary, such assets can be amortized for Dutch tax purposes. Note that a 0.55% Netherlands capital tax is due on the value of the capital contribution. If intangibles are transferred in exchange for shares in the Dutch subsidiary, the parent company is often not subject to taxation in its

home country upon receipt of such shares. Thus, depending on dividend policy, a tax deferral of up to 31.5% of the intangible asset value can be achieved. A branch of a foreign corporation is in essence entitled to the same tax treatment for intangibles, under the condition however, that the intangibles are allocable to the business activities of the branch.

Issues concerning the amortization of intangible assets can be discussed with the tax inspector and require justification of the amounts involved.

SUBSIDIARY COMPARISON

Pros	Cons
Liability of shareholders is limited to the extent of their capital contribution.	More expensive, complicated and time-consuming.
Unless agreed otherwise by contract, foreign parent company is not responsible for debts, obligations and liabilities of the Dutch subsidiary.	Withholding tax on remitted earnings (usually 5% on dividends).
Dutch nationals prefer dealing with a Dutch subsidiary as opposed to a foreign branch office.	Publication of financial statements in full is mandatory for a medium-sized or large company.
If no remittance of profits to the parent is necessary, further taxation can be deferred by reinvesting the subsidiary's earnings.	Liability to various Dutch taxes may arise when the company liquidates and the shareholders have not acted in good faith.
Intangible assets can be amortized for Dutch tax purposes regardless the business activities of the company	A capital registration tax of 0.55% is payable on the (value of) capital contributions.
	Appointment of at least one director is required by law.

BRANCH COMPARISON

Pros	Cons
Relatively easy to set up and costs are generally lower.	Operates as a foreign company and has no Dutch identity, so acceptance by Dutch nationals may be affected.
No withholding tax on remitted earnings.	Foreign parent company is fully responsible for debts, obligations and liabilities of the Dutch branch.
No requirement to publish the financial result of the branch (except foreign insurance companies and banks).	
Losses of Dutch branch may be offset against taxes/profits of the foreign head office.	

TRADE AND PROJECT FINANCING

DESCRIPTION OF BANKING SYSTEM

Banking and financing are important service industries in the Netherlands providing funds for international as well as domestic trade. The Dutch financial sector is dominated by three Dutch bank conglomerates - ABN Amro, Rabobank, and ING Bank - which have about 75 percent of total lending. U.S. financial services providers in the Netherlands play on a level legal field. The Finance Ministry and Central Bank grant full national treatment to foreign banks.

According to the Finance Ministry, Dutch legislation implements all existing EU law and regulations on the provision of financial services. Banks organized in the Netherlands as branches of a U.S. parent cannot benefit from the EU single banking passport and are subject to both U.S. and Dutch regulations.

Foreign financial services providers face no special conditions or restrictions, and receive full national treatment. However, one provision of the Dutch 1992 Banking Act does reflect the EU Banking Directive's "reciprocity" provision. The Finance Ministry says this section has never been used, and that all applications from non-EU parent banks are handled on a national treatment basis.

To locate Dutch banks with correspondent U.S. banking arrangements, contact:

The Netherlands Bankers' Association (NVB)
P.O. Box 3543
1001 AH Amsterdam
Phone: (31) 20 550 2888
Fax: (31) 20 623 9748.

Foreign Exchange Controls Affecting Trade

There are no foreign exchange controls in the Netherlands.

GENERAL AVAILABILITY OF FINANCING

Banking facilities for international transactions available in the Netherlands generally meet or exceed U.S. standards.

HOW TO FINANCE EXPORTS/METHODS OF PAYMENT

Financing is provided at market rates by commercial banks and (for a small part) by a specialized export financing company - NV Export Financiering Maatschappij, set up by the large commercial banks.

TYPES OF AVAILABLE EXPORT FINANCING AND INSURANCE

The Nederlandsche Credietverzekering Maatschappij NV (NCM), a private company owned by the Dutch banks, and a number of insurance and export finance companies, provides export credit insurance. NCM can be contacted at: Nederlandsche Credietverzekering Maatschappij NV, Keizersgracht 271-287, 1016 ED Amsterdam, Phone: (31) 20 553 9111, Fax: (31) 20 553 2811. Information on Eximbank programs can be obtained from the marketing department, Phone: (202) 566-8860. Eximbank also has a toll free number, Phone: (800) 424-5201, that provides information on its overall programs.

AVAILABILITY OF PROJECT FINANCING

Most projects are financed by public and private sector lenders at commercial rates.

TYPES OF PROJECTS RECEIVING FINANCIAL SUPPORT

As a member of the European Union, the Netherlands has access to EU-funded programs which provide a wide range of support in the form of grants, loans and co-financing for training, feasibility studies, infrastructure projects in the environmental, transportation, energy and other key sectors. EU initiatives are designed to support projects within its Member States and the EU-wide "economic integration" projects that cross over borders.

EU Structural Funds are available to assist economically depressed regions that require industrial restructuring and agricultural re-conversion. Tenders for such projects are subject to EU public procurement legislation, provided that the tender meets the EU threshold requirements. There are no overt prohibitions against the participation of U.S. firms. From a commercial perspective, these initiatives create significant market opportunities for European firms of American parentage.

LIST OF BANKS WITH CORRESPONDENT U.S. BANKING ARRANGEMENTS

The Dutch banking sector is dominated by three big Dutch banks: ABN Amro, ING, and Rabobank. Nonetheless, U.S. and foreign banks are represented. Important bank contacts:

ABN Amro Holding NV
P.O. Box 283
1000 EA Amsterdam
Phone: (31) 20 628 9898
Fax: (31) 20 628 7740

Internationale Nederlanden Bank NV (ING)
P.O. Box 1800
1000 BV Amsterdam
Phone: (31) 20 563 9111
Fax: (31) 20 563 5700

Rabobank Nederland
P.O. Box 17100
3500 HG Utrecht
Phone: (31) 30 290 9111
Fax: (31) 30 290 2672

Bank of America National Trust and Savings Association
P.O. Box 1638
1000 BP Amsterdam
Phone: (31) 20 557 18 88
Fax: (31) 20 557 16 00

Citibank NA
P.O. Box 23445
1000 DX Amsterdam
Phone: (31) 20 651 42 11
Fax: (31) 20 651 42 34

Foreign Bankers' Association
P.O. Box 19870
1000 GW Amsterdam
Phone: (31) 20 550 2888
Fax: (31) 20 623 9748.

MARKET RESEARCHREPORTS

Advertising Services
Agricultural Equipment
Air Pollution Control Equipment
Building and Construction Materials and Equipment
Business Travel
Casual Apparel
Computer Services
Defense Equipment
Dental Equipment and Services
Diagnostics
DIY & Hardware Products
Fast Food/Restaurant Franchise
Franchising
Garage Equipment
Home Health Care & Rehabilitation Equipment
Hotel, Restaurant & Catering/Food Processing Equipment
Household Consumer Goods

Internet Services
Laboratory Instruments
Logistics Services
Pleasure Boats
Recycling Services
Renewable Energy Technologies
Solar Energy Systems
Tourism Infrastructure Market
Trucks and Parts
Value-added Telecom Services
Visit USA Market
Water Pollution Control Equipment

Scheduled Industry Subsector Analyses 2001:

Internet Security Solutions
Liberalized Telecom Market
Medical related Biotech Products and Services
Automotive Tools & Equipment
Automotive Accessories
Logistics Services
Power Trading
Hazardous Waste Management and Disposal Equipment Technologies & Services
Aviation & Helicopter Services
Business Travel
Food supplements

Scheduled Reports 2004: (Foreign Agriculture Service)

Fresh deciduous fruits semi-annual
Livestock semi-annual
Livestock Brussels
Poultry semi-annual
Grain & feed annual
Forest products annual
Dairy semi-annual
Oilseeds & products annual report
Tobacco annual
Fairs: food/agriculture import regulations
Livestock annual
Poultry annual
Fresh deciduous fruit annual
Exporter guide
Competitor report
Seafood annual
Trade leads report
Foreign buyer list annual report
Frozen French fry annual
Dairy annual
Planting seed annual
Citrus annual report

PROPERTY AND OWNERSHIP LAWS AND REGULATIONS

NETHERLANDS INDUSTRIAL PROPERTY OFFICE

The Netherlands Industrial Property Office (NIPO) is responsible for granting patents in the Netherlands and for disseminating the technical knowledge stored in the patent literature. The NIPO is an independent part of the Ministry of Economic Affairs

The NIPO was founded in 1893 as executor of the Trademarks Act in the Netherlands. Within the NIPO the Patents Office has been granting Dutch patents since 1912 in accordance with the conditions formulated in the Patents Act of 1910. This is probably why you still know the NIPO under the name of the Patent Office (or 'Octrooiraad).

NIPO: EXECUTOR OF THE PATENT SYSTEM

Knowledge protection primarily means granting patents. This is a legal task of the NIPO. In addition, the NIPO maintains a register with countless data regarding patents applied for and granted. These tasks are carried out by the Patent Office and the Register and Publications department.

THE NIPO: DISSEMINATOR OF PATENT INFORMATION

The NIPO's second core activity is the distribution of patent information. The NIPO actively provides target group orientated information regarding the patent system, the data stored in the patent register and the extensive collection of literature in the field of industrial property. These tasks are carried out by the Library & Documentation department and the Marketing and Public Relations department.

. The NIPO is also responsible for registering topographies for semiconductor products rights (chips) and for receiving Benelux filings for trademarks, drawings or designs, which filing parties do not submit directly to the Benelux Trademarks Office or the Benelux Design Office

The 175 employees of the NIPO focus their service provision on entrepreneurs, service providers, scientists, researchers and students who:

- wish to have information about the patent system,
- want to file a patent application.
- want information from the patent register
- want to use the technical knowledge stored in the patent literature,

FAQ (FREQUENTLY ASKED QUESTIONS)

Question: I have an idea that I would like to protect. Can I do that?
Answer: Unfortunately, you can have a product or process protected, but not an idea..

Question: Does my invention already exist?
Answer: To find out if your invention already exists you can visit the Netherlands Industrial Property Office's Library, Patentlaan 2, in Rijswijk. You can look into everything that is known in a specific field in the more than 30 million unique documents, on paper, cd rom or via the Patent Inforamtion Online system. If you wish, the staff in the reading room will assist you during your search

Question: Does company X or person Y have patent rights?
Answer: You can look for names of companies and people in the public patent register via the NIPO's Public Information Service.

Question: Could I possibly be committing an infringement of an existing patent with my invention?
Answer: Your patent agent can investigate whether you are infringing an existing patent. Or, if the number of the patent publication concerned is known, it can be ordered in writing from the NIPO.

Question: I would like to know whether a specific trademark is registered with your Office.
Answer:You can contact the Benelux Trademarks Office, Bordewijklaan 15, 2591 XR The Hague, telephone +31 70 - 349 11 11. for information about protection of trademark. You can also contact a trademarks agent.

Question: What does it cost to obtain a patent?
Answer: The level of expense to obtain a patent depends on the number of countries in which you wish to apply for protection and whether you are using the help of a patent agent. In the Netherlands these costs (including the costs of employing a patent agent) amount to around NLG 5,000.= for a six year patent and around NLG 10,000.= for a twenty year patent

Question: Am I obliged to have my patent application filed via a patent agent?
Answer: No, it is not compulsory to have a patent application filed by a patent agent, although it is advisable. One of the things the patent agent can help you with is drawing up your patent application..

Question: f I file a patent application in the Netherlands, does this apply immediately to other countries?
Answer: No, a Dutch patent application only applies to the Netherlands and our overseas territories.

Question: I want a world patent!
Answer: A world patent (one patent for every country in the entire world) does not exist. This term is misleading. What you can do is apply for an international patent via the World Intellectual Property Organisation for many countries outside Europe. Naturally, you can also apply for a national or European patent

INTELLECTUAL AND INDUSTRIAL PROPERTY RIGHTS.

How do you protect your invention, the new name you have thought up for your product or the book that you have published about your new discovery? Dutch law offers you the possibility of protecting your new products or processes, such as protection by a patent or via copyright. But also the possibility of protecting a trademark or design.

The patent and design rights together with the plant breeder's rights and the topographies of semiconductor products rights (also referred to as 'chips') form the *industrial property rights*. The entirety of industrial property rights and copyrights are called the *intellectual property rights*..

These rights are explained below - click the desired subject on the chart below.

	Intellectual property rights	
1. Copyrights		for literary, artistic and scientific works
2. Industrial property rights	a. Patent rights	for new products or processes
	b. Trademarks	for text or image trademarks
	c. Designs	for the appearance of a utility object
	d. Plant breeder's rights	for crops
	e. Topografies of semiconductor products	for 'chips'

COPYRIGHT PROTECTION

The Copyright Act of 1912 protects 'literary, scientific or artistic works'. The creator is entitled to the copyright until 70 years after his or her death

By creating a literary, scientific or artistic work a claim can be made on copyright immediately, but there is only certainty after a legal judgement. Examples of what copyright can protect are: a text, a work of art, directions for use, brochures, videos and other promotional material, photographs ornaments, drawings, scale models, construction works, etc.

No costs are associated with copyright and the protection applies worldwide. The Copyright Manifestation Foundation, PO Box 2184, 1180 ED Amstelveen, telephone +31 20 - 347 04 05 can provide you with more information about forms of copyright protection

PATENTS

Companies that want to survive or grow must innovate. They will have to take advantage by introducing new products and processes to their changed economic and technical environment. A systematic approach to the innovation process maximizes the chance of success of such a new product or process. The patent system plays an important role in this. Knowledge of what is already protected or known is of crucial importance to succesful innovation..

There are two aspects to the patent system:

- knowledge protection
- dissemination of patent information

These are also the core tasks of the Netherlands Industrial Property Office in Rijswijk, the executive organisation for the patent system in the Netherlands. The NIPO aims to increase use of the patent system

THE REQUIREMENTS FOR OBTAINING A PATENT

The three intrinsic requirements that an invention must satisfy to be considered for granting a patent in the Netherlands are:

1. Novelty
2. Inventive step
3. Industrial applicability

Novelty is understood to be the fact that the product or process may never have been of public knowledge anywhere in the world prior to the date of filing the patent application, this too includes through the inventor himself/herself (for example because of a brochure or a presentation at a fair)

Inventive step means that the invention may not be obvious to the professional.

Industrial applicability means that the invention must involve a technically demonstrable operating product or production process: a perpetual motion machine for example does not satisfy this condition. Services, scientific theories, arithmetic methods, ideas that have not been fully worked out and aesthetic designs are examples of things that cannot be protected by patent. Other forms of protection may well apply to these, such as copyright or the right to protect designs.

THE 1995 PATENTS ACT

In 1995 the Dutch Patents Act of 1910 has been changed radically. The most important difference from the past is that patents are granted without being examined. The applicant can find out afterwards that he has had an invention protected that could no longer be patented, because the invention is not new. He may therefore be infringing the rights of others unconsciously. In that case he runs the danger of having to answer to the Court. This danger is not so great for those who possess a twenty year patent, because of the novelty search that provides some insight into existing rights.

The innovating employer will have to take stock of the consequences of his application himself. The applicant will have to determine the value or applicability of the desired or obtained patent himself or - preferably - along with his patent agent. This could also involve weighing up the advantages and drawbacks, the costs and the benefits. Proper, timely consideration (including timely referral to patent information) prevents incorrect expectations and will often result in a more conscious and better founded application

THE APPLICATION PROCEDURE

If you want a patent that applies for the Netherlands, the procedure startsat the Netherlands Industrial Property Office in Rijswijk, where you can request an application form. Although the intrinsic requirements (novelty, inventive step and industrial applicability) apply, they are not examined. This examination only takes place in Court if a conflict arises.

After filing the patent application you will have to opt for a patent with a maximum duration of six or twenty years. You have thirteen months to make this choice. If you want a twenty year patent you must ask for a novelty search within thirteen months.

The results of this provide an indication of what was already known. If you do not apply for a novelty search within thirteen months you will get a six year patent automatically. If you already know that you want a six year patent when you file or before the end of the thirteen months, you can of course indicate this in writing when you file or later on.

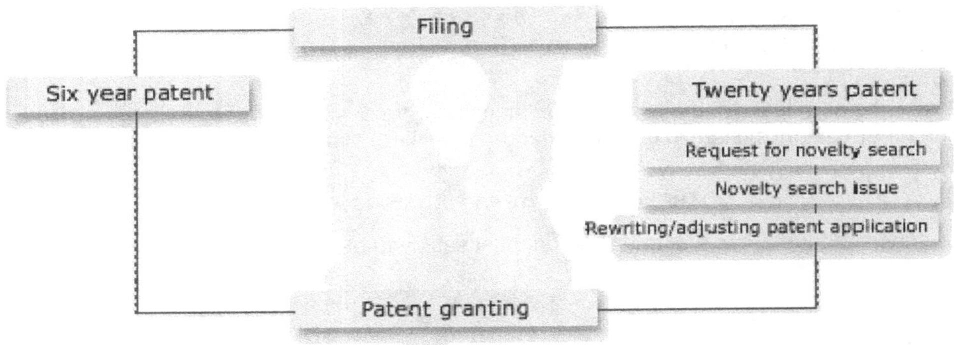

APPLYING FOR PATENTS ABROAD

Most countries recognise the priority or preference right. This is important if patent rights are to be obtained abroad and implies the following.

Once the first patent application has been filed, there is what is referred to as the 'preference or priority right' that lasts for one year. This means that you can file corresponding applications in or for other countries for a period of one year, and the filing date of the first application will be allocated to these. This date is called the preference or priority date.

The consequence of the preference right is that the application cannot be damaged during the entire preference year by publications or actions of others or of the applicant himself/herself, which could be detrimental to the aspects of novelty or inventive step.

The acquisition of patent rights abroad may be done in different ways. You can of course apply for a patent in each individual country, but there are also two other possibilities: via the European Patent Treaty or via the Patent Cooperation Treaty.

1. The European Patent Convention
SSince 1978 it has become much simpler to obtain patent rights in other European countries. Before that time patent rights had to be applied for separately in each country in accordance with the applicable procedures there. With the arrival of the European Patent Convention it is possible to obtain patent in many countries using one procedure. In 2009 nineteen countries are affiliated to this treaty: Austria, Belgium,

Cyprus, Denmark, Finland, France, Germany, Greece, Great Britain, Ireland, Italy Liechtenstein, Luxembourg, Monaco, the Netherlands, Portugal, Spain, Sweden and Switzerland.

The granting procedure is carried out by the European Patent Office (EPO). This procedure takes three to four years and results in a patent that is examined intrinsically on the novelty, inventivene step and industrial applicability requirements.

In diagram form the course of the European procedure runs as follows:

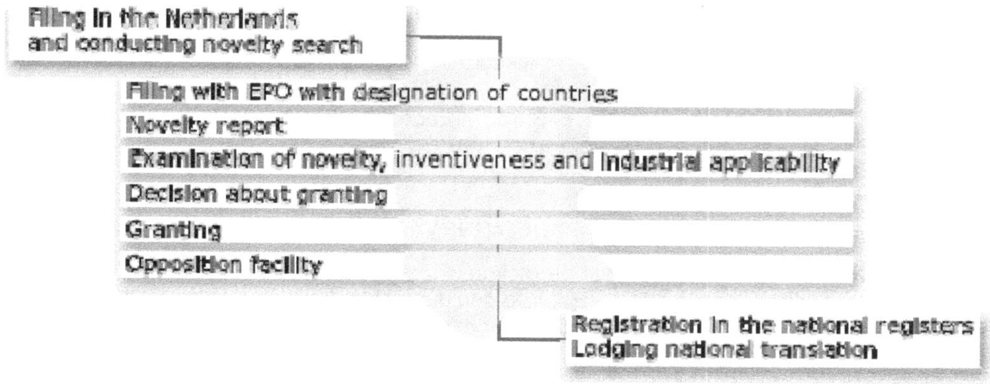

* It is also possible to file an application directly with the EPO. In that case the novelty search will still have to be conducted.

When filing the application, the countries in which the patent will be valid if it is granted must be designated. Acquisition of this European patent results in a collection of national patents. Th s means that after the EPO grants the patent it has to be converted into national patents which then fall under national legislation. This is important if legal action has to be taken abroad for example.

The costs of a European patent (assuming a patent that has to be granted in roughly eight countries, including the costs of an agent and national translations) amount to a minimum of NLG 50,000.=. This means that this procedure is worth the effort if one wishes to obtain patent in a minimum of three to four affiliated countries.

If a Dutch applicant follows this European route and designates the Netherlands (even if he has already applied for an unexamined patent in the Netherlands), he will obtain a soundly examined patent for the Netherlands and can allow the unexamined patent to lapse after granting.

2. The Patent Cooperation Treaty (PCT)
An international patent application can also be filed in accordance with the Patent Cooperation Treaty (PCT). More than 90 countries are now affiliated to this treaty. The affiliated countries which the application applies to must also be designated here.

However, contrary to the European Patent Convention this PCT procedure does not result in a patent being granted. The international application is followed by the international novelty search, a publication and if desired a provisional assessment. This procedure ends there. The results of the novelty search and any assessment can then be transferred to most national patent granting bodies or to the EPO, where the procedure can be completed.

TRADEMARKS

The Benelux Trademarks Act of 1962 regulates the protection of trademarks. This can involve a text trademark (whether or not linked to a special writing style), an image trademark or a combination of both. The trademark must have a sufficient distinguishing effect and may not be too descriptive.

Examples of text or image trademarks that have been protected are the name Shell, or the Shell 'shell'. But distinctive packaging, such as the packaging of a Coca Cola bottle or the Camping Gas blue colour can also obtain protection via Trademarks' rights.

A claim can be made on the right immediately after what is referred to as the 'depot', but there is only certainty following a legal judgement. The right lasts for ten years, and this can be extended without limitation. The costs of such protection in the Benelux territory amount to roughly NLG 1,500.=, including the costs of an agent.

You can contact the Benelux-Trademarks Office, Bordewijklaan 15, 2591 XR The Hague, telephone +31 70 - 349 11 11, for more information and to file your trademark.

DESIGNS

The Benelux Designs Act from 1966 regulates protection of the appearance of a utility object. The design must be new to Benelux during the last 50 years. You could consider here design protection of a vase, chair, car or a material pattern. However, design that determines achievement of a technical effect is not classed as design for the purposes of the Act.

A claim can be made on the right immediately after what is referred to as the 'depot', but there is only certainty following a legal judgement. The protection lasts for a maximum of five years, and this can be extended twice by five years. The costs of such protection in the Benelux territory are roughly NLG 1,500.= including the costs of an agent.

You can contact the Benelux Designs Office, Bordewijklaan 15, 2591 XR The Hague, telephone +31 70 - 349 11 11, for more information about filing your design.

PLANT BREEDER'S RIGHTS

The Plant breeder's rights consist of the rights that the 'owner' has to a plant strain and all of the rules based on which the plant breeder's right can be obtained and how it can be protected or maintained. You can apply to the Plant Breeder's Right Council, PO Box 6700 AC Wageningen, telephone +31 317 - 419 031 for the plant breeder's right

Plant breeder's rights protection can be applied for via the Plant Breeder's Right Act of 1966 for the cultivation material of each 'strain' belonging to the plant kingdom. In addition the protection extends to the actual use as a propagating medium for ornamental plants. The application must be valid and must contain a proposed name. It must also be a new product that is distinguishable, homogenous and durable.

BUSINESS TRAVELING TO NETHERLANDS

US STATE DEPARTMENT SUGGESTIONS

COUNTRY DESCRIPTION: The Netherlands is a highly-developed, stable democracy.

ENTRY REQUIREMENTS: A passport is required. A visa is not required for U.S. citizens for visits of up to 90 days. For more information concerning entry requirements for the Netherlands, travelers can contact the Embassy of the Netherlands at 4200 Linnean Avenue N.W., Washington, D.C. 20048, tel (202) 244-5300, or the Dutch consulate in Chicago, Houston, Los Angeles, New York, or San Francisco.

CRIME INFORMATION: While the rate of violent crime in the Netherlands is low, tourists are occasionally targeted, usually in conjunction with robbery attempts. Visitors to larger cities frequently fall prey to pickpockets, bag snatchers, and other petty thieves. While thieves may operate anywhere, the U.S. Consulate General in Amsterdam receives frequent reports of thefts from several specific areas:

- The train from Schiphol Airport to Amsterdam Central Station is particularly plagued by gangs of thieves, who often work in pairs. In those instances, one thief distracts the victim, often by asking for directions, while an accomplice moves in on the victim's momentarily unguarded handbag, backpack, or briefcase. The thieves typically time their thefts to coincide with train stops so they may quickly exit.
- Within Amsterdam, thieves are very active in and around the Central Train Station, the red light district, in restaurants, and on public transportation, especially Trams One, Two, and Five between the Central Station and the Museum District.
- Throughout the Netherlands, thefts of bicycles and of personal belongings from automobiles are very common.

The loss or theft abroad of an U.S. passport should be reported immediately to the local police and the nearest U.S. Embassy or Consulate. Useful information on safeguarding valuables and protecting personal safety while traveling abroad is provided in the Department of State's pamphlet *A Safe Trip Abroad.* It is available by mail from the Superintendent of Documents, U.S. Government Printing Office, Washington, D.C. 20402, via the Internet at http://www.access.gpo.gov/su_docs, or http://travel.state.gov.

MEDICAL FACILITIES: Medical facilities are widely available. Serious medical problems requiring hospitalization and/or medical evacuation to the United States can cost thousands of dollars or more. Doctors and hospitals often expect immediate cash payment for health services.

MEDICAL INSURANCE: U.S. medical insurance is not always valid outside the United States. U.S. Medicare and Medicaid programs do not provide payment for medical services outside the United States. Uninsured travelers who require medical care overseas may face extreme difficulties. Check with your own insurance company to confirm whether your policy applies overseas, including provision for medical evacuation. Ascertain whether payment will be made to the overseas hospital or doctor or whether you will be reimbursed later for expenses you incur. Some insurance policies also include coverage for psychiatric treatment and for disposition of remains in the event of death. Useful information on medical emergencies abroad, including overseas insurance programs, is provided in the Department of State, Bureau of Consular Affairs brochure *Medical Information for Americans Traveling Abroad*, available via its home page and autofax service.

OTHER HEALTH INFORMATION: Information on vaccinations and other health precautions may be obtained from the Centers for Disease Control and Prevention's international traveler's hotline at 1-877-FYI-TRIP (1-877-394-8747), via their autofax service at 1-888-CDC-FAXX (1-888-232-3229), or their Internet home page at http://www.cdc.gov.

TRAFFIC SAFETY AND ROAD CONDITIONS: While in a foreign country, U.S. citizens may encounter road conditions which differ significantly from those in the United States. The information below concerning the Netherlands is provided for general reference only, and may not be totally accurate in a particular location or circumstance.

Safety of Public Transportation: Excellent
Urban Road Conditions/Maintenance: Excellent
Rural Road Conditions/Maintenance: Excellent
Availability of Roadside Assistance: Excellent

In urban areas, motorists must be especially mindful of the priority rights of bicyclists. Lanes at the center of many urban two-way streets are reserved for buses, trams, and taxis. Pedestrians should pay particular attention not to walk along bicycle paths, which are often on the sidewalk and usually designated by red pavement.

Taxi service in the Netherlands is safe but expensive. Trams and buses are both convenient and economical, but they are frequented by pickpockets.

AVIATION SAFETY OVERSIGHT: The U.S. Federal Aviation Administration (FAA) has assessed the Government of the Netherlands' Civil Aviation Authority as Category 1 -- in compliance with international aviation safety standards for oversight of the Netherlands' air carrier operations. For further information, travelers may contact the Department of Transportation within the U.S. at 1-800-322-7873, or visit the FAA's Internet website at http://www.faa.gov/avr/iasa.htm. The U.S. Department of Defense (DOD) separately assesses some foreign air carriers for suitability as official providers of air services. For information regarding the DOD policy on specific carriers, travelers may contact DOD at 618-229-4801.

CRIMINAL PENALTIES: While in a foreign country, a U.S. citizen is subject to that country's laws and regulations, which sometimes differ significantly from those in the United States and may not afford the protections available to the individual under U.S. law. Penalties for breaking the law can be more severe than in the United States for similar offenses. Persons violating Dutch laws, even unknowingly, may be expelled, arrested, or imprisoned. Drug possession and trafficking are illegal in the Netherlands.

CUSTOMS REGULATIONS: Customs authorities encourage the use of an ATA (Admission Temporaire/Temporary Admission) Carnet for the temporary admission of professional equipment, commercial samples, an/or goods for exhibitions and fair purposes. ATA Carnet Headquarters, located at the U.S. Council for International Business, 1212 Avenue of the Americas, New York, NY 10036, issues and guarantees the ATA Carnet in the United States. For additional information call 212-354-4480, send an e-mail to atacarnet@uscib.org, or visit http://www.uscib.org for details.

CHILDREN'S ISSUES: For information on international adoption of children, international parental child abduction, and international child support enforcement issues, please refer to our Internet site at http://travel.state.gov/children's_issues.html or tel. (202) 736-7000.

EMBASSY/CONSULATE LOCATIONS/REGISTRATION: U.S. citizens are encouraged to register at the Consulate General in Amsterdam and to obtain updated information on travel and security in the Netherlands.

The U.S. Embassy is located in The Hague, at Lange Voorhout 102; telephone (31)(70) 310-9209. However, all requests for consular assistance should be directed to the Consulate General in Amsterdam at Museumplein 19, telephone (31)(20) 664-5661, (31)(20)679-0321, or (31)(20) 575-5309. The after-hours emergency telephone number is (31)(70) 310-9499. The U.S. Embassy and Consulate General website at http://www.usemb.nl answers many questions of interest to Americans visiting or residing in the Netherlands.

GETTING THERE

Air

The Netherlands' national airline is *KLM-Royal Dutch Airlines (KL).* KLM flies direct to all major European, North American and Asia-Pacific cities.

Approximate flight times: From Amsterdam to *New York* is 7 hours, to *Belfast* is 1 hour 5 minutes; to *London* is 1 hour; to *Manchester* is 1 hour 5 minutes.

International airports

Amsterdam (AMS) (Schiphol) (web site: http://www.schiphol.nl) is 15km (9 miles) southwest of the city (travel time by train - 20 minutes). *KLM* buses provide a daily service from 6 AM-12 AM departing every 30 minutes, stopping at the a selection of major hotels and returning to Schiphol. There is a direct rail link between the airport and Amsterdam *Centraal* Station, with trains every 15 minutes from and every hour through the night. Trains to *Zuid* station (Amsterdam South) run every 15 minutes from; return is from *Zuid* station, Parnassusweg/Minervalaan (via tram no. 5 from the city center). There is also a service to the RAI Congress Center every 15 minutes from. Return is from RAI station (via tram no. 4 from the city center). Plentiful taxis are available to the city.
Airport facilities include restaurants, duty-free shops, currency exchange machines (able to convert 17 different currencies), banks, an art gallery, baby rooms (free of charge and open 24 hours), showers, a business center (with fax, personal computer and telephone facilities), conference rooms and car rental.

Rotterdam (RTM) (Zestienhoven) (web site: http://www.schiphol.nl/rotterdamairport.nl) is 8km (5 miles) northwest of the city (travel time - 15 minutes). 24-hour flight information: (10) 446 0813. Bus no. 33 departs every 10 minutes. Return is from Central Station, Knisplein, from 0630-1830. Taxis to the city are also available. Airport facilities include restaurant, bank, outgoing duty-free shop and car rental.

Eindhoven (EIN) (Welschap) (web site: http://www.schiphol.nl/eindhovenairport) is 8km (5 miles) from the city. Coaches run every 15 minutes and taxis to the city are also available. Airport facilities include car rental and outgoing duty-free shop. Flight information: (40) 251 6142.

Maastricht (MST) (Aachen) (web site: http://www. schiphol.nl/maa) is 8km (5 miles) from the city. Airport facilities include outgoing duty-free shop.

Groningen (GRQ) (Eelde) (web site: http://www.schiphol.nl/groningen_airport_eelde) is 9km (6 miles) from the city.
Enschede (ENS) (Twente) (web site: http://www.schiphol.nl/twente_airport) is 8km (5 miles) from the city.

Sea

The major ferry ports are Vlissingen, Rotterdam and Hook of Holland (Hoek van Holland). Regular car and passenger ferries are operated from the UK to The Netherlands via the following routes and shipping lines:
StenaLine (tel: (0990) 707 070; web site: http://www.stenaline.co.uk): Harwich to Hook of Holland; journey time - 3 hours 45 minutes (day), 4 hours 30 minutes (night); 2 sailings daily.
P&O North Sea Ferries (tel: (01482) 377 177; web site: http://www.ponsf.com): Hull to Rotterdam (Europoort); journey time - 12 hours 30 minutes; 1 sailing nightly.
DFDS Seaways (tel: (01255) 240 240; web site: http://www.dfdsseaways.co.uk): Newcastle-Amsterdam (summer only); journey time - 16 hours.

Note: *P&O European Ferries* and *Hoverspeed UK* run services to The Netherlands via Belgium. French ports also provide connections.

Train

There are regular *Eurostar* trains from London to Brussels where a direct connection to a number of destinations throughout the Netherlands can be caught after a 30-minute wait. The entire journey takes a little over 7 hours (journey time from London to Brussels is 3 hours 40 minutes; from Brussels to Amsterdam is 3 hours. The national rail network (see *Travel - Internal* section) provides links to other major European cities, including Paris, Zürich, Frankfurt/M, Copenhagen and Luxembourg.
For more information and reservations, contact *Eurostar Enquiries*, Eurostar House, Waterloo Station, London SE1 8SE (tel: (01233) 617 599 (travel agents) *or* (0990) 186 186 (members of the public); web site: http://www.eurostar.com). For information on special fares for groups of at least ten people contact the *Eurostar Groups and Incentives Department* (tel: (0870) 600 0777; fax: (020) 7902 2355). Rail travellers not using the Channel Tunnel link need to cross the channel by some form of sea crossing, usually by ferry or hovercraft; for details on sea crossings see also under *Sea* above. The cost of the crossing is usually included in the price of the rail ticket. For information and reservations contact *Rail Europe* (tel: (0990) 848 848).

Road

The Netherlands are connected to the rest of Europe by a superb network of motorways. All roads are well signposted with green 'E' symbols indicating international highways, red 'A's indicating national highways, and smaller routes indicated by yellow 'N's. The national speed limit is 120 kph (75mph). Although frontier formalities between The Netherlands, Germany and Belgium have now all but vanished, motorists - particularly on smaller roads - should be prepared to stop when asked to do so by a customs official. The yellow cars of the *ANWB/Wegenwacht* (Royal Dutch Touring Club) (tel: (70) 314 1420) patrol major roads 24 hours a day with qualified mechanics equipped to handle routine repairs. For emergencies, dial: 60888 (within The Netherlands only).

Traveling from the UK, all road vehicles can be carried through the channel tunnel in *Le Shuttle* trains running between Folkestone in Kent (with direct access from the M20) and Calais (with links to the A16/A26 motorway; exit 13). All vehicles from motorcycles to campers can be accommodated. Passengers generally travel with their vehicles. Heavy goods vehicles are carried on special wagons with a separate passenger coach for the drivers. Terminals and shuttles are well-equipped for disabled passengers. Passenger Terminal buildings contain duty-free shops, restaurants, bureaux de change and other amenities. The journey takes approximately 35 minutes from platform to platform and about one hour from motorway to motorway. Shuttles run every 75 minutes, 24 hours a day and three to four trains run each hour at peak times. Services run every day of the year. By contacting *Eurotunnel Customer Information* in Coquelle (tel: (3) 21 00 61 00; fax: (3) 21 00 60 01) as they approach the French terminal, motorists can find out when the next shuttle leaves and how busy the service is. Motorists pass through customs and immigration before they board, with no further checks on arrival. Fares are charged according to length of stay and time of year. The price remains constant throughout the day and applies to the car, regardless of the number of passengers or size of the car. Off-peak fares are: Day Return: if booked one day in advance, £45 Mon to Sat, £20 Sunday; 5-Day Return: £159 (not available to travel agents); Standard Return: £239. Lower rates apply to motorcycles. There are also many promotional deals available, especially outside the peak holiday seasons. Tickets may be purchased in advance from travel agents, or from Eurotunnel Customer Services in France or the UK with a credit card. For further information, contact *Eurotunnel Customer Services* in the UK on (0990) 353 535 (brochures and reservations).

Coach

Eurolines run coach services from the UK to The Netherlands and from The Netherlands to various destinations throughout Europe. They have an office in Amsterdam at Rokin 10, 1012 KR (tel: (20) 627 5151; fax: (20) 627 5176; web site: http://www.eurolines.nl). Further information can also be obtained by calling Eurolines in the UK (tel: (020) 7730 8235 (reservations) *or* (0990) 143 219 (public reservations); web site: http://www.eurolines.co.uk).

Car Rental

Major companies can be found in the main cities, among them *Avis, Hertz, Budget* and *Europcar*.

GETTING AROUND

Air

KLM Cityhopper (WA) operates between Amsterdam and Eindhoven. *Transavia Airlines (HV)* (80% of which is owned by KLM) also runs scheduled flights. *Martinair Holland (MP)* operates passenger and cargo charter services. Enquire at KLM offices or at the Netherlands Board of Tourism for further information.

Sea

Ferry service to the Wadden Islands across the Ijsselmeer (former Zuyder Sea) and Schelde Estuary. There is also a service to the Frisian Islands across the Waddenzee. *Boat Tours* runs excursions from Amsterdam, Rotterdam, Utrecht, Arnhem, Groningen, Giethoorn, Delft and Maastricht. *StenaLine* operates a daily service for private cars, freight and trailers.

Train

The highly developed rail network, of which about 70% is electrified, is efficient and cheap, and connects all towns. Both Intercity and local trains run at least half-hourly on all principal routes. Rail and bus timetables are integrated, and there is a common fare structure throughout the country. *NV Nederlandse Spoorwegen* (web site: http://www.ns.nl) is the state-owned rail company and operates all lines within the country.

Cheap fares

Rail Rovers are valid for one day. *Public Transport Link Rovers* are issued in conjunction with *Rail Rovers*. These cover unlimited travel on all public transport buses and trams in town and country, and on the underground system in Amsterdam and Rotterdam. *Euro Domino* tickets are available for travel in The Netherlands, or The Netherlands and Belgium. 3-, 5- and 10-day passes are available. The *Benelux Tourrail Card* allows unlimited travel for any five days within a 1 month period, covering The Netherlands, Belgium and Luxembourg. Other deals include *Multi-Rovers, Summer Tour Rovers* and *Teenage Rovers*. Children under 4 years of age travel free on all journeys within The Netherlands. *Child's Railrunner* tickets are available for children aged 4-11 years traveling with a fare-paying adult (19 years or older), and include up to three children traveling with any one adult. Contact the Railway Authority of any of the participating countries for prices and further information.

Inter-Rail passes are also valid in The Netherlands.
Any UK enquiries about rail travel, the purchase of *Rail Rover* tickets and prices should be addressed to: Holland Rail, Gilbert Street, Ropley, Hampshire SO2 40BY (tel: (01962) 773 646; fax: (01962) 773 625; e-mail: hollandrail@ukconsultants.com).

Road

There is an excellent road system. Visitors to The Netherlands may use credit cards when obtaining petrol. The motoring association in The Netherlands is the *ANWB* (Royal Dutch Touring Club), Postbus 93200, 2509 XB The Hague (tel: (70) 314 1420).

Bus

Extensive regional bus networks exist. Long-distance coaches also operate between the cities, but costs are generally on a par with trains.

Taxi

Taxis have an illuminated 'taxi' sign on the roof and there are taxi ranks at railway stations and at various other points in the cities. Rather than hailing taxis in the street, it is more usual in The Netherlands to order a taxi by phone. Taxis should have meters inside to indicate the fare, including the tip.

Car rental

Available from airports and main hotels. All European car-hire companies are represented.

Bicycle rental

Bicycles can be hired from all main railway stations, but must be returned to the station from which they are hired. A refundable deposit is required.

Driving regulations

Driving is on the right. Drivers should be particularly aware of cyclists; often there are special cycle lanes. There is a chronic shortage of parking space in central Amsterdam, and the rush hours (7 AM-9 AM and 5 PM-7 PM) should be avoided throughout the whole country. Parking fines are severe. Headlights should be dipped in built-up areas, but it is prohibited to use sidelights only. Children under 12 should not travel in the front seat. Seat belts are compulsory. Speed limits are 80kph (50mph) on major roads, 120kph (75mph) on motorways and 50kph (30mph) in towns.

Documentation

An International Driving Permit is not required, as long as a driving license from the country of origin is held. EU pink format licenses are accepted. Trailers and caravans are allowed in without documents. A Green Card is advisable, but not compulsory. Without it, drivers with motor insurance policies in their home country are granted only the minimum legal cover in The Netherlands; the Green Card tops this up to the level of cover provided by the driver's own policy.

Urban

Public transport is very well developed in the cities and large towns. A *strippenkaart* national fares system exists - strips of 15 tickets each are widely available at railway stations, post offices and some tourist offices. These are accepted anywhere in payment of standard zonal fares. There are also individual and multi-day tickets for the cities. For more detailed information on travel within Amsterdam, Rotterdam and The Hague, see below.

Amsterdam: Amsterdam has an extensive network of buses, trams and underground *(GVB)*, with frequent services from early morning to about midnight. There are less frequent services throughout the night at a higher fare. Full information on services (including a map), day tickets and *strippenkaart* (strip-tickets) can be obtained from the GVB office in front of the Central Station (0700-2230 daily) or the GVB Central Office at Prins Hendrikkade 108-114.

Tram

Amsterdam's 17 tram lines provide a fast, frequent and reliable service, making the tram the best way to travel around the capital. Trams operate from 6 AM to midnight Monday to Friday (from 6.30 AM Saturday and 7.30 Sunday). The tram system (as well as the buses and the underground) enables reasonably quick travel even during the busiest periods of the day. Trams leave from Central Station: 1 and 2 traverse the main canals, 19 takes a route to Museumplein and Concertgebouw and 9 and 14 to the Muziektheater and Waterlooplein market. A new Circle Tram service has begun operating through central Amsterdam, taking in major attractions and hotels.

Underground

Amsterdam's underground lines all originate at the Central Station and serve the southeastern business district and the suburbs. Trains run from 6 AM to midnight Monday to Friday, from 6.30 AM Saturday and from 7.30 AM Sunday. The GVB is easy to use.

Taxi

These are fairly expensive. Booking is usually made by a phone call (tel: (20) 677 7777), but taxis can also be picked up at taxi ranks (Central Station, Rembrandtplein and Leidseplein). Fares are indicated by the meter; a small tip will be appreciated.

Car rental

The major European firms, including *Hertz* and *Avis*, are represented. Cars can also be hired through most hotels. Parking regulations are quite strict and failure to park in prescribed areas or to pay the parking fee can result in a fine and the prospect of the car being clamped or towed away.

Water travel

Canal Buses (every 25-45 minutes between Central Station and Rijksmuseum; children under the age of 5 travel free); Watertaxis (9 AM- 1 PM Monday to Sunday, carrying 8 to 25 passengers); Museum Boats (departing from Prins Hendrikkade every 30 minutes in summer and every 45 minutes in winter) and Waterbikes (for 2-4 people, with a route map provided) are all available.

Boat rental

Visitors can hire pedalos (also known as canal bikes) and boats to explore the canals.

Bicycle rental

This is an excellent way to travel around Amsterdam, and it seems nearly everyone is doing it. Cycle lanes are clearly marked by white lines - but visitors are advised to watch out for trams, cars and pedestrians. There are numerous companies renting out bikes (at a cost of approximately f10-f12.50 per day).

Rotterdam: The city has excellent bus and tram services and a 2-line underground network, which work on a zonal system. Information is available from the Central Station.

Car rental

The major European firms, including *Avis* and *Hertz*, are represented.

The Hague: The Hague has bus and tram services. Information is available from the Central Station, Koningin Julianaplein.

Journey Times

The following chart gives approximate journey times (in hours and minutes) from Amsterdam to other major cities in The Netherlands.

	Air	Road	Rail
The Hague	-	0.40	0.44
Rotterdam	-	1.00	1.00

Utrecht	-	0.25	0.30
Groningen	-	2.00	2.20
Arnhem	-	1.10	1.10
Maastricht	0.40	2.30	2.30
Vlissingen	-	2.00	2.45
Eindhoven	0.30	1.30	1.25
Breda	-	1.30	1.50

ACCOMMODATION

Hotels

The Netherlands has a wide range of accommodation, from luxury hotels in big towns to modern motels along motorways. The Netherlands Reservation Center (NRC) (*Netherlands Reserverings Centrum*) can make reservations throughout the country: Postbus 404, 2260 AK Leidschendam (tel: (70) 419 5500; fax: (70) 419 5519; e-mail: info@hotelres.nl; web site: http://www.hotelres.nl).

Grading

The Netherlands Board of Tourism issues a shield to all approved hotels by which they can be recognized. This must be affixed to the front of the hotel in a conspicuous position. Hotels which display this sign conform to the official standards set by Dutch law on hotels, which protects the tourist and guarantees certain standards of quality. Hotels are also graded according to the *Benelux* system, in which the standard is indicated by a row of 3-pointed stars from the highest (5-star) to the minimum (1-star). However, membership of this scheme is voluntary, and there may be first-class hotels that are not classified in this way. *Benelux* star ratings adhere to the following criteria:

5-star (H5): This is a new category signifying a luxury hotel. Amenities include private bath and/or shower, toilet, radio and TV in every room. 24 hour room service. Fax facilities in reception.

4-star (H4): First-class hotels. 80% of rooms have a private bath. Other amenities include night reception and room service.

3-star (H3): Half of the rooms have a private bath or shower. Other amenities include day reception and the sale of tobacco products.

2-star (H2): A quarter of rooms have a private bath. Other amenities include a bar.

1-star (H1): Simple hotel. No private baths, but hot and cold water in rooms. Breakfast available.

Cat H: Hotel with minimal comfort.

Cat O: Simple accommodation.
For further information contact the Netherlands Board of Tourism.

Guest-Houses

These are called *pensions* and rates vary. Book through local tourist offices.

Bed & Breakfast

Not as common a form of accommodation as it is in the UK but reservations can be made through Bed and Breakfast Holland, T. de Bockstraat 3, 1058 TV Amsterdam (tel: (20) 615 7527; fax: (20) 669 1573; e-mail: bbrholland@hetnet.nl).

Self-Catering

Farmhouses for groups can be booked months in advance via the local tourist offices. Holiday chalets, especially in the relatively unknown parts of Zeeland, can be booked through the local tourist office. Bungalow parks throughout the country can be booked through the Netherlands Reserverings Centrum (NRC). Most bungalow resorts offer a full range of recreational facilities including swimming pools, golf and tennis. Prices depend on size, quality of amenities and the time of year. To order a self catering brochure call the Netherlands Board of Tourism (see address section).

Camping

There are some 2500 registered campsites in Holland. Only 500 offer advanced booking, the others operate on a first-come, first-served basis. Off-site camping is not permitted. Prices are fairly high and it is often far better value to stay more than one night. A list is available from the Netherlands Board of Tourism (see address section) and reservations can be made through the *Stichting Vrije Recreatie*, Broekseweg 75-77, 4231 VD Meerkerk (tel: (183) 352 741/2/3; fax: (183) 351 234).

Youth Hostels

There are 34 hostels in various surroundings, from castles to modern buildings. People with a Hostelling International card pay approximately G20-30 for an overnight stay including breakfast (non-members pay G5 more). Information is obtainable from the Dutch Youth Hostel Association (*Stichting Nederlandse Jeugdherberg Centrale*), Prof Tulpstraat 2, 1018 HA Amsterdam; tel: (20) 551 3155; fax: (20) 639 0199; web site: http://www.njhc.org).

MONEY

Currency

Guilder (Dfl or Fl) = 100 cents. Notes are in denominations of Dfl1000, 250, 100, 50, 25 and 10. Coins are in denominations of Dfl5, 2.5 and 1, and 25, 10 and 5 cents.

Single European currency (Euro)

On January 1 1999, the Euro became the official currency of 11 EU member states (including The Netherlands). The Euro is currently only used as 'written money' (checks, bank transactions, credit cards, etc). The first Euro coins and notes will be introduced in January 2002; the Guilder will still be in circulation until July 1 2002, when it will be completely replaced by the Euro. 1 Euro = Dfl2.20371.

Currency exchange

Exchange offices are indicated by the letters GWK. GWK is a national organization with currency exchange offices at major railway stations, at Shiphol airport and at the border crossings with Germany and Belgium. Hotels tend to charge high commissions. *Verkoopt* means sell, while *Koopt* means buy.

Credit cards

MasterCard, American Express, Diners Club and Visa are accepted. Check with your credit card company for details of merchant acceptability and other services which may be available.

Travelers' checks

Widely accepted. To avoid additional exchange rate charges, travellers are advised to take travellers cheques in Dutch Guilders.

Exchange rate indicators

The following figures are included as a guide to the movements of the Guilder against the US Dollar:

Date	Oct '98	Jun '99	Nov '99	May '00
$1.00=	1.84	2.11	2.10	2.47

The following figures are included as a guide to the movements of the Euro against the US Dollar:

Date	Jul '99	Oct '99	May '00	Aug '00
1 Euro=	$1.02	$1.06	$0.89	$0.93

Currency restrictions

There are no restrictions on the import and export of either local or foreign currency.

Banking hours: 9 AM- 4/5 PM Monday to Friday.

PUBLIC HOLIDAYS

Jan 1 New Year's Day.
Apr 13 Good Friday.
Apr 16 Easter Monday.
Apr 30 Queen's Day.
May 5 National Liberation Day.
May 24 Ascension Day.
Jun 4 Whit Monday.
Dec 25-26 Christmas.

BUSINESS CUSTOMS

The Dutch market is a highly competitive market and the U.S. exporter must keep certain factors in mind to achieve maximum success. The "golden keys" of customary business is courtesy, especially replying promptly to requests for price quotations and to orders. These are a prerequisite for exporting success. In general, European business executives are more conservative than their American counterparts; therefore, it is best to refrain from using their first names until a firm relationship has been formed. Friendship and mutual trust are highly valued, and once an American has earned this trust, a productive working relationship can usually be counted upon.

Dutch buyers appreciate quality and service and are also interested in delivery price. Care must be taken to assure that delivery dates will be closely maintained and that after-sales service will be promptly honored. The Dutch and Europeans in general, are concerned that after placing an order with an American supplier, the delivery date will not be honored. While there are numerous factors that may interfere with prompt shipment, the U.S. exporter must allow for additional shipping time and keep in close contact with the buyer.

It is much better to quote a later delivery date that can be guaranteed than promise an earlier delivery that is not completely certain.

U.S. exporters should maintain close liaison with distributors and customers to exchange information and ideas. In most instances, mail, fax, or telephone communication is sufficient, but the understanding developed through periodic personal visits is the best way to keep distributors apprised of new developments and to resolve problems quickly. Prompt acknowledgment of correspondence by airmail or fax is recommended.

Further, U.S. exporters should seriously consider warehousing in the Netherlands for speedy supply and service of their European customers. A vigorous and sustained promotion is often needed to launch products because of buying habits. Products must be adapted to both technical requirements and to consumer preferences. It is not sufficient to merely label a product in conformity to national requirements for the development of the full market potential. Consumers must also be attracted to the product by label and packaging as well as ease of use.

TRAVEL ADVISORY AND VISAS

U.S. citizens are required to be in possession of a valid passport to enter the Netherlands. No visa is required for U.S. citizens visiting the Netherlands for less than 3 months, but one is required for longer periods. An American citizen entering the Netherlands for permanent residence must apply for a residence permit at the Dutch Aliens Police within eight days of arrival in the country. U.S. citizens planning to work are required to obtain a work permit from the Ministry of Social Affairs through the District Labor Bureau (Arbeidsbureau) or through the Netherlands Consulate General in their country of residence. Such permits must be obtained by the Dutch employer and are usually granted only for specialized work. Management and skilled workers have no difficulty in obtaining work permits. It is advisable for American citizens to register at the U.S. Consulate General if they plan to reside in the Netherlands.
The United States Embassy website is USEMB.NL and has additional information on the Netherlands and links to other useful sources. For general and country-specific travel information, see the Department of State's web site at http://travel.state.gov

LANGUAGE COMMUNICATION

English usually can be used in commercial correspondence. However, not all Dutch understand English and for retail products it is essential to provide advertising, labeling, and use instructions in Dutch. If such literature cannot be provided, the U.S. exporter should work with the Dutch importer or distributor to have the products labeled in the Netherlands.

While language barriers pose no problems, some expressions and terms may have different meanings from those in the U.S. To assure better understanding, it is well to define unfamiliar terms in commercial activities. By reference and the use of INCOTERMS in an agreement, both parties will be using the established international set of commercial terms which helps to reduce possible misunderstandings and promotes fair dealing.

HOUSING

Housing is often difficult to find and rents vary widely. Family housing of a size to which Americans are accustomed will be expensive in or near the larger cities. In many areas, furnished quarters are easier to find than unfurnished quarters. The term "unfurnished" must be taken literally. The tenant often must provide electric fixtures, stove, refrigerator, water heater, wardrobes, etc. Usually, the owner accepts responsibility only for exterior repairs; interior maintenance and repairs are usually at the tenant's expense. It might be necessary to engage a real estate agent (makelaar), although their fees are high. A municipal housing permit is required to occupy certain houses and apartments, and the landlord can advise you on this. Be aware that a verbal commitment can be considered a legally binding contract.

TRANSPORTATION

Rental automobiles are available at numerous locations. An international or state driving license is acceptable. Cars are driven on the right-hand side of the road. The national roads and highways are excellent. Newcomers may find driving in town a little disconcerting because of the many cyclists who often make unexpected turns or must be passed at close range. Some city streets have special bicycle paths. Right-of-way is that of the vehicle entering from the right unless the vehicle is coming out of a driveway. Roads posted with orange diamonds do not have to yield the right-of-way. The speed limit in the cities is 30 miles (50 km) per hour and on highways about 70 miles (120 km) per hour.

Most cities in the Netherlands have good public transportation systems (e.g. trains, buses, streetcars), and prices are reasonable. Taxis are available everywhere and the fare is comparable with other European cities.

HEALTH

Medical services are excellent and hospitals compare with those in the U.S. Common medical needs are readily obtained, and special supplies are normally available on short notice. An international certificate of vaccination is not required for travelers from the U.S. Drinking water is excellent, most pharmaceuticals are available, and sanitation is at American standards.

OTHER INFORMATION

With the ease of telephone communications, international calls are frequently the best method of arranging appointments and maintaining solid commercial relations. The Dutch are usually adept at handling business calls in English, but the American executive must be prepared to expect some language problems. The time zone for the Netherlands is Greenwich mean time +1, or 6 hours ahead of the U.S. eastern standard time (EST + 6 hours). Fax machines and E-mail have increased the speed and ease of international communications and should be used to maintain strong business ties. The electric current is alternating current, 50 cycle, 220 volts. American appliances, such as electric shavers and hair dryers do not work and will be damaged if used without a converter. Most hotels have a 110 volt outlet in the bathroom for U.S. electric shavers. Conservative business attire is recommended at all times. Business appointments are also required and visitors are expected to be punctual.

U.S. Business travelers are encouraged to obtain a copy of the "Key Officers of Foreign Service Posts: Guide for Business Representatives" available for sale by the Superintendent of Documents, U.S. Government Printing Office, Washington, D.C. 20402; Tel. (202) 512-1800; Fax (202) 512-2250. Business travelers to the Netherlands seeking appointments with U.S. Embassy The Hague officials should contact the Commercial Service in advance.

SUPPLEMENTS

BILATERAL CHAMBERS OF COMMERCE

Aken-Maastricht
CCI Aachen-Maastricht
www.cci-aachen-maastricht.com

Argentina
Argentinian-Dutch Chamber of Commerce
Avda. de Mayo 701, Piso 19, 1084 BUENOS AIRES, Argentinië
Tel: 00-54-1-3343247
Fax: 00-54-1-3427329
E-mail: camcom-arg-hol@infomatic.com.ar

Belgium
Belgian-Luxemburg Chamber of Commerce for the Netherlands
www.beluned.nl

Dutch Chamber of Commerce for Belgium and Luxemburg
www.nkvk.be

Brazil
Dutch-Brazilian Chamber of Commerce
Rua Marquês de Itú, 503 cj. 62, CEP 01223-001, São Paulo, SP, Brazilië
Tel: 00-55-11-2215899
Fax: 00-55-11-2219242
E-mail: hollbrazchamber@originet.com.br
www.dutcham.com.br

Office in the Netherlands
Bezuidenhoutseweg 181, Den Haag
Postadres: PO Box 10, 2501 CA Den Haag
Tel: +31 70 -3441589
Fax: +31 70 -3853531
E-mail: missions@nchnl.nl

Czech Republiek
Dutch Chamber of Commerce in Praha
Italská 17, 120 00 PRAAG 2 Czech Repuplic
Tel: 00-420-2-24222336
Fax: 00-420-2-24237579
E-mail: nlchamber@nlchamber.cz
www.nlchamber.cz

Office in the Netherlands
Bezuidenhoutseweg 181, 2594 AH Den Haag
Tel: +31 70 -3857587
Fax: +31 70 -3477975
E-mail: nl_kvkhth@wxs.nl

France
Dutch-French Chamber of Commerce
64 rue de Tocqueville, 75017 Paris
Tel: 00 33 147 66 83 75
Fax: 00 33 147 66 82 19
E-mail: ccfn@worldnet.fr

Office in the Netherlands:
Bezuidenhoutseweg 181, Den Haag
Postadres: PO Box 90852, 2509 LW Den Haag
Tel: +31 70 382 05 5'
Fax: +31 70 347 79 75
E-mail: nfkvk@nfkvk.nl
www.nfkvk-ccfn.com

French Chamber of Commerce in the Netherlands
Wibautstraat 129, 11e étage, 1091 GL Amsterdam
Tel: +31 20-5628200
Fax: +31 20-5628222
E-mail: cfci@cfci.nl

Germany
Dutch-German Chamber of Commerce
Freiligrathstrasse 25, 40479 Düsseldorf, Germany
Postadres: Postfach 320213, 40417 Düsseldorf, Germany
Tel: 00-49-211-4987201
Fax: 00-49-211-4920415

Office in the Netherlands
Nassauplein 30, Den Haag
PO Box 80533, 2508 GM Den Haag
Tel: +31 70-3114114
Fax: +31 70-3632218
E-mail: ndkvk@bart.nl
www.dnhk.nl

Hong Kong
The Dutch Business Association - DBA
Room 5702, 57th Floor, Cheung Kong Center, 2 Queen's Road Central, Hong Kong
Tel: 00-852-28152801
Fax: 00-852-28152173
E-mail: dba@hkstar.com
www.dba.com.hk

Indonesia
Indonesian-Dutch Association - INA
Citra Graha, 7th floor, room 703, Jalan Jendral Gatot Subroto Kav. 35-36, Jakarta 12950 Indonesia
Postadres: P.O. Box 4385, Jakarta 12043

Indonesia
Tel: 00-62-21-5200702
Telefax: 00-62-21-52009 69
E-mail: ina@ina.or.id
www.ina.or.id

Office in the Netherlands
Bezuidenhoutseweg 181, 2594 AH Den Haag
Postadres: PO Box 10, 2501 CA Den Haag
Tel: +31 70 -3441582
Telefax: +31 70 -3853531
E-mail: ina@nchnl.nl

Israel
Chamber of Commerce Netherlands-Israel
29 Hamared Street, Room 1230, Tel Aviv, Israel
Tel: 00-972-3-5173261
Fax: 00-972-3-5173283

Office in the Netherlands
Bankrashof 3, 1183 NP Amstelveen
Tel: 020-5038063
Fax: 020-5038064
www.kvknederlandisrael.nl

Italy
Italian Chamber of Commerce for the Netherlands
Laan v Meerderfort 52 kamer 21, 2517 AM Den Haag
Tel: +31 70 -3469220
Fax: +31 70 -3653286
E-mail: italiaansekvk@dataweb.nl
www.dataweb.net/~italiaansekvk/

Japan
Japanese Chamber of Commerce in the Netherlands
www.jcc-holland.nl

Poland
Dutch-Poolse Chamber of Commerce
Murmanskastreet 25, 04-203 Warschau, Poland
Tel: 00-48-22-5154170
Fax: 00-48-22-5154305
E-mail: pnig@polbox.com

Office in the Netherlands
Bezuidenhoutseweg 181, 2594 AH Den Haag
Tel: +31 70 -3352611
Fax: +31 70 -3477975
E-mail: nl_kvkhth@wxs.nl

Portugal
Dutch-Portugese Chamber of Commerce
Avenida Infante Santo 43-5, 1350 Lissabon, Portugal
Tel: 00-351-21-3955581
Fax: 00-351-21-3955582
E-mail: office@ccph.pt

Slovakia
Dutch Chamber of Commerce for Slovakia
Hradné Údolie 15, 81101 Bratislava, Slovakia
Tel: 00-421-7-54418721
Fax: 00-421-7-54418723
E-mail: nlchamber@nlchamber.sk

Office in the Netherlands
Bezuidenhoutseweg 181, 2594 AH Den Haag
Tel: +31 70 -3857587
Fax: +31 70 -3477975
E-mail: nl_kvkhth@wxs.nl

South-Africa
Dutch Chamber of Commerce for Zuid-Afrika
4rd Floor, Export House, Corner Maude & West Streets, Sandton 2196 Zuid-Afrika
Postadres: P.O. Box 781738, SANDTON 2146 South-Africa
Tel: 00-27-11-8842065
Fax: 00-27-11-8835573
E-mail: info@sanec.co.za
www.sanec.co.za

Office in the Netherlands:
Bezuidenhoutseweg 181, Den Haag
Tel: +31 70 -3470781
Fax: +31 70 -3352766
E-mail: info.nl@sanec.co.za

Sweden
Swedish Chamber of Commerce
www.swedishchamber.nl

Switzerland
Swiss Chamber of Commerce in the Netherlands
www.swisschamber.nl

Surinam
Surinam-Dutch Chamber of Commerce and Industry
Dr. J.F. Nassylaan 48b, Paramaribo, Surinam
Tel: 00-597-476909
Fax: 00-597-476909

Office in the Netherlands
Koningskade 30, 2596 AA Den Haag
Tel: +31 70 -3245005
Fax: +31 70 -3281094
E-mail: nedcar@xs4all.nl

Thailand
Netherlands-Thai Chamber of Commerce

(NTCC)
BB Building 19th floor, room 1909, 54 Sukhumvit, 21 Sukhumvit Road, Klongtoey Nua Sub District, Bangkok 10110 Thailand
Tel: 00-66-2-2607501
Fax: 00-66-2-2607502
E-mail: ntccbkk@ksc15.th.com

Office in the Netherlands
NTCC, c/o Nederlands Centrum voor Handelsbevordering, T.A.V. de heer Gerard Westenburg, Bezuidenhoutseweg 181, 2594 AH Den Haag.
Tel: 070-3441544
Fax: 070-3853531
www.ntcc.nl

United Kingdom
The Netherlands-British Chamber of Commerce
'The Dutch House', 307 High Holborn, London, WC1V 7LS United Kingdom
Tel: 00-44-207-4051358
Fax: 00-44-207-4051689
E-mail: nbcc@btinternet.com
www.nbcc.co.uk

Office in the Netherlands
Oxford House, Nieuwezijds forburgwal 328 L, 1012 RW Amsterdam
Tel: +31 20-4217040
Fax: +31 20-4217003
E-mail: nbccnl@btinternet.com

United states
American Chamber of Commerce in the Netherlands
Van Karnebeeklaan 14, 2585 BB Den Haag
Tel: +31-70-3659808
Fax: +31-70-3646992
E-mail: office@amcham.nl
www.amcham.nl

Dutch Chamber of Commerce for America
1 Rockefeller Plaza, Suite 1420, New York, N.Y. 10020 United States
Tel: 00-1-212-2656460
Fax: 00-1-212-2656402
E-mail: newyork@netherlands.org
www.netherlands.org

Office in the Netherlands
Bezuidenhoutseweg 181, 2594 AH Den Haag
Tel: +31 70-3478292
Fax: +31 70-3473732
E-mail: thehague@netherlands.org

Other addresses

Eurochambres
Box 4 - Rue Archimède 5 -B1000
Brussel (België)
tel:(+32-2)2820850
fax: (+32-2)2300038
eurochambres@eurochambres.be
www.eurochambres.be

Europese Kamer Unie (EKU)
Bezuidenhoutseweg 181
2594AH Den Haag
tel: +31 70-3820551
fax: +31 70-3477975
nfkvk@evd.nl
www.nbcc1.demon.co.uk/eku

IBCC/ICC, International (Bureau of) Chambers of Commerce
38, Cours Albert 1er, 75008 Paris
tel:33(1)49.53.2828
fax: 33(1)49.53.2942
ibcc@iccwbo.org
www.icc-ibcc.org

Overzeese Kamer Unie (OKU)
Overseas Chamber Union
Bezuidenhoutseweg 181
2594AH Den Haag, The Netherlands

World Chambers Network (WCN - ICC)
Paris
tel:33-1 49 53 2944
fax: 33-1 49 53 2938
helpdesk@worldchambers.com
www.worldchambers.com

LARGEST LAW FIRMS

Adriaanse & Van Der Weel, 35, Rouaansekaai, Middleburg, NL-4330 AE, Netherlands, Tel: 31118635365, Fax: 31118636178, Contact: Rikkert Hoekstra

Allen & Overy Nederland, Apollolaan 15 P. O. Box 75088, 3000 AB Amsterdam, Amsterdam, , Netherlands, Tel: 31-20 574 1200, Fax: 31-20 671 8775, Contact: Rob Abendroth

Arnold Siedsma, Sweelinckplein 1, The Hague, , Netherlands, Tel: 31 70 365 48 33, Fax: 31 70 361 50 54, Contact: Ir Prins

Baker & McKenzie, Leidseplein 29, Amsterdam, 1017, Netherlands, Tel: 31-20-5517555, Fax: 31-20-6267949, Contact: Peter Dekker

Barents & Krans, Parkstraat 107, The Hague, 2500 GL, Netherlands, Tel: 31703760606, Fax: 31703651856, Contact: Clemens Sevenaer

Beer Advocaten, Johannes Vermeerstraat 23, Amsterdam, 1071 DK, Netherlands, Tel: 31206732199, Fax: 31206758163, Contact: John Beer

Bierman AlofsWaiboer advocaten notarisssen, Lingedijk 58 PO Box 124, Tiel, Alaska 4191 KK, Netherlands, Tel: +31 344 618844, Fax: *31 344 612174, Contact: Theo Teeuwen

Boekel De Neree, Atrium Building, Strawinskylaan 3037, Amsterdam, NL-1077, Netherlands, Tel: 31204313131, Fax: 31204313143, Contact: J. Sigaar

Buruma Maris, Scheveningseweg 66, The Hague, 2517 KX, Netherlands, Tel: 31703529500, Fax: 31703503014, Contact: Cees Hagen

Clifford Chance LLP, Apollolaan 171, Amsterdam, , Netherlands, Tel: 31 -20 5777111, Fax: 31 20 5777222, Contact: Ruth Van Andel

CMS Derks Star Busmann Hanotiau, 4 Oude Enghweg, Hilversum, , Netherlands, Tel: 31 35 67 21 821, Fax: +31 35 67 21 888, Contact: J.W. Bouman

CMS Derks Star Busmann, Pythagoraslaan 2, Utrecht, 3584 BB, Netherlands, Tel: 31302121212, Fax: 312121222, Contact: E. Vile

De Brauw Blackstone Westbroek, 10th Floor, Coolsingel 139, Rotterdam, , Netherlands, Tel: 31-10 240 65 00, Fax: 31-10 411 35 48, Contact: Frederik Buijn

DE LA FUENTE ABOGADOS, Postbus 4397, Rotterdam, 3006 AJ, Netherlands, Tel: 31 10 2120273, Fax: 31 10 452 96 85, Contact: Eliseo De la Fuente Gonzalez, LL.M.

DeBrauw Blackstone Westbroek, Zuid Hollandlaan 7, The Hague, 2596 AL, Netherlands, Tel: 31703285328, Fax: 31703285325, Contact: Harro Knijff

Den Hertog & Kam, Lange Voorhout 70, The Hague, 2514 EH, Netherlands, Tel: 31703624187, Fax: 31703648447, Contact: Willem Kam

Dirkzwager, Office Building, Arnhem, 6824 BJ, Netherlands, Tel: 31263538300, Fax: 31263510793, Contact: Maarten Baneke

Dirkzwager, S. Mathonsingel 4, Nijmegen, , Netherlands, Tel: 31 24 322 66 41, Fax: 31 24 322 20 74, Contact: Til Kressin

Dolk-Verburg-Diamond, Cronenburg 75, Amsterdam, 1081 GM, Netherlands, Tel: 31203016161, Fax: 31206464716, Contact: F. Mulder

Freshfields, Apollolaan 151, Amsterdam, , Netherlands, Tel: 31 20 488 0900, Fax: 31 20 488 0901, Contact: Roger Berner

Fruytier Advacaten, Keizersgracht 221, Amsterdam, 1016 DV, Netherlands, Tel: 205304300, Fax: 206237129, Contact: Jan Groot

Fruytier Advocaten, Keizersgracht 221, Amsterdam, 1016 DV, Netherlands, Tel: 31206272088, Fax: 31206237129, Contact: Noel Ellens

Hoegen Dijkhof Advocaten, The Rembrandt Tower, 13th Floor Amstelplein 1, Amsterdam, 1096 HA, Netherlands, Tel: 31204624070, Fax: 31204624080, Contact: Hans Dijkhof

Houthoff Buruma, Scheveningseweg 66, The Hague, , Netherlands, Tel: 31-70 352 95 00, Fax: 31-70 350 30 14, Contact: C.J. Hagen

Houthoff Buruma, Weenatoren, Weena 355, Rotterdam, , Netherlands, Tel: 31-10 217 20 00, Fax: 31-10 217 27 00, Contact: Jacqueline Meyst-Michels

Houthoff, Parnassusweg 126, Amsterdam, 1070 AM, Netherlands, Tel: 31205772004, Fax: 31205772700, Contact: Reinout De Waal

Kernkamp Advocaten, Veerkade 5D, Rotterdam, NL-3016 DE, Netherlands Tel: 31104116471, Fax: 31104136923, Contact: Hein Kernkamp

Koster, Claasen & Smallegange, Boompjes 550, Rotterdam, 3000 AK, Netherlands, Tel: 31104132180, Fax: 31104122125, Contact: Johan Van Noort

Kupperman Van Der Wiel & Co., Parnassustoren, Locatellikade I, Amsterdam, 1070 LK, Netherlands, Tel: 312030512040, Fax: 31203052050, Contact: Erik Van Unen

Loyens & Loeff, Tripolis 300 P.O. Box 71170, Amsterdam, , Netherlands, Tel: 31 20 578 57 85, Fax: 31 20 578 58 00, Contact: Jeroen Ten Berg

Loyens & Loeff, Weena 325, Rotterdam, , Netherlands, Tel: 31 10 224 6224, Fax: 31 10 412 5839, Contact: S. Bertels

Nauta Dutilh, Prinses Irenestraat 59, Amsterdam, NL-1077 WV, Netherlands, Tel: 31205414646, Fax: 31206612827, Contact: R. Hooghoudt

Nauta Dutilh, Weena 750, Rotterdam, , Netherlands, Tel: 31-10 2240000, Fax: 31-10 4148444, Contact: Ch. Peter Bannier

Oppenheimer Wolff & Donnelly LLP, Viottastraat 42, Amsterdam, , Netherlands, Tel: 31-20-305-57 00, Fax: 31-20-305-57 90, Contact: Charles Moons

Parramore Advocaten Amsterdam, London Building, Burg. Stramanweg 102-H, Amsterdam, 1101 AA, Netherlands, Tel: 31204090038, Fax: 31206968581, Contact: Michael Parramore

Pels Rijcken & Droogleever Fortuijn, Koningin Julianaplein 30 A-Building, The Hague, 2502 AT, Netherlands, Tel: 31703488700, Fax: 31703477494, Contact: Leen Keus

Petten, Tideman & Sassen, Van Stolkweg 10, the hague, 2596hv, Netherlands, Tel: 0031(0)703504055, Fax: 0031(0)703506187, Contact: Bruno Tideman

Schut & Grosheide, Van Boshuizenstraat 12, Amsterdam, 1083 BA, Netherlands, Tel: 31205419888, Fax: 31206464966, Contact: W. Neervoort

Shutts & Bowen, B.V. LLP, Europa Boulevard 59, Amsterdam, , Netherlands, Tel: (31 20) 661-0969, Fax: (31 20) 642-1475, Contact: Rosemarie Schade

Stibbe Simont Monahan Duhot, Stibbetoren Strawinskylaan 2001 Postbus 75640, Amsterdam, 1070 AP, Netherlands, Tel: 31205460606, Fax: 31205460123, Contact: Niels Koeman

Ten Holter Advocaten, Oranjepark 9, Dordrecht, 3311 LP, Netherlands, Tel: 31786137177, Fax: 31786130171, Contact: Peter Van Gool

Trenite Van Doorne, Churchillplein 5, The Hague, , Netherlands, Tel: 31-70 338 3131, Fax: 31-70 358 4798, Contact: Derk Rijpma

Trenité Van Doorne, De Lairessestraat 133 P.O. Box 75265, Amsterdam, 1070 AG, Netherlands, Tel: 31206789123, Fax: 31206789589, Contact: Paul Witteveen

Trenité Van Doorne, Gebouw P.O. Box 190, Rotterdam, 3000 AD, Netherlands, Tel: 31104042111, Fax: 31104042333, Contact: JOS BOS

Udink, Gribling & De Jong, Alexanderstraat 2, The Hague, 2514 JL, Netherlands, Tel: 31703110711, Fax: 31703110722, Contact: Marc Udink

Van Anken Knuppe Damstra, Westblaak 180, Rotterdam, 3001 HA, Netherlands, Tel: 31102249224, Fax: 31104143644, Contact: Eltjo Rentema

Van Benthem & Keulen, Euclideslaan 51, Utrecht, 3584 BM, Netherlands, Tel: 31302528528, Fax: 31302528500, Contact: Cees De Jong

Van Der Steenhoven Advocaten, Roemer Visscherstraat 47, Amsterdam, 1054 EW, Netherlands, Tel: 31206077979, Fax: 31206831947, Contact: Jan Van Der Steenhoven

Van Dijk & Van Arnhem Advocaten Apeldoorn, Soerenseweg 146a, Apeldoorn, 7313 EM, Netherlands, Tel: +31 55 355 9899, Fax: +31 55 355 9818, Contact: Sipke W. van Dijk

Van Mens & Wisselink, Rivierstaete Building, Amsterdam, , Netherlands, Tel: 31-20-301 66 33, Fax: 31-20-301 66 22, Contact: K. L. H. Van Mens

Van Mens & Wisselink, Wilhelminapark 60-61, Utrecht, 3508 AL, Netherlands, Tel: 31302547947, Fax: 31302522552, Contact: Frans Duynstee

Van Riet & Associees, Einsteindreef 111 P.O. Box 9907, Utrecht, 3506 GX, Netherlands, Tel: 31302635051, Fax: 31302635060, Contact: Marie Cools

Van Schoonhoven In't Veld, Anrooygebouw, 7 Peter van Anrooystraat, Amsterdam, 1070 AZ, Netherlands, Tel: 31206796969, Fax: 31206764339, Contact: Ferry Van Schoonhoven

Van Wijmen Nouwen, Westplein 12-14, Rotterdam, 3001 KB, Netherlands, Tel: 31104364066, Fax: 31104360582, Contact: Rob Meijer

Wouters Advocaten & Notarissen, Oostmaaslaan 71, Rotterdam, , Netherlands, Tel: 31 10 880 1700, Fax: 31 10 880 1717, Contact: Pieter Bolland

Wouters Advocaten & Notarissen, Prof. W.H. Keesomlaan 8 P.O. Box 75381, Amsterdam, , Netherlands, Tel: 31 20 880 8700, Fax: 31 20 880 8787, Contact: Ton Nederveen

Wouters Advocaten, World Trade Center Eindhoven, Pastoor Petersstraat, Eindhoven, NL-5600 AT, Netherlands, Tel: 31402447260, Fax: 31202448745, Contact: Georg Van Daal

US AND COUNTRY CONTACTS

U.S. EMBASSY TRADE-RELATED CONTACTS

Terry Sorgi
Acting Senior Commercial Officer
The U.S. Commercial Service
American Embassy
Lange Voorhout 102
2514 EJ The Hague
APO address:
American Embassy
US & FCS The Hague
Unit 6707 – Box 039
APO AE 09715
Phone: (31) 70 310 9417
Fax: (31) 70 363 2985
E-mail: the.hague.office.box@mail.doc.gov
Website: www.uscs.nl

The U.S. Commercial Service
American Consulate General
Museumplein 19
1071 DJ Amsterdam
Phone: (31) 20 575 5351
Fax: (31) 20 575 5350
E-mail: amsterdam.office.box@mail.doc.gov

Mark A. Tokola
Counselor For Economic Affairs
American Embassy, The Hague
Unit 6707 – Box 039
APO AE 09715
Phone: (31) 70 310 9271
Fax: (31) 70 310 9348
Website: www.usemb.nl

Phil Letarte
Counselor for Agricultural Affairs
American Embassy, The Hague
Unit 6707 – Box 039
APO AE 09715
Phone: (31) 70 310 9209
Fax: (31) 70 365 7681

American Citizens Services
American Consulate General
Museumplein 19
1071 DJ Amsterdam
Phone: (31) 20 575 5309
Fax: (31) 20 575 5310
Website: www.usemb.nl

TRADE AND INDUSTRIAL ASSOCIATIONS IN KEY SECTORS

American Chamber of Commerce
Burg. van Karnebeeklaan 14
2582 BB The Hague
Phone: (31) 70 365 9808
Fax: (31) 70 379 6322

Holland International Distribution Council
P.O. Box 85599
2508 CG The Hague
Phone: (31) 70 346 7272
Fax: (31) 70 360 3698
Trade association for transport, logistics, and warehousing companies.

VIFKA
P.O. Box 220
3454 ZL De Meern
Phone: (31) 30 662 1515
Fax: (31) 30 662 1717
Trade association for office, information and (tele) communication industries.

Vereniging Federatie Het Instrument
P.O. Box 2099
3800 CB Amersfoort
Phone: (31) 33 465 7507
Fax: (31) 33 461 6638
Trade association for suppliers of instrumentation for industrial electronics, automation, laboratories and medical technology.

FARON/FME
Netherlands Association of Manufacturers of Electronic Equipment
P.O. Box 190
2700 AD Zoetermeer
Phone: (31) 79 353 1355
Fax: (31) 79 353 1365

FENIT - Federatie Nederlandse Informatie Technologie
P.O. Box 11760
1402 AT The Hague
Phone: (31) 70 385 7171
Fax: (31) 70 383 6931

VLM
P.O. Box 190
2700 AD Zoetermeer
Phone: (31) 79 353 1323
Fax: (31) 79 353 1365
(Association of Dutch manufacturers of pollution

control
Equipment)

GOVERNMENT OFFICES RELATING TO KEY SECTORS

Ministry of Economic Affairs
P.O. Box 20101
2500 EC The Hague
Phone: (31) 70 379 7169
Fax: (31) 70 379 8074

Ministry of Agriculture, Nature Management and Fisheries
P.O. Box 20401
2500 EK The Hague
Phone: (31) 70 379 3911
Fax: (31) 70 381 5153

Ministry of Transport
P.O. Box 20901
2500 EX The Hague
Phone: (31) 70 351 6171
Fax: (31) 70 351 7895

Ministry of Health, Welfare and Sport
P.O. Box 20350
2500 EJ The Hague
Phone: (31) 70 340 7911
Fax: (31) 70 340 7834

Ministry of Housing, Physical Planning and Environment
P.O. Box 20951
2500 BZ The Hague
Phone: (31) 70 339 3939
Fax: (31) 70 339 1280

Ministry of Social Affairs and Employment
P.O. Box 90801
2509 LV The Hague
Fax: (31) 70 333 4444
Phone: (31) 70 333 4040

MARKET RESEARCH FIRMS

To locate market research firms in the Netherlands contact:
The Netherlands Association of Market Research Firms (NVVM)
Hogehilweg 8
1101 CC Amsterdam Z.O.
Phone: (31) 20 697 6951
Fax: (31) 20 691 0433

COMMERCIAL BANKS

To locate Dutch banks contact:

The Netherlands Bankers' Association (NVB)
P.O. Box 19780
1000 GW Amsterdam
Phone: (31) 20 550 2888
Fax: (31) 20 623 9748

WASHINGTON-BASED USG COUNTRY CONTRACTS

Paul Dacher
Netherlands Desk Officer
U.S. Department of Commerce/ITA
Room 3042
14th & Constitution Avenue, N.W.
Washington, D.C. 20230
Phone: (202) 482 6008
Fax: (202) 482 2897

TPCC Trade Information Center
Phone: 1-800-USA-TRADE

U.S. Department of Agriculture
Foreign Agricultural Service
Trade Assistance and Promotion Office
Phone: (202) 720 7420

U.S. Department of State - Office of Business Affairs
Phone: (202) 746 1625
Fax: (202) 647 3953

AMERICAN STATE OFFICES IN THE NETHERLANDS

Indiana
World Trade Center
Strawinskylaan 305
1077 XX Amsterdam
Phone: (31) 20 571 1886
Fax: (31) 20 571 1889
Director: Mr. James Sitko

Maryland
Beurs - World Trade Center
Room 869
P.O. Box 30224
3001 DE Rotterdam
Phone: (31) 10 205 3860
Fax: (31) 10 205 5494
Director: Mr. Gary Kunkle

BASIC TITLES ON NETHERLANDS

IMPORTANT!

All publications are updated annually!

Please contact IBP, Inc. at ibpusa3@gmail.com for the latest ISBNs and additional information

TITLE
Netherlands A "Spy" Guide - Strategic Information and Developments
Netherlands A Spy" Guide"
Netherlands Antilles Offshore Tax Guide - Strategic Information, Regulations, Contacts
Netherlands Antilles Ship Registration, Merchant Shipping Regulations and Rules Handbook
Netherlands Banking & Financial Market Handbook
Netherlands Business and Investment Opportunities Yearbook
Netherlands Business and Investment Opportunities Yearbook
Netherlands Business and Investment Opportunities Yearbook Volume 1 Strategic Information and Opportunities
Netherlands Business Intelligence Report - Practical Information, Opportunities, Contacts
Netherlands Business Intelligence Report - Practical Information, Opportunities, Contacts
Netherlands Business Law Handbook - Strategic Information and Basic Laws
Netherlands Business Law Handbook - Strategic Information and Basic Laws
Netherlands Business Law Handbook - Strategic Information and Basic Laws
Netherlands Business Law Handbook - Strategic Information and Basic Laws
Netherlands Business Law Handbook Volume 1 Strategic Information and Basic Laws
Netherlands Business Success Guide - Basic Practical Information and Contacts
Netherlands Company Laws and Regulations Handbook
Netherlands Company Laws and Regulations Handbook - Strategic Information and Basic Laws
Netherlands Constitution and Citizenship Laws Handbook - Strategic Information and Basic Laws
Netherlands Country Study Guide - Strategic Information and Developments
Netherlands Country Study Guide - Strategic Information and Developments
Netherlands Country Study Guide - Strategic Information and Developments Volume 1 Strategic Information and Developments
Netherlands Country Study Guide Volume 1 Strategic Information and Developments
Netherlands Criminal Laws, Regulations and Procedures Handbook - Strategic Information, Regulations, Procedures
Netherlands Customs, Trade Regulations and Procedures Handbook
Netherlands Customs, Trade Regulations and Procedures Handbook
Netherlands Diplomatic Handbook - Strategic Information and Developments
Netherlands Diplomatic Handbook - Strategic Information and Developments
Netherlands Ecology & Nature Protection Handbook
Netherlands Ecology & Nature Protection Handbook
Netherlands Ecology & Nature Protection Laws and Regulation Handbook
Netherlands Economic & Development Strategy Handbook
Netherlands Economic & Development Strategy Handbook
Netherlands Electoral, Political Parties Laws and Regulations Handbook - Strategic Information, Regulations, Procedures
Netherlands Energy Policy, Laws and Regulation Handbook
Netherlands Export-Import Trade and Business Directory
Netherlands Export-Import Trade and Business Directory

TITLE
Netherlands Fishing and Aquaculture Industry Handbook - Strategic Information, Regulations, Opportunities
Netherlands Foreign Policy and Government Guide
Netherlands Foreign Policy and Government Guide
Netherlands Government and Business Contacts Handbook
Netherlands Government and Business Contacts Handbook
Netherlands Healthcare Sector Organization, Management and Payment Systems Handbook - Strategic Information, Programs and Regulations
Netherlands Immigration Laws and Regulations Handbook - Strategic Information and Basic Laws
Netherlands Industrial and Business Directory
Netherlands Industrial and Business Directory
Netherlands Insolvency (Bankruptcy) Laws and Regulations Handbook - Strategic Information and Basic Laws
Netherlands Internet and E-Commerce Investment and Business Guide - Strategic and Practical Information: Regulations and Opportunities
Netherlands Internet and E-Commerce Investment and Business Guide - Strategic and Practical Information: Regulations and Opportunities
Netherlands Investment and Business Guide - Strategic and Practical Information
Netherlands Investment and Business Guide - Strategic and Practical Information
Netherlands Investment and Business Guide - Strategic and Practical Information
Netherlands Investment and Business Guide - Strategic and Practical Information
Netherlands Investment and Business Guide Volume 1 Strategic and Practical Information
Netherlands Investment and Business Profile - Basic Information and Contacts for Succesful investment and Business Activity
Netherlands Investment and Trade Laws and Regulations Handbook
Netherlands Investment, Trade Strategy and Agreements Handbook - Strategic Information and Basic Agreements
Netherlands Labor Laws and Regulations Handbook - Strategic Information and Basic Laws
Netherlands Land Ownership and Agriculture Laws Handbook
Netherlands Mineral & Mining Sector Investment and Business Guide - Strategic and Practical Information
Netherlands Mineral & Mining Sector Investment and Business Guide - Strategic and Practical Information
Netherlands Mining Laws and Regulations Handbook
Netherlands Recent Economic and Political Developments Yearbook
Netherlands Recent Economic and Political Developments Yearbook
Netherlands Recent Economic and Political Developments Yearbook
Netherlands Space Programs and Exploration Handbook
Netherlands Space Programs and Exploration Handbook
Netherlands Starting Business (Incorporating) in Netherlands Guide
Netherlands Starting Business (Incorporating) in....Guide
Netherlands Tax Guide
Netherlands Tax Guide Volume 1 Strategic Information and Basic Regulations
Netherlands Taxation Laws and Regulations Handbook vol2
Netherlands Telecom Laws and Regulations Handbook vol1

TITLE
Netherlands Telecommunication Industry Business Opportunities Handbook
Netherlands Telecommunication Industry Business Opportunities Handbook
Netherlands Transportation Policy and Regulations Handbook
Netherlands: Business in Netherlands for Everyone: Practical Information and Contacts for Success
Netherlands: Doing Business and Investing in Netherlands Guide
Netherlands: Doing Business and Investing in Netherlands Guide
Netherlands: How to Invest, Start and Run Profitable Business in Netherlands Guide - Practical Information, Opportunities, Contacts

Equatorial Guinea Company Laws and Regulations Handbook
Eritrea Company Laws and Regulations Handbook
Estonia Company Laws and Regulations Handbook
Ethiopia Company Laws and Regulations Handbook
Falkland Islands Company Laws and Regulations Handbook
Faroes Company Laws and Regulations Handbook
Fiji Company Laws and Regulations Handbook
Finland Company Laws and Regulations Handbook
France Company Laws and Regulations Handbook
Gabon Company Laws and Regulations Handbook
Gambia Company Laws and Regulations Handbook
Georgia Company Laws and Regulations Handbook
Germany Company Laws and Regulations Handbook
Ghana Company Laws and Regulations Handbook
Gibraltar Company Laws and Regulations Handbook
Greece Company Laws and Regulations Handbook
Greenland Company Laws and Regulations Handbook
Grenada Company Laws and Regulations Handbook
Guam Company Laws and Regulations Handbook
Guatemala Company Laws and Regulations Handbook
Guernsey Company Laws and Regulations Handbook
Guinea Company Laws and Regulations Handbook
Guinea-Bissau Company Laws and Regulations Handbook
Guyana Company Laws and Regulations Handbook
Haiti Company Laws and Regulations Handbook
Honduras Company Laws and Regulations Handbook
Hungary Company Laws and Regulations Handbook
Iceland Company Laws and Regulations Handbook
India Company Laws and Regulations Handbook
Indonesia Company Laws and Regulations Handbook
InternationalCompany Laws and Regulations Handbook
Iran Company Laws and Regulations Handbook
Iraq Company Laws and Regulations Handbook
Ireland Company Laws and Regulations Handbook
Israel Company Laws and Regulations Handbook
Italy Company Laws and Regulations Handbook
Jamaica Company Laws and Regulations Handbook
Japan Company Laws and Regulations Handbook
Jersey Company Laws and Regulations Handbook
Jordan Company Laws and Regulations Handbook
Kazakhstan Company Laws and Regulations Handbook
Kenya Company Laws and Regulations Handbook
Kiribati Company Laws and Regulations Handbook
Korea, North Company Laws and Regulations Handbook
Korea, South Company Laws and Regulations Handbook
Kosovo Company Laws and Regulations Handbook
Kuwait Company Laws and Regulations Handbook
Kyrgyzstan Company Laws and Regulations Handbook
Laos Company Laws and Regulations Handbook
Latvia Company Laws and Regulations Handbook
Lebanon Company Laws and Regulations Handbook
Lesotho Company Laws and Regulations Handbook
Liberia Company Laws and Regulations Handbook
Libya Company Laws and Regulations Handbook
Liechtenstein Company Laws and Regulations Handbook
Lithuania Company Laws and Regulations Handbook
Luxembourg Company Laws and Regulations Handbook
Macao Company Laws and Regulations Handbook
Macedonia Company Laws and Regulations Handbook
Madagascar Company Laws and Regulations Handbook
Madeira Company Laws and Regulations Handbook
Malawi Company Laws and Regulations Handbook
Malaysia Company Laws and Regulations Handbook
Maldives Company Laws and Regulations Handbook
Mali Company Laws and Regulations Handbook
Malta Company Laws and Regulations Handbook
Man Company Laws and Regulations Handbook
Marshall Islands Company Laws and Regulations Handbook
Mauritania Company Laws and Regulations Handbook
Mauritius Company Laws and Regulations Handbook
Mayotte Company Laws and Regulations Handbook
Mexico Company Laws and Regulations Handbook
Micronesia Company Laws and Regulations Handbook
Moldova Company Laws and Regulations Handbook
Monaco Company Laws and Regulations Handbook
Mongolia Company Laws and Regulations Handbook
Monserrat Company Laws and Regulations Handbook
Morocco Company Laws and Regulations Handbook
Mozambique Company Laws and Regulations Handbook
Myanmar Company Laws and Regulations Handbook
Namibia Company Laws and Regulations Handbook
Nauru Company Laws and Regulations Handbook
Nepal Company Laws and Regulations Handbook
Netherlands Company Laws and Regulations Handbook
New Caledonia Company Laws and Regulations Handbook
New Zealand Company Laws and Regulations Handbook
Nicaragua Company Laws and Regulations Handbook
Niger Company Laws and Regulations Handbook
Nigeria Company Laws and Regulations Handbook
Niue Company Laws and Regulations Handbook
Northern Mariana Islands Company Laws and Regulations Handbook
Norway Company Laws and Regulations Handbook
Oman Company Laws and Regulations Handbook
Pakistan Company Laws and Regulations Handbook
Palau Company Laws and Regulations Handbook

Palestine Company Laws and Regulations Handbook
Panama Company Laws and Regulations Handbook
Papua New Guinea Company Laws and Regulations Handbook
Paraguay Company Laws and Regulations Handbook
Peru Company Laws and Regulations Handbook
Philippines Company Laws and Regulations Handbook
Pitcairn Islands Company Laws and Regulations Handbook
Poland Company Laws and Regulations Handbook
Polynesia French Company Laws and Regulations Handbook
Portugal Company Laws and Regulations Handbook
Qatar Company Laws and Regulations Handbook
Romania Company Laws and Regulations Handbook
Russia Company Laws and Regulations Handbook
Rwanda Company Laws and Regulations Handbook
Saint Kitts and Nevis Company Laws and Regulations Handbook
Saint Lucia Company Laws and Regulations Handbook
Saint Vincent and The Grenadines Company Laws and Regulations Handbook
Samoa (American) Company Laws and Regulations Handbook
Samoa (Western) Company Laws and Regulations Handbook
San Marino Company Laws and Regulations Handbook
Sao Tome and Principe Company Laws and Regulations Handbook
Saudi Arabia Company Laws and Regulations Handbook
Scotland Company Laws and Regulations Handbook
Senegal Company Laws and Regulations Handbook
Seychelles Company Laws and Regulations Handbook
Sierra Leone Company Laws and Regulations Handbook
Singapore Company Laws and Regulations Handbook
Slovakia Company Laws and Regulations Handbook
Slovenia Company Laws and Regulations Handbook
Solomon Islands Company Laws and Regulations Handbook
Somalia Company Laws and Regulations Handbook
South Africa Company Laws and Regulations Handbook
Spain Company Laws and Regulations Handbook
Sri Lanka Company Laws and Regulations Handbook
St. Helena Company Laws and Regulations Handbook
St. Pierre & Miquelon Company Laws and Regulations Handbook
Sudan Company Laws and Regulations Handbook
Suriname Company Laws and Regulations Handbook
Swaziland Company Laws and Regulations Handbook
Sweden Company Laws and Regulations Handbook
Switzerland Company Laws and Regulations Handbook
Syria Company Laws and Regulations Handbook
Taiwan Company Laws and Regulations Handbook
Tajikistan Company Laws and Regulations Handbook
Tanzania Company Laws and Regulations Handbook
Thailand Company Laws and Regulations Handbook
Togo Company Laws and Regulations Handbook
Tonga Company Laws and Regulations Handbook
Trinidad and Tobago Company Laws and Regulations Handbook
Tunisia Company Laws and Regulations Handbook
Turkey Company Laws and Regulations Handbook
Turkmenistan Company Laws and Regulations Handbook
Turks & Caicos Company Laws and Regulations Handbook
Tuvalu Company Laws and Regulations Handbook
Uganda Company Laws and Regulations Handbook
Ukraine Company Laws and Regulations Handbook
United Arab Emirates Company Laws and Regulations Handbook
United Kingdom Company Laws and Regulations Handbook
United States Company Laws and Regulations Handbook
Uruguay Company Laws and Regulations Handbook
Uzbekistan Company Laws and Regulations Handbook
Vanuatu Company Laws and Regulations Handbook
Vatican City Company Laws and Regulations Handbook
Venezuela Company Laws and Regulations Handbook
Vietnam Company Laws and Regulations Handbook
Virgin Islands, British Company Laws and Regulations Handbook
Wake Atoll Company Laws and Regulations Handbook
Wallis & Futuna Company Laws and Regulations Handbook
Yemen Company Laws and Regulations Handbook
Serbia Company Laws and Regulations Handbook
Zambia Company Laws and Regulations Handbook
Zimbabwe Company Laws and Regulations Handbook

www.ingramcontent.com/pod-product-compliance
Lightning Source LLC
LaVergne TN
LVHW080034210926
848481LV00011B/3190
* 9 7 8 1 4 3 3 0 7 0 3 8 9 *